Cultural Recycling in the Postdigital Age

Miriam Llamas Ubieto /
Johanna Vollmeyer (eds.)

Cultural Recycling in the Postdigital Age

PETER LANG

Lausanne - Berlin - Bruxelles - Chennai - New York - Oxford

Library of Congress Cataloging-in-Publication Data
A CIP catalog record for this book has been applied for at the Library of Congress.

Bibliographic Information published by the Deutsche Nationalbibliothek
The Deutsche Nationalbibliothek lists this publication in the Deutsche Nationalbibliografie; detailed bibliographic data is available online at http://dnb.d-nb.de.

Cover Illustration:
© shutterstock.com/CoreDESIGN

GOBIERNO DE ESPAÑA
MINISTERIO DE CIENCIA E INNOVACIÓN

UNIVERSIDAD
COMPLUTENSE
MADRID

Unión Europea
Fondo Europeo de Desarrollo Regional
"Una manera de hacer Europa"

This work was supported by the Spanish Ministerio de Ciencia e Innovación under Grant "REC-LIT. Reciclajes culturales: transliteraturas en la era postdigital"; Ref. RTI2018-094607-B-I00; (MCI/AEI/FEDER, UE).

ISBN 978-3-0343-4547-7 (Print)
E-ISBN 978-3-0343-4808-9 (E-PDF)
E-ISBN 978-3-0343-4809-6 (EPUB)
DOI 10.3726\b21438

Published by: Peter Lang Group AG, Lausanne, Switzerland

info@peterlang.com - www.peterlang.com

Table of Contents

Johanna Vollmeyer and Miriam Llamas Ubieto
Universidad Complutense de Madrid

Cultural Recycling in the Postdigital Age: An Introduction

This book attempts to provide an understanding of the possibilities and restrictions of current cultural recycling phenomena in the postdigital age. The contradiction of an age when massive digitisation projects make our cultural and literary heritage more accessible than ever is that the awareness of that heritage appears to be constantly shrinking. This poses new challenges in postdigital studies: understanding and analysing new continuities between the analogue and the digital (as well as the alterations of collective and identitarian narratives within them); new cultural recycling strategies and practices; and the traces that the postdigital leaves in the recycling processes and in their outcomes. We offer material for the exploration of how the awareness of the cultural heritage can be increased in a conscientious and meaningful way. This collection also contributes to a better understanding of the technological ecosystem in which we are immersed and to which we contribute through our practices. Finally, this volume interrogates specifically the possibilities of the literary within a postdigital framework.

The use of digital technologies has become a quotidian practice in which the analogue and the digital can no longer be seen as separate. Our lives are computerised in a way we have never experienced before, leading to a new analogue-digital continuum (constant connectedness, immediacy, accessibility etc.). However, the 'new' digital media have become less visible, and therefore less "new" the more they have become ubiquitous, due to their massive use since 2006/2010. This postdigital condition has provoked unprecedented qualitative changes in our daily cultural practices, in our media production and use, in the way art reacts to these changes, but also how art relates to these new technologies. For this reason, the digital should not be understood as something counter to our analogue reality, but as something that permeates it as our 'reality' is increasingly infused with digital information (Internet, algorithmisation, AI, big data, virtual simulations). In this process, the Internet itself has changed as we experience a growing personalization of the digital grid, we are moving in. We rely on semantic webs with platform structures that foster a culture of participation, propagation, and convergence, where we can observe content flows through multiple media. All information seems both personal and omnipresent concurrently. The postdigital condition implies the transformation of experience and perception, a transformation caused by technological changes that impact the forms of (tele)communication; the storage and reconfiguration of knowledge; and the production, reception, and circulation of cultural and literary elements.

Publications about similar concepts such as intertextuality, adaptation, appropriation, hypertextuality, transmedia, remix, sampling, etc. exist, but their conceptual approach and their epistemological conceptualization are different from 'cultural recycling'. We introduce an innovative way of conceptualizing these and other new phenomena. Our hypothesis is that 'recycling' is a notion that inherently implies time and memory (repetition, iteration, and dissemination) as well as movement (circulation), therefore going beyond similar studies noted above. Its potential for exploring cultural phenomena of the postdigital age has not previously been unveiled. It allows us to rethink this particularly extended tendency of 'putting into use again/reuse and relive' in our postdigital age. Not only is the bibliography relating to media studies considered, but also the (few) studies about 'recycling' and 'recycling'-discourses in other fields, such as economy, ecocriticism, and memory studies. What is particularly new in our interdisciplinary contribution is that it bridges the gap between cultural recycling, literature and the postdigital condition by providing an approach that unites the fields of media studies, cultural studies, and literary studies, which allows for the creation of a new research field where only a few, indirect contributions currently exist.

Cultural recycling is intimately related to the postdigital condition because it is one of its expressions. The replicative reproduction and circulation of textual production and visual content in the current media ecosystem have increased, since they are part of the altered communication methods that form the basis of the postdigital condition. We understand by postdigital recycling a processing action on a used material, waste, or product that implies its detachment from its initial context and its subsequent return to a new life cycle in ways affected by the postdigital condition. This operation implies circulation as well as revaluation. The action of processing can be creation from or reuse of something pre-existing. It involves a technical application and implies iterativity, because it circulates by replicating itself between producer(s) and receiver(s), albeit with variation. This variation can be minimal and be only a change of function, or it can be a transformation in production, circulation, or reception. The concept of postdigital recycling – understood as a typical cultural practice of the postdigital condition – allows the interrogation of practices that have become an everyday trend due to the specific form of reproduction and the form of postdigital recurrence. These characteristics of reproduction and recurrence are inherent to analogue-digital practices in the postdigital era, so that the notion of postdigital recycling is based on an important temporal component in a double sense: reiteration and circularity, situated between distribution and circulation, between event and continuity.

The book addresses academics and researchers from humanities and social sciences, students and university professors who might use this publication for educational purposes. It is also of interest for cultural and media institutions, as well as cultural agents that deal with digital media. It is particularly relevant to media studies, cultural studies, comparative literature, literary studies, arts and visual studies, communication studies and digital humanities.

The contributions of this volume focus on cultural recycling in the postdigital age articulating both theoretical approximations and case studies. The case studies gathered here provide a wide range of unique approaches, but they are all interrelated by highlighting characteristic features of postdigital recycling that differ from the qualities of recycling in previous periods. They are also bound together by the intention to illuminate how these phenomena have become global and how similar developments can be observed in different languages and cultural spheres.

In order to address each of the contribution's particularities with respect to the initial question, the contributions are structured so that more theoretical works appear first, followed by case studies. The first chapters deal with more theoretical approaches to postdigital cultural recycling and its impact on memory and history. Miriam Llamas Ubieto explores the development towards mass digitalisation and datafication that transforms our way of communicating and organising our knowledge in the postdigital age. Recycling has become a dominant trend because it is also part of the inherent dynamics of the postdigital age. Additionally, cultural recycling practices have acquired specific characteristics driven by unique features of the postdigital condition, including AI, platformisation, rendering, robotics, physics simulations, etc. The contribution first explains the notions of postdigital, recycling and cultural recycling and compares them with other associated terms. Then, it explores the specificities of the present phenomenon of postdigital cultural recycling. Finally, it addresses the epistemological productivity of the notion for understanding communicative phenomena characterised by the postdigital condition. For this purpose, Llamas Ubieto analyses various discourses and conceptualizations of the term 'recycling' and explores cultural and literary examples of postdigital cultural recycling applying a mediological,[1] a cultural theoretical and a philological approach.

The changes in postdigital culture described in the first chapter have an immediate effect on the way we do memory. Remembering and creating memory – be it individual or collective – is highly influenced and dependent on growing digitalisation and datafication. In her contribution, Johanna Vollmeyer puts the focus on literary texts as cultural products that are recycled in and through digital media and contribute to the creation of memory. Through two examples, she analyses how digital media appropriate these texts and adjust them to their algorithmic logic, and how literary texts reflect this process.

Linda Maeding deals with the past from a different angle. Her contribution focuses on history and its meaning in a postmodernist age. Through the Instagram account of Sophie Scholl, she raises questions about continuity in an age of radicalised technological reproducibility. Against the backdrop of Frederic Jameson's critique of postmodernism, Maeding elucidates how cultural recycling is now frequently conceived as an ahistorical practice that plays with nostalgia and retromania instead.

A strong focus on narratives is on the fore of Amelia Sanz's analysis of Amélie Nothomb's novels. Sanz focus lies on the clearly predigital narratives of the literary texts of this French author that nevertheless are made for a postdigital world. Taking advantage of the selective, performative, and collective features of the concept of recycling, Sanz examines how an author such as Amélie Nothomb, who determined to show herself as predigital, develops a storytelling by means of postdigital strategies for cultural recycling.

Questions about the use of canonical work in artistic practices for postdigital publishing are the topic of Maria Goicoechea's contribution. Taking Ulises Carrión's pioneering manifesto "The New Art of Making Books" (1975) as a starting point, she draws readers' attention to the work of artists that use canonical literature as raw material for their pieces, such as Jesse England's *E-Book Back Up* (2009), Jason Huff's *AutoSummarize* (2010), or Mimi Cabell and Jason Huff's *American Psycho* (2011). Goicoechea explores the different strategies involved in the process of cultural and literary recycling that these artists employ. A special focus lies on the use of print affordances as subversive and performative gestures that open a dialogue about contemporary notions of authorship, and originality.

1 A form of media theory that is based on the interdependency of technical mediality and semiosis. See Albrecht Koschorke: *Körperströme und Schriftverkehr. Mediologie des 18. Jahrhunderts*. Fink: Munich 1999, p. 11.

The presence and recycling of canonical works is also at the fore in María José Calvo's analysis "Besmette stad" (infected city), a *Gesamtkunstwerk* inspired by the poem collection *Bezette stad, 1921* (occupied city) by Flemish poet Paul van Ostaijen. His poems describe the German occupation of Antwerp during the First World War and are now recycled in such a way that the verses are reproduced unaltered but put into a new context – the Covid-19 pandemic. There they are remediated into new cross-media artifacts. As a result, the historical past is appropriated creatively by not only recreating the original in the present but also by embedding it into a new media context where a new message can arise.

The example of "Besmette stad" also shows how recycling can be understood as the basis for the creation of a canon. Adrián Menéndez de la Cuesta takes up this aspect of recycling processes when he focuses on how literary works are remediated in social networks through memes that help to reinforce or create a literary canon. He analyses how contemporary literature incorporates references to memes that, at least partially, have become 'canonical'. His research is guided by questioning which canon of literary works is most likely to be recycled and how do literature and memes interact in this recycling loop.

The importance of social media for the development of postdigital recycling is also highlighted by Antonio Domínguez Leiva. His case study deals with the proliferation of monoliths as an homage to S. Kubrick and A. Clarke's classic *2001 Space Odyssey* (1968). Only the massive distribution of images that show a monolith found in Utah made a meta-recycling of previous recycling processes employed by Kubrick and Clarke possible. This evokes a citational game that raises questions about classical issues of authorship and attribution. With Kubrick's monolith, contemporary art rediscovers some of its origins and evokes the original film and that of the works from which it was inspired by means of the same hypermodern quotation method.

Changes in the postdigital narratives are also at stake in Rafael Vidal Sanz' contribution about the recycling of 'the Ghostly' and Spiritism. Throughout time, 'the ghostly', the search for contact with a disappeared or invisible world, has found different media in which to nest. At the end of the nineteenth century, a new typology of photography emerged, 'spiritual photography', which through overexposure sought to print spirits on a photosensitive plate. Now, the new postdigital media, characterized by their virtuality, can serve as a medium for the ghostly. In his contribution Vidal Sanz analyses the way in which films, such as *Personal Shopper* (2016) by Olivier Assayas or *Host* (2020) by Rob Savage, introduce elements such as spiritism and ghosts into a recycling process by means of postdigital technologies.

The postdigital is also characterised by its interactivity and the double role of consumers as producers simultaneously. In this context, Silviano Carrasco analyses various recycling products of the fairy tale *Little Red Riding Hood* in board and video games. The author focuses on the active participation of prosumers in the development and marketing strategies of video games, hence in the creation of both the content and the appearance/design. Nevertheless, the same players seem to be hesitant when it comes to incorporating apps into classical board games that are frequently considered as invasive, for example.

Folktales not only play an important role in games, but in contemporary child literature, too. Teresa Cañadas García takes a closer look at the basic features of classical tales that are oral communication: universality and cohesive capacity. Both features that enhance their propensity for re-elaboration, re-appropriation, and re-use processes. In this context, recycling is nothing totally new but a typical narrative strategy in children's literature. However, recent remediation adapt traditional tales to today's world of technology in an unprecedented way as Cañadas shows.

Likewise, María del Pilar García-Carcedo is interested in a didactic approach towards the recycling of classical texts, in this case folk tales in social media. She analyses the production of memes created by students of the Faculty of Education at Complutense University, based on various versions of some of the best-known folk tales in the world (*Cinderella*, *Little Red Riding Hood* and *Sleeping Beauty*, as well as on a lesser-known tale in the Hispanic tradition, *Blancaflor*). By means of her student's production she shows how traditional folk tales have been the object of a wide variety of versions and transformations through the ages, but that their skeleton, structure, and archetypes do not vary. That converts the stories into perfect material for modern digital recycling.

Begoña Regeiro Salgado also puts predigital narratives at stake. Her case study focuses on texts written in a predigital age that are now recycled for educational purposes. She shows how cultural recycling has not only become a key mechanism in the processes of production and reception of literary texts but is also a key strategy in the didactics of literature. A frequent critique is that teachers often fail to present classical texts to students in an attractive or meaningful way. In her contribution she proposes that literary recycling with postdigital tools can help establish a contact with the text as it was originally conceived by the author.

This volume, along with the contributions contained in it, is the result of the studies carried out within the scope of the REC-LIT (REC-LIT Cultural Recycling: Transliteratures in the Postdigital Age, RTI2018-094607-B-I00) research project, funded by the EU's ERDF/Spain's Ministry of Science and Innovation – AEI: an interdisciplinary project based on theoretical and applied research, with the purposes to identify cultural recycling strategies of the literary, and to find traces of postdigital culture, as well as postglobal and postdata tendencies.

Miriam Llamas Ubieto
Universidad Complutense de Madrid

Postdigital Cultural Recycling

Abstract: Given that we are now in a postdigital condition (Cramer 2014, Cox 2014, Berry 2015, Jordan 2020) that affects all our daily cultural practices, we have to ask ourselves how this affects the production, circulation and reception of cultural elements. As the shift towards the postdigital condition involves using mass digitisation and datafication to transform the way we communicate and organise knowledge, these practices of production, circulation and reception show that content recycling is now the dominant trend. This trend is driven by several specific features of postdigital culture. This chapter investigates the extent to which these recycling practices and phenomena have acquired specific characteristics as a result of this postdigital condition. Using various discourses and conceptualisations of the term 'recycling' applied to culture, it addresses the question of whether "cultural recycling" is an appropriate and productive conceptualisation of certain communicative phenomena characterised by the postdigital condition.

Keywords: postdigital, cultural recycling, AI, literature, memory, circulation

> *"I've always said that creativity is the world's greatest recycling program."*
>
> *(Scott Belsky, Chief Strategy Officer and EVP, Design and Emerging Products, Adobe. In: "How Generative AI is Transforming the Creative Process: Fireside Chat with Scott Belsky (Adobe) and Bryan Catanzaro (NVIDIA)", Nvidia GTC 2023, retrieved 22.03.2023).*

1. Introduction

In a 2002 field study of memory, Neville and Villeneuve noted that recycling "has become the paradigm of cultural production today. If we thus recur to the notion of recycling, it is to address the necessary ambiguity that arises between value and void […] authenticity and 'simulacrum,' just as those between subject and objects at its disposal in cultural production, […] This explains why 'recycling' is inadequately comprehended within a positive or negative axiology." (Neville / Villeneuve 2002, p. 6). More than two decades have passed from since this consideration of recycling as a core element for explaining cultural production.

Belsky's contemporary phrase shows a similar relevance of recycling. In Belsky's conceptualisation, recycling is part of the current discourse that explains the interior operation of human beings by metaphors which suggest its similarity to digital technological productions. Like a hall of mirrors, these productions are positioned as though they are innate and inherent to humans, as a symbolic and cultural being (Cassirer [1944] 1996, p. 51), with the coinage of terms like (artificial) 'intelligence' or (machine) 'learning'[1] and many more. What is decisive about Belsky's statement is the awareness of those developing the technologies that shape our world and our reality that the great human process and great act of individual processing they are emulating – and simultaneously transforming – is precisely that of recycling.

Academics in the humanities demonstrated interest in cultural recycling. The concept appears in publications on cultural and media practices during the 1990s and early 2000s. Despite this interest, work on its conceptualisation seems to have been abandoned along with any in-depth interrogation of it as a critical tool to understand digital culture, precisely at a time when culture experienced the seismic shift of mass digitalisation.[2] In Media Studies, communications, studies of art and literature, philosophy, sociology and psychology, and even critical digital humanities, the dominant approaches to understanding digital culture have often focused two avenues: 1) either analysing notions inherent to technological infrastructure itself, which they see as an extreme materialised expression of prior concepts, as in the case of hypertext, virtuality and interactivity; or 2) they focus on the consequences of these infrastructures for the organisation of knowledge and communicative, social, identitarian, and everyday practices. Both approaches have deployed an arsenal of terminology that describe communicative phenomena in social networks and in a variety of logics of the digital media. As a result, terms that already existed in 20th-Century literary, linguistic, and artistic theories, such as intertextuality and adaptation, continued to be applied. Other terms, such as remix, mash-up, sampling, remediation, etc., have been reintroduced and adapted specifically to digital culture. They have expanded particularly in the field of media and popular cultural studies.

---

1 I will from now on generally refer to Artificial Intelligence as AI, and to Machine Learning as ML, although both terms, from the strict point of view of meaning, are not very appropriate for referring to these systems.

2 Of course, there are very honourable exceptions which link cultural recycling and digitality, including Ernst (2002), in the same volume of Neville and Villeneuve (2002) or those of Klucinskas and Moser (2004).

The aim here is not to question the validity and epistemological productivity of all of them, but it is striking that it is precisely 'recycling' which has been relegated to the background. In the best cases, it is used as a simple synonym for terms like remix.[3] In the worst cases, it is criticised as a term of infinite scope, rendering it semantically empty and unusable as a concept to understand cultural practices.[4] The primary aim of the present study is to rehabilitate 'cultural recycling' by demonstrating its epistemological productivity as a critical tool for reflecting on cultural processes, phenomena and practices. 'Cultural recycling' is particularly appropriate and operational when interrogating cultural phenomena and practices in the current media ecology due to the concomitances with it, and because it offers an angle of observation which does not appear in other more frequently used terms. The second objective is to explore the specific characteristics acquired by cultural recycling in the postdigital condition. The question is: What does cultural recycling consist of when it is steeped in the postdigital condition and affected by it? While this could be split into two questions, it is posed here as a single question precisely because of the intersections of the fact of the postdigital condition and the phenomena and practices that constitute this condition. Recycling is an operational term for some practices in the postdigital condition because recycling is a relevant element in the condition, but in which the recycling practices have subsequently mutated.

2. Postdigital condition and cultural practices

We are immersed in a situation which is conditioned by digital technological changes that affect all kinds of cultural practices in everyday life.[5] The (ontological) definition of 'medium' is a carrier of signs with three functions: storage, transmission and (today) calculation (based on data) (Wetzel 2017, pp. 467, 472). The profound change in current mediality lies in the fact that the calculation, which intersects with other functions, assists in two essential features of digital mediality: computation and subsequent automation. Starting with Wetzel's definition, I propose a variation: I distinguish between three modalities of the

---

3 For examples of the use in the area of Remix Studies of the term 'recycling', see Navas (2015, pp. 122, 123, 125, 126, 128); Navas (2022, pp. 5, 77, 199, 200); Navas / Gallagher / burrough 2021a, pp. 2, 4) or Gunkel (2006, pp. xviii, xxvii).

4 See: Kendall / Koster (2007) and Randall (2007).

5 'Cultural practices' are understood here from an intermediate position of social practices between the cultural dimensions of the individual, collective and material or practical, following the notion of social practices of Andreas Reckwitz ([2000] 2006, p. 559).

computerised medium, associated with its function: the medium as digital storage (sustained by databases and by programming using algorithms); the medium as telecommunication (remote transmission and hyper-connection); and the medium as carrier (i.e. the digital object, format, etc. which transfers signs or messages, but is now charged with computation and automation).[6] Given that medium as a carrier is essentially communicative, this change in its nature impacts the area of communication and processes, phenomena and practices associated with it (storage and transfer of signs of knowledge or of signs of significant and aesthetic creation). Thus, it also affects practices of organisation, access, transfer and reception of knowledge, which are in turn necessary for knowledge production processes or for communicative processes, such as creative-aesthetic processes.

We are dealing with cultural practices and manifestations of reception, production and circulation that change through the impact of recent technological and digital developments and the impact of a cultural sphere that has also been remodelled until it becomes a new medial/economic ecology that is based on logics inherent to advanced techno-capitalism. The industries and institutions of knowledge, information, production, creation (advertising, entertainment, art, etc.) have metamorphised into this economic-medial system that allows and, at the same time, restricts practices of reception, production, and circulation. In this new cultural regime, which once more engages with talent, ingenuity and newness and recapitalises them, there is an intersection of the popular or amateur and the professional; the industrial/mercantile and the heteronomous; rigorous knowledge and information with a background of lack of knowledge; the mechanical and the human; digital and analogue.[7] The operational basis of these practices (reception, production and distribution/circulation) is the same environment that unites them and has a certain logic and special features derived from digital mediality during its expansion in the 1990s and after. As well as the aforementioned computation (calculation and algorithm function) and automation (acting by itself following pre-programming), modularity (sectioning and reorganisation of information and data or fragmentation), composition (combination), numerical representation

6 For a detailed outline of the debate on the concept of 'media', see Burkhardt (2015).

7 The term should be understood in its common cultural meaning as a digital electronic system and not strictly in the physics-based distinction between discrete signs (whether binary or not) and other types of signals. For the difference between analogue and digital in both areas, see Cramer (2014).

(with computational codes based on mathematical functions) and digital mimetic (re)presentation (Manovich 2001, pp. 27–31)[8] of all kinds of virtual components are also noteworthy. The latter may be understood as representation or as digital configuration, which is computer-generated. Behind it lies a cultural reconfiguration based on computer/mathematical codes (for example, in Physics Simulation, which consists of modelling how objects would behave in real situations) and, as noted by Manovich, behind it lie aesthetic selections, the logic inherent to software (Manovich 2013), as well as logics inherent to the economic model which has been imposed over the last two decades. Today's technological sophistication and the concomitant sophistication of cultural industries mean that we are no longer dealing with a "metamedium" (Manovich 2013, pp. 83, 101–106),[9] but with a panmedial universe in which, as the prefix 'pan-' suggests, few practices without digital components are omitted in this panmedial universe. In one way or another, digital is the access point to the analogue (think about how often a card catalogue cabinet is consulted in a library to find a publication). Modern analogue, or neo-analogue, retro-analogue and even retro-paleodigital, reflect the digital or are related with digital, albeit as antithesis. In this way, this integrated digitality grows, "embedded" and "embodied" (Hine 2015), in everything, but goes beyond this integration because digitality has become a co-actant in an environment which is already a digital/analogue hybrid.

Not even the Internet can be explained simply as an infrastructure in the form of the web, network of networks, equivalent to hypertext.[10] In this panmedial environment, the amalgam that joins it together is constituted by digital infrastructures that are interconnected and enable the spread of elements (Jenkins / Ford / Green 2013) thanks to the interoperability of platforms and to their convergence (Jenkins 2006), which mould a form of participatory culture. The Internet has thus shifted since the boom of social networks and other services, from being an open network of networks to one of platforms (van Dijck 2013; van Dijck / Poell / De Wall 2018), and then to platformisation (Nieborg / Poell 2018), in which the platforms become dominant economic and social structures (Helmond 2015) that organise, design, guide and even direct practices

8 Manovich (2001) also includes variability and cultural transcodification among the characteristics.

9 This environment functions as metasystems which support many different types of information structures and can represent many other media, which are in turn reinforced with new properties and new tools for working with them (Manovich 2013, pp. 83, 101–106).

10 As Landow (1992 and 2006) said, borrowing the idea from Barthes.

of interaction and accessibility. In the new 'surveillance capitalism' (Zuboff 2019), companies' recapture of user data and the use of content and interactions which they create becomes a decisive element in the economic model. As García Arnau states, the consumption of these platforms is governed by their designs, whose aim is to maintain consumers hooked for as long as possible, articulating a new logic focused on the subject:[11] "They fight to ensure that it is not we who self-govern ourselves in consumption, but that we should be vulnerable to what they offer" (García Arnau 2020a), by what he calls "personalised mass directionality" (García Arnau 2015, pp. 373–381; García Arnau 2021). That is why, parallel to the "participatory culture" of Jenkins (2006), Shäfer shows how the industrial sequence of "design, affordance, appropriation by the users" becomes an interminable cycle in which the "[p]roducts that have been developed by users beyond established industries can in turn be implemented into those industries' business models. Further, modified products may be re-implemented by their original vendors as new or further developed design." (2011, p. 168).

Therefore, tools that are easy to use by users become key. The practices nevertheless are not as free as they appear, nor is the network they form so open as one may think just because it allows everyone to act, compared with the previous restrictive system of production, publication, and distribution. It is no coincidence that within the framework of the ELO (Electronic Literature Organization) there is already talk of the post-web (Monfort 2018) since Leonardo Flores (its then president) launched the idea of a third generation of electronic literature in 2018 (Flores 2019). It is therefore a case of the practices of cultural production and distribution[12] being created by using web 2.0 and the platforms, apps, availability of big data and the composition and postproduction tools (Bourriaud 2002) that do not require knowledge of computing, but of the operating codes that have been designed and are easy to use. Productions of this type reflect this new medial ecology of recent years. This may become conformist or, as indicated by Saum-Pascual, "maintain a hyperawareness of the capitalist commodification and datafication of human experience on the Web,

11 This characteristic of personalisation in the ecosystem of digital technology had already been announced by Manovich in 2001: "[…] new media follows, or actually runs ahead of, a quite different logic of post-industrial society – that of individual customization, rather than mass standardization" (2001, p. 30). But, as can be seen in current studies, being subject-centred does not imply there is no propagation at the same time as mass standardisation, due to the adoption of repetitive rules and practices inherent to this digital cultural order.

12 Although they refer to literary manifestations in this case, his proposal can be extended.

but [...] oscillates between defiance and conformism" (2020, p. 3) because "the rules of virality within the platform ended up defining and commodifying our participation" (Saum-Pascual 2020, p. 5).

Precisely at the time when digitality is passing through more layers of the everyday, i.e. both fixed and mobile practices and objects, the impact of this shift with respect to the form of communicating on the Internet is that it is becoming more invisible. In fact, the invisibility of this digital mediality, as well as the way in which it guides our actions and practices, is one of the first aspects that appear in the postdigital discourse: the awareness of being in a different situation with respect to the digital. In "Beyond Digital", Negroponte (1998) already predicted this very situation as one in which the medium becomes as "everyday" and transparent as water or air, as electricity in its time. Paradoxically at the time when digital technology is more omnipresent, ubiquitous and everyday than ever, it is rendered increasingly more transparent and invisible[13] and of course less "new". This has been the starting point in the history of the conceptualisations of the term 'postdigital', which first appears in the area of art and studies of electronic music circa 2000. It was introduced by Cascone in the academic field (2000), taking the idea of Negroponte (1998) of the end of the digital revolution once technology had become imperceptible. Cramer (2014) takes up the term for a condition after the perception of digital media as new, but, as in *post-apocalyptic*, with an understanding of the postdigital as a condition in which the digital has not been superseded (Cramer 2014) but has advanced from a past moment of rupture to a continuous state, implying a continuation of the consequences of the digital (albeit revised, and without having overcome said consequences).[14] Often in those years, this refers to artistic manifestations that criticise what is digital.

---

13 And it is this notion of invisibility which does not disappear but increases in discursive and colloquial forms that continue to convert technology into a spectral ghost. The comparison of AI of the last generation with a "blackbox" is a good example of this. In this way, the idea is created of inaccessibility and incomprehension, an enigma or a monster, the two limits of culture according to Ricardo Piglia, "El juego de organización — uno podría decir — de los límites de una cultura están dados por el enigma y el monstruo" ["The game of organising, one could say, the limits of a culture are provided by the enigma and the monster"] (1991, pp. 4–5), as if the attempt of all understanding must be aborted and remain on the surface of an irreflexive but fascinating use. (All Spanish sources are translated by the author.)

14 See the articles by Cox and Cramer in relation to the term 'post-digital' and the concept of the 'post-' prefix. Cramer mostly uses the term to refer to a condition or set of aesthetic and artistic trends that share two things in common: (1) they can only exist once the new media have ceased to be 'new' because they have become ubiquitous and

I have borrowed from Cramer (2014) and Jordan (2020, pp. 8–15) the notion of 'postdigital condition' to define this situation, albeit with certain qualifications. The aim of this definition is not only to emphasise the change of perception through the everyday aspect, intensification, ubiquity, and amount of the digital. I further consider that postdigital also refers to a modification of the digital technological qualities *per se*, which are the basis of this new situation of continuous mutation subject to the forms adopted by digital media ecology, in the unceasing creation of novelty, and to which we adapt. In line with Cramer (2014) and Cox (2014), I do not use 'post-' according to a logic of periodisation, as in post-history, where it would indicate that something had been overcome or had ended, because we are currently at a time of unprecedented computerisation and "digitization"· (Cox 2014). Rather I argue that the utility of post- (Latin 'behind, after' – in both the spatial and temporal sense) lies in the capacity it endows to (1) name something that occurs behind the digital revolution and is a consequence produced by and inseparable from it and (2) designate a later state, rather than an event, following the break with the analogue world induced by the digital revolution. Thus, one of the fundamental characteristics of the postdigital condition is the analogue-digital continuum, as Cramer suggested (2014). In other words, digital is no longer only an interface on the computer monitor (like a 'prothesis' of the analogue, in the sense indicated by McLuhan); rather, reality is increasingly perforated by digital information, from the Internet of things, moving through different forms of augmented reality or the implementation of data mining which affect everyday human actions, and including human-machine interactions in the physical environment.[15] In addition, there has been a mass digitisation of the real, modelled by computer programming languages and an algorithmisation that is nourished by enormous databases (big data), but which also leads to the generation and modelling of new virtual realities (for example, generative AI), the configuration of virtual simulation interfaces or an increasingly immersive virtual reality. They are different degrees of intensification

every day, and (2) they involve ways of overcoming the dichotomy between analogue and digital for this same reason. For a more detailed history, particularly in the spheres of art and culture, see Llamas Ubieto (2020).

15 The convergence between physical and digital "channels" has also been called in the commercial area for more than a decade the "phygital", referring to creating a customer experience in which the two converge (see Vate-U-Lan et al. 2016), but in the stricter sense the term is used for a type of interface and "tangible interaction where digital and physical contents are combined" (Gelsomini / Spitale / Garzotto 2021).

of the computational presence by which the boundary between the analogue and the digital becomes so blurred it practically disappears.

This transition to the postdigital condition may be dated to the middle of the first decade of the 21st Century, coinciding with the boom of digital capitalism (Betancourt 2016) and with the development and mass availability of pre-existing technologies (such as social networks) or smartphones.[16] It is continuing with what appears to be an unprecedented intensification of developments of what are called the "exponential technologies" (Bree 2023, p. 6): those which "allow the change to an accelerated velocity" by "cost reduction and substantial progress in areas such as computational power, bandwidth and data storage." (Bree 2023, p. 6). It is an incessant and permanent state of mutation by innovations in computation which improve its capacities and power within short periods and is the basis of what I have termed digital panmediality. What also substantially contributes to this is that developments in different areas converge (AI, robotics, rendering, Physics Simulation, new materials, and processors, etc.), which boost in their intersections the technological creations of hardware and software which would not have been possible years ago. It becomes a continuous incorporation of innovations in digital technology that bring with them transformations of practices and entire cultural spheres, often accelerated without sufficient time to adapt to each new point, because time itself is increasingly compacted. It is no wonder that their impact is said to be producing the fourth industrial revolution (Schwab 2017). In the cultural field, all of them can be understood as bases for the postdigital condition and the generation of new forms of knowledge and perception. In summary, the following developments can be highlighted: the sophisticated and intensified use of computation and algorithms (such as in the "sequential paradigm" of linear algorithms and in the "connectionist paradigm" of the so-called artificial neural networks included in different forms of AI),[17]

16 There is a time difference between the arrival and mass establishment of certain technological developments in different social strata and geographical spaces, depending on economic and geopolitical matters.

17 As Rodríguez explains in this respect, "an AI device is simply a computational architecture which aims to emulate the behaviour of the human brain by the design of systems of autonomous learning (machine learning and deep learning) based on the processing of large amounts of information in the form of data from which patterns are extracted by statistical induction processes. The output of AI, which in the common jargon we call 'decisions' is the result of a probabilistic calculation based on previously detected patterns incorporated into the operation of the computational system." (2020, pp. 24–25). Bajohr makes this division between two algorithmic paradigms (Bajohr 2022a).

combined with datafication, platformisation,[18] permanent hyperconnectivity, robotics and the developments in rendering, simulation, or virtuality.

The growing automation allowed by these algorithmic, datafication and virtualisation processes and the mix of them with analogue reality lead to two essential characteristics of the postdigital condition. First, the existence of an alternative virtual 'space' or dimension, a non-place, whose basis is computational and its form is that of logico-mathematical and topological infrastructures that carry out a number of operations: connect, process, analyse, generate, model and store based on data (including the real datafied elements and/or other data which, in a pseudo-mimetic relation, generate new inexistent modelling, for example, by rendering). Because of this logico-mathematical and topological nature, its materiality, which generates virtual productions, differs from previous means of virtual creation (such as the cinema, photography or the typewriter). Combined with the speed of automation, it brings with it the impression that it is in-material[19] or even invisible. The code and calculations are hidden and this logic does not tend to be visualised. Behind it the priority is for "an abstract unity of reified elements" (Berry 2015, p. 49) over meaning to the point that some tasks, due to speed, high resolution, or intangibility, are not seen, and are illegible or opaque, except for the ornamental surfaces of the software and interfaces. At times it even "requires the mediation of software, and hence a double-hermeneutic" (Berry 2015, p. 49). But this operation has associated patterns and logics of "commodification" (sometimes hidden) which can be historicised, and which are extended in everyday life, as well as specific means of aesthetic relation.

Second, the hybridisation with this alternative virtual space instantiates new communication environments, which may be understood according to the notion of "Mixed Reality"[20] presented as a Reality-Virtuality Continuum which consists of being an "environment as one in which real world and virtual world objects are presented together within a single display, that is, anywhere between the extrema of the RV continuum" (Milgram / Takemura / Utsumi / Kishino 1994, p. 283), but which I understand in a broader sense as

---

18 The first four correspond to the related pillars that are noted by Jin in his exploration of cultural production in the AI era (2021, pp. 7–8).

19 As Berry notes, "although not immaterial, the digital is constituted through a complex series of abstraction layers which actually do enable programmers to work and code in an abstract machine disconnected in a *logical* sense from the materiality of the underlying silicon" (Berry 2015, p. 46).

20 In the rest of the text, Mixed Reality will often appear abbreviated to MR.

a more or less immersive continuum according to the form of graphic virtual or voice/audio interface. I would add as diverse according to the relation of co-actantiality which is established with it. A fundamental role is played by feedback and hybridism between the virtual dimension (sometimes almost invisibly integrated in objects or in the environment) and the analogue physical dimension.

3. The need to recover the term 'recycling' for the postdigital condition

It is worth asking why we should use the term 'recycling' today. Neville and Villeneuve (2002) were already talking two decades ago of this as a new paradigm. In 2023, Belsky notes that recycling has always existed. The need for the term today is even more pressing, if possible, than in the early days of the massification of these technologies when Neville and Villeneuve were writing. Now neither the process of digitising huge amounts of cultural elements nor the remediation (Bolter / Grusin [1999] 2000) from analogue media to a metamedium are so novel. So today, in the postdigital condition, the practices and elements coexist in this panmediality affected by the same dynamics and logics of functioning which cannot be understood without recycling. Moreover, this is a key insight that allows us to understand how changes in cultural practices bring with them transformations in our forms of sensitive perception, thought and cognitive processing or imagination, and thus involve new conceptions and imaginaries of the real. It is pressing to return to the term 'recycling' today to capture in another way what is happening and reflect on it in a different fashion. Cultural factors, schemes and elements have always survived thanks to multiple acts of recycling, repetition with variability in a practice similar to that carried out by a different agent. So Belsky was not wide of the mark. Husserl had already noted that this practice of repetition was the basis of intersubjectivity ([1922–1937] 1988, p. 21), without which there would be no persistence of cultural knowledge over time, or synchronously between various humans. Repetition may be an act of "Responsivität" and of dialogue or it may be an automatism. But in this new medial-economic ecosystem, this repetition, if it is extended with the implications of the term recycling, not only lies at the heart of the cultural, but also at the foundation of the mathematical-algorithmic and aesthetic designs of functioning of this ecosystem which now enable and condition the cultural. That is why the phenomenon of recycling and its characteristics have changed, but the term is also essential for conceptualising these phenomena and practices marked by the postdigital condition.

Recycling is thus a key piece of the functioning of the ecosystem because the underlying logics of the ecosystem are based on constant feedback and recursiveness. As Beer stresses, "These are recursive processes with algorithms being measured, honed and refined to suit the systems of measurement and the story they fit within – 'the models analyze the world and the world responds to the models.'" (2013, p. 74).

Not only does the design cycle of the model of platforms incorporate recycling, as mentioned earlier, but the presence of digitality grows and increases the storage (with their divergencies, obsolescences, deletions, suppressions and forgettings) up to an amount which is impossible to absorb in a human period of cognitive processing and reception. Pre-programming with AI based on the database itself[21] or the Internet to filter, select and recycle elements, supposedly in a personalised or subject-centred way and according to other criteria which we do not know about as user-consumers. The specialised human filters of access to knowledge, legitimised by their own acquired knowledge which confers on them the authority to discern information, wisdom and truth, are replaced by new parameters programmed by humans and by other types of filtering parties used as gateways for access and propagation (amateurs, dilettantes, influencers, super-specialised auto-didacts, the masses who legitimate a theme with their *likes*). Inter-subjectivity and collectivity are mediatised and guided. This also happens with other media, but the digitalisation of life lays new ground in this regard.

In an unprecedented absorption, the knowledge and production created by many are recycled synthetically for forms of automatic generation (with AI), that are based on statistical probability and prediction when comparing enormous amounts of human productions (textual, visual, computer code, etc.). This happens in a way that appears to invert the relationship in the mediatisation. With the latest developments of neural networks and deep learning, the human subject adopts the role of mediator. It is this that mediatises, making incursions (by way of reinforcement and prompts) in the productions generated automatically by the digital medium. This is often carried out for profit or private interest and not necessarily guided by humanistic criteria,[22] raising diverse questions, such as: to

21 For a more detailed explanation of the term 'database', as well as the meaning and interrelations of the notions of 'datum' and 'information', see Burckhardt (2015, pp. 149–203).

22 There is talk in this respect of "collaborative" intelligence to refer to these productions created by many and accessible to many (including machines) and of "collective intelligence" created between humans and machines (Bree 2023, pp. 37–38). In this case, the absorption takes advantage of both types of phenomena.

what extent can concomitances and common features (of cultural practices) that have not been discovered so far be found by this mass comparison? Will the co-actantial interaction of human users and machines to generate inferences, predictive probabilities and preprogrammed patterns lead to a standardisation in production and reception practices, to a continuous repetition of the same thing?

Add to this that the term 'recycling' is pertinent for reflecting on the cultural phenomena affected. First, because among other qualities to be tackled, three relevant aspects are associated with these dynamics mentioned earlier: temporality, movement, and the action of use. Recycling also allows the exploration of temporality in a threefold way, as it implies 'returning to' (look back to something again, for example) something pre-existing; it implies repetition (present twice) in its use and cyclical time (something is incorporated into a new life cycle or the same cycle, but once more), which certainly alludes to the movement of circulation and duration. Second, to these three aspects we can add one more benefit: recycling may be understood at a 'micro' level, as the action and result of a use which is specific and singular in time (temporal and concrete), or at a 'macro' scale, allowing a focus from a temporal and spatial distance in multiple cycles and circulations of something, or in multiple reincorporations of something into the same cycle. Hence, it explores the phenomena of a continuum, incessantly reintroducing what preceded, and of a constant circulation, guided technologically by the mediality in the postdigital condition.

In line with these ideas, before going further into the singularities of postdigital cultural recycling, it is important to understand the history of the term and present the conceptualisation proposed here as a starting point.

4. From recycling to cultural recycling

4.1. The term 'recycling'

The word 'recycling' is a recent coining, as its use began to be extended in the 20th Century after its appearance in the 1920s in the English language.[23] It is made up of morphemes with an ancient etymology: the Latin prefix 're-' (an inseparable particle which is only found in combinations[24]), the Latin lexeme

23 In Spain, for example, its use can be seen in the CORDE corpus for the first time in 1968 in the field of energy, raw materials, and industry, through the translation of a UNESCO publication.

24 *Nuevo diccionario latino-español etimológico* by Raimundo de Miguel y de Morante, Leipzig, Brockhaus (1867, p. 783), https://latinonline.es/diccionario-latin-espanol/pagina-783/.

cyclus which comes from the Greek *κύκλος* (*kýklos*) and the suffix '-ing' from the Pan-Germanic '*-unga', '*-inga'[25] and which, as in the Spanish '-aje' (from the French '-age', in turn from the Latin '-atĭcus'[26]), forms substantives based on verbs to express the action or result attached to the verb.[27] Thus, recycling is defined as both an action and the result, effect, or product of that action. This gives rise to the dual implication of both an action and concurrently that this action produces something (effect or result). The action and its result are of a specific type, due to the meanings of the prefix 're-', when combined with verbs. In this case, it means 'repetition', which implies that something takes place twice by the same action. This follows the Latin word *repetĕre*[28], to 're-address something or bring something again' (i.e. make something return again or carry out an action to return again to something that has been left behind). This connotes movement back to a previous moment, which is repeated and is made present again. This shares a connection to both as in *restĭtŭo*[29] (making something return in a new time to its previous state) and as in *rĕcordor* (bring to the heart (*cor*), where the memory resides (remember)).[30] In some cases 're-' is associated with repetition that is used for intensification, as we all know from rhetoric.[31]

---

25 *Online Etymology Dictionary* compiled by Douglas R. Harper, https://www.etymonline.com/search?q=-ing.

26 *Diccionario de la Lengua Española*, Real Academia de la Lengua Española, Edición 23.6 (2022).

27 See 'reciclaje' in *Diccionario de la Lengua Española*, Real Academia de la Lengua Española, Edición 23.6 (2022) and 'recycling' in *Oxford English Dictionary Online*. March 2023. Oxford University Press, https://www-oed-com.bucm.idm.oclc.org/view/Entry/271857? Third Edition, June 2009; most recently modified version published online March 2023, retrieved 16.06.2023.

28 *Breve Diccionario Etimológico de la Lengua Castellana*, ed. by Joan Corominas, 3. ed, Madrid, Gredos (1987, p. 503).

29 *Nuevo diccionario latino-español etimológico de Raimundo de Miguel y de Morante*, Leipzig, Brockhaus (1867, p. 808).

30 *Nuevo diccionario latino-español etimológico de Raimundo de Miguel y de Morante*, Leipzig, Brockhaus (1867, p. 786). Thus, we can see the association between 'recycling' and 'record' (to keep something for the future, to bring it to remembrance). See: *Online Etymology Dictionary* compiled by Douglas R. Harper, https://www.etymonline.com/word/record and *Cambridge Dictionary Online*, Cambridge UP, 2023, https://dictionary.cambridge.org/es/diccionario/ingles/record.

31 See 're-' in *Diccionario de la Lengua Española*, Real Academia de la Lengua Española, 23.6 Edition (2022).

This action and its result, which can denote 'happen twice', 'return to' or 'make something from the past return', unite two-time nuances in that both repetition and the action of 'returning to' have to be associated with the notion of cycle or circle in its dimension of movement over time. This introduces a third time nuance, its duration. Already in classical Greek, *κύκλος* (*kýklos*) came to designate 'circular movement' and 'cycle of time',[32] also understood as a 'cycle of seasons or events' (i.e. a recurrence and ordered sequence of phenomena which occur in a circular form) by means of a metaphoric transfer of the specific to the abstract, from the 'circular object' of any kind, such as orbits. This series of phases through which a phenomenon passes form a characteristic and ordered set which, when it closes, means returning to the start. If we observe the terms etymological journey, by extension it carries with it the idea of periodic repetition of itself which is found in notions of 'cycle of seasons' and 'cyclical time'.

Thus, this action of recycling brings with it the existence of something on which one necessarily acts to make it return and repeat again. It is pre-existing; but it is also inserted, processed, or passed through a cycle[33] again. Even the cyclical process itself (to which something is subject) "of a fixed sequence of events"[34] may be one that is repeated, and the recycling may refer to the reiteration of a process from its start to the end, indefinitely.

The semantic component of 'cycle' is key for any definition of the term recycle because it contributes movement. What is repeated does not simply repeat at another point in time but moves by its insertion in a time circle through which it passes. By being put into orbit, something pre-existing is made circulate in a life cycle. For both meanings ("passed through a cycle again" and "repetition of a fixed sequences of events"), the action of resuming something prior and inserting it in a circular movement may imply that this is done in the same cycle (i.e. the material is reincorporated repeatedly into the same cycle, for example, to extend or increase the effects of this cycle)[35] or that the cycle itself is repeated.

---

32 *Diccionario griego clásico-español*, Madrid, Vox, ed. by José M. Pabón (1967, p. 359); and *Dicciogriego* by José Sánchez Sanz, in https://www.dicciogriego.es/index.php#esp?lema=617&n=617&s=ciclo%20(de%20tiempo), retrieved 16.06.2023.

33 *Random House Unabridged Dictionary of American English* (2023) https://www.wordreference.com/definition/recycle.

34 See the meaning of 'recycle' as noun in *Collins English Dictionary. Copyright HarperCollins Publishers*, https://www.collinsdictionary.com/dictionary/english/recycle, retrieved 16.06.2023.

35 See this meaning in *Diccionario de la Lengua Española*, Real Academia de la Lengua Española, 23.6 Edition (2022).

In the latter case, the material is incorporated repeatedly in a sequence of events, but in a new cycle with the same material.

In both cases, the material circulates again, once more passing through a cycle (whether the same or another), and therefore 'lives' a new cyclical sequence or episode of circulation, extending its life. It could be said that a new time cycle of life is given to the material.[36] The current connotation of 'something pre-existing' that is the object of the action as material is due to use in descriptions of the physical processes of the thermal, chemical and hydrocarbon industries of the United States, where it meant a re-introduction of a substance into a cyclical process (refining) to recover components (such as phenols from ammoniacal gas liquor).[37] It is no coincidence that the term arose with this literal meaning at the heart of the Second Industrial Revolution, as it was precisely the mass mercantile production of the technical-industrial revolution that transformed processes and actions on materials. A term was needed to name a new reality, technique, or cultural practice, but only the technical form and its potential had changed, as the separation and reincorporation of elements in processes were not intrinsically new. In its coinage, the 'action' component of the meaning acquired a strong association with production, especially within the framework of very specific processes. It already assumed an economic, productive, and technical type in the context of exponential increases in production and consumption of goods, as well as the generation of waste. Here we have the concurrent contemporary meanings of 'recycling': of the production of something new coexisting with the use of something pre-existing, which may even have been thrown away or taken out the system.

After the Second World War, it is unsurprising that analogous terms appear, as happens with cybernetics (and other systemic theories), and with 'feedback', a mechanism for feeding "a system or circuit by the return of part of its output."[38]

---

36 For example, to mitigate its impact on the environment and thus extend the duration and sustainability of the constant life cycle on earth, as happens with the current use of the term in ecological discourse. See Hauser (2010), Windmühler (2014) or Bühler (2015).

37 The *OED* thesaurus refers to the U.S. Patent 1,566,796 8/1 from 1925 (https://patents.google.com/patent/US1566796A/en?oq=1%2c566%2c796+1925) as the first documented use as a verb and noun in this field. This origin also appears in *Merriam-Webster*, and in Graeber (2012, p. 281); Windmühler (2014, p. 105) and Reynier (2022, p. 24).

38 See the meaning of 'feedback' as "a system or circuit created through the input of part of its output", in *Diccionario de la Lengua Española*, Real Academia de la Lengua Española, 23.6 Edition (2022).

This attributed movement in a circular loop of not only to raw materials and fluids, but to other types of materials, including information and electronic computer signals. Like 'feedback', 'recycling' will suffer a metaphoric shift in which it also refers to signs, symbols, and cultural materials. This extensive meaning of recyclable materials, whose sole condition for this capacity is having formed part of a cycle or processing, will be maintained here for the definition of cultural recycling. To understand how we reach this point, it is necessary to observe how the term 'recycling' has acquired other connotations as it continued its path to the current discourses of economic and industrial production.

In the 1960s and 1970s, resulting from growing concerns about environmental sustainability (negatively affected by industrialisation) and criticisms of consumerism, inspired by the theoretical and systemic explanations such as those mentioned, the discourse of ecology arose as a science of survival (Bühler 2015, p. 231). Within that discourse, the term 'recycling' nuanced again to acquire its current meanings. In the original Greek, economics consisted of the regulation or management of *οἶκος* (gr.) "the self-sufficient household" (Graeber 2012, p. 283). The term shifts during the industrial revolution from the self-sufficient and self-contained household to a larger industrial context. There appears as early as the 19th Century the image of circulation from nature to manufacturing, which reaches consumers through the market, including, according to Marx, the reintroduction of "Exkremente" in the circulation of production and consumption (Kirchmann 2006, p. 504). The ecology of the late 19th Century was also based on circularity in its object of study, *οἶκος*, now as the overall relations of the animal with its organic and inorganic environment (Graeber 2012, p. 284). From the 1970s, the pursuit of finding a balance in the relationship with nature was proposed as a new idea of circularity of production-consumption that restores the natural cycles interrupted by humans' linear production-consumption dynamics, which deplete and destroy the environment. As indicated by Bühler, it is at the crossroads between politics, science, and technology that this new acceptance of recycling arises (2015, p. 226). To this a legal status will be added in the 1970s.[39] Understood in this perspective, 'recycling' incorporates a material previously used or a waste product of the process of production and consumption

---

39 As a number of authors mention, of particular importance for this is the study of the Club of Rome on limits to growth (1972). The report has several precedents in programmes and legislation (Windmühler 2014, p. 107; Albrecht 2001, p. 11) for the organisation of sustainability of forests (in the 16th Century in Germany, according to Albrecht (2001, p. 10)) or household waste starting in the early 20th Century (Windmühler 2014, p. 106), to give two examples. This idea of "reprocessing waste

that is circulated in a natural life cycle in which it is reused.[40] It therefore confers a number of useful life cycles to this material. This re-incorporation often implies some type of processing of the material (such as oil refining), especially when it is waste material or even as hazardous. In the today's colloquial meaning, recycling also refers to the reuse or recovery of materials used, even if they do not have the status of waste.[41] It is worth highlighting that although practices of this kind are called recycling, they go back to prehistory and became more sophisticated with industrialisation.[42]

The change of ecological discourse turns recycling into a moral category and refers not only to manufacturing action, but also to the behaviour of individual consumers (Graeber 2012, p. 281). It differs from other forms of waste reclamation focused on economic goals by the incorporation of environmental sustainability objectives (Hoffmann 2001, p. 473).[43] The translation of the English word 'recycling' into German is insightful here. In the sense of *Wiederverwendung* (reuse) and *Wiederverwertung* (revaluation), one can explicitly appreciate that the act implies a change in value of materials subject to the new instantiation

---

materials when the productive process is carried out […]" appears in the *Diccionario panhispánico del español jurídico* (2023), https://dpej.rae.es/.

40 In this respect, it is worth noting the thesis of Bühler, who warns that the current ecological theories understand ecological space as a totality which differs from other ideas of space because the circulations are its constitutive organising element (2015, p. 234). The imaginary construct of these circulations is closed and human beings have a twin position in this respect: as part of the ecosystem (of nature and the cycle) they are objects of recycling and are affected by it; and in turn, as "Akteur", they interrupt or modify these cycles from which they take things which they place in them again, therefore from a position external to this 'cycling'. To this we can add that these circulations (*Kreisläufe*) are not closed, as it raises the question of the rest, or what is left outside the relations involved in these systems (Bühler 2015, pp. 228–231, 241) or the problems which the chemical process of recycling itself may generate for the environment (such as that of radioactive waste).

41 See 'recycling' in *Merriam-Webster Dictionary*, https://www.merriam-webster.com/.

42 For more information on the notion and history of the phenomena of recycling, see the bibliography on the discourse and cultural practices of waste, such as Albrecht (2001), Hauser (2010), Alexander / Reno (2012), Windmühler (2014), Bühler (2015), Fennetaux / Junqua / Vasset (2015), Fernández Mallo (2018), or Assmann (2020).

43 This is reflected in the popular 1970s American slogan "reduce, reuse, recycle" (Hoffmann 2001, p. 473). Moreover, as Windmühler notes, the term 'recycling' has now not only acquired a political and moral component, but an ideological one (2014, p. 106) with an utopian potential for improvement and a promise of salvation and the avoidance of destruction (2014, pp. 107–108), with connotations that are even religious.

(Albrecht 2001, p. 8, Hoffmann 2001, p. 472, Hauser 2010, p. 45, and Windmühler 2014, p. 104). In this intermediate state of the process or action of recycling, it leaves behind the status of waste to re-acquire a value of use (or at times also of the economy or market), but it also has been transformed by the relationship with the new situation (temporal, contextual) and acquires a different value. This dynamic is a cultural construct, and it is a critical component in defining 'cultural recycling'.

Recycling as an action may adopt different basic operations or strategies which lead to the incorporation and reuse of the material in a cycle. These are analogous to the procedures identified by the aesthetic: like the transfer to another context, classification, decomposition or separation, the reclassification, recombination and modification of the form or material (transformation). They may involve a manual action and/or a technical action. Their inherent iterativity also always implies variation, although it may be the minimum provided by the new moment when it is integrated. The fact that it always implies (re)covery and variation does not necessarily allude to a change in the ontological status of the material that is the object of recycling, rather simply to the function (for example, the bottle may serve as a jar or have the same function if it is used to drink another liquid). At other times, the transformation is such that the material is completely modified, or only a part is taken, and latent remains can barely be detected (as when obtaining new raw materials, obtaining new chemical components, or creating something using existing materials that are barely recognisable or have become energy). It may be that the new use has the same function as the recycled material (such as paper which comes from recycled paper). It should also be clarified that the recovery does not necessarily imply a loss of quality or devaluation of status; in fact, quite the opposite.

4.2. Cultural recycling

By means of a metaphorical shift, recycling becomes a category with a specific meaning in the cultural arena, designating cultural practices and productions in the broadest sense. In other words, it not only refers to industrial processes or economic and ecological recovery based on waste but maintains its semantic etymological load and connotes those uses. That is why some aspects implied in the restricted sense of recycling which have been covered in theoretical cultural studies may be useful, as we shall see below.

Artistic forms that have used remains have been known since Antiquity, as well as the avant-garde manipulation of throwaway elements. Already by the 1950s there were artistic manifestations which used waste with a critical ecological awareness. Even though recycling was transformed into an artistic cultural category starting in the 1990s, studies not only address this type of art, but open up other artistic and cultural manifestations (beyond the artistic canon) that recover preceding materialities. Of note regarding the introduction of this term in the area of cultural studies is, *inter alia*, the work of the research team of the University of Montreal.[44] Its aim has been to explain processes and modes of cultural production and the recovery of materials from a new epistemological perspective.[45] In both the Anglo-Saxon and French academic worlds, as well as the German *Kulturwissenschaft* linked to visual studies and studies of memory,[46] its appearance in the academic field of cultural studies, as noted by Rigeade, Latham and Marie, can be explained because "of the way a cultural production changes meaning when it is received in another cultural frame [...], Cultural Studies covers heterogeneous fields in art and culture, both highbrow and lowbrow, celebrated works of art as well as forgotten 'practices of everyday life'" (2022, p. 2). They allude to Klucinskas and Moser to note that in this frame "recycling is not only a current concern but also a fuel in western culture" (Rigeade, Latham and Marie 2022, p. 2). Due to globalisation, it is not only present in western culture.[47]

Beyond the studies in this academic field that have worked on practices and discourses of economic and ecological recycling and the category of waste as a cultural construct from the 1980s,[48] the term 'cultural recycling' is defined in the present work as the action of use and/or processing of a pre-existing cultural material, which implies its decoupling from a previous context and its placement again in a new life cycle (thus its circulation). It explains cultural processes (and therefore communicative processes) of reception, (re)production and circulation in a way which offers epistemological advantages. From its etymological roots, it derives this first possibility of understanding it as communicative cultural

44 The work was carried out above all from 1992 to 2001, although they continued publishing (see Klucinkas and Moser (2004, pp. ix-x)). Also of note in German is the work by Schneider (1997).

45 See Klucinskas and Moser (2004, pp. 1–29); Moser (2007).

46 See Hoffmann (2001); Kirchmann (2006); Jacke / Kimminich / Schmidt (2006) and Neville / Villeneuve (2002).

47 In the area of literary studies, worth highlighting apart from the works by Klucinskas / Moser (2004) and Moser (2007), are the publications by Kalaga (2011), Assmann (2019) and Rigade / Latham / Marie (2022).

48 For example, see Thompson (1979), Albrecht (2001), partly also Martin (2008), Hauser (2010), Alexander / Reno (2012) or Assmann (2020).

practices which return to something pre-existing, repeated in the present and enabled to circulate. It may be an interpretative reception made by a subject, which is therefore crossed by it, replicating it, and reacting to this query which comes from another time. In this way, it is of itself a new cultural production as an event or practice in a different context. This production may lead to a construction in the form of a new product more or less similar to a previous form.

It adopts four aspects from its industrial and economic meaning. 1. It is an action of use; 2. It is a process and an intervention which often has associated mechanical operations or symbolic cultural manipulations of use for iterative creation based on something or for its reuse with another function (similar or different to the previous source), which in the cultural field is equivalent to aesthetic-semiotic operations. 3. These processes are carried out on a material which is replicated in this new use, so that it is re-contextualised in a new production (also if it is a production as a communicative event, not only a new product) "sometimes referring to objects being turned into something entirely different, or sometimes to old objects remaining somehow enmeshed in the new" (Stanford in Wilson / Stanford 2022, p. 60) and 4. Its incorporation in this way into a new circuit or continuous surrounding circulation.

The question which arises, and is not present in these notions, is that of a "media-technological condition" (Moser 2007) in which the subject and the process are immersed. The afore-mentioned aspect of materiality, which is the object of recycling and the result based on it, is particularly dealt with in the field of the most modern economic and ecological sense of recycling. What is interesting in these studies is not so much considering it as waste or second-hand material, as that this consideration is a cultural construct which places recyclable material in a transitional or interim position, until it is reused in some way, as well as the status and value which is attributed to it according to what are also cultural conditioners.[49]

This aspect of the value possessed by the recycled material and its result have also been the subject of discussion. From the economic view of efficiency and utilitarianism, recycling will serve for upcycling, or intensifying a production cycle, and in the continuous recycling in the (post)industrial era of a material. The material may lose its quality in a kind of downcycling, and therefore the cultural recycling will become inseparable from the logic of the market and capitalism. That is why, according to Randall, "The *recycling* metaphor seems

---

49 As Randall explains, its greater or lesser value does not depend on the fact itself of having been recycled (2007).

here to be being stretched in two different directions at once; on the one hand, the raw material is waste, detritus or at the very least a useless surplus which is transformed into an object of value; on the other hand, the recycled product is itself inferior to the original [...]" (2007). According to Kendall and Koster "the discourse of recycling can promote a narrative of cultural production and progress that negates the idea of significant loss" (2007). As Randall states, "*recycling* supports rather than contests the dominant economic mode and it is primarily this consonance which makes it, for me, an uncomfortable metaphor" (Randall 2007). Moreover, recycling not only implies negating the idea of loss of signification, but also an "epidemic cultural amnesia" (Randall 2007), or, as Hoffmann warns, a culture based on memory is here confronted with the possibility of its *Entgeschichtlichung* (deshistorisation), as through operations inherent in recycling (classification, decomposition and reclassification) it is submerged in the destruction of the carriers and the connections of transmission with the source are dissolved, which becomes unclear and difficult, or prevents the recovery and recognition of what was (2001, pp. 473–474).

From the ecological perspective, what is positive about recycling is its contribution to the goal of returning to a natural equilibrium with a pre-modern cyclical order prior to the human intervention that destroys the environment. It would be a case of reaching a zero level. With respect to this latter question, Moser warns that the re-conceptualisation of recycling in the cultural sphere does not oblige "to adapt the implications of the figure of eternal return" because recycling "contains the idea of transformation and metamorphosis. It never brings a system, or a material, back to the same position [...] there is a new production or new meaning to be registered. In this sense, it can be combined with a modern theory of history, or a theory of modern history although it contradicts its ideological claim to a linear progression of the historical process" (2007). Moreover, he claims that recycling makes us aware in a critical form not only of the change, but also of the forgetting, of the destruction, and of the negative moment which the ecological use of the term tries to make us forget. Recycling begins with the destruction, the negation of what has been culturally formed, constituted, instituted (Moser 2007).

This ambivalence between creation and destruction of the term prevents the meaning from devolving into a negative and positive axiology[50] and from uncritically adopting the evaluation, devaluation, and revaluation processes of economic recycling. However, we cannot ignore the contents of the processes

50 This is what Neville and Villeneuve (2002) warn in the quote at the start of this chapter.

of valuation in each cultural field's context. Cultural recycling alerts us precisely to these processes. Without awareness of them, if we fall into the post-modern idea that the concept of recycling is always only levelling and places everything in the same spectrum, we run the risk of losing sight of a more nuanced vision (Larose 2004, p. 221) in which the construction of the cult value of something, or the aura, is changing, re-ritualising (García Arnau 2020b) and is not yet exhausted in an idealistic tradition of autonomy of art and genius (Barck 2004, pp. 92), just as the post-industrial era supressed the difference between original and copy, representing the loss [depletion] of the aura (Benjamin [1936; 1955] 2003, pp. 13–16) and even the actual abolition of the idea of value. There are trivialising and levelling recycling phenomena, but this neither implies that the concept is trivial or levelling, nor that it is aligned with the notions which understand everything as a continuous flow. Quite the opposite! The prefix 're-' incorporates a friction, the heterogeneity of criss-crossing temporalities (Robin 2004, p. 75) and the intervention of the specific event with each action.[51]

Another criticism of 'recycling' as investigative category argues that it is inseparable from capitalism, which converts everything into commodities within the cycle of production, use and consumption, and thus into its economic value. As Kirchmann notes, this must be qualified, given that the economic added value according to Karl Marx tends to zero in the case of "produktiv" (productive) consumption as against "industriell" (industrial) (2006, p. 504). In current terms, there would be not just economic exchange value or surplus value, but also a value of use, of symbolic capital with respect to communication, knowledge, or aesthetic experience. Although contemporary culture is practically impossible to dissociate from a capitalist, post-industrial frame of access and consumption, which turns the subject itself into a commodity and into a means of production and transfer of commodities, this does not imply that the notion of value "in both its economic and symbolic sense" (Perniola 2002, p. 135) has disappeared. In any case, returning to the question of pre-existing cultural materiality, this has been created and therefore used in the cultural-symbolic sense at least once. This use prior to its current context may leave traces, as may the process of recycling itself.

The metaphorical transfer of the physical-tangible material from the eco-industrial process to the cultural sphere has another important implication: unlike

51 On the differences between 'retro' and nostalgia in the interaction between past and present, see Keller (2006, pp. 320–332), and on the commodification of the past, see Fennetaux / Junqua / Vasset (2015, p. 4).

the above, the cultural material can be intangible in the abstract symbolic dimension of meaning (such as ideas, content, forms, concepts or figures), but their materiality resides both in the signifier and in the physical support which carries the signs, the medium, whether this is the space and the matter that allows the propagation of sound waves, a paper or digital materiality. In this way, the entity which may be recycled is a sign material and may be constructed with multiple layers, formats, or structures, but this leaves behind the idea of text as unity, only abstract, unique, or primary (as is inherent in intertextuality) without negating the use of the semiotic dialogic interaction to understand the recycling processes.

The processing of material always involves a new context of use. Its relationship with its context implies some type of significant production or additional semiotics. It also implies a return to something past, where a relationship of memory and reference exists, even if only in the replication by way of reaction of a replication as a hashtag or a response. Both make the action of recycling move between action (*Ausführung*) and presentation or staging of something previous (*Aufführung*).[52] Depending on the degree of transformation of the former, the recycled matter may delay or withdraw its substance (Pombo 1997, p. 14) and the preceding context, leading to a modification not only of the significance (semantic) but also of the type of sign itself (Dika 2003, p. 14) or re-semiotisation. It can even lose the memory of meaning and contextual relation, leaving only traces of it, converted into a new entity, an object with another substance, with a form and significant function completely different. It may even be a hapax, a remnant that can no longer connect with a context. In this way, the notion of recycling is separated from that of adaptation (Hutcheon 2006) and of its subcategory of appropriation (Nicklas 2012, p. 6). They coincide when recycling carries material across frontiers, but they are focused on its closeness to or distance from the original or on the implications and contributions of the new appropriationist version (Nicklas 2012, pp. 6, 10). Adaptation and appropriation cannot fully contain recycling's mnemonic articulating form or open reproduction to other times and to their collision (Stanford in Wilson / Stanford 2022, p. 58), to the footprint of what has been withdrawn or delayed in the event, or in terms of the circulation with which it is linked. This gives recycling

52 Both terms are understood here in the senses given by von Bernstorff (forthcoming) in the field of pragmatics. The performance character (*Aufführung*) arises from the iterativity of the factual action (*Ausführung*). What happens (the factual) serves to explore the potentials of the fictional (von Bernstorff).

increased relevance for the processes analysed by comparative literature and the studies of transculturality.

Understood at a 'macro' level, cultural recycling consists of the circulation[53] of one or more materials through multiple practical actions of repetition carried out by several agents. Its movement, continuity, and duration through time take place with this constant inter-subjective recurrence that always represents a return to something pre-existing. But although this phenomenon may appear like a flow of reused ideas *ad infinitum*, it is not the same as a continuous magma without internal differentiations, because for this circulation to take place specific actions are required: recycling events on a 'micro' level. On each occasion they imply both a new relationship with what is circulated as well as a friction (Tsing 2004, p. 6). Although it is merely an identical repetition of the material, it ties in every time with a different moment, with another temporal context. That is why the description of these circulations is more similar to what is shown by the figure of the network, with each of these recycling events as a micro-node.

However, this concept involves a danger. As in the case of post-structuralism, in trying to overcome dichotomic and hierarchical thought in order to manifest a more complex reality, it is possible to place everything in a fluid and continuous symmetry (which can at most only take into account the dialectic with what is outside it). However, circulation on the web is not free of rules or forms of power that regulate and condition frictions and movement. As Koschorke points out, the field of power is not simply weakened in them but is organised by way of complex rules. (2010, p. 23) The studies on digital platforms and social media demonstrate this well by foregrounding how they are full of regulations (Gießmann 2015, pp. 128–129). The studies of Internet infrastructures have also demonstrated that there is a tension between autonomous control and hierarchical control (Galloway 2004, p. 8). The distributive and horizontal movement of this flow overlaps with the hierarchical centralisation that underlies the circulation, as shown by Smith and Brown Jr. According to them, it is organised rather in an ambivalence between what is continuous and what is punctual (2018, p. 210–211). The latter corresponds to the notion used in this study of the specific, concrete, memory 'event', as implicit in it is the return to something pre-existing from a unique present, and therefore its repetition, but with variation (even if this is minimal).

---

53 The term 'circulation' is understood here in the sense given to it by Appadurai ([1996] 1998 and 2010).

5. Postdigital cultural recycling

Postdigital cultural recycling is the action of processing and using pre-existing cultural material, implying its decoupling from a previous context and placement in a new life cycle that is made possible by and is subject to the postdigital condition. To understand what happens with cultural recycling when it is postdigital, we have to separate the chain of steps involved in a recycling action (micro) that correspond to the factors of communication and the aspects seen on cultural recycling. This allows us to locate the way in which the postdigital media environment affects the chain.

First, there is (1) the pre-existing material, forming part of the network of surrounding materials in circulation, i.e. (2) a store or archive (if it is more organised or regulated) to which movement is inherent, which always involves in itself a memorial relationship between the past and present. (3) The actions of taking up again, using and processing are in turn triply temporal 'makings', as they imply 'returning' or 'making something past return' to the present, repeating it (receiving it or reproducing it) and as a result making it circulate (also in time). They involve an active relationship (between perpetration and representation) and a referential link with this pre-existing material and its context. These actions take place thanks to (4) aesthetic operations and strategies that comply with shared codes and a design (conditioned by a context) and a (5) present context (of a physical and symbolic type). The recurrence and friction with other elements (such as the present context) of these actions make the material circulate, give it a (6) value and make it a (7) resulting material with a significance or function. The value and significance depend on the interaction between the market conditions, the channel (the medium as transmitter), and the aesthetic operations of its processing.

Both the value and the meanings attributed are relevant (1) for something to be selected (from the storage) and processed in the reception-interpretation; (2) during the productive/creative processing and the substantiation of ideas or materials in friction; and (3) in circulation with the consequent redoubling and distribution, as this circulation confers a legitimising value on it. The visualisation of recycling is similar to that of a feedback loop, given that what is circulated comes to form part of the network of circulating materials (or store), as mentioned previously.

What happens to 'cultural recycling' when it is postdigital? Stressing the term 'postdigital' means adding another aspect to it: the technological mediatisation in the postdigital condition. Due to the specific forms of reproduction and recurrence of the postdigital mediatisation and due to the specific synergy between humans and such mediatisation, the components of cultural recycling (return to the past, processing repetition and circulation), located between the event and continuity, are affected. It is not simply a case of acceleration, intensification, or material expansion. The functionalities of cultural recycling are moulded in terms of their qualities.

The steps and factors of the cycle are now imbued with the same panmedial environment (mixed reality) which is a carrier, transmitter, and repository of signs. All the signs are computerised and automated. This means that the contextual situation of the act of recycling coincides partially with the same medium or channel, the environment of a hybrid-analogue MR. Moreover, it is through this same medium (as a transmitter) that the materials (as carriers of signs) circulate or are transferred and are the medium as storage. Access to the materials and to their contexts and their storage is intermediated by the same media channel. The codes (repertoire of rules and strategies of cultural practices) behind the practical operations for access as well as for processing and creating the processing operations owe it to this context of analogue/digital mixed reality and are now implemented with automated or semi-automated digital processes and tools. This is not trivial. Due to their aesthetic design qualities, the system of signs (codes) behind the operations using material is what allows the indexing to a present frame of reference or context (medial or mediatised) from which the pre-existing material is articulated or reproduced (is referred to). Therefore, the codification (aesthetic, based on designs and codes) with the media now redirects and includes a referential context-framework which is an MR (digital/analogue) and is therefore partially the same panmedial medium/environment and a personalised context. It is no longer an external context in which the channel-medium-transmitter was located 'alone' (which it refers to or external frame of reference), although it is also composed of symbolic aspects in the predigital era. The material[54] and its ontological status, as well as the referential relation, are also affected. Not only is it affected by its digital nature (partial or total), the material's conversion into a matter which travels with metadata (and not only those legible by humans such as the reference data of a book in a library) is influenced. The value is now generated by this mixture of codes (aesthetics) and contexts, so it also depends on a mixed-reality environment based on the co-actantiality of humans and digital technologies with different levels of human and machine synergy (assistance, complementarity or replacement of part of the human action and actions which go beyond what could be calculated by a single human due to the amount and speed).

54 'Material' is understood both in its tangible and intangible aspects.

Given the gravity of these ideas, it is important to clarify how this context is understood here. The term is used to maintain the descriptive relationship with the concept of 'context' normally used in both linguistic and communicative studies, understood as what surrounds the 'text' and is in turn articulated by or related to it; without it, the semiosis would not occur. However, given the complexity of the signifying layers of the materials in the digital environment, the classical notion of text is insufficient. It appears a contradiction here to use the term 'con-text', as it includes 'text', despite the units not being understood here as only text. That said, their use is maintained for the purpose of a common comprehension of what is understood by context, adapted here to an idea of 'con-material' or 'con-event'. The context alludes to different types and is therefore multiple, referring both to the notion of a physical and abstract communicative situation which implies a subjective mental model constructed by the participants (van Dijk 2008, p. 6) and to the linguistic context inherent to structuralism, i.e. the correlations, co-occurrences and relations of the message which surround an element within it (for example, other words after and before another one). With context the reference here is also to the horizon of expectations and symbolic sociocultural orders, which are discursive, of knowledge and imaginary, and which can be related to this material and shared collectively (as in the *Kulturwissenschaft*), symbolic codes of different levels (including the linguistic) which allow and restrict the understanding of sense, communication, and cultural practices. Nevertheless, context is also understood to mean the personalised and digitally codified personal context that incorporates data extracted by signals of the subject or the material (for example, the individual's metadata), the present interaction (and those extracted from this subject in the past, which are reapplied). They are data ('capta') handled relationally, combining mobile, local and social contexts (Snickars 2012).[55] Finally, the virtual-physical context in which the action takes place (for example, the interface of a platform or of the artefact[56] with sensors) is also considered.[57]

55 Following Snickars, the search for "coffee" when in the street, by relational inference, will lead as a result to a café in the area instead of a different result such as a brand or history of coffee, if one is at home; 'local' will imply relations with the linguistic, geographical, etc. environment; and 'social' with relations with others based on social interactions (friends, followers, etc.).

56 At times, this interface may be the size of a whole field, as in Topgolf (https://topgolf.com/).

57 It is worth pointing out that the last two kinds of digital or media context go further here than the "formal approach to context" of the branches of Computer Science and

5.1. Re-(cycling): repeating like the past that returns or that is returned to

Processing and using existing material in the postdigital condition consist of events of repetition (with greater or lesser variation), characterised by the reciprocal interaction between human and machine produced through the interface. These repetitive modes are directed and conditioned by both the computational operations of processing the datafied information and by the pre-programmed designs of the repertoire of practices and (semi-automatic) manipulations that are available to the user (such as the classic 'cut and paste'). They are now also linked to psycho-economic prescriptions. The key question for cultural recycling is how to establish relations with the existing material and its contexts. In other words, what is the memorial relationship with the past and how is meaning created based on that past. Although they are inseparable, the first points to questions dealt with from classic rhetoric to pragmatics and post-structuralism; the second points to the processes of semiosis and referentiality. For the question of significant relations with the past, it is worth noting that the form in which computational and aesthetic-technological procedures establish indexical inclusion of the present context is essential, as without contextual relations there would be no semiosis. Another key to understanding how

Artificial Intelligence, which are often based on contexts such as "formal models [...] reduced to a set of propositions" (van Dijk 2008, pp. 10–11). They try to transcribe the context of formally stable units using mathematical descriptions. They try to reproduce what happens in the mind. The basic theory of the representation of knowledge and reasoning in AI is based on Minsky's notion of "frame" ([1974] 1992), which sees it as a "structure" that the subject "selects from memory". According to Minsky, "A frame is a data-structure for representing a stereotyped situation, like being in a certain kind of living room, or going to a child's birthday party. Attached to each frame are several kinds of information. Some of this information is about how to use the frame. Some is about what one can expect to happen next. Some is about what to do if these expectations are not confirmed.

We can think of a frame as a network of nodes and relations. The 'top levels' of a frame are fixed, and represent things that are always true about the supposed situation." (Minsky [1974] 1992). These are stored in ontologies of sets or hierarchical taxonomies which organise information in the form of data. In some ways, they can be partially linked to the notion of 'schemes' in psychology. The development of languages of framework (like RDF) has been crucial for the semantic Web (focused on the fact that machines can 'read' the contexts in the Internet as data based on ontologies and relate them (linked data)) and for AI, together with other standard languages such as ones that are object-oriented (like OWL), based on semantic categories and modal logic.

recycling has been modified is that in the event of a postdigital human-machine link, the continuum between both has been altered by growing automation (the possibilities of executing complex programming operations autonomously through algorithms stemming from big data particularly once they are easily structurable, tokenizable, organisable, and linkable, with the form of a database).

To understand this relationship with the remnant past elements, we have to understand that the possibilities of repetition by processing of pre-existing materials (whether analogue-sensorised, digitalised, mixed or born digital) are not limited to the 'facilities' of edition offered to users; they are preexisting. The recipients of any digital material (for example, a text) are not therefore dealing with a static product; rather, an electronic process of generation (Ablitt 2019, p. 102) that is almost instantaneous and dynamic (i.e. a process of rendering, which is based on what is preceding and preexisting). As Ernst explains, it is a "metonymic transformation of non-intuitive data into graphics" (2002, p. 113) or into another type of sign. Behind each event that may repeat the symbolic material perceptible by humans with the same quality, the underlying code-based process (normally invisible) is not equivalent to the industrial reproduction of copies starting with a mould. It is sustained in a greater complexity, based on a system of computational logical/mathematical modelling that is located between *imitatio* and *inventio*. Starting with elements from the past and present of the physical world, the models emulate using mathematical and topological formulations, but they also incorporate the capture of physical signals directly by sensors and other proceedings that are translated into data. Because the mathematical/logical operations are broader than pre-existing reality (Flusser 1993, p. 263 ff.), the resulting virtual digital simulation includes architectural constructions that generate new elements, such as in videogames or in current post-representational (Steyerl 2014) and post-real photography of the apps that generate images artificially by using the filters for 'improving' an image. To these constructions which mix factuality and fiction based on recycled past data, we can add that the models are adaptable according to the materials or data that are incorporated in real time and that often proceed from a different temporal context, such as the integration of the interaction of a specific moment of a human with the system (a case of the recursivity of the system).

There is another key factor that happens with these ubiquitous and everyday simulations, modifying the possibilities of relations with pre-existing material. This medium, which is somewhere between machine action (*Ausführung*) and perceptible symbolic (re)presentation (*Aufführung*) by making present what is absent and by its characteristics of architectural and logical configuration, establishes a relationship of distance differently from other media with the references of the web in which it is placed (or pseudo-references if they are imaginary constructions). This substantively mixes the *phantasmata* of memory, in the sense of Aristotle's *De memoria et reminiscentia* (the images whose past reference is thought to have been lived, without having been so). The events are constructed not by the mental imagination, but by the adjustable mathematical model with the feedback with the physical environment that captures and emulates it. In other words, the computational operations and standardised programming languages obey a regime of logics and regulations which are used to translate the functioning of the physical and symbolic world. To model the material converted into information and the information into data, logical operations are used in mathematical language (to a great extent known since the rhetoric and heuristics of the Antiquity) of complex relations by similarity, identity, difference, causality, inference, indexical causal relations, contiguity, addition, deduction, division, escalation or multiplication, extrapolation, combination, frequency, correlation and, in particular, probability. This allows the information to be processed in the system and to reorganise it and generate other new information or imitate with statistical/mathematical forms the existing forms to predict the probable/real. Within the scope of the symbolic (as developed systematically in the humanities since structuralism), the inter-relations of elements of any code are essential for the production of semiosis, but it is also known and extended by semiotics and pragmatics that any element is susceptible to acquiring attribution of a sign and be susceptible to semiosis and that it is indissociable from the relationship with the world (leading to theories of referentiality). As explained by Bajohr (2023a, p. 61), not even the most sophisticated AI systems that imitate these processes of signification up to the multimodal form remain "grounded in the world", however much they may connect with the environment outside themselves and integrate in it by way of captures and sensors. Thus, the "indexical AI" (Bajohr 2023a, p. 64) has a relationship of connection and mathematical transcription in signs within the system which reproduce meaningful relations, but it is not an indexical signifier relationship in the strict sense that is established, as the causal or indexical semantics imply the sensory-experiential-symbolic comprehension of the elements involved as signs-meanings-referents integrated in an "Erfahrung" (or authentic experience) (Benjamin [1936] 2007, pp. 103–104). As Bajohr states, they generate a "dumb meaning" (2023a). The immediate consequence is that even the most automatic forms may generate materials with sign representation which is perceptible to humans and is possible for a human-receptor to attribute meaning to them when relating this element (which emerges from the latent and legible system by machine) with the world.

However, the underlying mathematical models and designs (largely profiled with criteria of economic capture) of surfaces or interfaces by their properties in the forms of reorganisation and modelling of informational material, as well as of leading practical actions, have a key impact on human-machine processes of significant relations with past elements. The logical relations have an enormous potential, not only for generating new connections but for finding "unsuspected latent connections" (Bajohr, 2023a, p. 66). Their *a priorisms* of segmentation and interrelation do not necessarily follow the criteria of pre-established predigital codes. They may tokenise the language or segment visual experience depending on other parameters or categories. In short, they are *a priorisms* established deductively that allow frequencies and even parameters to inductively be found. The relations and sequences of pre-programmable instructions (for example, using algorithms) may go beyond what can be realised in the current physical environment. In other words, the virtual environment may leave suspended the coordinates and categories with which signs in epoch x are compartmentalised and related. As emulators and captors of the past and present from which they receive feedback, they need to re-translate continuously the symbolic forms with which humans construct meanings and also produce perceptible signs and signals (i.e. in the domain of aesthetics). Although it is also true that latent modelling of logical/mathematical constructions may make diverse signifying modes equivalent and relationable: accounting for or not, giving value or not, differentiating between the visual and linguistic sign (as Bajohr explains regarding AI systems generating image/text (Bajohr 2023a, p. 66)). Thus, the contextual environment of mixed reality in which we carry out cultural practices is increasingly imbued with a twin logic in which distinctions such as fact and fiction or past/present/future, uniqueness and repetition, etc. may have or may not have at the same time a weight in the meaning. In any case, it is where the confluence between the present context of vital experience and remodelled elements based on the past is constant.[58]

Without reaching an exhaustive overview of all the possibilities of relations and signification of the past that returns, below are some examples of different options which could not have occurred before the postdigital condition[59] and

58 An interesting example of analysis of how the different levels of surface and algorithmic design of an app reconfigure with classifications and pre-model practice and memory may be seen in Smit (2023), to the point that the practices are adapted to the algorithmic logic which influences the construction of the individual memory itself.

59 The examples have been taken from a more extensive corpus analysing postdigital cultural recycling in literature and of literature recycled in the postdigital condition.

which highlight a common element in the practices and productions of all kinds within it: the emphasis on the aesthetic aspect brought about by mixed reality.[60]

With respect to the processing and use of pre-existing elements, I establish two criteria for dealing with the relations with the past and semiosis: 1) the level of automation and datafication in the human-machine synergy; and 2) the type of relations with pre-existing material and of the material with the contexts established through these synergies, as dependent on the ambivalent potential of the virtual infrastructures (between imitation-feedback and suspension of prior categories and coordinates). Broadly speaking, for this second distinction there are two possible relations between present contexts (of MR) and material from the

---

Limiting it to this scope is not only due to the impossibility of covering all the manifestations, but also to the fact that the technological developments of automation in the field of language are a fundamental part of the postdigital shift in recent years, due to the forms of mass communication through, among others, mobiles, platforms and automated text and image generators with AI. To this can be added the fact that due to the key role played by rhetorical operations and the surfaces of design linked to aesthetics in all the current postdigital culture, the scope of the studies of literature, which deal with both, and literature itself, as the art of language, have much to contribute to a reflection on this matter.

60 An analysis of the handling of taste in digital designs would exceed the scope of this study, but it should be noted that the designers in fact stress the idea of creating a world in which there are increasingly more aesthetically "beautiful" objects, and particularly in valuing that they should be "beautiful for me", in other words, in the unending aestheticisation and creative-productive generation, but personalised (Catanzaro (2023), in the talk with Bensky cited at the start). Reckwitz has also stressed this imperative of creativity as part of the economic system (2017) that imposes itself on the subjects. It is worth noting that the creativity associated with this aesthetic is understood as 'personalised beautiful taste' in these current designs, leaving aside the difference between the artistic and creative by industry, as indicated by Bajohr (2022b, pp. 265–266), as well as the fact that art and aesthetics do not have to be beautiful. That idea was superseded decades ago. They promote the idea of configuration and generation of the beautiful in a personalised way according to individual desire and taste (as stressed by Baßler and Drügh (2021, p. 289)). Paradoxically, this combines with a homogenisation and standardisation resulting from the redundancy of codes and repertoires of simulation and prior modelling of desire constructed by the media itself, as well as with the fact that it is the users (i.e. the collective) who are called to co-generate the metaverse with these automated tools for 'creative' generation, but also with the fact that the subjects are searching for a reference in others for their self-affirmation or to see themselves, and this is how the "Stilgemeinschaften" (style communities) (Baßler and Drügh 2021, p. 291) arise, according to the "Denkstile" (styles of thought) and their dynamics described by Fleck (1980).

past and its contexts.[61] The relationship may be of similarity with what is referred to, articulated or evoked (such as in metaphor), or of contiguity (as in reactions, comments or elements which emerge around it in contiguous or continuous relation, in metonymy). All these imply some type of re-contextualisation.[62] Among these forms of relations there are multiple options, but in the repository *Rec-Lit: Estrategias de reciclaje cultural y literario en la era postdigital*,[63] we distinguish for the first group between (1) appropriation (which implies a gesture of possession); (2) rewriting (which includes forms such as paraphrase and other presentations of previously written material) and (3) remediation (which alludes to the mediality of the material referred to, following the notion of Bolter and Grusin ([1999]2000)). To these I wish to add (4) 'multimodal replication', which may be generative (with algorithms and automatic). Within the second type of relations we can include: (1) recovery, as a form that is equivalent in terms of the gestuality it implies to the notion of appropriation, understanding here that the material is respected and its re-contextualisation by contiguity also rescues its prior contexts; (2) recreation, which implies a relationship of contiguity in which the material is revived in performance in the new context; and finally, (3) reproduction, which supposes a reiteration of the same material or a part, marking its material and symbolic limits with the surroundings in contiguity. To the latter are added relations by (1) circulation; and (2) re-circulation. It is worth noting that they are not self-excluding. For a detailed approach to the possible strategies and operations from zero to maximum transformation of material, as well as to the corresponding technological facilities which allow processing, repetition, and circulation, see the section of the glossary of definitions of 'recycling strategies' in the *Rec-Lit* repository and the remix studies that have dealt with them in depth.[64]

---

61 I am inspired in this distinction by the two forms of intertextual memory explained by Lachmann (2010), but without following it precisely, given that her starting point responds to the paradigm of intertextuality which places the text as a unit around which the rest is text. I am basically interested by the possibilities of relationship taken from rhetoric.

62 For an extension of this term, see the introduction of Meier / Viehhauser (2020, pp. 1–20).

63 The repository has been created inside the REC-LIT project and is coordinated by Llamas Ubieto and Goicoechea de Jorge (2022).

64 Glossary in *Rec-Lit*: http://repositorios.fdi.ucm.es/REC-LIT/view/generico.php?id=54&idpadre=54; see also Gunkel (2016), Navas / Gallagher / burrough (eds.) (2015); Navas / Gallagher / burrough (eds.) (2021b); Navas (2018); Navas (2022); Sánchez (2023); Waysdorf (2021).

I outline the examples from a lower to a higher level of automation. One of the most common forms for retaking former material (whether digital or digitised) consists of its inclusion in a digital interface, which becomes part of the present context from which the meaningful relations with it are established, as well as the application of digital post-production tools that affect its most superficial access layer and its materiality of the computer code below. Materials are constantly published and in circulation, for example, on social networking platforms. Thus, it may be a reproduction in which a significant new relationship has been created, re-functioning with the communitive aim of the current emitter, as happened with the verses of the poem that went viral, "El fin último de la (mala) literatura" (Ben Clark 2011),[65] whose initial context disappeared to the point where the title and author, time and thus ironic critical meaning of the original were lost in relation to these elements.

On the other hand, it may allow an enrichment of the material, as in the critical editions which transport the contexts of the past from the new contextual-medial presentation, marking an explicit separation. As Sahle explains, reception is prepared with a view to a "zeitliche Distanz" (time distance) (2020, p. 28). Ecdotics thus redoubles the contexts to ensure a better understanding, and the object or material acquires a new relational identity between the two (Sahle 2020, p. 30). The mixed analogue/digital environment is not only harnessed in the interaction of the reader with a text with layers of enrichment or explicative hypertext that would be the equivalent to the paratexts and notes of a traditional edition, not even in the digital tools for manipulating text such as *wreader* (reader and writer), but also in the possibility of implicit and explicit interconnections which demonstrate the automatic relations of this material with other online materials or with a corpus or interactions of other readers. For example, consider the enriched new edition of the short stories *Calleja interactivo. Plaga de dragones*;[66]

---

65 Published in his book of poems *La mezcla confusa* (Madrid, editorial Univ. Popular José Hierro), which went viral with more than a million reproductions, either literal or with variants, and reactions, on a number of social platforms and social networks. This is an example of popular appropriationism of verses which have become apocryphal on the web and were attributed to a number of authors, as well as having been decontextualised and re-semanticised, as most of the reproductions also lost the title, which implies the loss of irony, as remarked by Escandell (2019). For more information, see the file of Llamas (2022) in the *Rec-Lit* repository: http://repositorios.fdi.ucm.es/REC-LIT/view/cm_view_virtual_object.php?idov=339&seleccion=1.

66 Goicoechea de Jorge, María (ed.): *Plaga de dragones* [1923], in *Calleja interactivo* (2022) http://cuentoscalleja.com/editorial.html; https://www.ucm.es/edicionliterariaelectronica/plaga-de-dragones; https://reclit.hypotheses.org/226.

the collaborative readings with annotation tools; the use of physical public space for the edition with augmented reality of poems on buildings using mobiles or other devices such as *Het Poëzie Museum* (*The Poetic Museum*) (2017);[67] or the enrichment with AI based on the descriptive texts of the paintings in the Prado Museum[68] (Madrid). The key in the latter examples is that the marking and separation of the time contexts is not dissolved, but rather emphasised.

It is worth exploring the extent to which the hybrid media context generates another reading experience and how the transfer of contexts from the past occur, associating the material with elements of it. For example, consider the press or advertising of the time, such as in *Calleja interactivo*. Also worth considering is the buildings of the present (for example, *Het Poëzie Museum*), which co-constructed semiosis.

We might also ask what criteria in the present are used to generate notions or imaginations of the past in the training of AI to establish, recognise or detect elements with meaning of the past in texts and other artistic materials (for example, symbols and their meaning in different epochs) or in preparations with immersive simulations (i.e. exhibitions, video games, etc.)?[69] Also, what implications are there in the lexical and syntactic simulation of the historical context of a 16th Century author with a text generation tool based on the connectivist paradigm of algorithms?[70] The *phantasmata* of today allow the production of deep fakes and fake news that supposedly come from past sources.

---

67 See the entry in the *Rec-Lit* repository, created by M. José Calvo (2021): http://repositorios.fdi.ucm.es/REC-LIT/view/cm_view_virtual_object.php?idov=348&seleccion=1.

68 The Prado Museum, according to its own website, implemented in 2019 "an augmented reading on the descriptive texts of the works published on the website through a engine of 'Comprensión del Lenguaje Natural' (NLU) which recognises the entities and concepts addressed in them to provide a more contextualised reading for the user", retrieved 06.07.2023, from https://www.museodelprado.es/actualidad/noticia/el-bsc-y-el-museo-del-prado-ensean-a-la-ia-a/b3e3e805-5beb-cdda-f1a3-ddb4191be5ec.

69 In this regard, see the joint project between BSC and the Prado Museum launched in 2023 to recognise symbols of the past in the museum's paintings (retrieved 06.07.2023, from https://www.museodelprado.es/actualidad/noticia/el-bsc-y-el-museo-del-prado-ensean-a-la-ia-a/b3e3e805-5beb-cdda-f1a3-ddb4191be5ec) and the European project *INTAVIA In/Tangible European Heritage* (retrieved 06.07.2023, from https://intavia.eu/).

70 On the differences between the connectivist and sequential paradigm relative to algorithms, see Bajohr (2022a).

These, like those falsifiers of objects from Ancient Egypt for collectors of the early 20th Century, exacerbate the difficulty in determining authenticity.[71]

A further possibility opening up recently is of connection with the digital archive in which knowledge of the past is stored (i.e. connected to the Internet) with the present context in the form of data capture of events in real time. The interactions of reading with a text are processed and generate immediate reactions in the object-process of the read or heard text. A reflection on the inclusion of the present time context and its intersection with collective memory is critical to the kinetic poem by María Mencía *Gateway to the World* (2014),[72] which connects the movements of ships entering the port of Hamburg captured digitally with the entries in *Wikipedia* that correspond to the names of these ships. The collective-global memory is put into action and can be seen in one of the physical nodes of global trading exchanges. The relation with material referring to the past (the encyclopaedic and collaborative memory) of *Wikipedia* is, therefore, one of contiguity to a recreation that sets it in motion, but it can also be understood as a transforming appropriation. The example illustrates the automation of the connection of networks (the Internet and geolocalisation data of ships) and the typical automation of the multiple repetitive practices of automatic generation in which we intervene without noticing when introducing text into a social network platform, or by using automatic correction and translation tools.

The tireless return of what is similar in automated rewritings becomes the incommensurable saturation of similar content. This similarity is due in large part to the easy to use digital editing and production tools (such as apps to create memes or others for design and creation) and the functionalities integrated in a variety of platforms and software, whose predesigned possibilities impose themselves formally and aesthetically, colonising the global imaginary. Likewise, there is a propagation of contents caught in these formats. The pre-existing

---

71 One example of a factual representation (cartographic in this case) which has been re-appropriated to become a real space in fiction and blur the borders between the two is the anonymous insertion of the geo-localisable location of the fictional space "Camp Jupiter" (from the fictional children's and young people's saga by Percy Jackson which appears for the first time in *The Lost Hero* (2010)) in Google Maps, retrieved 07.06.2023, from https://goo.gl/maps/8d4XmBm2oaMAKG7c7; VR62+CG Orinda, California, U.S.A. The confusion is such that the comments below show that some people ask whether it is some type of leisure facility like a thematic park, or a real camp based on fiction.

72 https://www.mariamencia.com/pages/gatewaytotheworld.html.

information, whether from distant or immediate past, becomes uniform in these recontextualisations of format and platform with a contextual relationship that does not allow a distinction of the value of the content based on what surrounds it (paratextual functions, context of provenience, etc.). Its value is based now on hierarchies that respond to associations and connections programmed with algorithms according to the present context of the subject as the centre of the interaction and other parameters, such as an economic interest in viralisation. The referential relationship of previous material is decontextualised and recontextualised according to this target. Relations of contiguity with each present context of these reproductions are established, but redundance, seriality and explicit or implicit repetition are key. The same contextual frame of the software's platform or design become the semantic contextual space of permanent relations that frame the analogue variations (increasingly with the algorithmic personalisation). This leads to experimentation with continuity. The constant context in the time of the platform becomes a continuous present above the possible multiple contexts of the past transferred implicitly or explicitly (nickname, place, etc.) through posts and publications that fly at full speed compulsively with a minimum action (*Ausführung*) by the human agent (click and scroll), but with an interaction inherent to human reception which is absorbed in this rhythm.

These forms are illustrated by another literary practice that begs a metamedial query because it is supported by repetitions with permutation: literary bots. The past is here again and again regenerated with pre-programmed variations. As against the darkening of the relationship with the contextual past in the bots that proliferate on the Internet, some artistic bots use these forms of automatic combinatory writing, in the tradition of generative and conceptual electronic literature, highlighting the mediatised relationship with the contexts of past and present. *gomringador* by Kathrin Passig (2018)[73] is an example of this. Located in an analogue-digital continuum, it incorporates the exponential expansion in the media discourse on the polemical elimination of the verses on the facade of the Alice Salomon Hochschule (Berlin) in 2017 of the poem "Avenidas" (1951) by the Swiss-Bolivian poet Eugen Gomringer, on the grounds of sexism. *gomringador* is a bot based on the permutation of some words of the poem

73 Passig states on her website: "Twitterbot *gomringador* – Zufallsgedichte im Stil von Eugen Gomringers "avenidas", nach einer Idee von @axaneco", retrieved 06.07.2023, from http://www.kathrin.passig.de/texte.html. Published on https://twitter.com/gomringador.

with others from a number of lists, including the substantives taken from the tweets published in 2017 by the writer Clemens J. Setz.[74] By appropriation, rewriting and remediation based on permutation (sequential) algorithms, Passig not only recontextualises and transforms the poem's materiality; the re-semiosis maintains the memory and traces of the discursive facts. The metaliterary bot itself refers to the analogue past context (material, architectural and textual), but also to the media context of the polemic (Twitter), to which the same bot owes its beginnings, its existence, and its persistence.

This reflection leads to an important aspect of postdigital recycling, related to the origin and status of the material. Recycling refers to its previous existence. Its origin may be untraceable, but latently refers to a previous time before the specific recycling-event starts. As in the classic *topoi* and *loci*, the origin depends on the most distant trace of which there is evidence in the present from which it is recycled.

Thus, it links to the more automatic fourth type of postdigital recycling. The amount of recyclable material grows, and the automated operations intensify so that the time and material distances can be erased, diluting the contextual limits articulated by the materials. This happens with AI software with connectivist algorithms in which the "promptology" (Bajohr 2023a, p. 67) of the contextual linguistic and cultural moment of the human actant is the vertex to which they converge in a predictive and new text, as from a compost with parts of the materials with which the model has been trained.[75] Once more, literature allows us to reflect on this transformation of the semiosis with the past, particularly that which uses analysing code and programmes and generating automatic texts programmes. *Data Biography* (2019) and *Machine Biography* (2020), by Diego Díaz and Clara Boj, invite reflection on the datafication of subjects and on the creation by generative AI with transformer neural networks based on datafied materials without distinction between what deserves preservation and what does not. With generative multimodal replication, the materials used (all the data which the two generated with their mobile phones for a year and which they managed to extract) are loaded to generate a new multimedia text, applying a number of programmes such as GPT-2 and GAN to create some fictional

---

74 On this controversy, see the story on DW, retrieved 06.07.2023, from https://www.dw.com/en/poem-on-berlin-college-wall-sparks-sexism-debate/a-40384180. For more information on the details of the composition, see Schlesinger (2020), Navarro / Seemann (2019, p. 128) and Passig (2019, pp. 76–79).

75 On the impossibility of verification and of the distinction of the sample on which the concept of remix is based, thus exceeding it, see Ludovico (2022, p. 760).

biographies their lives in 2050. Not only their data, but the materials which the Spanish community in GPT-2 and others used to train the programme are the recycled indistinguishable compost for the production of the new text of prospective fiction that foregrounds their predictive and probabilistic nature. That is to say the automated production of each phrase, word or image as a future element, supposedly predictable, based on past material, emulates according to probabilities that also depend on the medial context of the present moment of production of each new linguistic context to which the software reacts. They used multimodal AI technology, incorporating image-text relations (for input and output) according to certain parameters which were established (Díaz / Boj 2023) so that a fictitious temporal chronology could be created. They problematise the converging generation of times and materials. They stress the latter with a retro-remediation act by printing the continuous text generated in an analogue segmenting format: 365 volumes on paper in a book format. These volumes convert the result into discretionarily separate, tangible units, as a gesture of human authorial reappropriation. Paradoxically, it also alludes to the question of the value of what is generated, as it is barely legible completely in human time and in terms of what they call the "datacene" (2023, p. 4). The growing creation only appears processible, and therefore legible, by the machines themselves for which time, however, lacks meaning.

5.2. (Re-)cycling: Repeating as circulation

It is precisely the substantial and expanding amount of material and data that make up the current digital medium in its storage quality which intersects with the quality of a remote transmitter by perpetual uninterrupted interconnection. The memory archive in the postdigital condition is processual and dynamic, not a simple accumulator. It also mixes forms of categorisation, organisation and hierarchisation which are emulated from predigital archives and others inherent to the priorities of computational reorganisation or of the economic model characterised by the mass personalised directivity with which a large number of peer-to-peer movements also intersect. This often involves difficulty discerning what is valuable from what can be eliminated, as well as the true from the false. In a world in which the materials created by anyone's invisible data accumulate, are analysed, linked with complex digital AI and ML tools and then used (and thus recycled) to feed algorithms that provide recommendations based on economic and emotional psychology criteria that serve, above all, to engage or capture attention and time, the construction of the individual and collective memory is affected. As Wieland notes, the archive and landfill, whose distance is so necessary for the ecology of memory, are drawing increasingly closer together (2020, p. 163).

What acquires value and stands out from the crowd depends on this design, with an aesthetic surface for our interaction and of the contextual capture of data of the present of the subject, but also of the processing of the previous ones. The circulation or multiple recycling through many subjects from a macro perspective functions by repetition of a material. This can be replicated in streaming by a device connected to a space 'in the cloud' of the Internet and in the platforms of social networks or over-the-top service platforms (OTTs) (Jin 2021, p. 2),[76] or within the memory of another device. The process of generating the layer of symbolic representation of the codified material can be carried out in it once downloaded or transferred there. Thus, the act of individual use that replicates something takes place when that something is transferred to the terminal. The guided retrieval and access modes include and combine the hierarchical distribution (of OTTs); the results offered by the semantic Web (depending on the taxonomies and other pre-selection criteria); the tools of discovery that make something arrive according to the pre-programmed and personalised algorithm; and the peer-to-peer transfers with automated facilities (resend, response, replication, record, etc.) in which the subjects are often the medium-transferrer.

The pre-existing element thus forms part of a collective memory shared by media and sustained as collective by its recurring transfer movements. These movements are produced thanks to techno-human synergies. As Hoskins indicates, these mediated memories are built through "emergences, enfoldings and interactions" (2016, p. 18). Thus, the storage of the circulating materials and their transfer are crossed with the context of MR (analogue-digital) of the users which have an ambivalent character (between simulation of prior coordinates and reorganisation according to other categories and criteria). Therefore, the materials assigned to a prior time and confirmed from the present as something with a mnemonic nature and even the 'memory practices', as noted by Jacobsen, "[they] do not remain fixed. Rather these can be shaped and re-ontologised by algorithmics technologies" (2020, p. 62). I would add, automatically "mediated memories have become *likely*, being variously resurfaced and vitalized by algorithmic processes" (Jacobsen 2020, p. 64). The pre-programmed dynamic movement is the key that makes elements from others emerge and co-construct our individual memory. They make elements generated from our past return (such as photos on a mobile phone or other data) which are then recollected.

76 YouTube is partly included in them.

This dynamism is organised by and modulates with algorithms, often by diverse associative relations of juxtaposition (such as the typical "other people who have seen this have also seen x") which is not based on a distinction of sense and non-sense. This has consequences. First, "the restructuring of our relationship with the past [...] the spacing of *différance*, of delay of perception, is being annihilated" (Ernst 2002, p. 116). It has the potential to create unsuspected connections, which I have called "volatile Mischungen" (volatile mixtures) (Llamas Ubieto 2023, pp. 14, 17). These have the possibility of a decontextualisation of past contexts, such that the datafied information decoupled from them become materials that only conserve part of their semantic traces, or are hapaxes disposed to attach to other contexts and dehistoricise themselves. A different way can also be produced by the reconnection with other elements associated with the same context of the past re-semanticises it [the material], making it exemplary material from a past moment for a community that revolves around this memoristic event. It functions in a way similar to a *semiophor*, material of the rubble or of the everyday liable to be forgotten that is transformed, as in the museum, into a sign which represents something broader (for example, the crafts of a period). Here it is transformed as part of the contextual media archive (which may be a shared space for sympathisers of something in a social network) and not in the museum.

The re-contextualisation of previously decontextualised objects in these volatile mixtures may also drive new meanings or new dialogues, opening spaces of *epoché* or of searching. In short, the 're-' of recycling, the friction in this circulating continuum of recycling is activated. In addition to its creative and heuristic potential, the danger of this disorder of *ἀρχή* (*arche*) is its facility to construct recontextualisations and mixtures of elements that are a lie on the materials of the past. Without being marked as such, counterfactual narratives go viral as truth at a time when the official institutions and the professional narratives of history are levelled in terms of their value with these works, due to the characteristics of the underlying techno-economic system.[77] We have known since Antiquity that plausibility and reasonableness do not ensure truth. The same is true with repetition, used in the art of persuasion to make ideas credible through on redundancy and their insistent persistence. This also happens with mathematical probability (increasingly common with generative AI with deep learning transformer architecture), which is no guarantee that the particular

77 These have been explained in the previous section in relation to the question of reference.

case has been produced or is produced or will actually be produced, as it can only guarantee the generation of a digitally codified representation which is statistically probable. One example of the devirtuation by expansion of the lack of verification, rigour and commodity is the example mentioned of the poem which went viral, and which demonstrates that the trend existed before the latest generation of AI.

The systematising of prior knowledge based on reasoned criteria of order according to a traceability to the source or start of the time path served as a basis for the progress towards the future from prior knowledge (information with contexts) on the world in various epochs (in Antiquity itself, but particularly starting from the 17th Century). These systems were based on archivists' need to know the systems of organisation and their standards (including the current international standards of bibliographical cataloguing) and partly by recipients, readers, scientists, etc. This required a language of labelling and interrelation comprehensible at a human scale, similar to how cartography integrated temporal incarnation; a *méthodos* (path), so that the development of knowledge is based on extending knowledge of the truth.

Today the most popular and extended systematic principle is based on actions of use for circulation or recirculation of something. This implies that the material element created, even in the analogue-digital sphere with the prior idea of being transferred by the web, is prepared to be findable and searchable in a different way, based on the structure of the semantic web. For example, witness the popular use of hashtags that group content together and have an indexical function or by means of other merchandising strategies to ensure they have a more visible, relevant or impactful position in the new hierarchy. The extent to which the analogue-digital continuum remodels analogue practices can be seen in "Acción poética" ("Poetic action").[78] What emerged as an activist artistic action that placed graffiti with literary fragments clandestinely on the facades of local physical public spaces as a form of artistic and popular re-appropriation in Mexico has become a movement that links these gestures with photographs of the graffiti that circulate through social media such as Instagram or Facebook at

78 For more information on this movement which was launched in 1996 in Monterey (Mexico) by Armando Alanís Pulido, see the interview with him by A. Rodríguez in 2016, retrieved 05.07.2023, from https://www.meer.com/es/22414-veinte-anos-de-accion-poetica and the article by C. Paul published in 2016 in the magazine *La Jornada* "Cumple Acción poética 20 años y crece de manera exponencial", retrieved 05.07.2023, from https://www.jornada.com.mx/2016/05/26/cultura/a03n1cul.

a global level. For this, the graffiti often now include in the analogue text of the corresponding Instagram account so it can be followed helping it to circulate.

Another formula which hybridizes the previous systematicy with current forms of order are the storage spaces and repositories created by independent communities or persons in popular culture, such as: Know your meme,[79] OTW[80] and Genealogy of Vidding,[81] as well as other social network spaces/platforms designed for access and sharing more than preserving, such as YouTube or Google Maps, but also parts of specialised platforms such as Wattpad or goodreads. All of the forementioned agglutinate content and reactions according to formats, themes, etc. These forms turn what would have otherwise been forgotten and would not be accessible (as it was not canonical and would not form part of a memory in deposit) into an active memory on an equal level with the canon,[82] not by the specialist filter of official archivists, but by the legitimacy granted to it by their persistence and popularisation (often directed algorithmically rather than based on the free and sovereign decision of the people, as pre-modelled taste).

In this way, what is placed in the circulating archive is liable to be reused again at any time, continuing to circulate. As Navas explains, "such objects are deliberately designed to circulate and be repurposed as much and fast as possible" (2018, p. 1). Given that this archive and the associated present medial context are re-updated constantly, at times the unexpected consequence is that current interest redirects the interest to what is recycled. By automatic association of what is recycled with something from the past, there is an encounter with the otherness of something which remained passive and even unknown in the repository, which leads to its rescue, recovery and even mass circulation.

There are still possibilities of exercising human control on the forms of recontextualising the material of the past and revivifying it (beyond the predesign in which humans intervene). An example of recovery (relation of contiguity) and recirculation (the current circulation of something which had circulated in another cycle of time) that is not fully guided by automation and reused for an unplanned use the semi-automatic system of interconnection of the Twitter

---

79 https://knowyourmeme.com/.

80 https://www.transformativeworks.org.

81 https://web.archive.org/web/20150512050651/http://video24-7.org/video/vidd ing.html.

82 I use here the conceptual division of Assmann (2010) between the past which becomes present by circulating and that which is conserved in the archive or deposit (situated between the canon and forgetting).

platform, was the viral phenomenon of the simultaneous collective reading of the *Divina Commedia* (1304–1321) by Dante Alighieri in 2018: #Dante2018. Many of those who became part of this community, which revolved around this hashtag and read one canto every day without the algorithm of positioning by the success which increased daily, would not have discovered Dante's work otherwise. The initiative came from a human being, Professor of Classical and Comparative Literature Pablo Maurette (Florida State University),[83] who recycled for another use marketing strategies extended in this postdigital environment: the 'challenges' of seriality and brevity. The digital medium thus intervenes in the reading reception and promotes a form of resuming it that revitalises the mediaeval text in the historical context different from that of its creation, as the participations, comments and notes mix erudition and professional reading on the text (with specialist collaborators) in relation to the context of creation with the recontextualisation through a connection by the users with the current context and forms of life, which revalue the text and its currency. The links with the present context, but also with the cultural archive (of epochs, cultural contexts, and diverse media) have been based on references, allusions and comments in the published tweets and shares.[84] The whole creates an enormous digital multimedia paratext. In many cases, the interventions are linked to each other, and in other cases the responses and commentary create other texts. The experience also raises the challenge and question of how far the platform's restrictions, including the brief format of the tweet, are an adequate hermeneutic tool to carry out an in-depth, meaningful, and contextualised reading of the work. Can a reading channelled, through a medium that tends to decontextualisation through brevity (rather than arguments developed in detail), dispersion and the never-ending number of publications, paradoxically, be an instrument to achieve a 'dense' reading of a literary work.[85]

---

83 The initiative had thousands of followers, above all from the Spanish-speaking world and many countries. At a given time, it had 4 million visualisations. For more information, see the file in the repository *Rec-Lit* by Llamas (2021), retrieved 06.07.2023, from http://repositorios.fdi.ucm.es/REC-LIT/view/cm_view_virtual_object.php?idov=336&seleccion=1 and https://twitter.com/maurette79.

84 These also include the register in some cases of own experience of reading, annotations and underlinings in the form of not only digital text but also photographing, and thus remediating the paper or themselves in the process, in a kind of reading selfie.

85 In a somewhat similar way, the composer and singer Jorge Drexler used his influence to recover and make a forgotten metric from the Spanish Golden Age recirculate, the *décima espinela*, when he invited people through social networks to share *décimas*

While phenomena of this type demonstrate that the heritage is being reappropriated by citizens in a re-contextualisation that allows the transfer of preceding contexts and the integration of the present context, a reorganisation of the circulating archive is occurring at another level, whose consequences for the configuration of knowledge, truth, memory and history are still uncertain.[86] First, the subject-centred ecosystem, which automatically redirects the materials that are made to return from the past to the subject according to the latter's contextual data, generate not only the famous 'filter bubble', but a difficulty for the encounter and dialogue with otherness. If we add to this that these materials may now be generated synthetically with AI tools in an interdependence with this subject, the possibility that one only accesses individualised content would consequently have a partial dissolution of the collective/shared memory. It would be partial because these productions may be based on the same materials with which a content-generation tool has been fed, and because the same materials generated may circulate when published, i.e. integrated in the dynamic archive which is still accessible collectively. If the institutions that oversee the preservation of materials and metadata no longer guarantee a world-grounded and referentially true relation to the preceding materials, or if they lose the legitimacy which they previously held, the possibility of knowing the provenance and context would be similar to that of platforms (such as YouTube) in which there are few and generally unreliable metadata. We would also lose the possibility of discerning or checking the origin, source, and truth.[87] This leads to the paradox: at a time when we have the greatest facility to reproduce material precisely, to transfer it unaltered and in which most material is easily available (Reynolds 2011, p. XXI), the traceability back to the initial reference disappears.

---

espinelas in homage to the painting Guernica (1937) by Pablo Picasso on its anniversary (2017). The result was a song based on material that circulated and its recording by Drexler in front of the painting, which also circulated. See the repository file *Rec-Lit* by Llamas retrieved 06.07.2023, from http://repositorios.fdi.ucm.es/REC-LIT/view/cm_view_virtual_object.php?idov=338&seleccion=1.

86 Another associated problem – the preservation and loss of quality of archived materials – cannot be addressed here due to the scope of the subject. Not only is the percentage of digitalised heritage still very small, but part of what has been digitalised is becoming obsolete and unusable with each exponential development of the systems.

87 The danger exists because the expansion of the capacity of leading information companies, such as the GAFAM, focuses on the model of propagation and attention, not one of distinction. If the post-modern carnivalisation destroyed the distinction between high and low, or between past and present, it was because this distinction was still recognised, but in this paradigm, the 'alter' is ignored and there is no distinction.

Today's automatic text and image generators of the connectivist AI paradigm, based on predictive statistics, obscure even more (if possible) the relationship with materials, dissolving the distinction between past and present.

With the inclusion of AI 'discovery tools' that search the bibliography to find what supposedly matches best what is searched for (deciding what is relevant)[88] and its integration in search engines (Google or Bing) and in bibliographic software (Clarivate[89]), we are now at a time of change which co-produces a new reality of what can be known and of the approximate relationship with what pre-exists, if the results are not specified or checked. As Waysdorf has said, "there is a loss of control inherent in digitization and accessibility, and with it a potential for use in unanticipated ways" (2021, p. 1141). The loss of control by users and the increase of enormous amounts of data produced with these synthetic formulas compared with "organic" materials make it increasingly difficult to tackle, manage and verify reliably. Is it really a good idea to relegate these actions to those systems which process, 'read' and select for us according to pre-programmed parameters that provide a diagram of relations among the materials, but whose rigour in results cannot be verified because it is not based on a good or bad reading comprehension of what is processed? What forms of printing fingerprints on material produced or searched in this way would allow control by citizens? As Bajohr has warned, "Whoever Controls Language Models Controls Politics" (2023b). What criteria and decisions on quality and truth will prevail in the constructions of future archives, including those created collectively? Those of the German *Wikipedia*, of the community which leads it in English, or those where it is managed in Spanish?[90] Will the trend continue for the ease promoted by the current techno-economic ecosystem in which the sources are referenced with increasingly less detail, making it even more difficult to check veracity? If the most powerful tools and the preservation of materials of global scope are managed increasingly by private institutions whose

88 They are based on the same logics of statistical probability, coincidence, and frequency. For example, ASReview (https://asreview.nl/), consensus (https://consensus.app/), elicit (https://elicit.org/) or scite (https://scite.ai/).

89 See Clarivate Plc, "Clarivate Announces Partnership with AI21 Labs as part of its Generative AI Strategy to Drive Growth, 22.07.2023, retrieved 14.08.2023, from https://www.prnewswire.com/news-releases/clarivate-announces-partnership-with-ai21-labs-as-part-of-its-generative-ai-strategy-to-drive-growth-301857301.html.

90 A comparison of the three demonstrates that *Wikipedia* in Spanish prioritises availability to a broad public and a decomplication of content, rather than the encyclopaedic and specialised spirit of the German version.

economic interest when offering debugged and quality databases prevails over an interest in education and access to general and open knowledge, as Rodríguez points out, "we must look for the notions of value and relevance that are being managed and proposed as a 'gold standard'" (2018, p. 6). The media context is updated and changes constantly, but the endless repetition of 'the same' leads to a standardisation of the similar.

6. Conclusion

Cultural recycling is becoming an essential concept if we are not to lose sight of the configurations and processes that underly the current media and economic ecosystem. Its threefold time aspect ('return to', repeat, circulation and duration) allows us to observe the temporal event it promotes and, at the same time, interrupts the constant circulation of materials. The feedback implicit in the concept is key for understanding the basis of the panmedial environment, as well as each digital-analogue event between human and machine, which is linked to the continuous return to the pre-existing: postdigital cultural recycling.

References

Abblitt, Stephen: "A postdigital paradigm in literary studies". *Higher Education Research & Development* 38(1) 2019, pp. 97–109, DOI: 10.1080/07294360.2018.1541313.

Albrecht, Helmuth: "Zur Geschichte der Begriffe 'Wiederverwertung, Abfall, Recycling und Nachhaltigkeit': eine Einleitung in das Tagungsthema". *Ferrum: Nachrichten aus der Eisenbibliothek, Stiftung der Georg Fischer AG* (73) 2001, pp. 4–11. http://doi.org/10.5169/seals-378351.

Alexander, Catherine / Reno, Joshua (eds.): *Economies of Recycling. The Global Transformation of Materials, Values and Social Relations*. Zed Books: London, New York 2012.

Appadurai, Arjun: *Modernity at large: cultural dimensions of globalization*. University of Minnesota Press: Minneapolis [1996] 1998.

Appadurai, Arjun: "Circulation ≈ Forms". *The Salon* (2) 2010, pp. 5–10. https://jwtc.org.za/the_salon/volume_2/arjun_appadurai_circulation_forms.htm.

Assmann, Aleida: "Canon and Archive". In: Erll, Astrid / Nünning, Ansgar (eds.): *Cultural Memory Studies: An International and Interdisciplinary Handbook*. De Gruyter: Berlin, New York 2010, pp. 97–108. https://doi.org/10.1515/9783110207262.2.97.

Assmann, Aleida: "Michael Cunningham' *The Hours*. Homage to the book in time of Media transformation". In: Schaefer, Heike / Starre, Alexander (eds.): *The Printed Book in Contemporary American Culture: Medium, Object, Metaphor*. Palgrave Macmillan: Cham 2019, pp. 139–154.

Assmann, David-Christopher (ed.): *Narrtive der Deponie. Kulturwissenschaftliche Analysen beseitigter Materialitäten*. Springer VS Wiesbaden: Wiebaden 2020.

Bajohr, Hannes: "Algorithmic Empathy: Toward a Critique of Aesthetic AI". *Configurations* (30:2) 2022a, pp. 203–231, retrieved 10.07.2023, from https://hannesbajohr.de/wp-content/uploads/2022/06/Algorithmic-Empathy.pdf.

Bajohr, Hannes: "The Paradox of Anthroponormative Restriction: Artistic Artificial Intelligence and Literary Writing". *CounterText* (8:1) 2022b, pp. 262–282, retrieved 10.07.2023, from https://hannesbajohr.de/wp-content/uploads/2022/07/Bajohr-Paradox-of-anthroponormative-restriction.pdf.

Bajohr, Hannes: "Dumb Meaning: Machine Learning and Artificial Semantics". *IMAGE The Interdisciplinary Journal of Image Sciences* (37:1) 2023a, pp. 58–70, DOI: 10.1453/1614-0885-1-2023-15452, retrieved 10.07.2023, from https://hannesbajohr.de/wp-content/uploads/2023/05/Bajohr-2023-Dumb-Meaning.pdf.

Bajohr, Hannes: "Whoever Controls Language Models Controls Politics", 08.04.2023 https://hannesbajohr.de/en/2023/04/08/whoever-controls-language-models-controls-politics/ [Translation]. Original: "Wer Sprachmodelle beherrscht, beherrscht auch die Politik". *Neue Zürcher Zeitung* 25.04.2023, 2023b, retrieved 10.07.2023, from https://www.nzz.ch/meinung/chatgpt-wer-die-ki-kontrolliert-beherrscht-kuenftig-die-politik-ld.1734342?reduced=true.

Barck, Karlheinz: "Revisiter le passé: réflexions sur la matérialité du recyclage". In: Klucinskas, Jean / Moser, Walter (eds.): *Esthétique et Recyclages Culturels: Explorations de La Culture Contemporaine*. University of Ottawa Press: Ottawa 2004, pp. 87–93.

Baßler, Moritz / Drügh, Heinz: *Gegenwartsästhetik*. Kontanz UP: Konstanz 2021.

Beer, David: *Popular Culture and New Media: The Politics of Circulation*. Palgrave Macmillan: London 2013.

Benjamin, Walter: "Das Kunstwerk im Zeitalter seiner technischen Reproduzierbarkeit". In: *Das Kunstwerk im Zeitalter seiner technischen Reproduzierbarkeit. Drei Studien zur Kunstsoziologie*. Suhrkamp: Frankfurt am Main [1936 French; 1955 German] 2003, pp. 7–44.

Benjamin, Walter: "Der Erzähler". In: *Erzählen: Schriften zur Theorie der Narration und zur literarischen Prosa* [*Ausgewählt und mit einem Nachwort von Alexander Honold*]. Suhrkamp: Frankfurt am Main [1936] 2007, pp. 103–128.

Betancourt, Michael: *The critique of digital capitalism: An analysis of the political economy of digital culture and technology*. Punctum books: Brooklyn, NY 2016. https://doi.org/10.21983/P3.0125.1.00.

Berry, David: "The Postdigital Constellation". In: Berry, David M. / Michael Dieter (eds.): *Postdigital Aesthetics. Art, Computation and Design*. Palgrave Macmillan: Houndmills, Basingstoke, Hampshire; New York 2015, pp. 44–57.

Bolter, Jay David / Grusin, Richard: *Remediation. Understanding New Media*. MIT Press: Cambridge [1999] 2000.

Bourriaud, Nicolas: *Postproduction: culture as screenplay: how art reprograms the world*. Lukas & Sternberg: New York, NY 2002.

Bree, Paco: "La transformación cultural y tecnologías exponenciales". *Anuario AC/E 2023 de cultural digital. Focus: ¿Viajan los contenidos culturales digitales en español?* Acción Cultural Española AC/E (ed.). ISSN: 2952-5276, 2023, pp. 25–39, retrieved 10.07.2023, from https://www.accioncultural.es/es/anuario2023.

Bühler, Benjamin: " 'Alles muss irgendwo bleiben.' Recycling und die Frage nach dem Rest in Wissenschaft und Kunst". In: Hahn, Daniela / Fischer-Lichte, Erika (eds.): *Ökologie und die* Künste. Fink: Paderborn 2015, pp. 223–243, retrieved 08.07.2023, from https://kops.uni-konstanz.de/server/api/core/bitstreams/66756ac1-8dbb-4305-bea6-75d9fc8eb63a/content.

Burkhardt, Marcus: *Digitale Datenbanken: Eine Medientheorie im Zeitalter von Big Data*. Transcript: Bielefeld 2015.

Cascone, Kim: "The Aesthetics of Failure: 'Post-Digital' Tendencies in Contemporary Computer". *Computer Music Journal* (24:4 Winter) 2000, pp. 12–18.

Cassirer, Ernst: *An Essay on Man. An Introduction to a Philosophy of Human Culture*. Yale University Press: New Haven 1996. [*Versuch über den Menschen: Einführung in eine Philosophie der Kultur*. Meiner: Hamburg 1944].

Cox, Geoff: "Prehistories of the Post-digital: Or, Some Old Problems with Post-Anything". *APRJA, A Peer-Reviewed Journal About* (3:1) 2014, http://www.aprja.net/prehistories-of-the-post-digital-or-some-old-problems-with-post-anything/.

Cramer, Florian: "What is 'Post-digital'?". *APRJA, A Peer-Reviewed Journal About* (3:1) 2014, http://www.aprja.net/what-is-post-digital/.

Díaz, Diego / Boj, Clara: "A critical approach to Machine Learning forecast capabilities: creating a predictive biography in the age of the Internet of Behavious (IoB)". In: Pau Alsina / Andrés Burbano (coords.). *"Possibles"*. *Artnodes* (31) 2023. Retrieved 06.07.2023, from https://doi.org/10.7238/artnodes. v0i31.405249; https://raco.cat/index.php/Artnodes/article/view/n31-diaz/506635.

Dika, Vera: *Recycled Culture in Contemporary Art and Film. The Uses of Nostalgia*. Cambridge UP: Cambridge 2003.

Ernst, Wolfgang: "Agencies of Cultural Feedback: The Infrastructure of Memory". In: Neville, Brian / Villeneuve, Johanne: *Waste-Site Stories: The Recycling of Memory*. State University of New York Press: Albany 2002, pp. 107–120.

Escandell, Daniel: *Crónica de un poema viral*. Ed. Delirio: Salamanca 2019.

Fennetaux, Ariane / Junqua, Amélie / Vasset, Sophie (eds.): *The Afterlife of Used Things. Recycling in the Long Eighteenth Century*. Routledge: New York 2015.

Fernández Mallo, Agustín: *Teoría general de la basura: (cultura, apropiación, complejidad)*. Galaxia Gutenberg: Barcelona 2018.

Fleck, Ludwig: *Entstehung und Entwicklung einer wissenschaftlichen Tatsache. Einführung in die Lehre vom Denkstil und Denkkollektiv*. Ed. by Schäfer, Lothar / Schnelle, Thomas. Suhrkamp: Frankfurt am Main 1980.

Flores, Leonardo: "Third Generation Electronic Literature". *electronic book review*, 4/7/2019. Retrieved 06.07.2023, from http://electronicbookreview.com/essay/third-generation-electronic-literature/.

Flusser, Vilém: *Schriften*. 3 vols. Ed. by Bollmann, Stefan / Flusser, Edith. Bollmann: Bensheim, Düsseldorf 1993.

Galloway, Alexander R.: *Protocol: How Control Exits after Decentralization*. MIT Press: Cambridge, Ma 2004.

García Arnau, Albert: *De la música y su reproducibilidad mecánica: una aproximación sociológica*. [PhD Thesis]. Universidad Complutense de Madrid: Madrid 2015. https://docta.ucm.es/rest/api/core/bitstreams/272fa524-f782-4779-9446-1a24080bc89d/content.

García Arnau, Albert: "Efecto Netflix: cambios macro y microculturales en la era de las plataformas de creación/distribución de contenido", 2020a, retrieved 08.07.2023, from https://2020.nodos.org/ponencia/efecto-netflix-cambios-macro-y-microculturales-en-la-era-de-las-plataformas-de-creacion-distribucion-de-contenido/, and from https://youtu.be/onoPZ-ljK44.

García Arnau, Albert: "El consumo digital entre los jóvenes: La era de la directividad masiva personalizada. Comunicación de Albert García Arnau". In: Llamas Ubieto, Miriam / Sánchez Gómez, Laura (eds.): *Rec Lit. Un blog sobre reciclaje literario postdigital*. 2020b, retrieved 08.07.2023, from https://reclit.hypotheses.org/80.

García Arnau, Albert: "¿Efecto Netflix? cambios macro y microculturales en la era de la directividad masiva personalizada". In: Bermúdez Vázquez, Manuel (coord.): *Luces en el camino: filosofía y ciencias sociales en tiempos de desconcierto*. Dykinson: Madrid 2021, pp. 1989–2010, retrieved 08.07.2023, from https://dialnet.unirioja.es/servlet/libro?codigo=791848.

Gelsomini, Mirko / Spitale, Micol / Garzotto, Franca: "Phygital interfaces for people with intellectual disability: an exploratory study at a social care center". *Multimedia Tools and Applications* (80) 2021, pp. 34843–34874. https://doi.org/10.1007/s11042-021-11164-9; https://link.springer.com/article/10.1007/s11042-021-11164-9.

Gießmann, Sebastian: "Internet- und Digitalisierungsforschung nach der Desillusionierung. Begriffe und Perspektiven". *Navigationen. Zeitschrift für Medien- und Kulturforschung* (15/1) 2015, pp. 118–135.

Graeber, David: "Afterword: the apocalypse of objects – degradation, redemption and transcendence in the world of consumer goods". In: Alexander, Catherine / Reno, Joshua (eds.): *Economies of Recycling. The Global Transformation of Materials, Values and Social Relations*. Zed Books: London, New York 2012, pp. 277–290.

Gunkel, David J.: *Of Remixology. Ethics and Aesthetics after Remix*. The MIT Press: Cambridge et al. 2016.

Hauser, Susanne: "Recycling, ein Transformationsprozess". In: Wagner, Anselm (ed.): *Abfallmoderne: zu den Schmutzrändern der Kultur: Tagungsband von Abfallmoderne, ein Symposium zu den Schmutzrändern der Kultur, an der Karl-Franzens-Universität Graz vom 3.-5. Juni 2008*, Vol. 4 Grazer Edition. LIT Verlag: Münster 2010, pp. 45–62.

Helmond, Anne: "The Platformization of the Web: Making Web Data Platform Ready". *Social Media + Society* 1(2) 2015. https://doi.org/10.1177/2056305115603080.

Hine, Christine: *Ethnography for the Internet: Embedded, Embodied and Everyday*. Bloomsbury: London, New York 2015.

Hoffmann, Christoph: "Recycling". In: Pethes, Nicolas / Ruchatz, Jens (eds.): *Gedächtnis und Erinnerung. Ein interdisziplinäres Lexikon*. Rowohlt: Reinbek bei Hamburg 2001, pp. 473–474.

Hoskins, Andrew: "*Archive Me! Media, Memory, Uncertainty*". In: Hajek, Andrea / Lohmeier, Christine / Pentzold, Christian (eds.): *Memory in a Mediated World: Remembrance and Reconstruction*. Palgrave Macmillan: Basingstoke 2016, pp. 13–35.

Husserl, Edmund: *Aufsätze und Vorträge (1922–1937), Husserliana XXVII. (Fünf Aufsätze über Erneuerung)*. Kluwer Academic Publishers: Dordrecht, Boston, London [1922–1937] 1988.

Hutcheon, Linda: *A Theory of Adaptation*. Routledge: New York 2006.

Jacke, Christoph / Kimminich, Eva / Schmidt, Siegfried J. (eds.): *Kulturschutt. Über das Recycling von Theorien und Kulturen*. Transcript: Bielefeld 2006.

Jacobsen, Benjamin N.: *"You Have a New Memory": Mediated Memories in the Age of Algorithms*. [PhD Thesis]. University of York, Department of Sociology 2020, retrieved 08.07.2023, from https://etheses.whiterose.ac.uk/28341/.

Jenkins, Henry: *Convergence Culture. Where Old and New Media Collide.* New York UP: New York, London 2006.

Jenkins, Henry / Sam Ford / Joshua Green: *Spreadable Media: Creating Value and Meaning in a Networked Culture*. (Postmillennial Pop). New York UP: New York, NY 2013.

Jin, Dal Yong: *Artificial Intelligence in Cultural Production. Critical Perspectives on Digital Platforms*. Routledge: New York 2021.

Jordan, Spencer: *Postdigital Storytelling: Poetics, Praxis, Research.* Routledge: London, New York 2020.

Kalaga, Wojciech / Kubisz, Marzena / Mydla, Jacek (eds.): *A Culture of Recycling / Recycling Culture?* Peter Lang: Frankfurt am Main 2011.

Keller, Katrin: "Wiederverwertungen. Retro und die Reflexivität des Reloads". In: Jacke, Christoph / Kimminich, Eva / Schmidt, Siegfried J. (eds.): *Kulturschutt. Über das Recycling von Theorien und Kulturen*. Transcript: Bielefeld 2006, pp. 320–332.

Kendall, Tina / Koster, Kristin: "Critical Approaches to Cultural Recycling: Introduction". *Other Voices* (3.1 May) 2007. Retrieved 08.07.2023, from http://www.othervoices.org/3.1/guesteditors/index.php.

Kirchmann, Kay: "Bildermüll und Wiederverwertung. Eine medientheoretische Perspektive auf Formen und Funktionen des Bilderrecyclings im Found-Footage-Film". In: Koebner, Thomas / Meder, Thomas (eds.): *Bildtheorie und Film*. Edition Text und Kritik: Munich 2006, pp. 497–512.

Klucinskas, Jean / Moser, Walter (eds.): *Esthétique et Recyclages Culturels: Explorations de La Culture Contemporaine*. University of Ottawa Press: Ottawa 2004.

Koschorke, Albrecht (2010): "Ein neues Paradigma der Kulturwissenschaften". In: Eßlinger, Eva / Schlechtriemen, Tobias / Schweitzer, Doris / Zons, Alexander (eds.): *Die Figur des Dritten. Ein kulturwissenschaftliches Paradigma*. Suhrkamp: Berlin 2010, pp. 9–31.

Lachmann, Renate: "Mnemonic and intertextual aspects of literature". In: Erll, Astrid / Nünning, Ansgar (eds.): *A Companion to Cultural Memory Studies.* De Gruyter: Berlin 2010, pp. 301–310.

Landow, George P.: *Hypertext: The Convergence of Contemporary Critical Theory and Technology*. John Hopkins University Press: Baltimore, London 1992.

Landow, George P.: *Hypertext 3.0: Critical Theory and New Media in an Era of* Globalization. John Hopkins University Press: Baltimore 2006.

Larose, Kim: "Topologies de la valeur". In: Klucinskas, Jean / Moser, Walter (eds.): *Esthétique et Recyclages Culturels: Explorations de La Culture Contemporaine*. University of Ottawa Press: Ottawa 2004, pp. 221–229.

Ludovico, Alessandro: "The vanishing of remix concept in machine-driven text". In: Barcelona Alsina, Pau / Vila, Irma / Tesconi, Susanna / Soler-Adillon, Joan / Mor, Enric (eds.): *PROCEEDINGS ISEA2022. BARCELONA 27 International Symposium on Electronic Art*. Universitat Oberta de Catalunya, and ISEA lnternational: Barcelona 2022, pp. 757–760, https://doi.org/10.7238/ISEA2 022. Proceedings, retrieved 11.07.2023, from https://isea2022.isea-internatio nal.org/wp-content/uploads/2023/02/ISEA2022-BCN-Proceedings.pdf.

Llamas Ubieto, Miriam: *Postdigital ahora*. (Serie: Cuadernos del ahora, n. 1). Docta Complutense: Madrid 2020, pp. 1–13, retrieved 01.08.2023, from https://hdl.handle.net/20.500.14352/11841; https://docta.ucm.es/rest/api/ core/bitstreams/8d8c81b0-a2a9-4341-9c86-dd40c8b849de/content.

Llamas Ubieto, Miriam: "Configurations of the Global in the Postdigital Era through 'Vor der Zunahme der Zeichen'". *Zeitschrift Archiv für das Studium der neueren Sprachen und Literaturen* (260:1) 2023, pp. 1–18. https://doi.org/ 10.37307/j.1866-5381.2023.01.02.

Llamas Ubieto, Miriam / Goicoechea de Jorge, María (coords.): *Rec-Lit: Estrategias de reciclaje cultural y literario en la era postdigital*. Repositorio institucional, Universidad Complutense de Madrid: Madrid 2022, retrieved 06.07.2023, from http://repositorios.fdi.ucm.es/REC-LIT/view/paginas/view_paginas. php?id=1.

Manovich, Lev: *The Language of New Media*. MIT Press: Cambridge, Mass.; London 2001.

Manovich, Lev: *Software Takes Command: Extending the Language of New Media*. Bloomsbury: New York, et al. 2013.

Martin, Sara (ed.): *Recycling Culture(s)*. Cambridge Scholar Publishing: Newcastle 2008.

Meier, Simon / Viehhauser, Gabriel: "Rekontextualisierung als Forschungsparadigma des Digitalen?", In: Meier, Simon / Viehhauser, Gabriel / Sahle, Patrick (eds.): *Rekontextualisierung als Forschungsparadigma des Digitalen*. Books on Demand GmbH, Norderstedt 2020, pp. 1–20, retrieved 10.07.2023, from https://kups.ub.uni-koeln.de/29390/1/SIDE14_Rekontextualisierung_ als_Forschungsparadigma_des_Digitalen.pdf.

Milgram, Paul / Takemura, Haruo / Utsumi, Akira / Kishino, Fumio: "Augmented reality: A class of displays on the reality-virtuality continuum". *Proceedings of SPIE – The International Society for Optical Engineering*, vol. 2351, 1994, pp. 282–292. DOI: 10.1117/12.197321.

Minsky, Marvin: "A Framework for Representing Knowledge". (MIT-AI Laboratory Memo 306, June 1974). Reprinted *in The Psychology of Computer Vision*, P. Winston (ed.), McGraw-Hill, 1975. Shorter versions in J. Haugeland (ed.), *Mind Design*, MIT Press, 1981, and in *Cognitive Science*, Collins, Allan/ Smith, Edward E. (eds.) Morgan-Kaufmann [1974] 1992, retrieved 11.07.2023, from https://web.media.mit.edu/~minsky/papers/Frames/frames.html.

Montfort, Nick: "A Web Reply to the Post-Web". *Post Position, Nick Montfort's personal blog*, 26.08.2018. Retrieved 06.07.2023, from https://nickm.com/post/2018/08/a-web-reply-to-the-post-web-generation/.

Moser, Walter: "Garbage and Recycling: From Literary Theme to Mode of Production". *Other Voices* (3.1) May 2007, retrieved 08.07.2023, from http://www.othervoices.org/3.1/wmoser/index.php.

Navarro, Fabian / Seemann, Selina: "Nachbericht zum Vortrag: Eloquentron3000 — Bots und Literatur". In: Golgath, Tabea (ed.): *Link – Kultur gestaltet Zukunft, Künstliche Intelligenz in Kunst und Kultur. Publikation der Tagung 15. – 16. Mai 2019*. Stiftung Niedersachsen: Hannover 2019, pp. 124–130. https://issuu.com/jjvhannover/docs/link_tagungspublikation_stiftung_niedersachsen_ein.

Navas, Eduardo: "Culture and Remix. A Theory on Cultural Sublation". In: Navas, Eduardo / Gallagher, Owen / burrough, xtine (eds.): *The Routledge Companion to Remix Studies*. Routledge: New York, London 2015, pp. 116–131.

Navas, Eduardo: *Art, Media Design, and Postproduction. Open Guidelines on Appropriation and Remix*. Routledge: New York, London 2018.

Navas, Eduardo: *The Rise of Metacreativity: AI Aesthetics After Remix*. Routledge: New York, London 2022.

Navas, Eduardo / Gallagher, Owen / burrough, xtine (eds.): *The Routledge Companion to Remix Studies*. Routledge: New York, London 2015.

Navas, Eduardo / Gallagher, Owen / burrough, xtine (eds.): "Introduction". In: Navas, Eduardo / Gallagher, Owen / burrough, xtine (eds.): *The Routledge Handbook of Remix Studies and Digital Humanities*. Routledge: New York, London 2021a, pp. 1–16.

Navas, Eduardo / Gallagher, Owen / burrough, xtine (eds.): *The Routledge Handbook of Remix Studies and Digital Humanities*. Routledge: New York, London 2021b.

Negroponte, Nicolas: "Beyond Digital". *Wired* 1998. Retrieved 06.07.2023, from https://web.media.mit.edu/~nicholas/Wired/WIRED6-12.html.

Neville, Brian / Villeneuve, Johanne: *Waste-Site Stories: The Recycling of Memory*. State University of New York Press: Albany 2002.

Nicklas, Pascal / Linder, Oliver: "Adaptation and Cultural Appropriation". In: Nicklas, Pascal / Linder, Oliver (eds.): *Adaptation and Cultural Appropriation: Literature, Film, and the Arts*. De Gruyter: Berlin, Boston 2012, pp. 1–14.

Nieborg, David B. / Poell, Thomas: "The platformization of cultural production: Theorizing the contingent cultural commodity". *New Media & Society* (20:11) 2018, pp. 4275–4292. https://doi.org/10.1177/1461444818769694.

Passig, Kahtrin: *Vielleicht ist das neu und erfreulich: Technik. Literatur. Kritik*. Droschl: Graz 2019.

Perniola, Mario: "Cultural Turning Points in Art: Art between Parasitism and Admiration". *RES: Anthropology and Aesthetics* (41 Spring) 2002, pp. 127–135.

Piglia, Ricardo: "La ficción paranoica". *Clarín. Suplemento Cultura y Nación*. Buenos Aires, 10.10.1991, pp. 4–5.

Pombo, Álvaro: "Prólogo", *Cuentos reciclados*. Anagrama: Barcelona 1997, pp. 7–16.

Randall, Marilyn: "Recycling recycling, or *plus ça change…*". *Other Voices* (3.1) May 2007, retrieved 08.07.2023, from http://www.othervoices.org/3.1/mrandall/index.php.

Reckwitz, Andreas: *Die Transformation der Kulturtheorien: Zur Entwicklung eines Theorieprogramms*. Velbrück Wissenschaft: Weilerswist [2000] 2006.

Reckwitz, Andreas: *The Invention of Creativity: Modern Society and the Culture of the New*. Polity: Malden, MA 2017 [Original: *Die Erfindung der Kreativität – Zum Prozess gesellschaftlicher* Ästhetisierung. Suhrkamp: Frankfurt am Main 2012].

Reynier, Christine: "Viginia Woolf's Radical Vision of Recycling". In: Latham, Monica / Marie, Caroline / Rigeade, Anne-Laure (eds.): *Recycling Virginia Woolf in Contemporary Art and Literature*. Routledge: New York, London 2022, pp. 23–35.

Reynolds, Simon: *Retromania: Pop Culture's Addiction to its Own Past*. Faber & Faber: London 2011.

Rigeade, Anne-Laure / Latham, Monica / Marie, Caroline: "Introduction: On Recycling Virginia Woolf in Contemporary Art and Literature". In: Latham, Monica / Marie, Caroline / Rigeade, Anne-Laure (eds.): *Recycling Virginia Woolf in Contemporary Art and Literature*. Routledge: New York, London 2022, pp. 1–19.

Robin, Régine: "Peut-on recycler le passé?". In: Klucinskas, Jean / Moser, Walter (eds.): *Esthétique et Recyclages Culturels: Explorations de La Culture Contemporaine*. University of Ottawa Press: Ottawa 2004, pp. 65–77.

Rodríguez-Ortega, Nuria: "Canon, Value, and Cultural Heritage: New Processes of Assigning Value in the Postdigital Realm". *Multimodal Technologies and Interact* (2:25) 2018, https://doi.org/10.3390/mti2020025.

Rodríguez, Nuria: "Inteligencia Artificial y campo del arte". *pArAdigmA. Revista Universitaria de Cultura* (23) 2020, pp. 24–43, retrieved 08.07.2023, from https://riuma.uma.es/xmlui/bitstream/handle/10630/19525/32.pdf?sequence=1&isAllowed=y.

Sahle, Patrick: "((Kontext (Text)) Edition) Rekontext". In: Meier, Simon / Viehhauser, Gabriel / Sahle, Patrick (eds.): *Rekontextualisierung als Forschungsparadigma des Digitalen*. Books on Demand GmbH: Norderstedt 2020, pp. 21–32, retrieved 10.07.2023, from https://kups.ub.uni-koeln.de/29390/1/SIDE14_Rekontextualisierung_als_Forschungsparadigma_des_Digitalen.pdf.

Sánchez Gómez, Laura: "Electronic literary creation: dialogues through cultural recycling", *Neohelicon* (forthcoming) 2024.

Saum-Pascual, Alex: "Is Third Generation Literature Postweb Literature? And Why Should We Care?", *electronic book review* 2020, retrieved 10.6.2023, from https://electronicbookreview.com/essay/is-third-generation-literature-postweb-literature-and-why-should-we-care/.

Schäfer, Mirko Tobias: *Bastard Culture!: How User Participation Transforms Cultural Production*. Amsterdam University Press: Amsterdam 2011. https://www.jstor.org/stable/j.ctt46n23s; https://doi.org/10.7273/60pg-1574.

Schlesinger, Claus-Michael: "Kafka stochastisch. Rekontextualisierung und Recodierung in computergestützten Textgeneratoren". In: Meier, Simon / Viehhauser, Gabriel / Sahle, Patrick (eds.): *Rekontextualisierung als Forschungsparadigma des Digitalen*. Books on Demand GmbH, Norderstedt 2020, pp. 97–105, retrieved 10.07.2023, from https://kups.ub.uni-koeln.de/29390/1/SIDE14_Rekontextualisierung_als_Forschungsparadigma_des_Digitalen.pdf.

Schneider, Manfred (1997): *Der Barbar: Endzeitstimmung und Kulturrecycling*. Hanser: Munich.

Schwab, Klaus: *The Fourth Industrial Revolution*. Crown: New York 2017.

Smit, Rik: "Die Plattformisierung des Erinnerns". In: Pentzold, Christian / Lohmeier, Christine (DFG-Netzwerk Kommunikationswissenschaftliche Erinnerungsforschung) (eds.): *Handbuch kommunikationswissenschaftliche*

Erinnerungsforschung. de Gruyter: Berlin 2023, pp. 471–493 [Supersvised automatic Translation by M. Menke and C. Pentzold], retrieved 10.6.2023, from https://doi.org/10.1515/9783110629743-023.

Smith, Dale M. / Brown Jr., James J.: "For Public Distribution". In: Gries, Laurie E. / Brooke, Collin G. (eds.): *Circulation, Writing & Rhetoric*. Utah State University Press: Logan 2018, pp. 208–224.

Snickars, Pelle: "If Content is King, Context is its Crown". *VIEW Journal of European Television History and Culture* (1:1) 2012, pp. 34–39. DOI: http://doi.org/10.18146/2213-0969.2012.jethc006.

Steyerl, Hito: "Postrepresenational: Politics of Post-Representation" [Interview]. *DIS Magazine*, Jun 2014, retrieved 11.07.2023, from http://dismagazine.com/disillusioned-2/62143/hito-steyerl-politics-of-post-representation/.

Thompson, Michael: *Rubbish Theory. The Creation and Destruction of Value*. Oxford UP: Oxford, New York 1979.

Tsing, Anna: *Friction. An Ethnography of Global Connection*. Princeton University Press: New Jersey 2004.

von Bernstorff, Wiebke: "Von fehlenden vierten Wänden und anderen Wahrheiten: Soziale Autofiktionen in Performance und Theaterpädagogik". [Forthcoming].

van Dijck, José: *The Culture of Connectivity: A Critical History of Social Media*. Oxford University Press: New York 2013.

van Dijck, José / Thomas Poell / Martijn de Waal: *The Platform Society. Public Values in a Connective World*. Oxford University Press: New York 2018.

van Dijk, Teun A.: *Discourse and Context. A Sociocognitive Approach*. Cambridge University Press: Cambridge, New York 2008. DOI: https://doi.org/10.1017/CBO9780511481499.

Vate-U-Lan, Poonsri / Quigley, Donna / Masouras, Panicos: "Phygital Learning Concept: From Big to Smart Data". *The Thirteenth International Conference on eLearning for Knowledge-Based Society*. Thailand: 15 December 2016, pp. 9.1–9.6, retrieved 11.07.2023, from https://repository.au.edu/server/api/core/bitstreams/7cbf882d-5c04-4550-8e7a-9c55eecc99dc/content.

Waysdorf, Abby S.: "Remix in the age of ubiquitous remix". *Convergence. The International Journal of Research into New Media Technologies* (27:4) 2021, pp. 1129–1144. DOI: 10.1177/1354856521994454.

Wetzel, Michael: "Medien". In: Kühnhardt, Ludger / Mayer, Tilman (eds.): *Bonner Enzyklopädie der Globalität*. Springer VS Verlag: Wiesbaden 2017, pp. 467–478.

Wieland, Magnus: "Ablagekulturen: Interdependenzen zwischen Archiv und Deponie". In: Assmann, David-Christopher (ed.): *Narrtive der Deponie*.

Kulturwissenschaftliche Analysen beseitigter Materialitäten. Springer VS Wiesbaden: Wiebaden 2020, pp. 149–165.

Wilson, Kabe / Stanford Friedman, Susan: "Of Words, Worlds and Woolf. Recycling *A Room of One's Own into Of One Woman or So*". In: Latham, Monica / Marie, Caroline / Rigeade, Anne-Laure (eds.): *Recycling Virginia Woolf in Contemporary Art and Literature*. Routledge: New York, London 2022, pp. 55–84.

Windmüller, Sonja: "Recycling". In: Samida, Stefanie / Eggert, Manfred K. H. / Hahn, Hans Peter (eds.): *Handbuch Materielle Kultur: Bedeutungen – Konzepte – Disziplinen*. Metzler: Stuttgart, Weimar 2014, pp. 104–109.

Zuboff, Shoshana: "Surveillance Capitalism and the Challenge of Collective Action". *New Labor Forum* (28:1) January 2019, pp. 10–29. https://doi.org/10.1177/1095796018819461.

Johanna Vollmeyer
Universidad Complutense de Madrid

Postdigital Recycling – Doing Memory and the Narrative

Abstract: Living in the postdigital age raises the question of how expanding digitalisation and datafication affects our way of remembering and creating memory, both individually and collectively. This contribution focuses on the recycling of "cultural products", particularly literary texts, in and through digital media. These cultural products form part of our communication, our collective memory and identity. When they are appropriated by hypermedia and adjusted to their algorithmic logic, they strongly transform processes of memory, as demonstrated by the diary app, *Journey*. Additionally, the literary text itself is profoundly modified by the changes of memory conceptions caused by algorithmic interventions, as demonstrated in Leif Randt's novel, *Allegro Pastell*.

Keywords: postdigital recycling, memory, narrative, app *Journey*, *Allegro Pastell*, Leif Randt.

1. Introduction

> *Nie nach Berlin gezogen zu sein, fühlte sich für Jerome so an, wie nie auf Facebook gewesen zu sein. Beide Entscheidungen hatten ihm viel Vergleichsdruck und narzisstische Kränkungen erspart, ihn vielleicht aber auch zu einem weniger akkuraten Zeitzeugen gemacht.*[1] *(Randt 2020, p. 118).*

Jerome's thoughts in Leif Randt's novel, *Allegro Pastell* (2019), are representative of the influence of the development of digital media on memory and the concept of memory. For Jerome, being an accurate contemporary witness is bound to a user's profile on social media, where all that has ever been posted is accurately archived. Thanks to Facebook's algorithm, the user is reminded periodically of exactly what happened a certain time ago. On the one hand, memory is perceived

1 Never having moved to Berlin felt to Jerome like never having been on Facebook. Both decisions had saved him a lot of comparative pressure, but maybe had made him a less accurate contemporary witness. (All translations from Johanna Vollmeyer).

as a stock of past events from where one can recover these events in an unaltered way in the present; on the other hand, platforms like Facebook help to structure and remind us of this apparently authentic memory content. These changes in our way of doing and understanding memory are taken up by contemporary authors and integrated into their literature.

This chapter analyses how literature reflects the modifications in the way of doing memory by media in the postdigital age. It demonstrates how our experiences are algorithmically processed and how this process is taken up by fictional texts. It also illuminates the effects of postdigital processes on memory on the original cultural artefacts, including long-written literary texts, when they are used and recycled in hypermedia production, even if those effects on tacit memory frequently go unnoticed.

To approach this complex situation, it will be necessary to define cultural recycling. Cultural content has been reused before the advent of the postdigital era via a myriad of recycling techniques and strategies. However, the postdigital era is characterised by profound quantitative and qualitative changes that demonstrate a paradigm shift from analogue, pre-digital, and digital ways of reusing pre-existing content. These insights will be contextualised within a theoretical framework that engages fundamental questions about waste, objects that are considered recyclable, different ways of recycling, the status of the original and its copy, etc.

Following the theoretical framework, this article discusses the changes that our personal and cultural memories have undergone since the start of the mass use of the smartphone in 2006. It includes an analysis of a digital media platform that focuses on literary text and a literary case study. Both provide insights into the transformation of doing memory in the postdigital age. Leif Randt's novel provides a clear example of how social media platforms change our perception of the world, of ourselves and ultimately of how we remember.

Another effect on many literary texts that will be observed in this contribution is a profound change on how memory is constructed. These changes are not only noticed in literary texts but also in digital media platforms themselves. They frequently make use of traditional genres that have nevertheless been adapted to the needs and conditions of the "new" media as can be observed in the case study of the diary app, *Journey*.

2. Theoretical framework: recycling as a way of doing memory

In this section, I unpack the term "cultural recycling," since it is crucial to determine what can be considered remnants in our society and which are worthy of reuse. Further insights into memory in the postdigital age will emerge through understanding what is considered a remnant and why that particular remnant is appropriate for reuse.

2.1. Cultural recycling

In his understanding of waste and its (re-)use, Agustín Fernández Mallo adopts the approach of complex systems to develop a general theory of waste. His monograph, *Teoría general de la basura* (2018), deals with waste in cultural production. He defines waste as any kind of remnant that provides stability and continuity, as well as the condition for the creation of anything new. Fernández Mallo, a physicist, illustrates this with the metaphor of a fossil: a fossil outlines the solid parts that are tangible, but requires the "soft" parts that must be added mentally to obtain a full picture. Our reality is constructed of existing solid parts, "waste", and soft parts, which we add to those pre-existing remnants. Further, remnants tell us nothing about the past; they are footprints that tell us what our present is like and that help us construct our contemporary identity (Fernández Mallo 2018, p. 11). Both our past and present are built out of pre-existing schemes (waste) that are completed by invented "new" matter (soft parts). Thus, we cannot understand our reality as fragmented, but as a kind of a hyperconnected network or grid (Fernández Mallo 2018, p. 19). Fernández Mallo calls this complex realism. For him, reality is the superposition of complex systems (Fernández Mallo 2018, p. 22):

> la realidad ni ha estado, ni está ni estará nunca, fragmentada sino organizada en red; la fragmentación tan sólo es una apariencia fruto de no haber cambiado la óptica de nuestro instrumento de visión. Lo que eran desdeñables residuos materiales o simbólicos que sin orden ni taxonomía se amontaban [sic] ante nuestros ojos, pasan, bajo esta nueva óptica y con tal de enfocar un poco mejor, a ser considerados como residuos complejos, coherentemente conectados en múltiples redes, no fragmentados, y por lo tanto culturalmente aprovechables de otro modo.[2] (Fernández Mallo 2018, p. 23).

---

2 "the reality was never, is not and never will be fragmented but is organised in a network; fragmentation is just an appearance as a result of not having changed the optics of our vision instrument. What were contemptible remnants or symbols that piled up in front of our eyes without any order or taxonomy are now, thanks to the new optics that allow us to focus a bit better, considered as complex remnants that are coherently connected in multiple networks, which are not fragmented and, thus, are culturally usable in a different mode." (Fernández Mallo 2018, p. 23).

To illustrate his approach, Fernández Mallo uses the beach as a metaphor. A beach is not just an accumulation of sand particles. In our modern times, it also consists of plastic particles and other remnants from other time periods that are superimposed, one on top of another. It is only in their entirety that they build what we call a beach. This insight leads to a new epistemology in which we understand our reality as a complex convergence rather than as dialectic, based on differences:

> el mundo es una suma de redes en la cual las cosas, los objetos, son subredes: nodos que son sustancias, y las relaciones, los enlaces, que se establecen entre ellos. [...] Ni es la estructuralista *manada* – conjunto de entes vivos que se mueven orientados bajo los designios de un líder o principio rector –, ni es el posmodernista *rebaño* – manso pastoreo neobarroco sin finalidad ni orientación vectora –, sino una individualidad que va introduciendo errores en el sistema externo, y por ello, de manera activa y determinante, pasa a formar parte de él sin por ello quedar subsumido como pieza ciega en él. [...] lo que importa es el modo en que [estas redes] coadyuvan a la existencia de un exterior a ellos, un paisaje, que más tarde o más temprano les devolverá materiales con los que ir rehaciéndose. El flujo vital del nómada.[3] (Fernández Mallo 2018, pp. 280–281).

Of particular interest in Fernández Mallo's explanation is the inclusion of non-human beings as active agents in the construction of our reality. However, he does not even consider the distinction between human and non-human as fruitful. He consistently references complex grids in which human individuals are only one more sub-grid. This allocates agency to any kind of matter, even algorithms. Fernández Mallo uses the term nomads, which are the flows in which networks are inserted and that they actually help to create. According to complex system theories, nomads provide a certain stability, but they are also open and connected to other systems, which allow their adaptation to external changes. Hence, in a continuous flow of change we find consistency where complex systems are based

---

3 "the world is the sum of networks in which things and objects are sub-networks: nodes that are substances, just as the relationships, the links that exist between them, are [...]. It is neither the structuralist *pack* – a set of living beings that move guided by the intentions of a leader or a guiding principle – nor the postmodernist *herd* – tame neo-baroque cattle without any destiny or structured guidance – but an individualism that is introducing mistakes into the external system, and accordingly becomes a part of it in an active and determined manner without being subordinated as a blind part of it. [...] what is important is the manner in which [these networks] contribute to an existence of the exterior, a landscape that sooner or later returns materials that serve for renewal. The vital flux of the nomad." (Fernández Mallo 2018, pp. 280–281).

on and evolve around these constants or, to use another term, remnants (as a physicist, he argues with Planck's constant or the speed of light in this context).

"Remnant" stems from Latin, meaning not allowing reality to move forward but to remain in a static position (Fernández Mallo 2018, p. 125). This is precisely the condition for change, because everything new only arises from pre-existing residues and not out of a void. Creating anything new implies the reappropriation of these solid parts. Only by virtue of this substrate can anything new evolve. It emerges by adding to this substrate, modifying it before it itself becomes the substrate for future creations (Fernández Mallo 2018, p. 127). The constant reusing of these cultural residues converts us into nomads (Fernández Mallo 2018, p. 131).

Fernández Mallo's insights are incisive for our understanding of the postdigital era. While earlier schools of thought like postmodernism have long reduced an understanding of our reality to the interpretation and performativity of text and language, the metaphor of our present seems to be one of networks and recycling. The networks and recycling metaphor not only refers to text and language, but also considers all kinds of materiality as described by Fernández Mallo's complex systems. This complex system theory clearly diverges from postmodernism in its approach to materiality. Thus, recycling has become the pertinent metaphor of the current moment, as Amelia Sanz Cabrerizo has pointed out. She draws our attention to important changes in the aesthetic-epistemological paradigms of understanding our reality,[4] which ranges from imitation – the predominant concept of the renaissance where imitating processes were understood as a reference to the original – ensued by the refusal of anything "old," which was characteristic of the era of romanticism with its idea of the genius creating artwork out of a void, followed by ideas of intertextuality attempting to provide us with the key for a better understanding of texts and the world, a concept that pointed more towards productivity, to our current postdigital discourse.

Postdigital discourse is characterised not so much by being concerned with concepts of understanding and interpretation as acting and performing. While the consumption of cultural or literary products were foregrounded in the 1990s, what is of interest now is the way available cultural matter can be reused. However, recycling does not bring all elements into a new lifecycle but only those

4 I would like to thank my colleague Amelia Sanz Cabrerizo for sharing her insights and research results on intertextuality and recycling in numerous meetings, workshops and emails with all members of the research group REC-Lit.

that are easily accessible and "to hand". Hence, this practice seems to promote a kind of presentism that challenges our concept of the past and the origin of things, and contains crucial consequences for the creation of memory.

Recycling implies, furthermore, the active participation of the consumer. This can be observed in everyday performances like the recycling of a plastic bottle, which can be considered an action to preserve our planet. Nevertheless, it frequently also conveys an almost theatrical act that refers to the importance of being seen, hence, the visibility of my own performance. Recycling in the context of environmental protection and economic sustainability is highly regarded in many societies to a point that it is increasingly considered a competitive edge in a global market.[5] Even if the motifs might be different, the self-staging aspect is also an important feature of cultural recycling. Many artists transform pre-existing art objects into something new or reintroduce them into the public domain, which frequently goes hand-in-hand with the aim to be seen and recognised as an artist. Recycling requires a collective dimension since it becomes particularly meaningful when many people undertake it. When we talk about recycling in the context of environmental protection, it would not make much sense if only a few people were active recyclers while the majority did not make any change. A similar mechanism can be observed in postdigital media. Only the reuse of a determined content by many makes this content especially visible (for example, poems that go viral). These changes in the performative act of producing cultural goods that imply an active prosumer who recycles what is at hand profoundly changes the way we do and perform memory, since the question of original and copy and the question of the author of a cultural artefact are continuously modified anew.

What does this mean for the creation of memory in the postdigital era? How does the recycling and reuse of available solid parts in digital media change our way of doing memory and the concept of memory itself?

2.2. Memory in the postdigital age

We largely acquire our worldly knowledge through the media and only a part of what we know stems from what we have learned by unmediated experiences.[6]

---

5 See, for example, Kolf (2021).

6 Here it is crucial to problematise the terms media and experience. Furthermore, language or any object that we manipulate and that might help us understand a certain situation or fact can be interpreted as media. In this contribution, what shall be referred to as media are all kinds of digital and non-digital communication tools, such as social

Memory plays a crucial role in the acquisition of knowledge because it assigns meaning and significance to both the mediated and the unmediated experiences. As José van Dijk (2007) argued in her reflections on mediated memory, media are not mere triggers or vehicles of memory content, but rather media and memory create each other mutually. This means that media are not acting in a unidirectional way on memory. Both media and memory arise from a reciprocal influence, from an intra-action[7] that results in the iterative stemming from both.

These insights about the entanglement of media and memory are not totally new, but in the case of digital media the way memory is created through this intra-action has changed significantly because the quantitative and qualitative characteristics of postdigital media differ profoundly from the media characteristics that could be previously observed. The following statements will clarify this development: (1) The use of digital media allows a growing "self-experimentation" (van Dijck 2007, p. 19) that is closely linked to immersive experiences. According to Steffi de Jong (2020), we have reached a digital-somatic phase, in which immersion will be a decisive way to experience and remember the past. Currently, this is "best" achieved through virtual reality (VR) apps that help dive into a past event and live it as if it were one's own experience. On the one hand, these immersive experiences might bring past events closer to the user and reinforce the awareness of certain historical events. On the other hand, they diminish the distance between emotional involvement and critical reflection. VR apps are usually based on immediacy that seems to shrink the temporal distance to the past, so that they will eventually change our perception of time and temporalities as well as our concept of testimony. These apps usually require the active participation of the user, which is another feature of digital media. (2) The user's role is increasingly changing from a simple consumer to

---

media platforms, mass media (online and analogue), apps, but also photographs that convey family awareness and so on.

7 The term "intra-action" is used according to Karen Barad's New Materialist approach towards agency and the entanglement of both human and non-human agents. According to her, our world emerges through intra-action, which is "the mutual constitutions of entangled agencies" (Barad 2007, p. 33). That is why she does not talk about inter-actions, because it could suggest that there are discreet entities that are able to take up contact but have existed in their current shape previously. On the contrary, she assumes that all beings, all matter, comes into being through intra-action with others. Thus, space, time and matter are produced through this "doing or being in their intra-activity" (Barad 2007, p. 178). (My special thanks to Dr. Marije Hristova for introducing Barad to the field of memory studies).

an active prosumer. The delineation between production and consumption is increasingly blurred since users are asked to actively engage with the content offered and, as in the case of social media platforms, they must first produce the content before others can access and consume it. (3) This new user profile leads to a stronger interlacing of the private and the public, since large parts of the published content derive from private spheres. Making it public implies another blurring, in this case of the delimiting of what has been considered private and public, with its consequent effects on the definition of private/personal and public/collective memory. The boundaries of these concepts have always been fluid but are challenged now more than ever. (4) Digital media stand out for being more participative, which could lead to an increasing democratisation of memory discourses. In fact, the Internet emerged with the promise of a more inclusive public memory that is able to permeate all social strata (Caron, Brown 2011, pp. 1–20). However, according to Meyer (Meyer 2009, pp. 175–206), this democratising effect is debatable, because of the question of who or which entity determines, for example, the results of our web searches and eventually our web queries about the past (Meyer 2009, p. 181). (5) That is why many authors diagnose a growing institutionalisation of the Internet due to the intervention of institutions and private enterprises which claim authority as gatekeepers of the information flow. These influences remain unnoticed by large parts of the user community since the algorithms that channel our web-based searches and our movement on digital devices remain invisible. (6) Users only move on the surface of an algorithm or software without the possibility of knowing the mechanism of the digital code that guides our behaviour, unless it is open source.[8]

Even though an algorithm is designed to be pragmatic and strictly formalised in order to always execute the same action, it is not free from social discourse. Although the algorithm is decontextualised and its aim is not to provide sense or significance, it has its own historicity since it has not been created out of a void but from a certain socio-technological context. In addition, algorithms are thought to create patterns that reconnect with the current moment, a process for which they need to revert to bits of this "reality", that is, data that have previously been collected or created themselves by technological processing (Vollmeyer / Maeding / Calvo 2020, p. 1). These patterns are created by executing the same process repeatedly, leading to a form of redundancy or repetition that eventually

8 Even in the case of an open-source programme/algorithm, the user needs to possess sufficient technological knowledge to be able to understand and interpret the digital code.

creates a certain reality. They decide which information is at hand and in what way; thus, what is going to be remembered or forgotten.

This kind of manipulation (7) is not only carried out by invisible algorithms; manipulation or modification is one of the main characteristics of the postdigital age. Data are constantly altered thanks to re-editing, remixing techniques, overwriting and consciously intended manipulation of data. All these interventions are mechanisms of forgetting and remembering simultaneously, since they pick up data (remembering) that are transformed into something new or different, often without indicating the initial source (forgetting) (Vollmeyer / Maeding / Calvo 2020, p. 3). Due to these manipulative processes, the perspective of our world is distorted. But frequently it does not remain a simple distortion. New information can be added that need not be factual. Thus, our world acquires (8) a new quality that can be considered postfactual.

(9) The omnipresence of digital media in our daily lives opens up the chance to access information almost anytime and anywhere. A growing amount of information is available to many people constantly and immediately. Thus, Andrew Hoskins talks about the "on-the-fly-memory" (Hoskins 2009, p. 91). The current moment is connected to the moment that has just passed, so we can talk about an omnipresence of the past. At the same time, digital media provide a simultaneity of events, experiences and places, such that media represent the real world in real time (Wilson 2009, p. 190). This leads to a broadened present and a disconnected past. Of course, the situation is even more multi-faceted, since the Internet is frequently perceived as an immense archive (10) from where the stored information can be retrieved in its original shape. This is how platform users frequently conceive of the Internet and is also one of the reasons why they consider events that pop up, for example, "On This Day" on Facebook (renamed "Memories" later), as truthful memories.[9] Here we must again ask who is administering this "stock," who is able and allowed to access it, what is considered part of the archive and what is rejected.

All these changes in media determine how memory is done and how the very concept of memory is perceived.

---

9 The "On This Day" Engineering Manager has declared that Facebook developed certain automatic filters that bring certain memories to the surface in the News Feed that users will most likely consider as meaningful. For the filter's design, the user's feedback had been fundamental (Aziz/ Paluri 2016).

2.3. Memory and recycling processes

Media and media use in the postdigital age is characterised by immediacy, personalisation, the changing role of a passive consumer to a more active prosumer and interconnectivity, to mention just some of the most important ones. Our reality is marked by a constant input of information, whether via mass media or social media. The latter particularly foster communication between users and the exchange of content that consumers have previously produced themselves. This makes these kinds of platform and their recycling methods highly self-referential. Interestingly, much of the content is used without authorial claims. Memes are a good example of this phenomenon. Even if it is obvious that their content requires "solid" parts, which means that it only works by appropriating already existing content, such as an image or a statement, it is frequently unclear where this material stems from. Its origin can hardly be traced back, but the author of the meme itself is also usually unknown. Authorship does not seem to matter, either for the appropriated content or for the meme itself. More interestingly, the attempt to find the "original" author of the appropriated content does not make much sense since this content has already been taken from other sources. This phenomenon challenges our conventional concept of original and copy (Gunkel 2016). A successful meme requires something more. Not only is the act of appropriation and rearranging important, a meme also aims to *circulate* the recycled content in its new form. The spread and collective use of the meme is a crucial postdigital feature and eventually the meme's *raison d'être*. Because of this, when a meme does not go viral it has floundered in some way. These processes of constant appropriation and reuse regardless of origin seem to lead to a certain kind of cultural subconscious: artefacts and the literary are recycled without an awareness for their origins. This creates a "cultural memory"[10] that is nevertheless not visible or at least not consciously referred to most of the time.

These changes in our media use and perception do not occur in a purely democratic way. Not everybody has the chance to access and use digital media evenly. Economic and social differences, to mention only two, create and widen digital gaps that can be found within societies as well as between different regions of the world. Even if people have the necessary digital devices available and a reliable Internet connection, not all segments of society are of interest for the algorithm-driven Internet. "Algorithms are [...] power-ridden.

---

10 The term in this context does not mean the concept forged by Aleida and Jan Assmann. Here it is limited to "cultural" content.

Options for self-presentation offered by preformatted template structures on social networking sites are limited in order to channel behaviour and facilitate the generation of consumer profiles" (Leurs 2015, p. 252). This has an effect on what is consumed and recycled. The race for likes is a good example to illustrate what Koen Leurs describes as channelled behaviour. On the one hand, users are encouraged to produce content that is more likely to get the audience's approval; on the other hand, what is liked and retrieved more frequently is also put on top of search results or news feeds, etc. What does not spark much interest disappears very soon and is lost to oblivion. Only what is at hand and made visible is normalized as a reference while all other content is dumped. This has immediate effects on our collective cultural memory, for example, through the establishment of a determined canon. Once content is introduced there, it is much more prone to be recycled again. This process not only determines the content that we can find on digital media; algorithms largely exceed the purely digital sphere since they already act at a much earlier stage, that is, content production already outside digital media and our own behaviour inside and outside the Internet. This characterises the postdigital age and thereby the cultural production of our present time.

3. Case studies

The following case studies provide further insights into the growing entanglement of the analogue and the digital and its effects on memory. They show how our way of doing memory is changing. These changes can be observed in hypermedia productions themselves and in "classic" literature productions that reflect these developments. Of special interest are changes in our narrative strategies that are applied to building memory. Finally, they show how literature persists and is recycled in hypermedia as proven narrative strategies, genre models, etc., are taken on by hypermedia productions.

3.1. The datafication of memory – *Journey*

Digital platforms, including social media platforms, aim to connect people, to empower them to do business and exchange information "while circumventing corporate or state intermediaries" (van Dijck / Poell / de Waal 2018, p. 7). At first glance, this implies democratising effects since platforms allow users to interact deliberately and independently. However, this seemingly democratising target is not the platform's only one. Their *raison d'etre* lies in the collection and trading of the content and user data that is pre-requisite for growing online connectivity (van Dijck / Poell / de Waal 2018, p. 9) – and also for profitable business. The other platform myth assumes that "platform services are 'free' because many do not charge for their services." However, most online social networks are "monetised through automating connections between users, content, data and advertising" (van Dijck / Poell / de Waal 2018, p. 10). In this context, algorithms are a tool to define a platform's "connective architecture [...] and to transform input data into a desired output" (van Dijck / Poell / de Waal 2018, p. 9) that will eventually provide us with personalised content and publicity. Personalisation and the entanglement of algorithms and user data show that platforms are not simply a technological invention to improve connectivity. They have a much stronger impact since they "shape the way we live and how society is organized" (van Dijck / Poell / de Waal 2018, p. 9).

The transformative power of platforms also affects the way of doing memory: platforms participate in an active memory task by archiving and structuring memory content. They do not do so neutrally. Platforms transform experience into behavioural data to generate a determined output, often closely linked to sales strategies. This has its effects on both collective memory (more influenced by platforms like YouTube) and individual memory (Facebook, diary apps, etc.). According to Nieborg and Poell, "cultural production is progressively 'contingent on', that is dependent on a select group of powerful digital platforms" (Nieborg / Poell 2018, p. 4276). Market consolidation by digital platforms conditions "[p]roducts and services offered and circulated... [so] that they are malleable, modular in design, and informed by datafied user feedback, open to constant revision and recirculation" (Nieborg / Poell 2018, p. 4276). In essence, platforms require the (re-)use of pre-existing content to function.

Rik Smit has shown in his analysis of diary apps how these mechanisms work. Apps like *Dayone*, *Universal Diary* or *Journey* reify the classical format of a dairy written by hand where one takes note of what has happened to him/her or was on his/her mind and seemed to be worth writing down. In the classical form, content depended almost exclusively on the author, whether in a handwritten diary or by typing the text on a computer. In contrast, apps like *Journey* do not leave any entry to chance. The app is promoted as being "more than just a journal, or a diary; we're your own motivational coach and happiness trainer. Let's embark on a fabulous journey of self-improvement today" (*Journey*). While the classical diary was thought to be a means for reflection, it now advances a claim for self-improvement: "Join millions of Journey users and create a healthier, happier mind. A sanctuary for your mind and soul, Journey will help increase your positive energy, be more grateful and a calmer mind by building healthy thinking through journaling" (*Journey*). The app is inspired by positive psychology, which is frequently misunderstood as a means of self-optimisation in neoliberal societies.[11] Self-improvement is positioned as a happiness project that can be achieved by following an algorithmic "if…then" logic, as Rik Smit (Smit 2023) has argued. If I do more of X, this will lead to more happiness. To reach this state of happiness through self-optimisation, the app offers a range of features: you can keep a record of your fitness level, your mood states, happy moments (pictures), and receive advice from a "coach", etc. To make the app even more complete and user-friendly, it encourages the use of other apps such as Google Maps, Siri Shortcuts and an email account service to accurately tag one's location in the entries, creating entries with Siri without even opening the diary app and composing texts via the email service for "quick and easy writing on the go" (*Journey*).

Nevertheless, the app's functions only work when they are filled in with the user's content, which is then recycled to produce a certain output. Thus, memories are transformed into data bits that feed the system in order to transform this data into mood overviews, "throwbacks", and "often together" collages. The application recycles and reconstructs experiences of the past to create the present and the future (Smit 2023). By doing so, the algorithm behind the platform becomes an active agent that preconditions what content is needed for the app to work properly and to produce the desired output. In contrast to classic diaries, entries are neither deliberate nor free, but they must fulfil certain functional aspects for their further recycling (data about fitness, friends, locations, etc.). The app is not only a tool for capturing one's own performance but it is an actively engaged agent that manipulates and transforms the data into a supposedly meaningful arrangement of recollections that determines what the user can consider appropriate for keeping. Hence, memory is constructed by an algorithmic logic that exemplifies the datafication of memory making. The term datafication in this context allows a two-fold interpretation. On the one hand, memory objects enter the formatted structure of the platform and are converted into data that "can be sorted, reorganised and re-presented in various forms by the app" (Smit 2023), and thus be recycled. On the other hand, users already preconfigure their memories for subsequent processing, adjusting their memories to an algorithmic logic even before transferring them to the platform. Furthermore, only what is "at hand" is recycled. Only the most recent past is taken into account while more remote events are not of real interest. This remote

11 See as a critical publication towards this interpretation of positive psychology Cabanas / Illouz (2019).

past is not necessary for tracking the user's performance and would lead to a more analytic design than just the simple if-then logic.

The *Journey* app clearly shows the transformative potential of platforms for society. Therefore, it is no surprise that these changes have also influenced literature production, as the following example will show.

3.2. Algorithmised memory in literature – *Allegro Pastell*

Leif Randt's novel, *Allegro Pastell* (2020), was first published in 2019. It illuminates the long-distance relationship between the novelist Tanja Arnheim, who lives in Berlin, and Jerome Daimler, a web designer from Frankfurt am Main. Their relationship is described as flawless, where nothing is left to chance. Both take care to keep a perfect balance between distance and proximity which finds expression in the careful choice of their communication channels. Even if they haven't agreed on any "information policy" (Randt 2020, p. 30), both prefer to write a classical email to express deeper reflections and more extended comments. The email is more characteristic of the digital age while apps, such as iMessenger or Telegram, are representative of the postdigital age since they rely on and foster a constant connectivity and immediacy. Tanja and Jerome opt for those applications when they want to share a present moment and expect a (more) instant reaction, where the communication tool itself is measured, as well as the frequency and the mode of their messages (voice or text message, length, emojis, etc.).

In this context, it is interesting that the veracity of email communication is questioned in the novel.[12] "Oft erzählte er von Freunden, die Tanja noch gar nicht persönlich kannte, theoretisch hätte er sich diese Charaktere also auch einfach ausdenken können, aber sie vertraute ihm [...]. In ihren E-Mails erzählten sie einander die Wahrheit, wenn auch nicht alles"[13] (Randt 2020, p. 31).

Since emails require more lengthy and in-depth expressions than a simple Telegram message, the main characters in Randt's novel consider them as prone to the introduction of fictional or at least non-factual content. Instant messages, in contrast, are understood as a more faithful expression of immediate thoughts

---

12 In contrast, in debates outside the novel, postdigital messenger services rather than emails are usually blamed for the creation of postfactual content. See the ongoing debate in the mass media and secondary literature about the creation of a postfactual reality through postdigital media (Perendia 2017; Montoya Camacho 2019).

13 "He frequently talked about friends that Tanja hadn't met so far; theoretically he could have just invented them but she trusted him [...]. In their emails, they told each other the truth, even if not the whole." (Randt 2020, p. 31).

and feelings. Despite this initial perception, emails are eventually accepted as being more authentic because their format is not as restricted as instant messaging. The narrator suggests that Jerome's emails to Tanja compensate for the dairy that he has never kept (Randt 2020, p. 31). Tanja also regards emails as more personal and free-floating narrations that do not require "proof-reading" before sending. In contrast, communication that takes place via more postdigital tools is described to be diametrically opposed in the way it is used,

> Die Fahrt mit dem Elektroscooter bis zur Allegro-Grundschule kostete Tanja 6,80 €. Auf den letzten Metern hatte sie ein anspruchsvoll zu filmendes Handyvideo von sich auf dem Roller gedreht und kurz danach entschieden, es niemandem zu schicken. Sie würde nie wieder den ganzen Weg von Neukölln bis Tiergarten auf einem Elektroscooter zurücklegen.[14] (Randt 2020, p. 264).

The decision not to send this video to anybody or to upload it to a social media platform is based on its representability. It does not represent Tanja's ordinary activities and she does not want to create the false impression of using the electro scooter as a common vehicle. This shows how much the character's behaviour is conditioned by social media platforms and postdigital communication tools. These tools exist not only for the exchange of information, ideas, feelings, etc., but always contain an important dramaturgic component that is the self-staging of the user for the public. Conversation partners are not taken as mere interlocutors but as an audience for which a play is staged. Like *Journey,* potential content is adjusted to this logic before it is uploaded and even produced.

Another example of this self-staging-mode is a picture that Jerome had taken while he was jogging. Even if he is sweaty, he has chosen a favourable angle that makes him look more masculine (Randt 2020, p. 31). This is not only related to vanity but to the fact that all content that circulates on digital media is produced for posterity. The visual and textual content that the characters send to each other is prepared for display to a wider public. This is even more evident in the case of social media platforms that merge the private and the public sphere. They reinforce this dramatic moment of staging which is also an important feature of the gesture of recycling. For any kind of recycling, it is crucial that others can observe the action. Thus, any act of recycling implies the creation of a past to be

---

14 "The ride with the electro-scooter to the Allegro elementary school cost Tanja €6.80. During the last few metres, she took a mobile phone video of herself on the scooter that was difficult to shoot and shortly after she decided not to send it to anybody. She would never travel again the whole way from Neukölln to Tiergarten on an electro-scooter." (Randt 2020, p. 264).

shown to a future audience. This is also the logic of social media platforms and their algorithms. Following their patterns makes it important to create content that is meaningful for the audience. Algorithms are designed to evolve and to be able to integrate the audience's reaction: the more likes a new entry receives, the longer it will be at the top of the recommended content. This shows that algorithms are actively adapting to the tastes of the platform's users but also subtly and strongly influence the user's behaviour, who adapts to the algorithmic logic in their content creation. This adaption finds expression in the increasingly important role of outward appearance. Social media users do not usually want to show themselves in an unfavourable manner. This shows the power of algorithms and their recycling structure.

Furthermore, the author of a digitally uploaded picture, video, or text, etc. does not possess full ownership over the content, neither legally nor technologically. Many apps oblige users to transfer the copyright of their contributions to the app-provider[15] but it is also easy for others to copy and redistribute the content even if it could still legally belong to the author. This results in contradictory behaviour by the characters. On the one hand, they produce digital content that is meant to stand the test of time, making the present into a production of a future past. On the other hand, their attentiveness culture strengthens their wish for immersion into the present moment that is detached from both past and future. Thus, whatever Jerome and Tanja do is based on careful decisions.

Whenever Tanja, Jerome, and other characters in the novel use social media they seem to weigh up the suitability for accurately representing the present moment as a meaningful future past. Hence, all content produced is thought to be a potential solid part of a fossil as Fernández Mallo has described it, which can later be recycled by appropriation through others or the author her or himself. In this context, social media are taken as faithful archives that store the present realistically and from which memories can be retrieved unaltered. This explains why Jerome, who has never had a Facebook account, considers himself a less accurate witness in the opening quotation of this contribution. Striving to leave an impression for posterity converts Tanja, Jerome and other characters into good observers, both in regard to the communication code applied and its decryption. They also observe themselves constantly from a supposedly objective angle located outside themselves. This leads to a distanced and analytical perspective of their own lives:

> Jerome kokettierte mit der Rolle des überglücklichen heterosexuellen Partners. [...] Jerome mochte den Gedanken, dass er sich selbst gegebenenfalls unerträglich finden

15 Normally a user must accept the terms and conditions of the app when she/he signs up.

würde, könnte er sich hier in der U4 von außen sehen. Einen Gedanken zu mögen, der andere verunsichern würde – das war typisch für den neuen Jerome, der mittlerweile spielerisch unterschied zwischen einer inneren Persönlichkeit, die nur er selbst kennen konnte, und einer äußeren Persönlichkeit, die sich aus den Zuschreibungen der Umwelt zusammensetzte.[16] (Randt 2020, p. 11).

This hyper-reflexivity does not prevent the characters from failing in their relationship. Soon Tanja breaks out of the couple relationship, puzzled by the proximity she has experienced with Jerome. After the (temporal) end, Jerome starts dating another woman. During their first meeting, he decides to wear sombre colours because she had dressed in sombre colours the weekend before when they met at a party. But now, she is wearing a bright yellow coat because she wanted to adapt to him and his style. "'Zwischen Samstag und Dienstag haben wir jetzt Cross-Partnerlook gemacht.' Der Irrsinn war, dass Marlene sofort verstand, was er meinte"[17] (Randt 2020, p. 129).

In this example, the characters decode every word or gesture correctly, but they are also aware of the code itself and its allusion. This causes a kind of recursiveness similar to an algorithmic logic. As explained in Chapter 2.2 on memory, algorithms are designed to correctly execute the same action repeatedly, regardless of contextual changes. To do so, they must be decontextualised and de-historised. The same happens to Jerome and Marlene, who do not ask for the historicity of the codes they use. They do not reflect on its origins but understand their behaviour as a kind of enhanced attentiveness that they experience as something positive. Leif Randt himself calls this attitude of his generation "*post-pragmatic joy*" (Hamm 2021). It is characterised by hyper-reflectivity, self-design and self-monitoring. Even the unconscious is perceived as an intended estrangement. This attitude fosters a desire to live an "absolute now" (Mangold 2020), a broadened presence, detached from the past, "Jerome sagte sich, dass sie in der totalen Gegenwart angekommen waren" (Randt 2020, p. 148).[18]

16 "Jerome flirted with the role of the overjoyed heterosexual partner. [...] Jerome liked the idea that, if he could watch himself from outside here in the U4 [metro line 4], he could find himself unbearable. Liking an idea that would unsettle others – this was typical for the new Jerome, who by now was able to differentiate playfully between an inner personality that only he could know and an external personality that was made up of the subscription to his environment." (Randt 2020, p. 11).

17 "'Between Saturday and Tuesday, we have made cross-matching clothes.' The madness was that Marlene immediately understood what he meant." (Randt 2020, p. 129).

18 "Jerome told himself that they had reached the absolute present." (Randt 2020, p. 148).

This present is directly linked to digitality in the novel. In another scene, Tanja is dancing in a club where she is taking synthetic drugs while she is simultaneously chatting on FaceTime with Jerome who is following her drug experience online:

> In der Griessmühle geschah, was meistens geschah, wenn Tanja auf Tanzflächen auf ihr Handy starrte – Leute gaben ihr durch Blicke und Gesten zu verstehen, dass sie doch jetzt bitte im Moment ankommen und das Handy wegpacken solle, aber diese Leute verstanden wenig. Sie hatten keine Ahnung, dass dies gerade für Tanja der schönste Moment war – high auf das Tor zur Welt in ihrer Hand blicken, mit denjenigen kommunizieren, die sie am meisten mochte, auf die Weise, die sie am besten beherrschte. Es war fantastisch, ein Handy zu besitzen, es war fantastisch, Menschen zu kennen, die man liebte. Tanja trug ihr Hemd nun um die Hüfte gebunden und tanzte im Sport-BH. Sie hob die Arme in die Luft, sie schloss die Augen. Ihr Telefon hielt sie die ganze Zeit fest.[19] (Randt 2020, 39).

Postdigital communication is described as the gateway to the world, to real experiences, to being present in the current moment. In this sense, Leif Randt's novel shows similarities to the case study of the diary app, *Journey*. Both present the promise of a better life through a positive psychology based on a high degree of attentiveness and mindfulness. However, living in the present implies a disconnection from the past and the future. Ironically, apps like *Journey* require *a priori* recyclable content to produce meaningful output that creates the state of self-consciousness from previously-created data. Similarly, Randt's characters behave as if they were users of the diary app.

The past that is produced by platforms is usually based on the recent experiences of its users. Only nearby moments are of interest, while more remote events fall between the cracks and escape the algorithmic cycle. As such, a "long-term memory" that comprises more than the last few years is not constructed. It comes as no surprise when the novel's characters do not dig deeper into their individual or family biography at any time. Despite all efforts at

19 "In the Griessmühle, what usually happened when Tanja stared at her self-phone in the middle of the dancefloor took place – the way they looked at her, people made her understand that she should live in the moment and put her mobile phone away, but these people understood little. They had no idea that this was precisely the most beautiful moment for Tanja – being high, watching at the gateway to the world in her hand, communicating with those that she liked most, in a way that she mastered the best. It was fantastic to own a phone; it was fantastic to know people who one loved. Tanja was now wearing her shirt tied to her hips and was dancing in a sports bra. She raised her arms into the air, closed her eyes. She held the phone tight all the time." (Randt 2020, 39).

self-consciousness, both Tanja and Jerome always remain on the surface and do not immerse themselves profoundly into critical self-analysis.

4. Conclusion

Leif Randt's narrator describes Tanja and Jerome as strongly self-optimising and self-monitoring. Attentiveness and mindfulness play a crucial role in their lives and are elevated to a kind of personal everyday philosophy. This is not because they are able to truly disconnect from the past and the future and focus only on the present, even if they believe that. Rather, they produce data that can be exploited in the future. Behavioural patterns like those of Jerome and Tanja are algorithmised behaviour. Both characters follow the algorithmic logic of social media platforms, where all content is produced to be converted into a potential solid part or residue that might be recycled in the future. Nevertheless, these solid parts never reference a more remote past; they are comprised of recent events which are easily "at hand".

What is at stake here is nothing less than a profound shift in our time perception, of what might be considered as past, present and future, indeed, of time itself. It is out of the question that time is not a constant or universal physical variable. Time has always been culturally encoded. I am pointing to the datafication and algorithmisation of societies that strongly impact how time and memory are perceived and constructed. Recycling strategies of different kinds of content play an important role in this. As demonstrated, online strategies exploit a user's data to create a determined past and future within the frame of selected "traditional" genres. The analysis of the diary app illustrated the diary genre being transformed into something very different. To borrow from Fernández Mallo once more, the diary genre represents the fossil's solid parts, while its adaption are the soft parts that must be added to construct the new whole. Genres, narrative strategies, and literary texts have always provided stability, but they have also always been adjusted and redefined. The novelty of the postdigital redefinition is the adaptation to an algorithmic logic.

This is reflected in literary production itself, as demonstrated by Randt's *Allegro Pastel*. The way people are represented and constructed adapts to the postdigital age. Not only does the plot depend on the postdigital communication tools and strategies that the characters apply, the character's construction of identity strongly depends on the algorithmic logic of producing the past in the present moment for the future. In other words, everything a person does is examined to be a potential and meaningful past for a future audience that might recycle this content. In the case of Randt's novel, the narrator does not seem to critically question these changes. The changes in doing memory and eventually in creating identity are rather taken as something given and ineluctable. Rather than achieving deeper insights into the origins of their emotions and behaviour, they simply fulfil certain patters as if their lives exist for the purposes of the diary app itself. In doing so, they never explore the deeper meaning of their lives. The novel is restricted to the surface, in the interface, to use a computational term, so that their lives remain enigmatic to a certain extent, just as the algorithms that underlie all social media platforms and apps that shape our daily lives in the postdigital era do.

Acknowledgement

I want to thank Dr. Miriam Llamas Ubieto, leader of the research project REC-LIT, for the numerous lectures, workshops, meetings but also phone calls and personal debates in which I had the chance to discuss my research in progress. Her always constructive comments and critical questions have contributed to producing my work.

References

Aziz, Omid / Paluri, Manohar: "Engineering for nostalgia: Building a personalized 'On This Day' experience" 2016, retrieved 05.02.2022, from https://research.facebook.com/blog/2016/03/engineering-for-nostalgia-building-a-personalized-on-this-day-experience/.

Barad, Karen: *Meeting the Universe Halfway*, Duke University Press: Durham/London 2007.

Cabanas, Edgar / Illouz, Eva: *Manufacturing Happy Citizens: How the Science and Industry of Happiness Control our Lives*. Polity Press: Cambridge 2019.

Caron, Daniel J. / Brown, Richard: "The Documentary Moment in the Digital Age: Establishing New Values Propositions for Public Memory". *Archivaria* (71) 2011, pp. 1–20.

de Jong, Steffi: "Witness Auschwitz? How VR is changing Testimony". *Public History Weekly* 2020 8(4), retrieved 04.02.2022, from https://public-history-weekly.degruyter.com/8-2020-4/witness-auschwitz-vr/; DOI: dx.doi.org/10.1515/phw-2020-15689.

Fernández Mallo, Agustín: *Teoría general de la basura (cultura, apropiación, complejidad)*. Galaxia Gutenberg: Barcelona 2018.

Gunkel, David J.: *Of Remixology. Ethics and Aesthetics after Remix*. The MIT Press: Cambridge *et al.* 2016.

Hamm, Simone: "Ziemlich nice. Die Gegenwart von Leif Randt ist pastellfarben". *Deutschlandfunk* 2.7.2021, retrieved 11.2.2022, from https://www.hoerspielundfeature.de/die-gegenwart-von-leif-randt-ist-pastellfarben-ziemlich-nice-100.html.

Hoskins, Andrew: "Digital Network Memory". In: Erll, Astrid / Rigney, Anne (eds.): *Mediation, Remediation and the Dynamics of Memory*. de Gruyter: Berlin 2009, pp. 91–106.

Journey, Web of the App, retrieved 8.2.2022, from https://journey.cloud/.

Kolf, Florian: "Aldi und Lidl müssen zu Entsorgungsunternehmen werden". *Handelsblatt* 2021, retrieved 25.02.2022, from https://www.handelsblatt.com/meinung/kommentare/kommentar-aldi-und-lidl-muessen-zu-entsorgungsunternehmen-werden/27674488.html?ticket=ST-1769368-psQKhyFZi7KORph9zgmF-ap6.

Leurs, Koen: *Digital Passages: Migrant Youth 2.0. Diaspora Gender and Youth Cultural Intersections*. Amsterdam University Press: Amsterdam 2015.

Mangold, Ijoma: "Das absolute Jetzt". *Die Zeit* 4.3.2020, retrieved 8.2.2022, from https://www.zeit.de/2020/11/leif-randt-allegro-pastell-rezension-buch-literatur?utm_referrer=https%3A%2F%2Fwww.startpage.com%2.

Meyer, Erik: "Erinnerungskultur 2.0? Zur Transformation kommemorativer Kommunikation in digitalen, interaktiven Medien". In: Meyer, Erik (ed.): *Erinnerungskultur 2.0. Kommemorative Kommunikation in digitalen Medien*. Campus Verlag: Frankfurt/New York 2009, pp. 175–206.

Montoya Camacho, Martín: "The era of post-truth, post-veracity and charlatanism". Universidad de Navarra 2019, retrieved 25.02.2022, from https://www.unav.edu/web/ciencia-razon-y-fe/the-era-of-post-truth-post-veracity-and-charlatanism.

Nieborg, David B. / Poell, Thomas: "The platformization of cultural production: theoriying the contingent cultural commodity". *New Media & Society* 20 (11) 2018, pp. 4275–4292, retrieved 11.2.2022, from https://doi.org/10.1177/14614448187696.

Perendia, George: "Media in a 'post-factual' age. Do social media have a monopoly on fake news?". *Wall Street International* 8.6.2017, retrieved 25.02.2022, from https://wsimag.com/economy-and-politics/26769-media-in-a-post-factual-age.

Randt, Leif: *Allegro Pastell*. Kiepenheuer & Witsch: Cologne 2020.

Smit, Rik: "Die Plattformisierung des Erinnerns". In: Pentzold, Christian / Lohmeier, Christine (DFG-Netzwerk Kommunikationswissenschaftliche Erinnerungsforschung) (eds.): *Handbuch kommunikationswissenschaftliche Erinnerungsforschung*. de Gruyter: Berlin 2023, pp. 471–493. [Supersvised automatic Translation by Manuel Menke and Christian Pentzold], retrieved 10.6.2023, from https://doi.org/10.1515/9783110629743-023.

van Dijk, Jose: *Mediated Memories in the Digital Age*. Stanford University Press: Stanford 2007.

van Dijck, Jose / Poell, Thomas / de Waal, Martijn: *The Platform Society*. Oxford University Press: New York 2018.

Vollmeyer, Johanna / Maeding, Linda / Calvo María José: *Memoria en la era postdigital*. (Serie: Cuadernos del ahora n. 4) 2020, pp. 1–8, retrieved 01.08.2023, from https://docta.ucm.es/entities/publication/46e2c614-c4e3-49a7-bf16-b5bf7303ad2e; https://docta.ucm.es/rest/api/core/bitstreams/c0655212-8f2c-4755-8070-70051c9890b7/content.

Wilson, Shaun: "Remixing Media in Digital Media". In: Garde-Hansen, Joanne / Hoskins, Andrew / Reading, Anne (eds.): *Save As… Digital Memories*. Palgrave Macmillan: Basingstoke UK 2009, pp. 184–197.

Linda Maeding
Universidad Complutense de Madrid

Whatever Happened to History? Cultural Recycling and Notions of the Past since Postmodernism

Abstract: Fredric Jameson diagnosed postmodernism as "the disappearance of a sense of history" (1985, p. 125), implying its inability to retain its own past. This chapter raises the question of the continuity of this particular understanding of our time, which was paradigmatic of postmodern cultural recycling as it was practised in the last few decades of the twentieth century. In the age of radicalised technological reproducibility, the phenomenon of cultural recycling is more ubiquitous than ever, but has it changed in quality? Against the backdrop of the above, I will discuss the extent to which Jameson's critique of postmodernism still captures the (post)digital present. In my thesis, cultural recycling in popular cultural forms is these days often conceived of as an ahistorical practice that hides its apparent "ideologyless" consumer ideology behind nostalgia and retro phenomena. Nonetheless, the potential of cultural recycling in digital spaces will also be identified. To this end, I will dedicate some reflections to the relation between the present and the historical past, as visualised in cyberspace. To support my perspective on the subject of cultural recycling and history, I will focus on the Instagram series @ *ichbinsophiescholl* as an example of contemporary cultural practices on the Internet that correspond to the theoretical concepts suggested above.

Keywords: postdigital recycling, postmodernism, history, Instagram, *@ichbinsophiescholl.*

1. After Digitalisation: The Archive of the Past

"Always historicize!" (Fredric Jameson: The Political Unconscious).

"[T]here has never been a society in human history so obsessed with the cultural artifacts of *its own immediate past.*" (Reynolds 2011, p. xiii). Nostalgia and the urge to look back have frequently been mentioned when describing the period from the 1990s to the present. Music critic Simon Reynolds adds a concretisation to this widely accepted diagnosis: the chronic "retro-consciousness" he sets out in an extensively read essay, nowhere more dominant than in pop music (Reynolds 2011, p. xviii), refers to a relatively recent past and, unlike Victorianism's love of antiquities, is not purist but often ironic. "It uses the past as an archive of materials from which to extract subcultural capital [...] through recycling and recombining: the bricolage of cultural bric-a-brac." (Reynolds 2011, p. xxxi).

The materials that compound this archive of the immediate past are available more widely than ever before. Retro-consciousness as understood by Reynolds "seeks to be amused and charmed" (2011, p. xxxi) by the past, and to this end, "the very media it is dependent on and disseminated through – records and television – enable the Event [sic] to become permanent, subject to endless repetition. The moment becomes a monument." (Reynolds 2011, xxxvi) Digitalisation has further accelerated and fuelled the cultural dominant of recycling, precisely by making popular culture products accessible with an intensity not seen until now. This has also changed patterns of consumption and distribution, further encouraging the escalation of retromania, "We've become victims of our ever-increasing capacity to store, organise, instantly access, and share vast amounts of cultural data." (Reynolds 2011, xxi).

Nowadays, the past seems to be ready to be captured at any moment. With digitalisation, it seems to come nearer and nearer until it forms part of an enlarged present, while at the same time the conception of history is undergoing profound changes. In this process, the breach between "past" (as something immediate and near) and "history" (as something artificial and remote) is becoming greater. This hypothesis forms the starting point for my reflections on the relevance of cultural recycling; that is, the practice of reusing cultural material in the new millennium, and the practice's relation to contemporary experiences of history as well as popular reconceptualisations of (or often, disillusionment with) history in the postdigital age. To shed light on this nexus, my chapter first assesses the validity of postmodern theory by analysing the continuity of current postmodernism and by examining its relation to the postdigital. To this end, I will rely strongly on Fredric Jameson's materialistic theory of postmodernism. The German Instagram series @ichbinsophiescholl will serve as an example to substantiate my theoretical argument about the potential continuity of postmodern temporality.

2. Is the postdigital postmodern?

The American poet Ezra Pound's imperative "Make It New" expressed the key message of modernist art:

> This slogan compels the writer to create out of the material of art work that is distinctively innovative. [...] These 'new' modern works cannot be wholly autonomous, however, as

> they must consider the aesthetics of the past in the context of the present moment [...]. (Bledsoe 2016).

The nexus between innovation, artistic autonomy and the consideration of tradition ("the past") is at the heart of modernism. It is at stake, again, in postmodernism, although its components are then in a process of profound re-evaluation, doubtlessly at the expense of innovation or newness. However, "Make it new" might also be read as a strikingly postmodern slogan as it quotes the nature of recycling: There is no new material in postmodernism, but we make it look (or work) as if it were new.

In what follows, I will not go into the well-studied differences between modernism and postmodernism, but rather centre on a more recent development: from postmodernism to postdigitality. I will draw a line from Fredric Jameson's critique of postmodernism to the analysis of the postdigital to argue that the postmodern and the postdigital share many basic characteristics that let us think of a continuous temporality, or in any case, of overlapping temporal, social and cultural regimes.

Postmodernism has been closely related to the new form of multinational consumer capitalism that is becoming more sophisticated in a digitalised network society. Curiously, the ideological dimension that informs this variant of "late capitalism" is often not considered to be such: postmodernism was meant to imply not only the end of history, but also of ideologies. In this context, the relevance of Jameson's contribution is said to be found in the fact that it did not limit itself to describe postmodernism as just a set of styles (as was the case with other theories of postmodernism), but to recognise its relation to a certain economic logic and its effects on the conceptualisation of historical experience. "Jameson was really the first major critic to insist on seeing postmodernism as a manifestation of certain political and historical circumstances" (Roberts 2000, p. 119). In this way, according to the Marxist thinker, postmodernism articulates economic forces on a cultural level. In his seminal essay "Postmodernism, or The Cultural Logic of Late Capitalism", first published in 1984 and then republished in an extended book form in 1991, Jameson stresses "the radical distinction between a view for which the postmodern is one (optional) style among many others available and one which seeks to grasp it as the cultural dominant of the logic of late capitalism" (1991, p. 45). This second approach conceptualises the theory of postmodernism as "a genuinely dialectical attempt to think our present of time in History" (1991, p. 45–46). In a famously concise definition, Jameson pinpoints the particularity of postmodernism as "the consumption of sheer commodification as a process" (1991, p. x).

Reconsidering the social effects of globalisation and the concentration of global capital, in his later work *Signatures of the Visible*, Jameson states our incapacity to think the category of totality:

> The truth of our social life as a whole – in Lukács' terms, as a totality – is increasingly irreconcilable with the possibilites for aesthetic expression or articulation available to us […]; and if we can grasp the truth about our world as a totality, then we may find it some purely conceptual expression but we will no longer be able to maintain an imaginative relationship to it. (2016, p. 74).

For Jameson, this observation is indeed problematic, as we can only perceive the present in fragments of a rather chaotic nature. The fragments do not form a complete puzzle any more, they are just pieces without context.

It is possibly precisely because of the fundamental fragmentariness of our present, obscuring the view of the whole, that Jameson sees postmodernism as characterised by a predominant preoccupation with itself. This finding is initially quite similar to Reynolds' theses on "retromania", which is ultimately more a preoccupation with oneself than with the past. Unlike Reynolds, however, Jameson does not judge this finding, "The point is that we are *within* the culture of postmodernism to the point where its facile repudiation is as impossible as any equally facile celebration of it is complacent and corrupt" (1991, p. 62). This is not about condemning or celebrating postmodernism. I shall affirm the same for the postdigital: it is not about evaluating this era positively or negatively, but about analysing it critically.

Jameson's problematisation of history in postmodernity is central to a discussion under postdigital auspices: about history as experience as well as concept. The erosion of grand narratives (Lyotard) like "progress" or "freedom" is usually interpreted as the end of modernity. This end was accompanied by a change in the experience of time, described by Jameson as the "disappearance of a sense of history". This development now consists of

> the way in which our entire contemporary social system has little by little begun to lose its capacity to retain its own past, has begun to live in a perpetual present and in a perpetual change that obliterates traditions of the kind which all earlier social formations have had in one way or another to preserve. (1985, p. 125).

I would like to highlight two points here: firstly, the idea of a "perpetual present", a broad present that grows at the expense of what Jameson calls the sense of history. History no longer offers any resistance to this present. Secondly, it is important to distinguish between history and the past. History unfolds its meaning in the present, not in the past. The disappearance of the sense of history, according to Jameson, now leads precisely to the perception of contemporary events as recent past (not historical) and in this way neutralises them for the present – they are no longer experienced as connectable to it. "The present has been colonised by 'pastness', displacing 'real' history" (1991, p. 20).

Against this background, and transferred to the cultural sphere, it also becomes clear why bricolage is one of the central cultural-artistic procedures of postmodernism. Postmodern artists "no longer 'quote' such 'texts' as a Joyce might have done, or a Mahler; they incorporate them, to the point where the line between high art and commercial forms seems increasingly difficult to draw" (Jameson 1985, p. 2).

In retrospect, the definition of the cultural logic of postmodernism may at the same time be called a prophetic foresight of the postdigital era. The incorporation of cultural material (digital and analog) into the holdings of the Internet archive is commonplace today; the tearing down of the boundaries between "high" and "low" culture in the "culture industry", already suspiciously observed by the Frankfurt School, has now prevailed on a broad front. However, since the turn of the millennium, this intermixing has certainly also been associated with hopes that digitalisation would democratise cultural and aesthetic judgements.

The changed concept of history and the impossibility of grasping the social as a whole (as embodied, for example, by communism, but also by the social market economy) led Jameson to diagnose postmodernism with a depthlessness (1991, p. 6) that can be understood both literally (flat screens) and metaphorically. In the latter sense, it corresponds to a culture of the image, which has since then spread and intensified rapidly through the Internet. Depthlessness, however, means superficiality in a formal sense, not as a judgement of content, as is often expressed in relation to popular cultural formats.[1] Jameson takes up Jean Baudrillard's concept of simulacrum and states that in the postmodern world, it is hard to distinguish the real from the simulated. There is no doubt that this blurring of the boundaries between "real" and "simulated" has increased with the digital turn, but it is precisely from the perspective of the postdigital that the concept of simulacrum can be questioned. What was once understood as simulacrum, we could say, is now quite real. Let us think of it as augmented reality. So "simulacrum" cannot be understood here as an illusion; rather, digitality does indeed have an effect on the real (and *vice versa*).

---

1 Jameson compares Van Gogh's painting of the worn-out *Shoes* with Andy Warhol's *Diamond Dust Shoes*, to illustrate this new depthlessness. According to the critic, in Warhol's artwork, there is neither depth nor context (1991, pp. 8–9).

For Jameson, pastiche as the aesthetic procedure of postmodernism *par excellence* also corresponds to its depthlessness. Unlike parody, which he contrasts with pastiche, the latter lacks the satirical impulse. In this sense, Jameson describes pastiche as "a neutral practice [...], without any of parody's ulterior motives" (1991, p. 17), which mixes styles of the past without hesitation. In this regard, it can also be linked to the weakening of history: that is, distance as an aesthetic effect (for instance, the viewer in front of an "old" work of art) was abandoned (Jameson 1992, p. 48). The result of this abandonment of distance and the dominant procedure of pastiche described in Jameson's theory is succinctly summarised by Felluga (2011), "We can no longer understand the past except as a repository of genres, styles, and codes ready for commodification." This assessment could also proceed from the Frankfurt School and might well overlook the contemporary role of "stylistic communities" as analysed by Baßler and Drügh. According to these critics, these often virtual communities are continually expanding the scope of aesthetic judgements. I concur with Jameson's view on postmodernism, however, that this occurs at the expense of history and in particular of historical agency. Everything is subjected to the regime of the aesthetic: food preferences, hobbies, the use of gendered language. Baßler and Drügh's point, in any case, is that these (aesthetic) judgements are themselves historical in nature (Baßler / Drügh 2021, pp. 129, 131).

So, what can we conclude about the relation between postmodernism (according to Jameson) and the postdigital present in terms of their notion of history and historicity?[2] It is quite obvious that Jameson's findings are still astonishingly topical today. Against this backdrop, I hold that the postmodern dilation of the present[3] has been radicalised in a postdigital present dominated by the aesthetic regime and that this is not necessarily a contradiction of the much-cited diagnoses of "retromania" or "nostalgia obsession". The quintessence of these is precisely that there is no discernible effort to capture the past epistemologically, but rather that this past is shaped according to the needs of the present, any distance between past and present being erased. Authenticity has clearly lost value in this culture; a development that the media philosopher

2 To my knowledge, the issue of their linkage has rarely been explicitly addressed in discussions of the postdigital. Cox is an exception, as he asks whether (and in what ways) Jameson's theory on postmodernism is also of use for the postdigital (2016, p. 72).

3 In their *Gegenwartsästhetik*, Baßler and Drügh (2021) make use of the term "broad present".

avant la lettre Walter Benjamin already noted and by no means condemned in the 1930s with regard to the cinema. However, from this situation we cannot deduce that contemporary cultural production only perpetuates a form of cultural amnesia (Cox 2016, p. 71). Instead, I would now like to examine briefly in what ways the postdigital present imagines history and what role cultural recycling might play in it.

3. Cultural recycling as (a)historical practice?

The postdigital present is said to be installed in a culture of presentism, as impressively described by Douglas Rushkoff, "If the end of the twentieth century can be characterised by futurism, the twenty-first can be defined by presentism" (Rushkoff 2013, p. 3). As for critics like Jameson, there is no contemporary imagination of a future in positive terms because of our postmodern inability to think of society as a whole and not as fragments. "Presentism" means that the nearer past is incorporated into the present in the mode of an extension. This is a profoundly ahistorical operation, and also the reason why, according to Reynolds, retro-phenomena always refer to a near past. It is also where today's nostalgia differs from the retrospective view celebrated by historicism. Within the latter frame, cultural recycling is most often thought of as an ahistorical concept, even an anti-historical one. Indeed, this is what Reynolds' essay about retromania suggests when analysing the 2000s as "a simultaneity of pop time that abolishes history while nibbling away at the present's own sense of itself as an era with a distinct identity and feel." (2011, p. XI). But it is also the cyclic process associated with recycling that seems not to go along with historical thinking but rather evokes Nietzsche's "eternal return of the same". Especially in popular cultural forms (Hollywood remakes, pop remixes), the (re-)circulation of well-known cultural figures, plots and other material can be described as an ahistorical practice that hides its apparent "ideologyless" consumer ideology behind nostalgia and retro phenomena. Thus, digitality, the constant looking back, and the impression of a timeless present enter into a strange and, moreover, so far rarely thematised combination. This was pointed out by Andreas Huyssen in an interview,

> The shift in the 20th century from a progress – and future – oriented sensibility up until 1968, to a memorial orientation towards the past since then is indeed remarkable and deep. Today, however, we may have to ask whether both futures past and present pasts have been replaced by present presents run by invisible and unknowable algorithms, the eternal now of an ever churning media and consumer culture, which neither knows the past nor imagines a future.

> In other words, we have to ask how digital technologies and social media affect the very capacity of human beings to live in an extended timeframe, rather than merely in an eternal here and now. (Huyssen 2018).

In this way, our representation of history is not only deprived of depth, but also of sharpness. This phenomenon goes hand in hand with the dominance of the category of space over that of time, as Jameson described it for postmodernism, "our daily life, our psychic experience, our cultural languages, are today dominated by categories of space rather than by categories of time, as in the preceding period of high modernism" (1991, p. 16).

It is doubtful whether the weakening of historicity is actually rooted in the medium at all – nowadays, the medium of the digital space. On the other hand, I argue that the immediacy of the digital and also the archival nature of the Internet as a gigantic repository without obvious criteria of order run counter to an elaborated sense of history, while at the same time these characteristics do indeed promote cultural recycling. This form of recycling is to be thought of as a practice in the social framework of a consumer society. To a certain extent, cultural recycling blurs the frontiers between production and consumption. In this way, however, cultural recycling also obscures the nexus that connects it with late capitalist ideology.

I have spoken of the weakening sense of historicity in cultural recycling and only briefly mentioned examples such as (retro-)remakes, and more generally a proliferation of retrophilic phenomena that fall under this practice. These phenomena are, however, by no means specific to postdigitality; they have already been critically analysed in postmodern theory. The point is that their presence is far greater in contemporary art and culture.

Cultural recycling is a vague term, one that has so far been a rather undertheorised concept. By this term, I simply understand the re-use of already existing cultural material (tropes, figures, plots, works of art, etc.). Now, however, we add the term "postdigital" to it as a description of our time, and thus point out that today, reality can no longer be understood as if it were independent of the digital or as if it were in opposition to it, since the digital permeates it (Llamas Ubieto 2020, p. 2). If, as Llamas Ubieto states, there has been a mass digitalisation of the real and an unprecedented remediation of reality, we must assume that the manners of mediation between subject and world have also changed. The Internet can today be seen as the principal mediator between the single subject and the world. It is also the place where many diverse practices of cultural recycling are located. So, coming back to the notion of "*postdigital* recycling", from a Cultural Studies approach we can for now operate with the following definition,

> We understand by postdigital recycling a processing action on a used material, waste or product that implies its detachment from an initial context and its return to a new life cycle. This operation aims at circulation as well as at re-evaluation. (Llamas Ubieto 2022; my translation).

Detachment, circulation and re-evaluation are terms of crucial importance here. It is commonplace to find that aesthetic categories that have prevailed since the Enlightenment (originality, aura, genius, etc.) are rapidly losing importance. In addition, however, the boom of recycling in the cultural sphere, in line with the loss of classically modern value categories, also leads to a certain sociocultural exhaustion, perceivable in the widespread impression of contemporary culture's lack of novelty and originality. Frequently, newness is only attributed to technical advances, devices, software, virtual media, etc.

The omnipresence of recycled materials can also be interpreted as a symptom of the crisis of posthistoire: the loss of grand narratives intensifies with the digital availability of everything (Baßler / Drügh 2021, p. 126). Extending Jameson's critique of postmodernism to postdigitality, the dissolution of grand narratives leaves fragments that are recycled and reused without taking the context into account. In other words, contemporary practices often dismiss the horizon of expectations (in the words of Reinhard Koselleck) that originated the work. While related cultural practices such as imitation or reproduction still preserve the original, this is not necessarily the case with recycling. Marilyn Randall pointed this out:

> In the metaphor of *recycling*, however, the recycled material is consumed and transformed, leaving nothing if not more detritus/garbage in its wake and producing a new product which, however similar or different to the old, must by definition replace it. […] And yet, this cyclical nature of recycling and its propensity to eliminate its origins makes the metaphor, for Moser, for example, particularly pertinent to the present cultural and historical moment: "Inside such a system one could theoretically recycle indefinitely. Temporal differences (past-present, present-future) as well as historical dynamics (the present overtakes the past by realising it; the future is the utopic projection of present projects) would also be practically abolished. This is what throws modern history into crisis". (Randall 2007).[4]

The act of recycling, then, *replaces* its source and invites us to a never-ending action, which levels the different temporal dimensions. Moser's argument on recycling as challenging the modern understanding of history is particularly

4 The paragraph cited contains a quotation from Walter Moser's study *Recyclages: Economies d'appropriation culturelle* (1996, p. 39), as translated by Randall.

interesting here. Actually, one could amend Jameson to the effect that it is not the sense of history *per se* that is weakened by recycling, but specifically the teleologically-oriented one that we generally identify with the still powerful modernity. In this sense, today's recycling trends are linked to the disintegration of grand narratives inaugurated by postmodernism. In *The Political Unconscious*, Jameson argues that narratives play a crucial role in mediating between the individual and society, or what he calls social totality, "according to a process of what he calls transcoding – the translating into an accepted code (which consists of certain narrative patterns and expectations) of social and historical reality to make it accessibly mediated for the individual" (Roberts 2000, p. 78). Although the use of narratives is timeless, it is not emptied of history. Hypothetically, we can state that despite the frequent populist attempts to recycle grand narratives (for instance nation, *Volksgemeinschaft*), micro-narratives dominate in (post) digital space, corresponding to the existing fragmentation on a social level. There are also formal reasons for this, as Internet (sub)genres like blogs and twitterature encourage short forms.

Long before the Internet became widely established, it was George Steiner who thought about "Real Presences" in a book of the same title (1985). There, he regretted a phenomenon that we can today connect to the recycling boom: the "disappearance of the primary under a mountain of secondary literature" (quoted from Kuhlbrodt 2019, p. 38).[5] This originally literary evaluation, thought of today, refers to the possibilities of the medium (to link and re-link, to twitter and re-twitter), and hence, to the nature of cultural recycling. I myself direct the gaze in this contribution to re-use, not primarily to *what* is being re-used. In this way, recycling comes into view as a process of change in the material used. The relation between result and source, however, becomes blurred and secondary.

The big question, which my contribution can only make explicit but not answer, is how to make sense of the past against this backdrop. How to think historically in a present which has unlearned to think of the past in terms of alterity: distances are thus being erased and the past is "incorporated" into the present. In order to approach this question, not only through the many criticisms of the recycling concept that have already been voiced, we need to take a look at the potential of the term. Sonja Windmüller has pointed out that

5 Kuhlbrodt's thesis is that "it is precisely through the Internet that the supposedly secondary takes on a new rank. […] The secondary has emancipated itself and has become primary itself, so to speak." (2019, p. 39; my translation).

"recycling" can be thought of utopically as a promise of salvation that survives destruction (2014, p. 108). However, recycling is not necessarily required for this promise to be fulfilled; memory as a possible umbrella term is also often ascribed this power of salvation. As Randall makes clear, recycling erases rather than commemorates the traces of what it was originally based on (2007). However, we do conceive of self-reflexive references that manifest themselves in practices of recycling and thus refer to the past in an innovative way, beyond retromania. In this context, we can think of the "power of recontextualisation" (Cannon 2002, here with regard to the artist and activist Steev Hise).

Such recontextualisation is not only semantic, but also technically facilitated by social media and the platformisation of the Internet. Victoria Walden Grace (2021) has researched this effect. Although her research deals with Holocaust memory and not with the generic recycling of cultural material, the logic she describes is certainly significant for our context because it points at the opportunities of digital recontextualisation:

> One of the ways digital media are having an increasingly powerful affect on Holocaust memory is through the use of **networked logics**, drawing together fragments of testimony, material evidence and other sources into **mapping projects** either of specific sites [...] or bringing a variety of sites together through **hyperlinks** [...]. These experiences open up space for users to follow particular threads, compare different narratives, and to be led by their particular interests. **Connectivity** of different material elements is key here, but there is rarely any sense of a closed-text or resolution offered. (2021).

The potentials of digital Holocaust archives listed above are also those of (post) digital recycling. The logic of the network and the focus on connectivity also show the emancipatory promise of digital media: the use and processing of abundant materials, the connection of which turns the subject from a mere consumer into a self-determined subject.

Before I now turn to one specific case of cultural recycling and its processing of history in the postdigital space, it should be stated that in my opinion, the concept of recycling primarily makes sense at a macro level, in reference to a phenomenon or trend that says a lot about cultural understanding and society, but is less practicable at the level of micro-analysis, where the concept of recycling has little ahead of advantage intertextuality and intermediality. The term would be too unspecific to have value for analysis at a micro level. A question of interest is whether and how recycling (as an umbrella term for different strategies and actions in the cultural sphere) could be accomplished as a *historical* practice despite its close ties to postmodern perspectives.

4. "Imagine it is 1942 on Instagram": A postdigital series and its mediation of history

Let us return to Jameson's observation of a "weakening of historicity, both in our relationship to public history and in the new forms of our private temporality" (1991, p. 6). This trend would go hand in hand with a fascination for the (extended, long) present and a disinterest/lack of interest? in the *historical* past. It can also be perceived in our standards for authenticity and originality as well as their (dwindling?) appreciation and has profound consequences for art and aesthetics. As Moritz Baßler and Heinz Drügh write, in the digital age, no one expects "an unadulterated reproduction of reality" from media that are actually considered guarantors of reality, such as photography (2021, p. 271). This development cannot remain without consequences for the understanding of history implicit in cultural products.

In this context of a renegotiated relation between fact and fiction, history and entertainment, I briefly introduce the Instagram series *@ichbinsophiescholl* (https://www.instagram.com/ichbinsophiescholl/), which comprised a weekly episode from 30 April 2021 to 22 February 2022: it ended on the anniversary of the execution of Sophie Scholl, who was killed by the Nazis on 22 February 1942 at the age of only 21 for her resistance actions. Produced by the public broadcasters Südwestrundfunk (SWR) and Bayerischer Rundfunk (BR), the series was not conceived as a commercial product, but has a didactic-historical mission that adds an innovative chapter to the history of the public commemoration of Nazi victims and the reconsideration of this period. What is being "recycled" here is a historical personality as well as historical material around which numerous narratives and a cult of personality have developed surrounding the anti-Nazi resistance group *Die Weiße Rose (The White Rose)* of the Scholl siblings.

If by "postdigital condition" we understand an unprecedented daily presence of the digital and computerisation, for its ubiquity (integrated in the environment and in the subjects) as well as for new continuities that blur the clear separations between "analogue" and "digital" (cf. Llamas Ubieto 2020), we can capture the sense in which *@ichbinsophiescholl* is a postdigital product *par excellence*. An analogue figure is "platformised" here: we observe a media product developed on the basis of original historical material that adapts to social media practices (including, for instance, numerous selfies of the protagonist). The format enables and promotes interaction between user and content, while at the same time exposing itself as formally "chic". What Jameson observed for postmodern culture applies here: the "history of aesthetic styles" "displaces 'real' history" (1991, p. 20). The philosopher interpreted this situation as a "symptom of the waning of [...] our lived possibility of experiencing history in some active way" (1991, p. 21). He saw this symptom paradigmatically represented in a genre, the "nostalgia film".[6] Today, the longing to experience history "in some active way" may be found in particular on social media platforms on the Internet.

An emotional approach is deliberately chosen, suggesting insights into Sophie Scholl's inner life: we see her crying, laughing, dancing and cooking; we see her despairing over the horrors of war and experiencing love, all from the character's perspective, looking directly into the camera. The posts are short; each weekly episode is around five minutes long and there is a great emphasis on Instagram-typical visual stories (even iconic food images are included), underpinned with short statements by Scholl in vintage lettering: "This regime is putting all our lives in danger! Enough is enough! I cannot continue to be idle"[7] (Week 17, 16.8.1942, posted 31 August 2021).

The motto (and premise) of the series, with which it was advertised on social media, is accordingly congruent. It also implies a specific approach to the past: "Imagine it's 1942 on Instagram...". (posted on 30.04.2021, https://www.instagram.com/p/CSwq6GqME2x/). New here is not the genre of some kind of "docu-fiction" that fictionalises real figures and events. What is new is that in a historical series, the present of social media, and no longer the past, is taken as the primary reference and measure. It is no longer about "how it really was", but rather conditionally about "how it might have been" if Instagram had already existed in 1942. Sophie Scholl, played by Luna Wedler, thus becomes a figure of the present, regardless of the historical costumes and the setting, based on the "then". This is also the intention of the series. "On the occasion of her 100th birthday on 9 May, the Instagram project by SWR and BR brought the resistance fighter out of the history books and into the here and now" (*Instagram project on Sophie Scholl*, my translation).[8] This "visualisation" was also suggested by the comments on the total of 401 posts on the Instagram channel. Many preferred

---

6 For Jameson, this includes films like *Blade Runner*, which combine a sophisticated aesthetic with a wistful (non-historical) look at the past.

7 All the episodes, combining written and visual material, are available in the ARD Media Library, retrieved 12.05.2022, from https://www.ardmediathek.de/video/ich-bin-sophie-scholl/woche-17-ploetzlich-ist-der-tod-so-nah/swr/Y3JpZDovL3N3ci5kZS9hZXgvbzE1MjI1NjQ.

8 See the producers: "Sophie Scholl, on Instagram, in real time", retrieved 12.05.2022, from https://www.swr.de/unternehmen/ich-bin-sophie-scholl-stimmen-der-macher-100.html.

the grammatical present tense and tried to warn Scholl of all kinds of dangers;[9] dangers that the historical figure had actually taken on many decades ago and whose outcome we know.

What specific role do social media[10] play in the series? The episodes were not only "liked", but also received lively commentary, with the character executed in 1942 replying.[11] Reading the comment section on Instagram, there seems to be an unwritten pact that what actually happened (Scholl's arrest and execution) is still only virtual and hence changeable. At some points, the Instagram stories together with the user content even suggest a counterfactual scenario. Repeatedly, the users warn "Sophie" not to risk her life, to be careful and to retreat. In other words, all empathising reactions that result from identifying with "Sophie", but which counteract the historical figure. What does the young woman stand for, what is she remembered for, if not for having put her life on the line while she and her companions demanded the end of the war and denounced Nazi crimes in their flyer campaigns?

The reactions to the series documented in the comments are most appropriately interpreted when taking into account the intended target audience. The producers' declared aim was to reach a younger audience and thus also to continue the German culture of remembrance in a contemporary way.[12] Significantly, "contemporary" ("new", say the producers) is here apparently synonymous with platformisation, i.e. the shift of public remembrance to the socially-shaped Internet. More aptly, it is about a postdigital space of memory that blends the *Lebenswelt* with the Internet, as it corresponds to the experience of the initial 750,000 followers[13] of the Scholl series. The understanding of history cultivated here, made explicit in the accompanying material to the series, cannot truly be separated from the memorial regime that stresses the affective dimension and experience of history. It might have benefited the project to differentiate more clearly between historical and memorial discourse. In this

---

9 See (aleatorically extracted) the comments on the following reel, retrieved 12.05.2022, from https://www.instagram.com/reel/CYQ_hKXFoPF/.

10 For our purposes, the definition of Seargent / Tagg serves, according to which social media can be conceived of as "any digital environment which involves interaction between participants" (2014, p. 14).

11 See the extremely interesting contribution by Stephens (2021) on "Playing Pretend on Social Media".

12 The producers, "We can bring Sophie Scholl to life on Instagram for a new generation – in a way you've never seen before", retrieved 12.05.2022, from https://www.swr.de/unternehmen/ich-bin-sophie-scholl-stimmen-der-macher-100.html.

13 After the end of the series, it still registers 717,000 followers (as of 16.5.2022).

sense, Richard Crownshaw wrote the following on recent Holocaust literature, but in my view applicable to the context presented here as well,

> What is needed is a dialectic between memory and history that, in delimiting the horizons of memory, does not lose sight of the cultural realities of over-identification, nor of the possibilites of the affective transmission of Holocaust memories. (Crownshaw 2010, p. viii).[14]

There is no doubt that the project is historically soundly researched; historians were involved as advisors. Besides, the makers seek to reflect on the specific form-content relation. Concerning their choice of the social platform, they state, "Instagram is no longer just a place full of cute dog pictures and food shots, but rather a world stage for activism and thus a 'place' where we would certainly have met Sophie Scholl." (*Stimmen der Macher*innen*).[15]

The series, however, conceptually evokes the "culture of the simulacrum" (Jameson 1991, p. 18) attributed to postmodernism,[16] which challenges the concept of the real. This is also one of the reasons for the criticism that the project has sparked, in addition to the applause for the innovative format.

@ichbinsophiescholl suggests authenticity, among other things through the exact dating of the episodes to the period 1941–1942, but incorporates deliberate references to the present. It is also characterised by omissions[17] and some incorrections (such as the wearing of gas masks in the German air raid shelters [Luftschutzkeller] during the bombings), which are not, however, exhibited as fiction. In one post (18 May 2021), the slogan "Make love not war" is used,[18] borrowed from the protest of the student movement against the Vietnam War and without any connection to the Nazi era. Media scholar Eva Hasel sees a danger in these "creative freedoms" because in the final instance, they could even lead to the denial of the Holocaust. In an interview, she commented on this:

> I don't like the idea of creating an illusion of reality. Or the feeling of "bringing something back to life". [...] If you start like that, then people who don't mean well can say, Oh, so if that's not true, what else is not true? And I don't think it's a good idea to fill in these

---

14 See also Crownshaw (2010, p. vii-viii): "the pursuit of historical anchorage further displaces historical understanding, substituting memory or 'hypermemory' for it".

15 *Stimmen der Macher*innen des Instagram-Projekts*, retrieved 12.05.2022, from https://www.swr.de/unternehmen/ich-bin-sophie-scholl-stimmen-der-macher-100.html.

16 Jameson adopted the concept from Jean Baudrillard and made it a central aspect of his theory of postmodernism.

17 Most strikingly the crimes committed against the Jews.

18 In the original: " Liebe machen statt Krieg", *@ichbinsophiescholl,* 18.5.2021.

> historical gaps that we definitely have with fantasy or with your own creation. (Quoted in Hespers 2022, my translation).[19]

The technical potential of the digital medium, the emotionalisation of content on social media, the possibilities of interaction with users are thus double-edged. On the one hand, they empower the individual user, in that the platform removes him or her from a purely passive approach; on the other hand, "history" is in a sense separated from "factual reality" and can now be experienced in a radically subjective and user-centric way,

> the postmodern subject can cut and paste its own reality together. In the face of a globalised media, the electronic archive, new media technologies and their collective information overload, the ability to surf, sample and mix one's way through these appears to define our agentic potential. (Spencer 2008, p. 195).

The question that I draw from my presentation of the Scholl series is whether we can possibly think of cultural recycling as a critical construct. As we have seen, today this practice is intimately linked to the (post)digital sphere. Nonetheless, the (post)digital is ideological and not exclusively a question of technology. This is why, if we want to unravel the commodity nature that often characterises cultural recycling, we also need to uncover the ideological implications of the (post)digital itself. It is not so much the content as the *aesthetics* of the Instagram series that makes this abundantly clear through the visualisation of Sophie as a character, open to fiction and hence proximity. Approaches to a history (not historiography) "from below" that have been transferred to the Internet could possibly point to alternatives here. I am thinking, for example, of the project "Open Memory Box" (https://open-memory-box.de), launched in 2013 and conceived by Alberto Herskovits and Laurence McFalls. The project makes private film recordings from the German Democratic Republic accessible: scenes from everyday life, holidays, family celebrations; without sound and commentary, which are left to the user.[20] This website does not enable users to have the communal experience that *@ichbinsophiescholl* offers, as they do not get in touch with each other. It can, however, get along without emotionalisation and abridgement. Unedited material on the Internet today may just hit us over the head like a *Stolperstein*[21]

19 See also, for severe public criticism, comedian Jan Böhmermann, who dedicated an episode of the popular *ZDF Magazine Royale* to the series (18.02.2022).

20 For additional information on this project, see Fürstenau (2013).

21 Literally meaning "stumbling stone", the word refers to a widely known initiative in public space that commemorates victims of Nazism. Their names are engraved in brass cubes that are installed on the pavement, normally in front of the houses from where they were once deported.

and in this way lead to the shocking approach of dealing with history in the way that the materialist philosopher Walter Benjamin had in mind when fleeing from the Nazis.

5. Conclusion

In his desperate condensed reflections *Über den Begriff der Geschichte*, written in 1940 and published posthumously in 1942, Walter Benjamin wanted to uncover the forces of history that have been put to sleep in the "once upon a time" of linear historical narrative.[22] This certainly utopian claim can only be fulfilled with difficulty by postdigital formats that deal with historical material. Due to the possibilities of digital participation, but also thanks to the accessibility of their sources, these formats undoubtedly have potential for activating the historical "narrative". However, the affectation of social media channels and the questionable separation of "history" ("cold" and distant) and "reality" (near and immediate) in the age of radicalised technological reproducibility are obstacles to this.

Using the example of *@ichbinsophiescholl*, but also Jameson's theory of postmodernity, my contribution has particularly highlighted the critical aspects that go hand in hand with the postmodern and now postdigital representation of history, without, however, ignoring the opportunities. So far, it is Holocaust research that has dealt intensively with the advantages and disadvantages of digital media in confronting us with genocide. What is needed, however, is a theoretical examination of concepts of history that are often only implicit in postdigital environments, as well as an informed criticism concerning the abolition of the distance between past and present that is often perceived here. Doubtlessly, this erasure stands in the way of a deeper understanding.

Technological developments initiated by the digital revolution have radicalised and further sophisticated the exposed characteristics of postmodernism, including its ahistorical understanding of time and its devaluation of newness. By referring to Jameson's seminal writings and comparing them with digital media discourse, I have shown that postmodernism and not postdigitality meant to signify the real break for our "sense of history".

22 On Benjamin's conception of history, diametrically opposed to the postmodern variant, see Opitz / Wizisla (2000, p. 419).

References

Baßler, Moritz / Drügh, Heinz: *Gegenwartsästhetik*. Konstanz University Press: Konstanz 2021.

Bledsoe, Eric Matthew: "'Make It New'." *The Routledge Encyclopedia of Modernism*. Taylor and Francis: Routledge 2016, retrieved 12.05.2022, from https://www.rem.routledge.com/articles/make-it-new.

Böhmermann, Jan: *ZDF Magazin Royale* 18.02.2022, retrieved 12.5.2022, from https://www.zdf.de/comedy/zdf-magazin-royale/zdf-magazin-royale-vom-18-februar-2022-100.html.

Cannon, Rebecca: *Detritus – Copyleft In Action* 2002, retrieved 12.5.2022, from http://cordite.org.au/features/rebecca-cannon-detritus-copyleft-in-action/.

Cox, Geoff: "Prehistories of the Postdigital: Or, Some Old Problems with Post-Anything". *APRJA* 3(1) 2014, pp. 70–75, retrieved 12.5.2022, from https://aprja.net//issue/view/8400.

Crownshaw, Richard: *The Afterlife of Holocaust Memory in Contemporary Literature and Culture*. Palgrave Macmillan: Basingstoke 2010.

Felluga, Dino: "Modules on Jameson: On Pastiche". In: *Introductory Guide to Critical Theory*. Last Update: 31.01.2011, retrieved 18.3.2022, from http://www.purdue.edu/guidetotheory/postmodernism/modules/jamesonpastiche.html.

Fukuyama, Francis: *The End of History and the Last Man*. Free Press: New York 1992.

Fürstenau, Marcel: "Digitales Heimkino: Die DDR in privaten Filmaufnahmen". *Deutsche Welle* 24.9.2013, retrieved 18.3.2022, from https://www.dw.com/de/digitales-heimkino-die-ddr-in-privaten-filmaufnahmen/a-50553640.

Herskovits, Alberto / McFalls, Laurence: *Open Memory Box*, retrieved 1.4.2022, from https://open-memory-box.de/.

Hespers, Nora: "Nach zehn Monaten 'Sophie Scholl' auf Insta: Lernen, wie man es nicht machen sollte". *Über Medien*, retrieved 1.4.2022, from https://uebermedien.de/68879/nach-zehn-monaten-sophie-scholl-auf-insta-lernen-wie-man-es-nicht-machen-sollte/.

Huyssen, Andreas: "State of the art in memory studies. Interview with Patrick Eser". *Passés futurs* (3) 2018, retrieved 12.5.2022, from https://www.politika.io/en/notice/state-of-the-art-in-memory-studies-an-interview-with-andreas-huyssen.

Jameson, Fredric: "Postmodernism and Consumer Society". In: Foster, Hal (ed.): *Postmodern Culture*. Pluto: London 1985, pp. 111–125.

Jameson, Fredric: *Postmodernism, or The Cultural Logic of Late Capitalism*. Duke UP: Durham 1991.

Jameson, Fredric: *Signatures of the Visible.* Routledge: New York 2016.

Kuhlbrodt, Jan: "*Von realer Gegenwart*". In: Lange, Katrin / Zapf, Nora (eds.): *Screenshots. Literatur im Netz.* Edition text + kritik: Frankfurt a.M. 2019, pp. 38–44.

Llamas Ubieto, Miriam: *Postdigital ahora*. (Serie: Cuadernos del ahora, n. 1) 2020, retrieved 01.08.2023, from https://docta.ucm.es/entities/publication/cfb16b9c-fa20-4922-ab25-053e7d33d133; https://docta.ucm.es/rest/api/core/bitstreams/8d8c81b0-a2a9-4341-9c86-dd40c8b849de/content.

Llamas Ubieto, Miriam: "Glosario: Reciclaje postdigital". In: Llamas Ubieto, Miriam / Goicoechea de Jorge, María (coords.): *Rec-Lit: Estrategias de reciclaje cultural y literario en la era postdigital.* Repositorio institucional, Universidad Complutense de Madrid: Madrid 2022, retrieved 06.07.2023, from http://repositorios.fdi.ucm.es/REC-LIT/view/generico.php?id=54&idpadre=54.

Opitz, Michael / Wizisla, Erdmut: *Benjamins Begriffe*. Suhrkamp: Frankfurt a.M. 2000.

Randall, Marilyn: "Recycling Recycling or plus ça change…". *Other voices* 3(1) 2007, retrieved 12.5.2022, from http://www.othervoices.org/3.1/mrandall/index.php.

Reynolds, Simon: *Retromania. Pop Culture's Addiction to its Own Past*. Faber & Faber: London 2011.

Roberts, Adam: *Fredric Jameson*. Taylor & Francis Group: London 2000.

Rushkoff, Douglas: *Present Shock: When Everything Happens Now*. Current: London 2013.

Seargeant, Philip / Tagg, Caroline: "Introduction: The Language of Social Media". In: Seargeant, Philip / Tagg, Caroline (eds.): *The Language of Social Media: Identity and Community on the Internet.* Palgrave Macmillan: Basingstoke 2014, pp. 1–21.

Spencer, Douglas: "Outside the Kaleidoscope: From Cut'n'Paste to Generative Process". In: Martin, Sara (ed.): *Recycling Culture(s).* Cambridge Scholars Publishing: Newcastle 2008, pp. 191–200.

Stephens, Carmelle: "Playing Pretend on Social Media". In: Walden, Victoria Grace (ed.): *Digital Holocaust Memory, Education and Research*. Palgrave Macmillan: Basingstoke 2021, pp. 237–265.

SWR / BR: *@ichbinsophiescholl*, retrieved 12.5.2022, from https://www.instagram.com/ichbinsophiescholl/.

SWR / BR: *Instagram-Projekt zu Sophie Scholl von SWR und BR*, retrieved 12.5.2022, from https://www.swr.de/unternehmen/ich-bin-sophie-scholl-projekt-100.html.

SWR / BR: *Stimmen der Macher*innen des Instagram-Projekts,* retrieved 12.5.2022, from https://www.swr.de/unternehmen/ich-bin-sophie-scholl-stimmen-der-macher-100.html.

Walden, Victoria Grace: *Holocaust Remembrance in a Digital Future: Towards Deep Truth or Deep Fake?*, retrieved 12.5.2022, from https://reframe.sussex.ac.uk/digitalholocaustmemory/2021/02/12/holocaust-remembrance-in-a-digital-future-towards-deep-truth-or-deep-fake/.

Windmüller, Sonja: "Recycling". In: Samida, Stefanie / Eggert, Manfred K.H. / Hahn, Hans Peter (eds.): *Handbuch Materielle Kultur. Bedeutungen, Konzepte, Disziplinen.* Metzler: Stuttgart, Weimar 2014, pp. 104–109.

Amelia Sanz Cabrerizo
Universidad Complutense de Madrid

Predigital Narratives for a Postdigital World: The Case of Amélie Nothomb

Abstract: We are heirs to key concepts such as intertextuality and interdiscursivity and, on this basis, we propose another conceptual metaphor that provides a different position and focalisation to analyse postdigital culture: recycling. Taking advantage of the selective, performative and collective features of this concept, we examine how Amélie Nothomb, who is determined to represent herself as predigital, develops her storytelling by means of postdigital strategies for cultural recycling.

Keywords: intertextuality, interdiscursivity, cultural recycling, Amélie Nothomb.

1. Recycling: neither quoting nor transmitting

More than ever, the transgenerational stability of knowledge has been broken in the postdigital, postglobal era. Arjun Appadurai already stated: the reproduction of cultures is becoming problematic, as much as cultural transmission.[1]

Every episteme always chooses a singular conceptual metaphor to represent, understand and realise its relationship with the past. *Ancien Régime* western cultures used *imitatio*, which means going back to and reverencing the sources. The New Romantic Regime felt the 'anxiety of influence' for the benefit of the singular and unique genius fighting against the paternal figure. 20th Century formalisms were committed to intertextuality and productive trans-textual relations. Perhaps it is time to move towards a new metaphor to redefine our relationships with cultural memory, in general, and to cultural memories, specifically.

Contemporary critics and scholars matured within the intertextual paradigm. It is not easy to get rid of this, considering the content of this major theoretical proposal, and we should not do so. Julia Kristeva (1974) provides a most interesting

1 As Appadurai points out (Appadurai 2005, pp. 84–55), following the debates generated by the famous Walter Benjamin's essay "The Work of Art in the Age of Mechanical Reproduction" (1935). We are following the French Appadurai work version, due to the translator's nuances, that we accept.

contribution analysing transposition and productivity as well as displacement and condensation, based on Freudian selection rather than Bakhtin's dialogism. Within this epistemological framework, *textum*'s meaning is in back of, around, and essentially hidden behind, in such a way that the different layers of sense must be discovered and interpreted, heuristics and hermeneutics aligning with each other.

In Kristeva's work, two main interpretations were highlighted for intertextuality, the history and the development of this concept being very well known. First, the narrow approach is exemplified by Foucault, Genette, Riffaterre and Bloom. They described a geological or archaeological representation of writing, digging vertically into sources, looking for metatextual marks to make intertexts visible, pointing out a right form of interpretation. Second, the very broad view is espoused by the late Barthes, Culler and Grivel, Derrida, Deleuze and Guattari. For them, the intertext became a rhizome from which genealogy is not possible.

In practical terms, both issues become useless. The restricted version of intertextuality is not enough for us. On the one hand, critics are always looking for analytical methods to identify intertexts; on the other hand, they have already produced a plethora of intertextual typologies.[2] In fact, this restricted definition avoids substantial textual dimensions such as communication, subjectivity, ideology and intentionality. The broader version of intertextuality is based on a textualising perspective: life is a text and texts are… *textum*, a fabric, a web. In both cases, some major risks arise: first, to make intertextuality the main criterion of literality; second, to enlarge the metaphor until the whole world becomes a text.

A possible issue to explore could be interdiscursivity theories: from Bakhtin to Marc Angenot, Dominique Maingueneau and Pierre Bourdieu for French scholars to Terry Eagleton, Luis Prieto, Edward Said, Robert Scholes and Hyden White in the Cultural Studies framework. All of them advocated the benefits of an interdiscursive approach which provided analytic-descriptive models suited to reformulate the place of literature in social discourse. They reintroduced communities of practice and (re)located codes, performativity and subjectivity in such a way that readers regained an active role. Moreover, a certain horizontality was proposed: discourse only makes sense in the contiguity of other discourses. Nevertheless, we still need a whole theory to integrate intertextuality in the framework of all kinds of intercontextual relationships,

---

2 This is the distance travelled between Duchesne (1984) and Mason (2019), for example.

particularly in multimedia environments and more so when they are digital and postdigital environments.

Since then, hypertexts arrived in our computer environments, allowing non-sequential access to a vast amount of loosely structured text in electronic formats. The dream of a fully revealed intertextuality seemed at last to become a reality to a post-structuralist, such as George Landow in the 1990s. Unfortunately (who would have thought it!), it seems that this (the hypertext) will kill that (the intertext), as Victor Hugo would like to say. In fact, the dream of a whole digitised world has not been realized,[3] but readers, users, and consumers think that it has, especially our own young students. For them, everything is on the Web, and what is not present there, does not exist and will never exist.

We agree that there has never been so much cultural heritage available, in such a way that

> the past is now not a land to return to in a simple politics of memory, but a synchronic warehouse of cultural scenarios, a kind of temporal central casting, to which recourse can be taken as appropriate, depending on the movie to be made, the scene to be enacted, the hostages to be rescued (Appadurai 1990, p. 30).

Everything seems to be within our grasp, ready to be reused, repeated, consumed in our digital capitalist cultures[4] in postdigital times. Contiguity is the key concept.

Remix, remediation and recycling have become major characteristics of the contemporary pop cultural ecosystem, which has been studied mainly for the digital and mass media age.[5] New digital spaces have opened up where popular culture can presume to be culture with a capital C. The appropriation of the fragment and insertion into other contexts thanks to the copy-paste command is becoming the most usual *modus operandi*. We would be facing a certain 'memetic culture' where a creation is appreciated not because of its originality, but because of the combination and even the automation of the processes of selection and composition: the 'new' would not be possible, or, at least, not necessary. Displacements and inconsistencies do not matter. In fact, we are all of us duplicators or recyclers.

---

3 Just 10 % of analogue collections have been digitally reproduced in Europe. See Europeana (2017, p. 28).

4 As Fredric Jameson already observed in 1979 (Jameson 1990, pp. 11–46). Cultural recycling is resolutely modern, but not in the elitist sense of Baudelaire, but as a mass cultural phenomenon, following Le Goff (2019 [1988], pp. 59–103).

5 We echo the positions of Klucinskas and Moser (2004), Jenkins (2006), Reynolds (2011) and Navas (2015).

In our postdigital era, a cultural object or a practice seems to be legitimised if and almost only if it deserves to be duplicated, repeated, recycled, going transmedial, viral, global, not just translated and circulating between national cultures, as in eras of print-culture dominance.[6]

Recycling, as a conceptual metaphor, can take advantage of the three R principles already incorporated in our daily lives: reduce, reuse, recycle. Strategies of recycling involve: first, selective operations that allow intentionality to be reintroduced in such a triage; second, 'horizontal' operations, as only available materials can be recycled; third, collective operations, since mass and shared practices are a *conditio sine qua non* for effective recycling. The fine line between private and public seems to be blurring. Recycling is a kind of performative act where a certain awareness and activism are explicit as soon as the speech act has consequences and the will of recycling is marked as such. This is how prosumers (and w-readers and authors) are regaining their active role in our postdigital life. So, 'revival', 'remake', 'sampling' and 'copy-art' are not just recent terms to evoke older terms such as 'rewriting', 'recreation', 'pastiche' and 'parody'. Words matter.

Recycling lets us keep on linking with Kristeva's transtextual productivity and Bakhtin's interdiscursivity, but with some important nuances in our postdigital and postglobal culture. There is a different positioning and focalisation regarding the past and the technologies of memory. Any operation of recycling not only focuses on the connection of two texts, but on the immediate output wherever the sources could come together since very often the connection seems invisible after recycling. No specific genealogy needs be established; the source is not the marked term. It is the very act of dialogue. Intertextual perspectives stressed divergent and differential temporalities, but in recycling operations the links may not work and the anchorages appear broken in such a way that misprision may matter while deliberate misinterpretation does. Cultural recycling focuses on the act of recycling and, by doing so, it becomes a way to be aware of the detachment.

Intertexts are reflexive thematisations of tracing the otherness and of the relationship with the structure of discursive authority, while postdigital recycling thematises the repetition. The identification of a particular intertextual source is not so relevant for recycling, but rather the more general structure to which the new production belongs. In fact, intertextual and recycling strategies are both governed by the rules of the discursive formation within which they occur.

---

6 See Hutcheon and Valdés (2002) for a complete overview of printed circulations in history.

But recycling is considered a collective and mass operation that legitimises a discourse and naturalises its acceptability in the postdigital era.

This begs the question: could the conceptual recycling metaphor provide an important perspective to understanding a cultural phenomenon such as Amélie Nothomb's narrative?

2. What's a predigital author like Amélie Nothomb doing in a postdigital world

Nothomb is becoming a canonical writer: a member of the Royal Academy in Belgium, praised for "son rayonnement international"[7] (Nothomb 2016, p. 6). Some works such as *Stupeur et tremblement* (1999) are part of the syllabus of the French Baccalaureate. She wrote her first best-seller at age 24 and from 1992 onwards she published a volume every autumn, with clockwork regularity: stories of about 150,000 words to be read on the Thalis route Paris-Brussels, whose rights make publishers scramble at the Frankfurt Book Fair. She has (or had?) become a serial writer!

Critics were unanimous and enthusiastic about her first novel *Hygiène de l'assassin*, which was awarded the Prix Alain Fournier in 1993, translated, and transmedialised in theatre play, film, opera, audio-book, etc. Decried by some and appreciated by others, she is on her way to becoming part of world literature today (Martiny 2016). "L'écrivaine au curieux chapeau a son armée de lecteurs fidèles qui l'achèteront, quoiqu'il arrive" (Duplat 2012).[8] She received the prestigious Renaudot Prize in 2021. Amélie Nothomb has become integrated into the star-system of authors. Her public appearances and the media show a woman wearing black clothing.[9] From the numerous gatherings in bookshops for presentations and signings, the correspondence with her readers by handwritten letter, to her repeated interviews on TV and radio shows (and on YouTube afterwards): they are curious *in presentia* meetings in the Internet era. She delivers herself to be read by a community of spectators eager to know everything about her (Robert 2018) in such a way that her first-person feminine

7 "her international outreach". (Nothomb 2016, p. 6).

8 "The writer with the curious hat has her army of loyal readers who will buy her works, whatever happens." (Duplat 2012).

9 Fabienne Claire Nothomb was born in Etterbeek (Brussels) on 9 July 1966, according to the *Etat Présent de la noblesse belge* (1995), and not in Japan (Clemmen 2014, pp. 447–454).

singular has become a postdigital social persona. In fact, the author is not dead, she is coming back.

In fact, Amélie Nothomb can no longer operate just in the frame of print capitalism, but in an electronic format, a new transmedial format. She also integrates the collective experiences of sharing: reading books, watching interviews, exchanging opinions and advice, sending messages-letters. Nevertheless, scholars tend to read Nothomb's works from the perspective of *Hygiène de l'assassin* (1992) and its manifesto rhetoric. We have identified more than 70 papers and reviews that have explored Nothomb's deconstruction of canonical models and all kinds of intertextual relations from a postmodern and metaliterary point of view. Without any doubt, *Hygiène* (1992), *Les combustibles* (1993), *Attentat* (1997) and *Mercure* (1998) proposed what critics wanted to read in the 1990s.[10] They seemed to enjoy finding the most amazing intertexts[11] and for good reason[12] they considered Amélie Nothomb to be a 'quotationist', even a decadentist at the turn of the millennium (Kemp 2013, pp. 237–250).

Some intertexts are so hidden that they are only identifiable by very skilled readers. By contrast, most of Nothomb's quotations in her narrative are explicit and more accessible to the average reader who has studied at secondary school in France or in French-speaking Europe.[13] Nothomb has always engaged the cultural stereotypes of mass culture: Pompey, Easter Island statues, Egyptian pyramids or the Turin shroud in *Péplum* (Nothomb 1996, p. 37). Her already canonical novels, like *Stupeur et tremblement* (1999), rely on the expectations

10 Even later, for example, regarding *Attentat* (1997): Miernowski (2014) or Cadeddu (2016).

11 Just a few examples, all national sources put together: Brainbrigge (2003, pp. 114–126); Oberhuber (2004, pp. 111–128); Dewez (2007, pp. 291–130); Seybert (2013, pp. 249–256); Signori (2013, pp. 74–91); Murphy (2016, pp. 151–161); Madigan (2017, pp. 64–74).

12 In *Attentat* (1997), she quotes Víctor Hugo and *Notre Dame de Paris*, Baudelaire, Gérard de Nerval, Oscar Wilde, Diderot and *L'Encyclopédie*, Sade, Stendhal and *La Chartreuse de Parme*, Jeronimus Bosch, Pierre Louÿs, George Bataille, Henryk Sienkiewicz and *Quo vadis?*, Nero, Homer, Virgil, Dalí, *The Elephant Man, Taran,* Victor Hugo and *Les Misérables,* Mishima, Venus, Apollo, Alfred Jarry, Kant and *The Critique of Pure Reason*, Cendras and *La Prose du Transibérien,* Balzac and *Eugénie Grandet,* Sherezade, Schiller and *Hymn to Joy*, Marx, Jesus, *Apocalypse*, Edmond Rostand and *Cyrano de Bergerac, Doctor Zhivago,* Orpheus, Euridice…

13 Many readers, Latin and Greek enthusiasts from their teenage years in high school, are still able to recognise Cicero's quotation, 'Quousque tandem abutere, Catilina, patientia nostra?' the first line of Marcus Tullius Cicero's *Against Catiline* (63 B.C.).

of an average French reader, including references to Molière, Prévert, Sisiphe, Bernanos, Nietzsche…

She made her choice a long time ago. Debating two scholars in front of a university audience, her position was clear: "Et je me suis retrouvée devant le public qui était conquis, évidemment"[14] (Nothomb 2018, pp. 73–74). However, there is always something for everyone. Miernowski (2014) is able to point out that Epiphane Otos, the protagonist of *Attentat* (1998), evokes the Greek root 'outis' meaning 'nobody' in Homeric literature, in moral German and Flemish poetry, in Verne's *Captain Nemo*…, but the protagonist has to accept that people will refer to Otis elevators! (Nothomb 1997, p. 11).

Nothomb relies on the general culture of her community of readers, more than on elite culture.[15] For example, it is no coincidence that Esmeralda appears in *Attentat* (1997), just one year after Disney's *The Hunchback of Notre Dame*. In fact, this novel draws on *Quo vadis*, Sinkiewicz's novel (1896) in the protagonist's mind, Mervyn Leroy's film (1951) for readers (*Attentat*, Nothomb 1997, pp. 27–33). Audio-visual media leave their mark everywhere.[16] Scenes from *Splendeur* (Nothomb 1999) seem to come directly from a film, even "films de samouraïs" (1999, 171) and not surprisingly the novel was made into a film. Film and TV frames are the core questions in *Acide sulfurique* (2005) from the very first sentence, but no challenging narrative style is used.[17] Any reader can identify some Hollywood film frames in *Tuer le père* (2011), also in *Frappe-toi le coeur* (2018); one would expect a difference between the storylines in the 1970s and in 2007, but there is none.[18]

---

14 "I found myself in front of such an audience and I won over all this people, of course". (Nothomb 2018, pp. 73–74).

15 She does not care about erudition, "Je ne crois pas tellement aux enquêtes, je ne crois pas tellement à la documentation; je me documente très peu, car l'écriture est surtout un moyen d'investigation du réel, vu de l'intérieur, pris de l'intérieur." (Saunier 2014, p. 95).

16 From *Le sabotage amoureux* (Nothomb 1992, pp. 49–50).

17 In contrast to other authors such as Jean-Philippe Toussaint in *Télévision* (2004), or Chloé Delaume in *J'habite dans la télévision* (2006), who modified their narrative (DalMolin 2012, pp. 151–163).

18 No interest apparently: "B.L.: Pourquoi avoir situé l'action de votre roman dans la France des années 70 à 2000? A.N.: C'est une époque que j'ai connue et, dès lors, c'était plus facile pour moi. Aussi je crois que, jusqu'en 1975 environ, nous étions encore dans un temps où l'on ne vivait pas dans le culte de l'enfant chéri" ("B.L.: Why did you set your novel in France between 1970 and 2000? A.N: It is a time I knew and, from then

Nothomb's narrative has never rejected modern communication devices. In *Attentat* (Nothomb 1997, pp. 113–141), the protagonist needs to use the fax for immediate communications. Telephone, fax and computers play a role in *Stupeur* (Nothomb 1999, p. 58). In *Le fait du* Prince (2008), some phones calls and phone numbers launch the story.

Nevertheless, Nothomb has repeatedly stated her rejection of digital technology, as a deliberate position she is proud to display.[19] She refuses to thematise digital environments in her novels, and while she claims her right to be predigital, autumn after autumn we look forward to a novel that deals explicitly with the digital world. In vain! By so doing, her narrative becomes the imprecator of her generation, such as Prétextat Tach did previously in *Hygiène* (Nothomb 1993, p. 89).

In any case, computing metaphors slip in between the lines from time to time.[20] As much as Amélie Nothomb wants to willingly live in a predigital narrative universe, postdigital reality is there. In *Une forme de vie* (2010), she took up the challenge of writing an epistolary novel in the context of the Iraq war. An American soldier sends her handwritten letters from Baghdad in such a way that the allocations of places and dates, the vocabulary of the posts, the rhythm of the mails by return post strictly respect the epistolary tradition. Turning herself into a character in her own novel displays her ignorance regarding e-mail addresses, and she is proud of herself for doing so (Nothomb 2010, pp. 93–94). Handwritten letters are prized (Nothomb 2010, pp. 55–57, 63–67, 86–87), but they will turn out to be false, since they were sent digitally by e-mail, copied, scanned. The novel is about the authenticity of (hand)writing and of (paper) reading in the postdigital era.[21] Nothomb is perfectly aware of the

---

on, it was easier for me. So, I think that, until about 1975, we were still in a time when we did not live in the cult of the cherished child.") (Nothomb 2017, p. 26).

19 See Nothomb (2012), or Robert (2018, pp. 22, 46, 51 and 75). More recently, "Ne m'envoyez pas un mail, je ne recevrai pas. Si vous m'envoyez une lettre, une vraie lettre écrite avec du papier, avec votre adresse, bien sûr, pas d'adresse mail, s'il vous plaît, je vous répondrai." ("Don't send me an email, I won't receive it. If you send me a letter, a real letter written on paper, with your address, of course, no email address, please, I will answer you.") (Nothomb / Pàmies, 2022).

20 For example, *Stupeur et tremblement* (Nothomb 1999, p. 81 and 88), *Le voyage d'hiver* (Nothomb 2009, p. 49), *Soif* (Nothomb 2019, p. 88).

21 The question is so burning nowadays that it is hard to believe that the transposition mail-social media has not been sought, "même si vos lettres ne m'arrivaient que scannées, elles me paraissaient si formidablement réelles." ("even though your letters only arrived scanned, they seemed so real to me") (Nothomb 2010, pp. 114); "pourquoi les individus seraient-ils forcément plus vrais quand on les a en face de soi? Pourquoi

era we live in[22] and this is precisely why she thematises reading and writing: she has become a kind of believer…in reading.

3. Nothomb's storytelling

The question "what is reading?" runs through the whole of Nothomb's work, with very negative overtones in her first few novels (*Hygiène de l'assassin* 1992; *Les combustibles* 1994), but as a fanciful triumph in *Les áerostats* (2020). Something happened in-between.

After the author's solipsism and contempt for the readers of Prétextat Tach (Nothomb 1992), and the cynical literature professors who particularly despised readers' desire for fictional immersion (Nothomb 1994, p. 56),[23] reading became one of the core thematic pillars of Nothomb's works, and readers play more and more active roles. In *Attentat* (1997), *Le voyage d'hiver* (2009) and *Pétronille* (2014), the characters need to be read and even the act of reading can be read (Nothomb 2009, p. 80). In *Robert des noms propres* (*Nothomb* 2002, pp. 51–53), the protagonists discover that they will exist by reading fairy tales or Ionesco's theatre plays (Nothomb 2002, pp. 152–56) and they succeed in acting as these fictional figures. Reading is also the salvation for the protagonist of *Antéchrista* (2003, pp. 144–145). In *Une forme de vie* (Nothomb 2010), the readers are in search of an author and the different authors are in search of their readers: everything leads us to think of the unfold w-readers or prosumers of our postdigital world.

Something happened. If in *Hygiène de l'assassin*, Homer was read by "les rares lycéens endormis qui annônent encore Homère" (Nothomb 1993, p. 55), in *Le Voyage d'hiver* (Nothomb 2009) the protagonist spent his time translating the *Iliad* and the *Odyssey*. Finally, in *Les áerostats* (Nothomb 2020, pp. 47–49), a teenage digital weapons enthusiast almost miraculously overcomes his reading difficulties, since he reads *The Iliad* in one night! There is no cause-and-effect

---

leur vérité n'apparaîtrait-elle pas mieux ou tout simplement différemment, dans l'épître?" ("Why should individuals necessarily be more truthful when they are in front of you? Why shouldn't their truth appear better, or simply differently, in the epistle?") (Nothomb 2010, p. 79).

22 *Journal d'une hirondelle* (2006) is a novel around a personal diary on paper: "En cette époque où la moindre adolescente exhibe son blog, peut-être n'y a-t-il rien d'aussi désirable que cela: un secret." ("In an age when every teenage girl exhibits her blog, perhaps there is nothing so desirable as that: a secret.") (Nothomb 2006, p. 990).

23 A certain "betrayal of clerks" (the critics, the academics) is denounced by a young student who advocates a kind of resistance by reading, by teaching or by wearing a coat (Nothomb 1994, p. 12, 16, 17, 20 and 23).

relationship; it is just a matter of fact! After Homer, the young guy reads Stendhal, Kafka, Radiguet, Mme de Lafayette and the whole repertoire of canonical French readings within the reach of the middle-class reader who took the Baccalaureate exam in French. Extraordinary!

In parallel, the reappraisal of fiction, the pleasure of storytelling and the increased confidence in her writing become evident throughout Nothomb's works. More and more she displays a tone of tales: the rhythm and the length of the sentences, the symbolical or allegorical content.[24] There are many allusions to fairy tales in her novels. Some scenes are presented as such in *Le Robert des noms propres* (Nothomb 2002, pp. 52–55, and p. 22, 27, 33), *Biographie de la faim* (Nothomb 2004, p. 22) and, of course, in *Barbe bleue* (Nothomb 2012) and *Riquet* (Nothomb 2016). Schéhérazade is at the heart of *Une forme de vie* (2010) since she (the fat in the soldier's body!) and the soldier and the narrator (A. Nothomb) feed their own lives with those letters: stories!

4. Storytelling: some strategies for recycling

After *Les combustibles* (Nothomb 1994), Amélie Nothomb became a determined storyteller, not a poet. Since traditional short stories belong to the public domain, authors can reuse them, transform them, recycle them. Nothomb, like Mme d'Aulnoy or Mme Leprince de Beaumont and many other women writers in the history of French literature, asserts her right to reuse tales as authors and as narrators because of her skills and experiences. They do so in their paratexts in the olden days and in interviews now (Nothomb 2016b). Tales are considered an authority.

Nothomb is recycling a type of narrative (short stories, tales) and to do so she uses different strategies. In one strategy, she reduces the narrative matter to fit the number of hours for a Thalis route Paris-Brussels; abbreviation is the first step for transformation. Her novels develop just one narrative goal announced from the opening sentences in such a way that the whole story will be a development of a riddle that is launched (Nothomb 1996, p. 5), a secret that is proposed to be unveiled (Nothomb 1997, p. 7), the assertive narrative position of the characters.[25]

---

24 Just an example: *Acide sulfurique* (Nothomb 2005, pp. 207–209).

25 The examples are numerous from the beginning of her career: *Les Catilinaires* (Nothomb 1995, p. 9), *Mercure* (Nothomb 1997, p. 7), *Le Voyage* (Nothomb 2009, pp. 7,65, 74, 133), *Le crime du comte Neville* (Nothomb 2015, p. 7).

Her incipits echo from the tales, but also the characters: their names are taken from literary tradition, or they are just invented following in the footsteps of the best story tellers, like Mme d'Aulnoy.[26] No descriptive breaks either for the characters or for the landscapes: the story just focuses on one character's feature and on the facts, without secondary narrative lines. Narrative ellipses are very well managed: Nothomb masters the narrative time from the first sentence, in such a way that a well-paced story, even the discursive rhythm, does not allow the reader to feel bored.

These narrative processes of abbreviation are used time and time again when Nothomb develops some privileged, traditional plots: as toxic character roles in *Le sabotage* 1993, Catilinaires 1995, *Robert des noms propres* 2002, *Antéchrista* 2003, *Acide sulfurique* 2005, *Petronille* 2014, *Frappe-toi le coeur* 2017, *Les prénoms épicènes* 2018, deformity and the sublime (e.g. beauty and the beast) in *Attentat* 1997, *Mercure* 1998, *Barbe bleue* 2012, *Riquet à la houppe* 2016, and even in her own life in *Le Sabotage amoureux* 1993, *Stupeur et tremblement* 1999, *Métaphysique des tubes* 2000, *Biographie de la faim* 2004, *Ni d'Ève ni d'*Adam 2007, *La nostalgie heureuse* 2013.

Another strategy for recontextualisation is to over-locate these themes. Nothomb's novels are always located in specific places and dates from the incipits through the entire narrative development.[27] This is not restricted to autobiographic stories[28] (Tien An Men in 1974 in *Le Sabotage amoureux* (Nothomb 1993), maps in *Biographie* (Nothomb 2004: pp. 7–9)), but also appears in recycled tales, such as *Barbe bleue* (Nothomb 2012) and *Riquet à la houppe* (Nothomb 2016), which are very well located in our contemporary Paris. In fact, the social dimensions of the space are very important in Nothomb's narrative. All these locations let her build a contiguity between fictional and real locations, between the author and the narrator, providing a link for her readers.

Even the imaginary island called "Mortes-Frontières" in *Mercure* (Nothomb 1997, p. 8) is easily identified as somewhere in Normandie and 1923 is pointed

26 Just an example in *Le crime du compte Néville* (Nothomb 2015): the fortune teller is called Rosalbe Portenduère; one of the daughters, Sérieuse; the sister and the brother, Oreste et Electre.

27 Locating in a timeline is used to mark fiction as science-fiction in *Péplum* (Nothomb 199). Even the airports as 'non-lieux' are pointed out as places from the beginning to the end in *Cosmétique de l'ennemi* (Nothomb 2001) and *Le Voyage d'hiver* (Nothomb 2009, pp. 7, 65, 74, 133).

28 For example, from the first sentence in *Stupeur et tremblement* (Nothomb 1999, p. 7) until the end: 14th January 1991, 15th, 17th, 18th…

out as the date when the action takes place. The same applies to *Le crime du Compte Néville* (Nothomb 2015), where readers should be able to recognise a castle in the Ardennes or Luxembourg (Bastia 2015). This is something remarkable for our postdigital and postglobal era: Fabienne Nothomb's life, as much as Amélie Nothomb's works, could endorse Hazel Englert's words in *Mercure*, "Ce qui me frappe, dans ma vie, c'est qu'elle n'a pas cessé d'aller vers le rétrecissement géographique"[29] (Nothomb 1997, p. 27). In recent decades, her novels have presented characters set in a particular time and location rather than travelling, which is relevant in our postglobal era in which technologies 'fold' the space more than ever.

In a third strategic move, Nothomb focuses her novels on new semantic and ethical polarisations as a strategy of re-composition to connect with her readers and undertake a collective recycling operation. This paper has previously demonstrated her appeals to the average ability of a French, francophone, or global reader who should be able to identify cultural references on different levels. When the reference to the plot is well known and announced openly (Perrault's tales in *Barbe bleue* (2012) and *Riquet à la houppe* (2016), Jesus Christ's last hours in *Soif* (2019)), the objective is to recompose the narrative plot based on different values. The "misappropriation" (Bloom 1973), or even reversal, of values is permitted in *Métaphysique des tubes* (2000) to *Soif* (2019).[30] In *Barbe bleue* (2012) and in *Riquet* (2016), a feminist revisionist mythmaking is fashioned on the legend of Bluebeard and on the beauty of a princess (Martini 2013).

What happens when one of the aesthetic, semantic, ethical poles that the characters or the narrator have chosen are no longer valid? This is the core point of many of Nothomb's novels, particularly *Le crime du comte* Néville (2015), where the young daughter attacks the father's *raison d'être* repeatedly: "C'est l'un des principes aristocratiques. On s'inspire des actes des anciens"[31] (Nothomb 2015, p. 127). The daughter issues further reproaches, such as:

---

29 "What strikes me in my life is that it has not stopped moving towards geographical shrinking."

30 From the beginning: "Au commencement il n'y avait rien" ("In the beginning there was nothing") (Nothomb 2000, p. 5), to the end: "Souviens-toi que tu es tube et que tube tu reviendras." ("Remember that you are a tube and to a tube you shall return.") (Nothomb 2000, p. 145). Or from the first sentence: "J'ai toujours su que l'on me condemnerait à mort." ("I always knew I would be sentenced to death.") (Nothomb 2019, p. 7), to the last one "Cela s'appelle solitude." ("This is called solitude.") (Nothomb 2019, p. 152), and, in between, the discovering of the human senses.

31 "This is one of the aristocratic principles. We are inspired by the acts of the ancestors." (Nothomb 2015, p. 127).

> De nos jours, dans le monde réel, qui n'est pas le tien, papa, quand une gosse de 12 ans se conduit, sans le savoir, avec cet art de la séduction qui lui vient d'un père trop courtois, c'est interprété de façon atroce et ça entraîne des conséquences.[32] (Nothomb 2015, pp. 95–96).

Something happened and the characters think that their time is over,[33] but perhaps not. This is the point: the Néville's castle will not be sold and the murder will not take place in this novel in 2015.

5. Recycling: the happy nostalgia

Many of Nothomb's characters are aware of the importance of memories and memory. The protagonist of *Le fait du prince* (2008, p. 92) knows that there is a repertoire out of order (the museums), but many others are available (performances of contemporary art) (Nothomb 2008, pp. 139–40). In *Biographie de la faim* (Nothomb 2004, p. 66), an atlas, a dictionary, and the Bible were the reservoirs where a little girl could draw on in the 1970s. Today, availability is different, as in *Les aerostats* (2020), where a character is fascinated by a collection of porcelain on the Internet, "Vous les avez achetés sur Internet et ils y sont toujours! Ce 'y', renvoyant à ce point vague, était le noeud du problème."[34] (Nothomb 2020, pp. 76–77).

Everything is there to be re-used. Notice the number of titles coming from the old days of authors and works[35] or the number of pages saturated with authors' names.[36] For readers in the postdigital era, culture has become less a *habitus* and more an arena for choices and representations. Nothomb, too, is aware that a temporal continuity has been disrupted and the earlier way of life no longer exists.

The source is dead, long live the source, which is always available. Why not use Quasimodo to call Épiphane, even if nobody knows Victor Hugo in *Attentat*

---

32 "Nowadays, in the real world, which is not yours, Dad, when a 12-year old girl unwittingly behaves with the art of seduction that comes from an overly polite father, it is interpreted horribly and has consequences." (Nothomb 2015, pp. 95–96).

33 Time is over, see Nothomb (2015, pp. 20, 81–83, 109, 126).

34 "You bought them on the Internet and they are still there! This "there", referring to this vague point, was the core of the problem." (Nothomb 2020, pp. 76–77).

35 Mainly in the last decade: *Le voyage d'hiver* (2009), *Barbe-bleue* (2012), *Le crime du compte Néville* (2015), *Riquet à la houppe* (2016), *Frappe-toi le coeur* (2017).

36 As much in *Péplum*: Zola, Dostoyevsky, Baudelaire, Radiguet, Roché, Voltaire, Thomas Aquinas, François Truffaut, Bulwer-Lytton, Suetonius, Tacite (Nothomb 1996, pp. 46–47), as in *Les aérostats* pages (Nothomb 2020).

(Nothomb 1997, p. 9)? Why not keep in mind Schubert's *Winterreise* during the attack on the Eiffel Tower since "il n'y a aucun rapport entre cet acte et cette musique"[37] (Nothomb 2009, p. 130)? The same thing goes for Olivia, the professor who steals ideas, papers and sentences from her PhD student and from Musset. The poet belongs to everybody in *Frappe-toi le coeur* (Nothomb 2017, p. 113)! It is the "principe de la quandoquité"[38] (Nothomb 1996, p. 32) that is always at work in Nothomb's most recent novels. She remembers, even if most of her readers do not.[39]

Digging into the historical repertoire has become a technical standard of any cultural production, but also a way of underlining the ephemeral character of the present.[40] It is fashionable consumerism, a remix. Similarly, Nothomb does not polish the objects' patina with reverence (since there are no users to be concerned with), but she re-circulates literary materials. In so doing, the author, her readers and her characters are engaged in a performative act. Cultural-literary recycling is a committed act: the selection and the reuse involve an action and generate a work for our postdigital and postglobal prosumers. It is an operation that exceeds the personal author's will and becomes a repeated, collective, socially-recognised act. Are there any consequences from these recycling-writing-reading acts?

The question was already posed in *Hygiène de l'assasin* (Nothomb 1992): can a Nobel Prize-winner be a murderer? It returns in *Petronille* (Nothomb 2014) and finally in *Les aerostats* (2020), "mon impact sur lui avait consisté à le transformer en lecteur de grande littérature.... Je n'avais pas empêché un innocent de devenir un assassin."[41] (Nothomb 2020, p. 173).

---

37 "There is no connection between this act and this music."

38 Following 'ubiquité' (ubiquity), 'quanticité' is an invented word to say 'in different moments at the same time'.

39 It is something that Nothomb repeats very often in her interviews, for example in Nothomb (2016b) or Robert (2018, p. 154) about Wim Mertens: ·Ce que j'aime, c'est le côté néogothique, néobaroque de cette musique. On ressent également l'influence de Haendel ou encore de Purcell." / "What I like is the neo-gothic, neo-baroque side of this music. The influence of Handel and Purcell can also be felt."

40 Remember the reflexions on time in *Le fait du prince,* particularly « L'exposition s'appelle 'Un milliard d'années, une seconde.' Il s'agit de faire ressentir le temps." / "The exhibition is called 'One billion years, one second.' The aim is to make people feel time." (Nothomb 2008, p. 101).

41 "My influence on him had been to transform him into a reader of great literature.... I had not prevented an innocent man from becoming a murderer." (Nothomb 2020, p. 173).

Twenty years after Nothomb's first novel, what happened? Is her time over? Checkmate to literature? We are awaiting Nothomb's new novel in the autumn.

References

Appadurai, Arjun: "Disjunture and Difference in the Global Cultural Economy". *Theory, Culture & Society* (7) 1990, pp. 295–310.

Appadurai, Arjun: *Après le colonialisme. Les conséquences culturelles de la globalisation*. Payot: Paris 2005.

Bastia, France / Goosse, André: "Amélie Nothomb, *Le crime du comte Neville*". *Revue générale*. Bruxelles CLI (9–10) 2015, p. 101.

Bloom, Harold: *The anxiety of influence: A Theory of Poetry*. Oxford University Press: New York 1973.

Brainbrigge, Susan: "Monter l'escalier anachronique: Intertextuality in *Mercure*". In: Brainbrigge, Susan / den Toonder, Jeannette (eds.): *Amelie Nothomb: Authorship, Identity ans Narrative Practice*. Peter Lang: New York 2003, pp. 114–26.

Cadeddu, Paola: "Sublime e grottesco nella escritura di Amélie Nothomb". In: *Variazioni sul ritmo. Da Paul Valéry ad Amélie Nothomb*. Franco Angeli: Milan 2016, pp. 47–72.

Clemmen, Yves-Antoine: "Sur les traces d'A. Nothomb. Cohérence des fragments". *Contemporary French and Francophone studies* (XVIII) 2014, pp. 447–454.

Dal Molin, Eliane: "Contemporary French fiction in and out of screens". *Studies in twentieth and twenty-first century literature* (XXXVI) 2012, pp. 151–163.

Dewez, Nausicca: "*Mercure* d'Amélie Nothomb au miroir des livres". *Versants: Revue Suisse des Littératures Romanes* (53–54) 2007, pp. 291–30.

Duchesne, Antoine: *Petite fabrique de la littérature*. Magnard: Paris 1984.

Duplat, Guy: "Le 21e Amélie Nothomb fait pschitt". *Libre Belgique* 21 août 2012, p. 449.

Europeana: *D4.4. Report on ENUMERATE Core Survey* 4, 2017, retrieved 2.2.2022, from https://pro.europeana.eu/files/Europeana_Professional/Projects/Project_list/ENUMERATE/deliverables/DSI2_Deliverable%20D4.4_Europeana_Report%20on%20ENUMERATE%20Core%20Survey%204.pdf.

Hutcheon, Linda / Valdés, Mario (eds.): *Rethinking literary history: a dialogue on theory*. Oxford University Press: New York 2002.

Jameson, Fredric: "Reification and Utopia in Mass Culture". *Signatures of the Visible*. Routledge: New York, London 1990, pp. 11–46.

Jenkins, Henry: *Convergence Culture Where Old and New Media Collide*. New York University Press: New York, London 2006.

Kemp, Anna: "Amélie the Aesthete. Art and politics in the world of Amélie Nothomb". In: Damlé, Amaleena / Rye, Gill (eds.): *Women's writing in twenty-first-century France. Life as literature*. University of Wales Press: Cardiff 2013, pp. 237–250.

Klucinskas, Jean / Moser, Walter (eds.): *Esthétique et Recyclages Culturels: Explorations de la Culture Contemporaine*. University of Ottawa Press: Ottawa 2004.

Le Goff, Jacques: "Antique (ancien) / modern". *Histoire et mémoire*. Paris: Gallimard 2019 [1988], pp. 59–103.

Madigan, M. Kathleen: "The challenges of childhood in a comic light in Amélie Nothomb's *Métaphysique des tubes*". *French Review* XC (4) 2017, pp. 64–74.

Martiny, Erik: "Nothomb, Barbe bleu". *World literature today* 87(1) 2013, p. 66.

Mason, Jessica: *Intertextuality in practice*. John Benjamins: Amsterdam, Philadelphia 2019.

Miernowski, Jan: "Le roman face à la beauté. Le grotesque en quête du sublime". In: *Le Sublime et le grotesque*. Librairie Droz: Genève 2014, pp. 297–317.

Murphy, Carol J.: "Chutes et échelles. Intertextes camusiens dans *Stupeur et tremblements* d'Amélie Nothomb". *Revue des sciences humaines* 324 (oct-déc) 2016, pp. 151–161.

Navas, Eduardo / Gallagher, Owe / xtine burrough (eds.): *The Routledge Companion to Remix Studies*. Routledge: New York, London 2015.

Nothomb, Amélie: *Hygiène de l'assassin*. Albin Michel: Paris 1992.

Nothomb, Amélie: *Le sabotage amoureux*. Albin Michel: Paris 1993.

Nothomb, Amélie: *Les combustibles*. Albin Michel: Paris 1994.

Nothomb, Amélie: *Les catilinaires*. Albin Michel: Paris 1995.

Nothomb, Amélie: *Péplum*. Albin Michel: Paris 1996.

Nothomb, Amélie: *Attentat*. Albin Michel: Paris 1997.

Nothomb, Amélie: *Mercure*. Albin Michel: Paris 1998.

Nothomb, Amélie: *Stupeur et tremblement*. Albin Michel: Paris 1999.

Nothomb, Amélie: *Métaphysique des tubes*. Albin Michel: Paris 2000.

Nothomb, Amélie: *Cosmétique de l'ennemi*. Albin Michel: Paris 2001.

Nothomb, Amélie: *Robert des noms propres*. Albin Michel: Paris 2002.

Nothomb, Amélie: *Antéchrista*. Albin Michel: Paris 2003.

Nothomb, Amélie: *Biographie de la faim*. Albin Michel: Paris 2004.

Nothomb, Amélie: *Acide sulfurique*. Albin Michel: Paris 2005.

Nothomb, Amélie: *Journal de l'hirondelle*. Albin Michel: Paris 2006.

Nothomb, Amélie: *Ni d'Eve, ni d'Adam*. Albin Michel: Paris 2007.

Nothomb, Amélie: *Le fait du prince*. Albin Michel: Paris 2008.

Nothomb, Amélie: *Le voyage d'hiver*. Albin Michel: Paris 2009.

Nothomb, Amélie: *Une forme de vie*. Albin Michel: Paris 2010.

Nothomb, Amélie: *Tuer le père*. Albin Michel: Paris 2011.

Nothomb, Amélie: *Barbe bleue*. Albin Michel: Paris 2012.

Nothomb, Amélie: "La Cause de Barbe-bleue est juste, on a tous le droit au secret". *Le Progrès* 19 août 2012 retrieved 2.2.2022, from https://www.leprogres.fr/france-monde/2012/08/19/la-cause-de-barbe-bleue-est-juste-on-a-tous-le-droit-au-secretv.

Nothomb, Amélie: *La nostalgie heureuse*. Albin Michel: Paris 2013.

Nothomb, Amélie: *Pétronille*. Albin Michel: Paris 2014.

Nothomb, Amélie: *Le crime du comte Néville*. Albin Michel: Paris 2015.

Nothomb, Amélie / de Decker, Jacques: *Discours de réception d'Amélie Nothomb à l'Académie royale de Belgique accueillie par Jacques de Decker*. Albin Michel: Paris 2016a.

Nothomb, Amélie: *Riquet à la houppe. Interview* (07.09.2016), 2016b retrieved 2.2.2022, from https://youtu.be/8-H2A6pLuHs.

Nothomb, Amélie: *Riquet à la houppe*. Albin Michel: Paris 2016c.

Nothomb, Amélie: *Frappe-toi le coeur*. Albin Michel: Paris 2017a

Nothomb, Amélie: "Amélie Nothomb, Personne n'est obligé d'aimer". *Lire* 458 (sept) 2017b, p. 26.

Nothomb, Amélie: *Les prénoms épicènes*. Albin Michel: Paris 2018.

Nothomb, Amélie: *Soif*. Albin Michel: Paris 2019.

Nothomb, Amélie: *Les aérostats*. Albin Michel: Paris 2020.

Nothomb, Amélie / Pàmies, Sergi: "La set d'escriure" (02.02.2022), Centre de Cultura Contemporània de Barcelona, retrieved 2.2.2022, from https://www.cccb.org/ca/multimedia/videos/amelie-nothomb-i-sergi-pamies/238111.

Oberhuber, Andrea: "Réécrire à l'ère du soupçon insidieux: Amélie Nothomb et le récit postmoderne". *Etudes françaises* 40 (1) 2004, pp. 111–28.

Reynolds, Simon: *Retromania: Pop Culture's Addiction to its Own Past*. Faber & Faber: London 2011.

Robert, Michel: *Amélie Nothomb. La bouche des carpes*. Entretiens avec Michel Robert. L'Archipel: Paris 2018.

Seybert, Gislinde: “Surrealistische Lektüre des Romanwerks von Amélie Nothomb”. In: *Geschlechter-F(r)iktionen. = F(r)ictions des genres. Geschlechterphantasien im literarischen Diskurs = Fantasmes des genres dans le discours littéraire*. Frankfurt: Peter Lang 2013, pp. 249–256.

Signori, Lisa F.: “Mirrors in the text. Amélie Nothomb's *Mercure*”. *Studies in twentieth and twenty-first century literature* 36 (1) 2013, pp. 74–91.

María Goicoechea de Jorge
Universidad Complutense de Madrid

The New Art of Making Books Revisited: Postdigital Recycling of the Literary

Abstract: This chapter revisits Ulises Carrión's pioneering manifesto "The New Art of Making Books" (1975) with the purpose of providing a critical framework that will be used to shed some light on contemporary artistic practices in the field of postdigital publishing. Attention will be paid to the work of artists that use canonical literature as raw material for their pieces, such as Jesse England's *E-Book Back Up* (2009), Jason Huff's *AutoSummarize* (2010), or Mimi Cabell and Jason Huff's *American Psycho* (2011), exploring the different strategies involved in the process of cultural and literary recycling. In an age when print competes with digital technology, its physical format appears to be more alive than ever, with artists using print affordances as subversive and performative gestures that open a dialogue about contemporary notions of authorship, originality and the evolving nature of contemporary reading habits and media consumption.

Keywords: postdigital publishing, recycling strategies, algorithm, appropriation, authorship.

1. Introduction

In 1975, Mexican conceptual artist Ulises Carrión published his literary and artistic manifesto "The New Art of Making Books", which proved highly prophetic and anticipated with great accuracy the artistic practices of future generations of creators who have reflected on publishing formats and literary culture during the first two decades of the 21st Century. Revisiting his seminal text from the perspective of a postdigital sensitivity can help us illuminate the practices of contemporary artists who have experimented with literary writing, reading and editing conventions, often using canonical works of literature as raw material for their new pieces.

Postdigital recycling carries with it the sign of the times, the overwhelming feeling that everything has already been said or done; therefore, it is impossible to generate original content *ex nihilo*, since every act of creation constitutes a particular type of recycling, of recontextualisation and processing of materials, which makes them useful again and integrates them into a new cycle.

Contemporary artists depend on our knowledge of our literary heritage to subvert and parody the act of literary creation through a myriad of strategies that combine digital technology with analogue craftmanship in conceptual books that challenge our notion of reading: using search engines, word processing programmes and email as automatic writing agents, subjecting illustrious novels and plays to different procedural transformations, challenging in the process the traditional concept of the book as the right container for the literary text and also posing questions regarding the state of creativity in digital culture.

Through the analysis of artistic proposals in the field of postdigital publishing, such as Jesse England's *E-Book Back Up* (2009), Jason Huff's *AutoSummarize* (2010), Mimi Cabell and Jason Huff's *American Psycho* (2011), Stephanie Syjuco's *Re-Editioned Texts: Heart of Darkness* (2011), Tom Scott's *Shakespeare.txt.jpg* (2013), or Almudena Lobera's *Superficial Reading* (2013) and *Technical Images* (2020), this chapter explores the different strategies involved in the process of cultural and literary recycling. In an age when print competes with digital technology, its physical format seems to be more alive than ever, with artists using print affordances as subversive and performative gestures that open a dialogue about contemporary notions of authorship, originality, analogue and digital constraints and potentialities, and the evolving nature of contemporary reading habits and media consumption.

2. The new art of making books revisited

Ulises Carrión (1941, San Andrés Tuxtla, Mexico – 1989, Amsterdam, Holland) studied philosophy and literature at the National University of Mexico. After publishing two anthologies of short stories and having established himself as a promising young writer, he decides to travel to Europe with a grant to study French at the Sorbonne and German at the Goethe Institute in Achenmühle. He finally completed his master's degree in English Literature at the University of Leeds with a thesis entitled "Judas' Kiss and Shakespeare's *Henry VIII*" (Reijnders 2017). At some point in his life, however, he discarded literature in favour of freer art forms (artists' books, performances, installations), even though literature and particularly the book were essential categories in his artistic production.

"The New Art of Making Books" summarises the paradigmatic change he envisions with respect to the future of the book as a technology that transcends its content, be it literary or otherwise, and which can be playfully altered to question traditional notions regarding the production, dissemination and reception of knowledge. Carrión conceives the book as an "autonomous space-time sequence" (1975, p. 1), as if he had anticipated the emancipation of the book as a container from its text, a tension between the text and its material support that has been made more conspicuous with the arrival of electronic textuality and the liquid nature of the digital text. In Carrión's words, "Books existed originally as containers of (literary) texts. But books, seen as autonomous realities, can contain any (written) language, not only literary language, or even any other system of signs." (1975, p. 1). So, the medium – the book – emerges as an artistic form to which the text is subsidiary, and language itself has become a source of investigation:

> New art's language is radically different from daily language. It neglects intentions and utility, and it returns to itself, it investigates itself, looking for forms, for series of forms that give birth to, couple with, unfold into, space-time sequences.
> [...]
> The words in a new book might be the author's own words or someone else's words. (1975, p. 4).

Moreover, in "The New Art of Making Books" the author becomes responsible for the whole process, making sure that the design of the book is in accord with its content and that both establish a symbiotic relationship. Liberating books from becoming the container of traditional literature, and the words from their meaning and intentionality, has given way to experimentation with other sign systems, which in recent years has meant opening the door to hybrid compositions that are half-human/half-machinic.[1]

As the book as an artifact gains relevance, the text recedes in importance, to the point that one can be the creator of a book yet write very little or nothing at all. Furthermore, since it is the book in its totality that is significant and words have been divested of intentionality, the book's content is not meant to be read in the traditional way but understood as part of a structure. Thus, with these new books come new reading habits; or should we say non-reading habits? Recently Goldsmith tweeted, "No need to read. A sample of the work suffices to authenticate its existence" (Soulellis 2019, p. 230). Ulises Carrión anticipated this change in reading, but contrary to his famous aphorism, "Dear reader. Don't read" (1973), reading has remained, of course, a crucial activity, though the conditions for it have changed: in the new art every book requires a

1 Along these lines, we find Flarf poets, like Nada Gordon, K. Silem Mohammad and Gary Sullivan, who often use Google search engine results as a primary text to create poems, mining the Internet with odd search terms and then filtering the results, a technique closely connected to 'found poetry' but introducing the machinic protocols and their incongruous juxtapositions.

different reading, being able to "read" it is already a sign that one has understood it. Reading, however, does not need to be completed since the reader can stop whenever he or she feels that the structure, the idea of the book, has been fully grasped. Reading, consequently, has incremented its speed (as we will see, his clairvoyance with respect to reading acquires a new degree of precision in light of electronic literature and postdigital publishing artifacts).

This line of thought has also led to one of the most frequently quoted aphorisms of this manifesto, "Plagiarism is the starting point of the creative activity in the new art" (Carrión 1975, p. 5), since texts have become surplus material. Following the path unlocked by Carrión's exhortations, we can find many exponents of conceptual poetry, including the "uncreative writing" movement championed by Kenneth Goldsmith, according to whom, "[w]ith the rise of the Web, writing has met its photography" (2010, p. xvii), alluding to the way in which a superabundance of text made available by the Internet will inevitably cause disturbances in the literary system. Conceptual poetry, in fact, has applied the same rationale to poetry that Sol Lewitt applied to conceptual art, "When an artist uses a conceptual form of art, it means that all of the planning and decisions are made beforehand and the execution is a perfunctory affair. The idea becomes a machine that makes the art" (1967).

Copying-and-pasting, transcribing, transcoding, and republishing large amounts of text is the common *modus operandi* of postdigital artists who have found in the analogical publishing of artists' books a new way to react to the Web's incommensurable and intangible nature. As is often the case in conceptual poetry, reading the text is not necessary to appreciate the work, since it is the idea of the text that is the essence of the whole project, whose outcome does not need to be pleasing either to the eye or to the soul; the text can be quite meaningless or emotionless. Confronted with such an overwhelming abundance of texts, the writer faces the dilemma of the impossibility of ascertaining the originality of his or her contribution. Carrión and Goldsmith's responses, at different times in history, are one and the same: "Dear writer. Don't write". The writer only needs to "borrow" the text to make it his or her own through a series of recycling procedures that have become the new aesthetic principles of our postdigital age. Postdigital creativity lies in the processes of de/recontextualisation, postproduction, republishing and the recirculation[2] of texts. By introducing

2 Recirculation is a term coined by Miriam Llamas Ubieto (2022) and borrowed from the glossary of the archive Rec-Lit. "It is a specific form of postdigital circulation in which something with mass circulation in other periods alongside other media through multiple spaces, borders and points is incorporated into a new life or cycle of

well-known texts into new contexts, a series of features that had been taken for granted or had passed unnoticed come to the foreground and allow us to see them afresh.

However, these recycling practices pose a challenge for critics as there are implications not only regarding notions of authorship and originality, but also with respect to the categorisation of the works according to their genre and artistic discipline. In *Against Expression*, Craig Dworkin discusses how assembling texts for an anthology on conceptual writing from the spheres of literature, music and the visual arts provided him with an argument to advocate a "theoretically-based art that is independent of genre", as he became aware that critics and readers need to open up to other disciplines and their traditions to be able to identify the family resemblances among pieces belonging to different artistic categories but stemming from similar conceptual fields (2010, p. xxiii). It can become quite impossible, for instance, to differentiate a poem from a work of conceptual art that uses text. To bring these works together under one category, Dworkin coined the portmanteau term "conceptual writing" (2010, p. xxiii), which assimilates both traditions.

Meanwhile, Carrión's point-by-point aphoristic description of artists' books circulated for years in several languages, but in the last decade it has seen its popularity increase exponentially thanks to the ways it resonates with contemporary artistic practices and to its dissemination on the Internet. The article was first published in Spanish in 1974 in the Mexican journal *Plural*, edited by Octavio Paz, and in 1975 in English in the prestigious art magazine *Kontexts*, and it has since acquired the status of a manifesto. And as with all manifestoes, the interest resides in knowing to whom the manifesto was addressed: did its intended audience already exist at the time of publication, or did it develop thanks simply to the existence and circulation of the manifesto?

Carrión's passion for these heralded new books was manifested in his life-long dedication to his pioneering bookstore and gallery, which he ran in Amsterdam from 1975 to 1979, creating, selling, and collecting artists' books that fit in with his conceptualisation. Eventually, he turned his artists' books shop – Other Books and So – into an archive, Other Books and So Archive (OBASA), creating a centre of artistic experimentation and publication around

---

mass, but postdigital, circulation over time. It is not just about taking it back from our heritage, as in the case of recovery, but rather what is stressed is the fact that it becomes a dynamic phenomenon that moves it again through new circuits." (My translation). http://repositorios.fdi.ucm.es/REC-LIT/view/generico.php?id=40&idpadre=40.

it, and thus transforming the conventional associations elicited by the concept of the archive into a more relational and lively institution. He closely identified with the archive, to the extent that he could not imagine it would continue to exist without him, and so he decided that after his death the archive's contents should be dispersed, and he gave the complete contents of the archive to his friend Juan J. Agius – an antiquarian specialising in avant-garde publications (Agius 2016).

The physicality of printed books and their collection in physical/virtual archives has been revived in the postdigital era: Silvio Lorusso and Juliette Pépin's Post-Digital Publishing Archive (P-DPA), Paul Soulellis' Library of the Printed Web, LEETHI's Rec-Lit: Estrategias de Reciclaje Cultural y Literario en la Era Postdigital, even Carrión and Co.'s own early initiative at an independent artists' centre in Amsterdam in 1972 – the In-Out center – has been resurrected in the form of a digital archive.

As Juan J. Agius, Carrión's trustee, and Heriberto Yépez begin to reprint the complete works of Ulises Carrión in Mexico, a generation of new authors of artists' books flourishes in the wake of a postdigital nostalgia for the material. For Paul Soulellis, postdigital publishing refers to "web culture articulated as printed artifact" (2019). His Library of the Printed Web is an archive of archives where the return to an analogue object after gathering, harvesting and compiling on the Web, is the prerequisite for occupying its shelves. Some of its pieces bear a certain connection to the Internet-based art of the 90s and early 2000s, while others find their roots in uncreative writing and appropriationism.

The artists united under the label "postdigital" show an enthusiasm for self-publishing and its accessibility, but publishing becomes a performative act full of subversion rather than an attempt to reach a wider audience. Just like Ulises Carrión did, they too turn to books and printing as forms of artistic practice. The collection of pieces that I would like to discuss here emerges from a very specific moment in time, providing a frozen image of the technological possibilities available through the advent of the Web 2.0 and a particular, irreverent attention to our literary heritage.

Carrión's seminal text finishes with an appeal for a democratising new book art, not addressed to a particular group of intellectuals ("In order to be able to read the new art, and to understand it, you don't need to spend five years in a Faculty of English" (1975, p. 7)), but to humans' common ability to create and interpret signs. He also announces the impossibility of creating new literature, since, according to his conception, literature as a form of communication belongs to the past:

> There is not and will not be new literature any more.
> There will be, perhaps, new ways to communicate that will include language or will use language as a basis.
> As a medium of communication, literature will always be old literature. (1975, p. 4).

Literature of the past, on the other hand, has become the raw material for the postdigital books we present in this chapter, manifesting a resilience to dying out or disappearing that testifies to some extent to its ongoing communicative properties. In 2008, Sarah Schmelling, for example, transposed Shakespeare's famous play in her *Hamlet (Facebook News Feed Edition)*. One year later, Alexander Aciman and Emmett Rensin, both students at the University of Chicago, did the same with Twitter and Penguin published their results in their collection *Twitterature: The World's Greatest Books Retold Through Twitter*. In their histrionic introduction, they compare themselves to Martin Luther and his translation of the Bible into vernacular German, since their Twitter versions of the classics aim to bring solace to those who find the great works of literature hard to understand:

> so many modern people find the great works of literature inaccessible, overwhelming, and even, perhaps, dull. It is not a defect of their character, nor any special ineptitude that has disposed them in this manner; rather, these great texts – timeless as they may be – are, in their present form, outdated. (Aciman / Rensin 2009, p. 1).

Notwithstanding their generous dedication, it is difficult to conceive of a fully engaged readership for these abridged versions that is able to find them funny or merely entertaining without knowing first-hand the original literary works they parody. The significance of their proposal lies in the details. We can read fast, but our attention does not need to stop once the structure and the technique underlying the work has been discovered – be it a compression algorithm, an email transcription or a processed text subjected to a sequence of procedures – the interesting part lies in the details. The examples of postdigital publishing we will discuss, as conceptual writing, are less theoretical than one would expect and highly intuitive, but the point being made here is that through a playful and irreverent manipulation of the literary they have inadvertently arrived at the same reading mechanics that machine reading does so well, distant reading techniques that identify the keywords in a corpus, their underlying structures and connections, in ways they had not been perceived before.

3. Postdigital recycling of the literary

Jesse England, an artist and educator based in Portland, Oregon, provides the context and most probably also the inspiration for his piece *E-Book Back Up*

(2009) on his webpage, where photographs of his work appear next to a link to *The New York Times*' article "Amazon Erases Orwell Books From Kindle," published in July 17, 2009. In it, customers who had both digital copies of *Animal Farm* and *1984* complained about a sudden disappearance of these titles from their digital libraries. The company alleged that the sellers of those copies did not hold the copyright over those works (actually, copyright for *1984* had expired in other countries, including Canada, but not in the United States). Students lost their notes together with their digital copy, and one customer noticed that his digital version of *1984* appeared to be a scan of a paper edition, "If this Kindle breaks, I won't buy a new one, that's for sure", he said. A very ironic twist of fate for Orwell's creatures, the idea of returning to print as a back-up copy of the e-book version is Jesse England's postdigital stratagem to denounce the authoritarian power harnessed by companies such as Amazon and the volatile nature of digital assets. Moreover, a second hardcover backup was made with the help of an online self-publishing house. England warns users, though, that the back-up is best viewed (not read!) on paper format (Fig. 1).

Fig. 1. Cover and inside of Jesse England's *E-Book Back Up* (2009).

The recycling strategy in this piece involves a particular type of retrograde remediation (Bolter / Grusin 1999, p. 147): it does not incorporate elements of the new media in the older medium to help the old medium appear more attractive to contemporary consumers, but to appraise the affordances of the old over the new. For its interpretation, it also requires the audience's memory of *1984* and its message regarding authoritarian regimes and their surveillance and censorship methods, including the memory hole – the incineration chute fed with news articles that did not conform to Big Brother's interests. This work is also in line with uncreative writing, since it appropriates Orwell's novel in full, but its publication is a gesture, a performative act that does not require any amount of devoted reading from the spectator. "Dear reader", Carrión would say, "don't read".

In this trend, we also find other examples of postdigital publishing. To some extent, they all depend on the reader's previous knowledge of the original literary works for their effect.

Spanish artist Almudena Lobera's *Superficial Reading* (2013) gives another twist to McLuhan's aphorism that the content of one medium is in itself another medium (1994, p. 8) by using another type of remediation: in this piece, Lobera transforms the concept of the book by eliminating its pages. Her pieces are wooden frames with just three "readable" spaces: the front and back cover, and the spine. The front cover contains a selected quote from the original work, not printed but hand-drawn imitating print type face and using a variety of techniques; the back cover offers a translation of the quote in either Spanish or English, and the spine is reserved for the book's original title and author, these last two spaces using pyrography with a laser cutter. Her work is an instantiation of Carrión's statement, "To make a book is to actualise its ideal space-time sequence" (1975, p. 1). By abbreviating the original work's content to a single quote, Lobera thus feeds us with the concentrated wisdom the book has to offer for our hurried time, this way allowing us to absorb the telegrammatic messages of a life's readings in just a few moments. However, upon a closer inspection, those quotes are hand-drawn recreations of print, bringing to the foreground that writing is like drawing, the visual representation of a language, and that the visible and legible dimensions of perception are interconnected in both literature and the visual arts. Among the titles chosen, three classics of literature in English stand out: James Joyce's *Ulysses*, William Shakespeare's *Hamlet*, and William Faulkner's *The Sound and the Fury* (Fig. 2).

Fig. 2. Almudena Lobera, *Superficial Reading*, 2013. Installation. Drawing on paper and laser engraved frames. Variable dimensions between 20 and 43 cm.

Whereas Jesse England's work acquires its eccentricity through undertaking the seemingly inane activity of photographing Orwell's novel page-by-page, Almudena's approach painstakingly reverts the speed of print through a return to the craftsmanship of the pencil and the virtuosity of the artist, although her result resonates with Carrión's perception that "[t]he new art makes it possible to read faster than the fast-reading methods" (1975, p. 6).

Also in line with this compression, we find Jason Huff's *AutoSummarize* (2010). Huff's selection of literary works for his piece does not entail any actual recollection of past readings, but follows a more procedural mode, "the top 100 most downloaded copyright free books" comprise his own book of arch-summarised novels, including *Dracula*, *The Count of Montecristo*, and *Emma*, which he has compressed into a few lines using Microsoft Word 2008's AutoSummarize 10-sentence function. He then organised the titles alphabetically to form the book's chapters. The result is quite hilarious, yet again one must have a good knowledge of the original novels' content to find the outcome significant. In this work, the classics are not being remediated but fully transformed by a mechanical writer (Fig. 3).

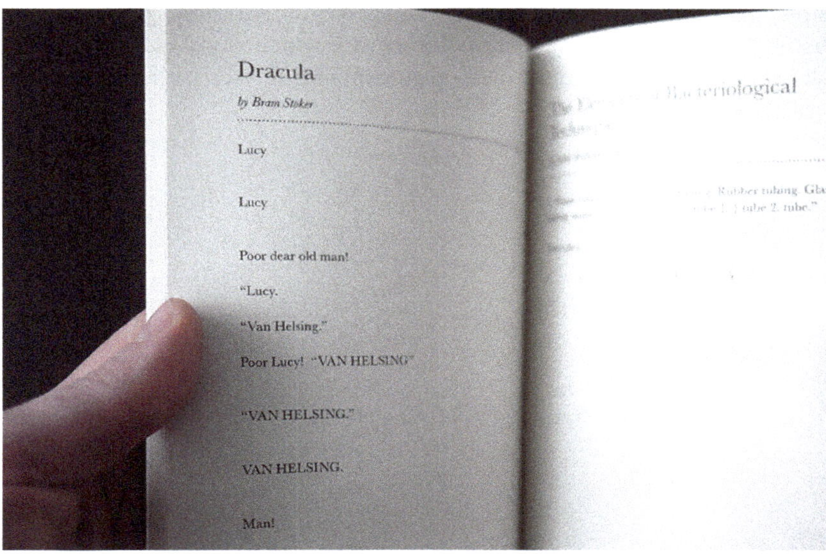

Fig. 3. *AutoSummarize* (2010) by Jason Huff. Photo by Paul Soulellis.

Stephanie Syjuco's *Re-Editioned Texts: Heart of Darkness* (2011) and Tom Scott's *Shakespeare.txt.jpg* (2013) represent further experiments with literary transformation through algorithmic processing. In Syjuco's "novel", Conrad's original text is reprinted on demand in 12 different iterations, altered by the different service chosen for online publishing, which gives each version its title, for example *http//sunsite.berkeley.edu/Literature/Conrad/HeartOfDarkness/03.html*. Each copy retains the errors and transformations of the digitisation of the novel: different fonts, the amount of content per page, and the inclusion of Google ads and mistakes, all communicating a feeling of progressive corruption and demystification of the original. It also highlights issues regarding authorship and appropriation, emphasising the loss that takes place in the translations from analogue to digital to analogue, as if a sort of mechanical rewriting of the text takes place in every transition. The titles inform the reader of the digital nature of the books, however something in these printed artifacts is unsettling. We cannot help but feel that the distance between the original text and what we have in our hands continues to stretch *ad infinitum*. As Paul Soulellis (2014) points out, "[t]he fish is out of the water", meaning that these works seem to inhabit an "in-between-state" that he relates to Duchamp's concept of the infrathin, which is described as "the immeasurable gap between two things as they transition or pass into one another" (Tucker 2009, p. 77). Regardless of their materiality, these works are not fully functional in their printed state – they seem like zombies, both dead and alive.

Fig. 4. Tom Scott's *Shakespeare.txt.jpg* (2013).

In Scott's *Shakespeare.txt.jpg*, a similar process is undertaken, in this case an experiment in applying a JPG compression algorithm at varying levels of quality to a literary text, Shakespeare's *Romeo and Juliet*, where the result is also the progressive corruption of the original text until it has been rendered completely unreadable. As Scott himself explains in his web presentation of the piece, "JPEG image compression is lossy. Every time you edit and save a picture, some of the original content is lost. But it's difficult to see that with the naked eye, so I compressed Shakespeare instead". What is recycled here is not only Shakespeare's play, but the compression algorithm itself, which is meant for compressing images without a significant alteration (a minute change in colour that would be nearly undetectable to the naked eye), whereas, even at 'maximum' quality, when it is applied to text, it leads to almost all characters being replaced by their neighbour in the alphabet. In this manner, Shakespeare's tragedy becomes the object of an experiment in "confused" transcodification: applying an algorithm aimed at a specific type of encoded data to another kind. Moreover, the action of transferring these experiments to print has been referred to as "transduction" – normally defined as the transfer of genetic material from one microorganism to another by a viral agent; in this case, it is used to describe the technique of mixing, blending and embedding digital processes into traditional print, the two forming a hybrid character (Soulellis 2014).

This procedure is also put to the test by Almudena Lobera in her series *Technical Images* (2020), where she uses Photoshop to smoothly translate the colour code palette of a painting into ASCII code; or records computer codes being ritually reproduced in traditional Japanese ink calligraphy; shifts from a music score played on a computer keyboard to typing text on a piano. For many years now, Almudena Lobera has been committed to exploring "the capacity of human perception and its relationship with the construction of biological, economic and socio-cultural structures" (Ramos-Izquierdo 2020, p. 1). In *Technical Images*, she experiments with disrupting two of the coordinates of classical communication: firstly, the use of the same language, which in this case she splits into three: English, Japanese and computer code, and, secondly, transmission through different media carrying out a two-way transfer between traditional and analogue actions, between mechanical and digital ones. As Oulipo members could see for themselves, she devises a procedural set of operations as a mode to trigger (as well as to contrain) her creativity, and she later twists the results in search of an aesthetically pleasing composition, devoid of intentionality in the conventional sense but deeply evocative.

From the myriad of texts that comprise the *Technical Images* exhibit, the book is a ritualised medium to which she grants a privileged status, placing it as a singular group of objects in the eclectically updated Japanese domestic altar or *tokonoma* that opens the exhibit. Normally comprised of three objects that are placed in a harmonious relationship alongside each other to provide a space for meditation and contemplation, in Lobera's intervention on the traditional *tokonoma* she has introduced an element of distortion that references to the digital transformations and the strange symbols and recodification of digital life. The spines of the stacked books are decorated with illegible musical and typographic symbols, disconcerting the spectator rather than inducing in him or her a state of profound meditation (Fig. 5). As in *Superficial Reading*, in this installation the book is not used as a container but as an external surface, an object of decoration that merely demands a quick glance at its cover or spine, but which is still mired in mysticism and ritual.

Fig. 5. Almudena Lobera, *Line Spacing*, 2019. Books with painted cloth binding. 37 x 40 x 30 cm.

Mimi Cabell and Jason Huff's *American Psycho* (2011) also involves the intervention of algorithms for its composition. For this piece, Cabell and Huff rewrote Bret Easton Ellis's novel by sending emails to each other, page-by-page, and collecting the Google ads that appeared next to their emails. The final product retains the cover of the novel[3] but replaces its original pages with blank lines with a few scattered footnote numbers next to the empty spaces where the words that triggered the ads should be located and a list of footnotes at the bottom with the Google ads (Fig. 6). The result exposes two different types of intervention, firstly it brings the role of Google's web crawlers to the foreground, the way they peruse private correspondence to suggest ads related to its content and, secondly, it presents another type of appropriation of the original literary work, which becomes conspicuous by its absence and by the eerie and disturbing associations the advertisements create with the violent content of this piece's raw material. The empty signifiers of Bret Easton Ellis' novel, combined with the incongruous narrative that the list of advertisements fabricates, nevertheless portrays a poignant image of American culture in the first decade of the 21st Century: brutally insensitive towards violence, racism, and sexism, obsessed with physical appearance and material goods, and on the quest for a quick fix to obtain happiness. The original novel, published in 1991, becomes the processed medium that has been recuperated, recycled and placed in circulation again with an updated portrayal of its protagonist – Patrick Bateman – through contextual advertisements of the 21st Century, presenting a frozen picture of a unique intersection in space and time.

3 They retained the design of the cover letters of the series version of Vintage Contemporaries Book, albeit eliminating the background photograph.

Fig. 6. A page from Mimi Cabell and Jason Huff's *American Psycho* (2011).

4. Conclusions

The collection of pieces discussed in this chapter are also fruits of a very specific moment in the history of literature and the history of print, a moment of transition between a fully digitalised process and the coexistence of analogue and digital products, an "in-between-space" in which a traditional reading is not always required but knowledge regarding the specificity of this postdigital era is essential to understand these printed artifacts – the "hybrid" creatures that Ulises Carrión anticipated and that digital technology has helped to conceptualise and embody.

What connects all these artists is that they use, as raw material for their transformations, literary texts found on the Internet, which acquire the status of pure data, disconnected from the time of their composition and reception, with the irreverence of one who uses Shakespeare's complete plays to light a fire. It could have been any other text gathered from the vast stacks of the Internet, but the fact that they use canonical works of literature testifies to the ongoing communicative value of these texts. The artists' playful provocations resonate far longer than they themselves had anticipated, which proves that they have hit a nerve. The literary and art critics that review these works, such as me, normally a generation older than the creators, cannot help but fear that they themselves are a species in danger of extinction, born in an analogical world and trained for a digital one, we might be the last ones to be able to share the appraisal of the canonical works of literature (we have actually read them) and to wonder at the transformative potential of digital media.

What remains constant is the phenomenon of change, which applies to everything in life including literary texts, since everything is in a constant state of transformation and every end anticipates a new beginning, from creation, development, maturity, decadence, dissolution and eventually recreation.

As Ulises Carrión anticipated with his Other Books and So Archive (OBASA) and Paul Soulellis, an archivist of archives, corroborates, contemporary artists have also developed the sensitivity of archivists:

> These are artists who ask questions of the web. They interpret the web by driving through it as a found landscape, as a shared culture, so we could say that these are artists who work as archivists, or artists who work with new kinds of archives. Or perhaps these are artists who simply work with an archivist's sensibility – an approach that uses the dynamic, temporal database as a platform for gleaning narrative. (Soulellis 2019, p. 229).

The countercultural effects of these proposals reside in their potential to continue recycling and therefore keep the conversation surrounding the great works of literature alive in a movement that diverges from the image-dominated culture that the web represents, or using Craig Dworkin's words, these works are set "to challenge the retinal imperative of art with a deskilled anti-aesthetic" (2010, p. xxxv) that borrows canonical literature and inflicts all sorts of transformations upon these well-known texts, inserting them in new cycles of life and dissemination. These movements of decontextualisation and recontextualisation refresh our view of these familiar works, making them significant again in their new context.

References

Aciman, Alexander / Rensin, Emmett: *Twitterature: The World's Greatest Books Retold Through Twitter*. Penguin: UK 2009.

Agius, Juan J: "On Other Books and So Archive". *Archivo Electrónico de Ulises Carrión,* July 29, 2016, retrieved 31.03.2022, from https://ulisescarrioncom.wordpress.com/2016/07/29/on-other-books-and-so-archive-agius/.

Bolter, Jay David / Grusin, Richard: *Remediation: Understanding New Media.* Cambridge: MIT Press 2000.

Cabell, Mimi / Huff, Jason: *American Psycho*. 2011, retrieved 31.03.2022, from http://p-dpa.net/work/american-psycho/.

Carrión, Ulises: "Dear Reader. Don't Read" 1973, retrieved 31.03.2022, from https://www.moma.org/collection/works/218144.

Carrión, Ulises: "The New Art of Making Books", *Kontexts* (6–7), Maastricht, 1975, retrieved 31.03.2022, from https://www.are.na/block/884513.

Dworkin, Craig: "The Fate of Echo". In: Dworkin, Craig / Goldsmith, Kenneth (ed.): *Against Expression: An Anthology of Conceptual Writing*. Northwestern University Press: Evanston Illinois 2010, pp. xxiii–liv, retrieved 02.08.2023, from https://ubu.com/concept/AgainstExpressionTOC-Essays.pdf.

England, Jesse: *E-Book Back Up*. 2009, retrieved 31.03.2022, from http://www.jesseengland.net/project/e-book-backup/.

Goldsmith, Kenneth: "Why Conceptual Writing? Why Now?", In: Dworkin, Craig / Goldsmith, Kenneth (ed.): *Against Expression: An Anthology of Conceptual Writing*. Northwestern University Press: Evanston Illinois 2010, pp. xvii–xxii, retrieved 02.08.2023, from https://ubu.com/concept/AgainstExpressionTOC-Essays.pdf.

Huff, Jason: *AutoSummarize*. 2010, retrieved 31.03.2022, from https://jason-huff.com/projects/autosummarize/.

LeWitt, Sol: "Paragraphs on Conceptual Art". *Artforum* vol. 5, no. 10, Summer 1967. Republished by *Art Theory*, retrieved 31.03.2022, from https://theoria.art-zoo.com/paragraphs-on-conceptual-art-sol-lewitt/.

Llamas Ubieto, Miriam: "Recirculación". In: Llamas Ubieto, Miriam *et al.*: *Glosario de estrategias de reciclaje*. In: Llamas Ubieto, Miriam / Goicoechea de Jorge, María (coords.): *Rec-Lit: Estrategias de reciclaje cultural y literario en la era postdigital*. Repositorio institucional, Universidad Complutense de Madrid: Madrid 2022, retrieved 06.07.2023, from http://repositorios.fdi.ucm.es/REC-LIT/view/generico.php?id=40&idpadre=40.

Lobera, Almudena: *Superficial Reading*. 2013, retrieved 31.03.2022, from http://www.almudenalobera.com/

Lobera, Almudena: *Technical Images*. 2020, retrieved 31.03.2022, from http://www.almudenalobera.com/

McLuhan, Marshall: *Understanding Media: The Extensions of Man*. MIT Press: Cambridge, MA 1994, p. 8.

Ramos-Izquierdo, Marta: "Technical Images: Preamble". *Technical Images Exhibition Catalogue*. Ministerio de Cultura y Deporte 2020, p. 1.

Reijnders, Tineke: "Ulises Carrión and the In-Out Center". *In-Out Center Archives* 2017, retrieved 31.03.2022, from https://inoutcenterarchives.nl/text/ulises-carrion.

Schmelling, Sarah: *Hamlet (Facebook News Feed Edition)*. July 30, 2008, retrieved 31.03.2022, from https://www.mcsweeneys.net/articles/hamlet-facebook-news-feed-edition.

Scott, Tom: *Shakespeare.txt.jpg*. 2013, retrieved 31.03.2022, from https://www.tomscott.com/romeo/.

Soulellis, Paul: "Performing Publishing: Infrathin Tales from the Printed Web". *Hyperallergic*, December 2, 2014, retrieved 31.03.2022, from https://hyperallergic.com/165803/performing-publishing-infrathin-tales-from-the-printed-web/.

Soulellis, Paul: "Search, Compile, Publish". In: Pichler, Michalis (ed.): *Publishing Manifestos. An International Anthology from Artists and Writers*. MIT Press: Cambridge, MA 2019, pp. 228–232, retrieved 31.03.2022, from https://soulellis.com/2013/05/search-compile-publish/.

Syjuco, Stephanie: *Re-Editioned Texts: Heart of Darkness*. 2011, retrieved 31.03.2022, from http://p-dpa.net/work/re-editioned-texts/.

Tucker, Thomas Deane: *Derridada, Duchamp as Readymade Deconstruction*. Lexington Books: Plymouth 2009, p. 77.

María José Calvo González
Universidad Complutense de Madrid

Postdigital Remediation and Recycling off the Page: The Collaborative Work *Besmette Stad*[1]

Abstract: In his poems *Bezette stad* (*Occupied City*) Flemish poet Paul van Ostaijen views the Great War as essential for the transition from the old world to the new. A century later, the multimedia artistic project "Besmette stad" was inaugurated and can be read as is an artistic recreation of van Ostaijen's poems in the postdigital age. This contribution aims to detect and classify the types and strategies of recycling which have been used in the re(use) of specific poems in the anthology *Bezette stad*.

Keywords: Great War, pandemic, *Bezette stad*, Paul van Ostaijin, "Besmette stad", recycling strategies.

1. Introduction

The collection of poems *Bezette stad* (*Occupied City*) ([1921] 2021), by the Flemish poet Paul van Ostaijen, published in 1921, depicts the circumstances before, during and after the occupation by the German Army of the Flemish city of Antwerp during the First World War. Its verses, typography and layout reflect a space of horror, desolation, absence and despair, without giving up dreams of a better society and a different life.

Van Ostaijen viewed the war as essential for the transition from the old world to the new. In Berlin, after the end of the Great War, he began to search for a new humanity, culminating in the creation and publication of his famous avant-garde work.

One hundred years later, the poetic work of Van Ostaijen and the concept of city embodied in it have taken centre stage again as a reference in a completely

1 I would like to thank those responsible for the project "Besmette stad", Matthijs de Ridder and Willem Bongers-Dek, who have shared their enthusiasm for this chapter; for reviewing the chapter and for their collaboration in granting permission for and facilitating the publication of the illustrations.

Moreover, this contribution has been possible, in part, thanks to the financial assistance of *Taalunie*.

different context: the start of a global pandemic triggered by the COVID-19 virus. Despite the new setting, the comparable elements are substantial: a city once more filled with solitude, emptiness, uncertainty, death and vulnerability. This affinity prompted the historians of literature Willem Bongers-Dek, Director of the Flemish-Dutch cultural centre deBuren and Van Ostaijen's biographer Matthijs de Ridder for a series of podcasts dealing with what they called "Besmette stad" ("Contaminated city").

This initial idea led to individual reading workshops of each poem in Van Ostaijen's collection. From the start of the lockdown in the spring of 2020, the workshops were carried out in a streaming format with an audience loyal to the reading sessions. The sessions are now stored on the website of the Flemish/ Dutch cultural centre deBuren.[2] In conjunction with the readings, De Ridder and Bongers-Dek assigned a poem from *Bezette stad* to each of more than a hundred artists who were part of the livestream audience at the literary workshops, with the main objective that they use the poem assigned to them to give an artistic response to the crisis of the pandemic. While *Bezette stad* can be considered a multi-media work, in which the poet reflects, among others, the films of the time, popular songs (French, Dutch, German and even Spanish), advertising slogans, collage, etc. the idea of the leaders of the macro project "Besmette stad" tended towards a *Gesamtkunstwerk*, in the sense that the relation between different arts in the work as a whole would aspire both to the elimination of the barriers that separated them, as well as to the overcoming of the limits of art itself (Bryant 1997, 59). The artists were asked to be aware of their time and space, reflecting the fears and dreams of the present and future of the pandemic and bringing their productions to life in accordance with the *ad-hoc* circumstances and conditions of the 21st Century. The collective work included artists from many different areas of the culture and arts of Flanders and the Netherlands, such as writers, musicians, composers, illustrators, visual artists, etc., who created a variety of productions in the form of poems, songs, performances, stories, interactive drawings, posters, illustrations, documentaries, recitals and exhibitions.

The inauguration of the multimedia artistic project "Besmette stad" took place on 8 June 2020, with the participation of the Ministers for Culture of Flanders (Jan Jambon) and the Netherlands (Ingrid Engelshoven). It featured the public

2 deBuren: *Leesateliers Besmette stad*, 26 June 2020, retrieved 17.01.2023, from https://deburen.eu/magazine/2788/leesateliers-besmette-stad.

performance of artistic projects that were being created based on the poems of Van Ostaijen.[3]

Additional elements were included on the project website, such as a map of a fictitious city called "Besmette stad", designed by the illustrator Dieter de Schutter.[4] The map is characterised by a visual and dynamic language in which the reader moves via the screen from one neighbourhood to another of the city, gaining access in individual files to van Ostaijen's poems, the individual workshops and the artistic manifestations based on those poems, which were created for the project in multiple media and devices.[5]

In addition, the artist De Schutter designed the poster for the "Street route workshops" *Eén, twee marsj*, which began in autumn 2020 as a follow-up to the reading workshops. In these walking tours, Matthijs de Ridder, sponsored by deBuren, guided the participants walking through the Antwerp of *Bezette stad* via three routes: the city of the war, the ideological city and the city's night life.[6] Beginning in 2021, these routes are available to be followed thanks to the mobile app *ErfgoedApp* (FARO 2021).

After a year of plans and further initiatives revolving around *Bezette stad* and the "Besmette stad" project, the Flemish/Dutch centre deBuren and the Paul van Ostaijengenootschap, coordinated by Matthijs de Ridder and Willem Bongers-Dek, jointly organised a 24-hour Paul van Ostaijen event (from 10 p.m. on 21 February to 10 p.m. on 22 February 2021) in commemoration of the 125th anniversary of the poet's birth and the 100th anniversary of the publication of his collection of poetry. In these 24 hours, the celebrations were broadcast live from the house where Paul van Ostaijen was born (and which is now the home of Matthijs de Ridder). During the event, the studio played host to a few experts in the work and life of Paul van Ostaijen as well as some of the artists who have based their creations on his works. The final hours of this event were broadcast from two emblematic venues: the *Elckerlyc* theatre in Antwerp and

3 deBuren: *Officiële opening Besmette stad*, 04 February 2021, YouTube, retrieved 17.01.2023, from https://www.youtube.com/watch?v=2d6vUxs5I8Q.

4 Verve built the *Besmette stad* website and Dieter de Schutter illustrated it.

5 deBuren: *Kaart Besmette stad*, 2020, retrieved 17.01.2023, from https://deburen.eu/besmette-stad.

6 deBuren: *Één-twee-marsj | Teaser 1: wandel mee!*, 27.11.2020, YouTube, retrieved 17.01.2023, from https://www.youtube.com/watch?v=O9k8uoTIsho&list=PLgxbksat77le-Kt2S05xOaaIgc2G1yhFb&index=2; *Één-twee-marsj | Teaser 1: de kunstenaars*, 27.11.2020, YouTube, retrieved 17.01.2023, from https://www.youtube.com/watch?v=vdlW6tqEh0U&list=PLgxbksat77le-Kt2S05xOaaIgc2G1yhFb&index=2.

the Flemish Cultural Centre *De Brakke Grond* in Amsterdam, on whose stage some of the artists participating in the "Besmette stad" project performed live.[7] This event celebrated on the same day the transfer of the manuscript of *Bezette stad* to the Flemish Community, to be exhibited and digitalised so that it can be available to anyone interested (Vlaanderen.be 2021).[8] Also announced was the publication of Matthijs de Ridder's *Boem. Paukeslag. Op strooptocht door Paul van Ostaijens* Bezette stad (Pelckmans 2021), which provides a historical, literary and critical review of the experimental work *Bezette stad.* Additional cause for celebration was the publication of the anthology of the project responding to the coronavirus crisis by De Ridder/Bongers-Dek: *Besmette stad. Vijfenzestig kunstenaars antwoorden op* Bezette stad *van Paul van Ostaijen* (Pelckmans 2021).

The exhibition "Boem Paukeslag. Bezette stad 100!" was held from 27 March to 27 June 2021 in the House of Letters in Antwerp (Letterenhuis), most of the space being dedicated to *Bezette stad*, but also including some of the artistic manifestations created for the *Besmette stad* project. It is now possible to take a virtual tour of the exhibition.[9] From March 2021 to November 2022, part of the exhibition (precisely the part dedicated to the new artistic manifestations based on *Bezette stad*) has become a type of travelling exhibition across Belgium and the Netherlands. Five young artists, most of them members of the "Besmette stad" project, were chosen for this multimedia exhibition. As of January 2023, the exhibition is rented to be shown in other cultural spaces.[10]

Having served as the starting point for the "Besmette stad" project, *Bezette stad* achieved a resonance and recognition at least comparable to the new project. Thanks to the new project, a collection published one hundred years earlier is now the subject to a (re)discovery of great transcendence, achieved by involving numerous artists who have disseminated it very widely through their joint work.

For example, there has been a re-publication of the facsimile edition of *Bezette stad* (Van Ostaijen 2021) used as a reference for this chapter, with an epilogue by the poet Erik Spinoy, who, after years of research on the work of Paul

---

7 deBuren: *Finale van de marathonuitzending 'De 24u van Paul van Ostaijen'!* 23 February 2021, YouTube, retrieved 17.01.2023, from https://www.youtube.com/watch?v=KRY9bb5IKHs.

8 The press conference was a part of the marathon.

9 Letterenhuis: *Boem Paukeslag. Bezette stad 100! Afgelopen expo-bezoek digitaal* (n.d.), retrieved 17.01.2023, from https://letterenhuis.be/nl/expo/boem-paukeslag.

10 Letterenhuis: *Boem Paukeslag: Bezette stad X 5* (n.d.), retrieved 17.01.2023, from https://letterenhuis.be/nl/boem-paukeslag-bezette-stad-x-5.

van Ostaijen, also created an online project in 2021 dedicated to *Bezette stad*, including its text, cultural and historical references and bibliography.[11]

Coinciding with the end of the toughest period of the pandemic and being aware that no solution had yet been found for the crisis itself, the coordinators of the "Besmette stad" project wished to close the project's circle by establishing a connection with the final poem in *Bezette stad*: "De Aftocht" ("The Withdrawal"). The poem represents the withdrawal of the German Army and the departure of Paul van Ostaijen to Berlin. In it can be discerned the liberation of the city of Antwerp at the end of the First World War. At the same time, it displays the widespread despair that this liberation has not brought change and a new reality appears very distant. For this reason, taking with reference the last poem "De Aftocht" in *Bezette stad* – which is very long – those managing the project "Besmette stad" were interested in including artistic manifestations not only from the Netherlands and Flanders, but also from Germany. The artists taking part asked themselves very similar questions to those proposed by Van Ostaijen in his last poem: What are the consequences of the crisis we are experiencing? What awaits us now? A liberation, a revolution? A return to normality or a new abnormality? Can we continue to act as before and during the crisis, or has the time come to determine some lessons and conclusions?

The first episode of the "De Aftocht" Festival took place on 22 February 2022. It was a celebration developed around the final poem, offering live music, poetry and performance in the form of a music-hall by artists in Dutch and German.[12] There was also a launch of the publication *De Aftocht* (Eble et al. 2022), which includes 35 artistic contributions in Dutch and German.

The publication on paper of *Besmette stad* and *De Aftocht* (De Ridder / Bongers-Dek 2021 and Eble et al. 2022) contains 65 and 35 artistic manifestations, respectively, in the form of texts, illustrations and drawings. Certain works were selected for these publications, as those created in audio(visual) format could not be included, although fortunately they are available on the website of deBuren.[13]

---

11 University of Liège. Faculty of Philosophy and Letters: *Bezette stad*, 2021, retrieved 17.01.2023, from http://web.philo.ulg.ac.be/bezettestad/.

12 deBuren: *Slotshow Paul van Ostaijenjaar: De Aftocht,* 22 February 2022, retrieved 17.01.2023, from https://deburen.eu/programma/5353/slotshow-paul-van-ostaijenjaar-de-aftocht; *Final show of the Paul van Ostaijen year: The Withdrawal*, 23 February 2022, YouTube, retrieved 17.01.2023, from https://www.youtube.com/watch?v=HlbXT-6FNAA&t=1190s.

13 deBuren: *Besmette stad* (n.d.), retrieved 17.01.2023, from https://deburen.eu/besmette-stad.

However, a large number of creations are not included either inside or outside the book, such as those presented on a stage in live performance, or those spread through social media, exhibitions, presentations or musical events, etc., which have to be viewed and listened to via other media and devices.

The aim of this chapter is to study some of the special creations that are outside the book of the collective phenomenon of "Besmette stad", with the premise that "Besmette stad" is an artistic creation of the postdigital age, and with the aim of detecting and classifying the types and strategies of recycling which have been used in the re(use) of specific poems in the anthology *Bezette stad* by Paul Van Ostaijen.

Based on the starting point that there has been a process of postdigital recycling, I have adopted the statement postulated in an article by Florian Cramer, that: " 'Post-digital' thus refers to a state in which the disruption brought upon by digital information technology has already occurred" (2014, p. 17). So, "postdigital" is in direct opposition to the notion of "new" technological media. Once these new media were diluted with old or previous ones, the analogue disrupting the digital, the notion of new media was superseded (Andersen / Cox / Papadopoulos 2014, p. 5). This process began in the first and second decade of the 21st Century.[14]

2. Analysis of the artistic creations in "Besmette stad"

2. 1. General comments

To classify the types and strategies of recycling, a specific nomenclature has been used with the corresponding definitions, as present in the repository and research space "Strategies of cultural and literary recycling in the postdigital era".[15]

Before starting to analyse the recycling of a selection of poems of the collective project "Besmette stad", I would like to make it clear that a general postdigital collaborative reading strategy of recycling has been used, mainly in the virtual reading workshops (deBuren *Leesateliers Besmette stad* 2020) directed by Matthijs

14 For a definition of the concept, a systematisation of the state of the question and an essential bibliography with commentary about the postdigital condition, see the article published by Llamas Ubieto (2020).

15 Within the REC-LIT project: *Cultural recycling. Transliterations in the postdigital era* (RTI2018-094607-B-100), financed by the ERDF/Ministry of Science and Innovation – State Research Agency. PI: Miriam Llamas. See: Llamas Ubieto / Goicoechea de Jorge (2022): http://repositorios.fdi.ucm.es/REC-LIT/view/paginas/view_paginas.php?id=1.

de Ridder, where the poems of *Bezette stad* were read and interpretations (of the poems) were shared and commented on. This served as an inspiration for the creations of the artists. In addition, the content of these literary meetings gave rise to the work of literary criticism on *Bezette stad* (De Ridder 2021).

Throughout the project there has also been a postdigital recycling strategy of collaborative writing to create a collective artistic product, including what appears both inside and outside the book giving one or more answers to the same poem, often with artistic duos collaborating, or producing diverse artistic creations in a new medium and time, through multiple media.

The original production had to serve, according to the coordinators of the "Besmette stad" project, as an element of inspiration for the creation of an artistic work in a new context. In this respect, Van Ostaijen's anthology has been recycled, firstly, through a process of decontextualisation, given that it has been removed from the context in which it was created; and, secondly, by recontextualising the poems it contains, which thereby acquire a new meaning.

Finally, this collective work has involved a type of recycling of the reproduction of the original work (Van Ostaijen's poem). The original work has been interpreted individually by the Flemish theatre actor and director Tom van Bauwel and included on the audio platform Soundcloud.[16] It may, however, be argued that there has been an appropriation of the original poem in his act, since there is not much transformation in his interpretation of the poem.

2.2. "Bedreigde stad" (Paul van Ostaijen) versus "Besmette stad/ Bedreigde stad" (Lucky Fonz III)

The poem "Bedreigde stad" ("Threatened city")[17] portrays the invasion of Belgium on 4 August 1914 by the German Army, and its triumphant entry into Brussels, reproducing the fires and bombardment of Antwerp at the start of October 1914 and the explosion of thousands of bombs dropped from zeppelins. This attack led to the complete destruction of the city: "Visé marsj Luik mortieren" [...] "défilé van éen dag en éen nacht door Brussel" [...] "het flak kerend land / de verre toren

16 Souncloud: *Album Bezette stad*, 2021, retrieved 17.01.2023, from https://soundcloud.com/search?q=Bezette%20stad.

17 The poem "Bedreigde stad" by Paul van Ostaijen can be accessed on: Van Ostaijen (2021, n.p.) and in deBuren: *Bedreigde stad* (2020), retrieved 17.01.2023, from https://deburen.eu/besmette-stad/10/bedreigde-stad-paul-van-ostaijen; and a critical study of the poem in: De Ridder (2021, pp. 95–120). The English translation is of the original work of Paul van Ostaijen (Colmer 2016).

en de laai ende brand" […] "de débâcle".[18] The poet uses the occlusive sounds [k], [t], [p], creating the sound of successive explosions, which helps express a world of noise and tumult: "*knal knal kneppert klettert knepperen klettert knallen*".[19]

These days are described as traumatic, full of fear and uncertainty, "Het sta**PP**en van de stad / *de forten zullen houen zullen vallen zullen houen zullen vallen* / het sta**PP**en van de stad in angst",[20] in a stifling landscape of survival. Chaos is represented in verses which are placed randomly on the page and move in different directions, reflecting explosions, flight, the noise of sirens, scattered bodies and limbs everywhere (Figure 1).

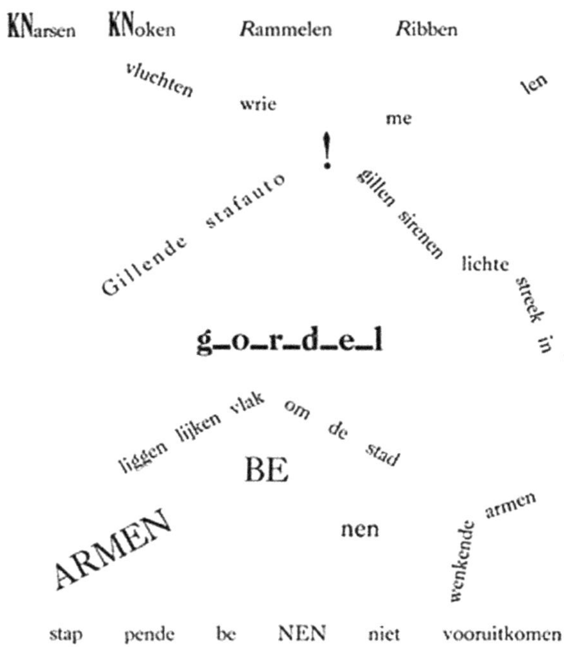

Fig. 1. Fragment of the poem "Bedreigde stad", in: Van Ostaijen (2021, n.p.; De Ridder 2021, p. 113).

---

18 "Visé march Liège mortars" […] "March-past through Brussels all day and all night" […] "the flickering hoRIzon / the distant tower and blazing FIRe"[…] "the debacle".

19 "*bang bang crump crackle crumping crackle crash*".

20 "The paCing **C**ity / *the forts will hold they'll fall they'll hold they'll fall* / the paCing fearful **C**ity".

"Bedreigde stad", as is the case in many of the poems in *Bezette stad*, naturally uses the three languages French, Dutch and German, which were used, read, heard and spoken back then. Popular operettas were also mixed with famous German army songs "Puppchen Du bist mein Augenstirn / Puppchen mein liebes Puppchen / Heil Dir im **Siegerkranz**"[21] (De Ridder 2021, p. 102).

On 9 October 1914, the Van Ostaijen family fled the Netherlands, as did many citizens of Antwerp. Amidst the chaos, the German Army moved from Brussels to Antwerp, which became a mecca for prostitutes from the whole country, because as well as fear there was also desire: "Alle hoeren uit het gehele land / en dat marsjeert dat doet de truk / langs de boulevards" […] "angst en begeerte".[22] Female literary and operatic characters from Puccini, like Manon and Mimi, enter scene; the war has not left them indifferent either: "tul goud zilver voile Mimi Manon pailjetten en tanden / de patronne en grande soirée / men heeft niet de tijd zich om te kleden / de obus valt / zonder / *un client mesdames voyons*".[23] Van Ostaijen also brings into his poem the iconic character from the mid-19th Century Juliette Récamier (1777–1849), the organiser of a famous literary salon in Paris. There is no money to flee, but if there were, where could she find a couturier to dress her?: "Gaby-Récamier heeft geen poen te vluchten / tailleur te ouderwets trimmen uitgesloten / Ah c'est la merde merde pour les Boches merde pour tout le monde".[24]

The end of the poem, located once again in an Antwerp now completely overtaken by the occupiers, demonstrates the counterpoint between the losers and winners, between exodus and victory: "verslagen leger / zegevierend leger" […] "EKSODE /!**SIEG**!"[25]

In the marathon homage to Paul van Ostaijen on 22 February 2021, the actor Tom van Bauwel read, on the stage of the *Elckerlijk* theatre of Antwerp, an extract from "Bedreigde stad" by the Flemish poet.[26] Then, as part of the same event,

---

21 "Puppchen Du bist mein Augenstern / Puppchen mein liebes Puppchen / **Heil Dir im Siegerkranz**".

22 "All the whores of the whole country / and they do well it does the trick /along the boulevards" […] "fear and desire".

23 "tulle gold silver voile Mimi Manon sequins and teeth / the madam up to the nines / no time to change / the shell falls / without / *un client mesdames voyons*".

24 "Gaby – Recamier no dough to flee / suit way out of style streetwalking impossible / Ah c'est la merde merde pour les Boches merde pour tout le monde".

25 "defeated army / victorious army" […] "Exodus /!**SIEG**!".

26 deBuren: *Boem Paukeslag!,* 23 February 2021, 2m38s-6m34s, YouTube, retrieved 17.01.2023, from https://www.youtube.com/watch?v=KRY9bb5IKHs. It can also be listened to on *Soundcloud*: Van Bouwel "Bedreigde stad" 2021.

Lucky Fonz III, a Dutch singer, composer and performance artist, staged his artistic creation called "Besmette stad / Bedreigde stad", at "De Brakke Grond", the centre of Flemish culture in Amsterdam, with a mixture of recital, musical performance and singing.[27] In the performance he says he feels caught up in the spirit of experimentation transmitted in the Van Ostaijens' poem, which inspired his own artistic production. Voice and electric drums helped him reproduce the military sounds and gunshots; these aggressive sounds are, according to him, present in the whole *Bezette stad* collection. The crash of the sounds is already audible at the start of his own poem:[28] "Granaten groot groter GROOTST…/ Groot = gevaar / Groter = gevaarlijker / En grootst = gevaarlijkstst".[29]

Lucky Fonz III created his work at the start of the pandemic. In his piece, he notes that two contrasting associations are already apparent in the first wave of lockdown: it appears that we are on holiday and it appears that we are at war, "Het lijkt wel vakantie" […] "Het lijkt wel oorlog".[30] In the act of recycling, Lucky Fonz establishes a parallel between the war in the original poem and the idea that the situation of the pandemic suggests that "it's like a war". Both situations were new experience for both artists. Like the war, lockdown produced a commotion. It was unexpected and inexplicable; understanding it required new words to explain it, to talk about it, and that is where the new parallel with the work of Paul van Ostaijen was established. Throughout his anthology the Flemish poet uses language associated with war films, as well as highlighting cinematographic techniques to show the war, with a new and explosive language. The artist Lucky Fonz III was struck by this journalistic approach in the work *Bezette stad* by Paul van Ostaijen, so his artistic response creates a of record of images of certain places and situations in the city under lockdown which have impacted him. He does so by means of impetuous and energetic poetics, with a story in which cinema also plays an important role, just as it did one hundred years ago in a new art form in the work of Van Ostaijen (Pakhuis de Zwijger 2020, 45m40s-59m19s).

Lucky Fonz observes that, having so much free time during the pandemic and at the same time nothing to do, "Hoe minder je beweegt hoe beter / Zeker

27 deBuren: *Boem Paukeslag!*, 23 February 2021, 7m11s-15m22s, YouTube, retrieved 17.01.2023, from https://www.youtube.com/watch?v=KRY9bb5IKHs.

28 The subsequent verses, unless specified otherwise, correspond to the work of Lucky Fonz III "Besmette stad / Bedreigde stad": De Ridder / Bongers-Dek (2021, pp. 49–53.

29 "Grenades Big Bigger BIGGEST…/ Big = Danger / Bigger = More Dangerous / And Biggest = Most Dangerous". The translation into English of the Dutch verses of "Besmette stad /Bedreigde stad" (De Ridder / Bongers- Dek 2021, 49–53), is my translation. I would like to give my warmest thanks to Harry Rijnen for revising the translation.

30 "It looks like a holiday" … "It looks like war".

als je het al hebt / We verslaan door met z'n allen / Zo min mogelijk / Zo min mogelijk / Zo min mogelijk / Te doen",[31] people resume activities that used to be undertaken in the past, like board games, "ik hoorde dat de bordspellen weer populair worden",[32] as if horror and entertainment were reconciled. They are thus recovering a situation in which the analogue world predominated. The language of war is also used by the artist with analogue board games or pre-digital video games of the 1980s or 1990s: Risk and Stratego (games of strategy), video games, both non-violent (PacMan, Tetris) and violent (Fifa, Call of Duty). By using the language of war, like "Granaten", "afvuren", "landmijnen", "dynamiet", "opgegroeid met oorlogskreten"[33] he portrays a situation of contamination, disease and defencelessness. When the first wave of the pandemic begins to recede, and people begin to return to the streets little by little, he calls on historic moments, referring to the fact that no fighter planes are seen any more: "Er is geen Spitfire ...", and uses the cinema, mentioning the artificial intelligence aircraft which represent a deadly threat: "... of Stealth meer te zien".[34]

Lucky Fonz III worked on his artistic piece by searching for appropriate terms for the situation experienced in the pandemic. He ironically shows how the government uses expressions in English and not Dutch to explain the current situation: "We flattenen the curve / Flattenen the curve / Flattening the curve / Dat kan alleen in het engels",[35] giving free rein to a parody in the style of an advertisement: "'Quarantaine! Garçon! Garçon! Quarantaine pour tout le monde!'" By turning the government's words into an advertisement, "RECLAME ...", he ironically criticises the idea that all together we can defeat the virus; and that money is being paid to those who had failed earlier to manage the arrival of the pandemic: "Samen zullen we dit! En samen zullen we dat! / Samen zullen we ons geld uitgeven / Aan de beste provider / De beste voorziener / Die dit ook niet ook had kunnen voorzien".[36] In the sung verses, which are the chorus of the poem, he says that the robbers no longer rob, and those who cry end their grief, and if you want to be with someone, the best thing is to remain as far away as

31 "The less you move the better / Especially if you've already got it / We defeat by all together doing / As little as possible / As little as possible / As little as possible".

32 "I heard board games are getting popular again".

33 "Grenades", "firing", "land mines", "dynamite", "raised with war cries".

34 "There is no more Spitfire or Stealth to be seen".

35 "We flattenen the curve / Flattenen the curve / Flattening the curve / That only works in English".

36 "Together we will do this! "Together we will do this! / Together we will spend our money / With the best provider / The best fore / Who neither couldn't have foreseen this either".

possible: "De rovers stoppen met roven / En de huilers met hun verdriet / Wil jij er ook zijn voor iemand? / Wees er nu dan niet".[37]

While the performance of the actor Tom van Bauwel of the poem "Bedreigde stad" may be considered a type of 'remediation', in which the poem of Van Ostaijen acquires a new significance in a new medium in the postdigital age, the artist Lucky Fonz III uses both remediation and re-creation as a type of recycling in his response to the coronavirus crisis, because by updating the reference poem he is not making a copy. He says explicitly that he uses the poem as an inspiration in its documentary aspect and images, in the warlike language, in the parody, in the clashing noises and contradiction between the fear of war/disease and the desire/pleasure of brothels/games and videogames. From his choice of title it is clear that a parallel is established between the modern-day contaminated city ("Besmette stad") and the threatened city of one hundred years ago ("Bedreigde stad"). The strategy of recycling which dominates the poem by Lucky Fonz III is transformation, as existing materials have been considered in its creation, but they have been altered, giving rise to a result that is different from the original. His response to Van Ostaijen's poem is a performance, whose text is now included in the volume *Besmette stad* (De Ridder / Bongers-Dek 2021, 49–53).

2. 3. "Rouwstad" (Paul van Ostaijen) versus "Ragtime Nightmare" (Shamisa Debroey)

The poem "Rouwstad" ("City of grief") by Paul van Ostaijen[38] refers to the aircraft bombings in October 1917 by the English allies; the order is for the lights to be put out. However, there are flashes of lights in homes and cafés; and as if the city residents were on a site where they couldn't move, the artillery can be heard, "VLIEGERAANVALLEN / Burgers sirenen verwittigd / moeten / 1 2 3 / overal donkerte / Licht in de kamer toontinteling van violet naar **Zwart** / op linnen en papier / kaffees= / onbewegelike pantersauto's / licht geschut".[39] From the outside, the glass of the windows reflects the few lights that can be seen outside; and if you

37 "The robbers stop robbing / And the howlers with their grief / Do you want to be there for someone too? / Then don't be there now".

38 The poem "Rouwstad" of Paul van Ostaijen can be accessed at: Van Ostaijen (2021); deBuren: *Rouwstad* (2020), retrieved 17.01.2023, from https://deburen.eu/magazine/rouwstad; the critical study of the poem is available at: De Ridder (2021, pp. 197–202). The English translation is of the original work by Paul van Ostaijen (Colmer 2016).

39 "A E R I A L AT TA C K S / Civilian sirens must be / notified / 1 2 3 / darkness everywhere / Light in the room tints flickering violet to Black / on linen and paper / cafés = / unmoving armoured cars / light artillery".

enter the café you see through the windows the same image that you see from the outside, but the light is being extinguished and the blue colours are becoming black and dominating the obscurity and the penumbra, "al de vensters zien straat door kleurglasbrillen" [...] "blauw-zwart zinken van gedoofde dingen / Vult / dieper **DONK**er **d**e **d**uistere straat / vallen".[40] The poem expresses the cries in the street and the trembling, followed by silence, obscurity and fear in a phantom city: "**Gil** / straat / ik / trem / geruisloos / valt de gil / **S**pokend straat / **S**piegel / me zelf / was ik **b**ang / dan zou / **A**ngst / niet zijn".[41] The image of tenuous light, obscurity, penumbra and, again, flickering light appears to indicate what the city looks like wherever gazes or passes the poetic 'I'. And the silence increases, yet in a misty, dull boom we hear modern music, ragtime; and simultaneously the ear hears and the eye sees the silence that seems to come from a cafe where, on the contrary, popular music can be heard, where the light is warm and there are people who are drinking and listening to music, with the tables adorned with flowers. Outside, however, there is sadness: "hebben scheppen lantaarns fluweel rondom / dansende krans / donkerte om / licht / trems scheppen om zich hun duisternis / meeschuivende duisternis met licht / geruislozer / zinnen simultaan / het oor hoort –het geruisloze– dat / het oog Ziet" [...] "dof echoëren in mist / **RAG** / fluwelen rijtuig / **RAG TIME**" [...] "warm licht / reuk van guitaren / horen van whisky en / verwelkte roos / *je bloem Musette* / is het triestig buiten / *Il fait si doux près de toi* / want / Jaarsma / warmt goed".[42]

In Soundcloud: *Rouwstad* (2021) the actor Tom van Bauwel recreates the poem Rouwstad by Paul van Ostaijen. The illustrator Shamisa Debroey's drawing "Ragtime Nightmare" is a graphic response to the poem by Paul van Ostaijen[43] (Figure 2).

---

40 "all windows see street through coloured glass / windows like German professors / blue-black sinking / of extinguished things / Filling / deeper **DARK**ness **d**im **d**ismal street / Falling".

41 "**Scream** street / ME / tram / noiseless / scream falls / **S**pectral **S**treet/ reflecting / me myself / if I were / **S**cared / **F**ear /would not be".

42 "streetlamps creating velvet surround / d a n c i n g c o r o n a / darkness surrounds/l i g h t / trams creating their darkness around them / darkness sliding along with light / less noise / senses simultaneous / the ear hears – the noiselessness – / the eye Sees"... "muffled echoes in mist / **R A G** /velvet carriage /
R A G T I M E" [...] "warm light / smell of guitars / sound of whisky and / wilted rose / *your flower Musette* / if it's miserable outside / *it's lovely near you* / because / Jaarsma / warms well".

43 deBuren: *Ragtime Nightmare,* 03.06.2020, retrieved 17.01.2023, from https://deburen.eu/besmette-stad/33/shamisa-debroey; De Ridder / Bongers-Dek (2021, pp. 140–141).

Fig. 2. Shamisa Debroey: "Ragtime Nightmare". In: De Ridder / Bongers-Dek (2021, pp 141–142).

In the illustration "Ragtime Nightmare", Shamisa Debroey depicts a protest. She chooses a quote from Van Ostaijen's poem: "IK / BEN / DE / STRAAT",[44] in which the poet wants to become one with what is happening on the street. Debroey uses these words as a text on a protester's banner, because he wants the street to be heard against injustice, inequality and repression. One of the first things that catches her attention in Van Ostaijen's poem is the reference made to the musical genre 'RAG TIME' and for the artist this evokes the title of the song "Ragtime Nightmare" by Tom Turpin, which lends its name to the title of her drawing. She adds that for a pianist it is very difficult to play this music, which is cyclical, and may lead to confusion because it is played so quickly. Shamisa Debroey relates it to the disasters of war in the poem by Van Ostaijen, and, in the period when she created her work, to the pandemic and the difficulties of emigration, elements that are repeated throughout history. Shamisa Debroey states that when she created this artistic work, she was very affected by the movement *Black Lives Matter*, so she could not ignore the emotion it provoked in her. The central character in the drawing is wearing a T-shirt with the slogan "I CAN'T BREATHE"; this links it not only to the time referred to in the poem "Rouwstad" of being enclosed and unable to breathe and the idea of being isolated, but also establishes a parallel with the death of George Floyd at the hands of the police on 25 May 2020.[45] In addition, what interests her in Van Ostaijen's poem is the chaos, the hustle and bustle of the city and the screams. The same word is used both in his poem and the illustration: "Gil". With "De duisternis dringt" she also makes clear that the darkness is imposed, referring to the poet's verse saying that in the depths of the penumbra darkness dominates: "Dieper in Duisternis Dringt Donkerte".[46] There are also images in the illustration of Debroey which reference the poem of Van Ostaijen in the verses: "masker / **O** / masker / op / mij /toe /**!**",[47] as if he were a soldier approaching the poetic "I" with a mask of war, one imagines to alleviate the tear gas and other toxic substances. The illustrator relates this giant "o" of Van Ostaijen to the "o" in the word "mond" (mouth) and in "mondmasker" (mask), and in this way portrays the mouths of the demonstrators covered with masks against the virus, and as masks to alleviate political repression. At the same time, she relates having to wear a mask to not being able to breathe, to the closed city

44 "I / AM / THE / STREET". The translation into English of the Dutch verses of "Ragtime Nightmare" (De Ridder / Bongers-Dek 2021, 140–141), is my translation.

45 deBuren: *Officiële opening Besmette Stad*, 04.02.2021, 03m04s-04m12s Youtube, retrieved 17.01.2023, from https://www.youtube.com/watch?v=2d6vUxs5I8Q&t=339s.

46 "Dark Driving Deeper into Darkness".

47 "**Mask / O**h /mask / to / wards / me!".

with people who look out from the inside and who, despite everything, go out to see what is happening. This gives rise to a drawing where the past and the present coincide, where they have a great deal in common. Her intention is to show how the two contexts correspond and to motivate the public about the reality of inequality and injustice.[48]

A kind of remediation recycling has been applied in Debroey's work, inasmuch as the content of Van Ostaijen's poem is represented in another medium. Quite a few of the characteristics of the old medium have been incorporated into the new, with the use of the verses: "Ik ben de straat", "Het oog ziet", "De duisternis dringt",[49] for example. These serve the artist's purpose of making her own recreation, that is, the updating of the original work. Similarly, when the drawing is viewed everyone has new experiences and interpretations, which gives a new life to the street, and at the same time appeals to some elements present in Van Ostaijen's poem. In this sense, Debroey's artistic work uses a strategy for transforming the original poem into a different medium with a different meaning, and with the intention that the new material should be manipulated and open to different interpretations and perceptions. Her chosen strategy of decontextualisation uses elements of the original poem to place the recycled element in a new social and historical context, giving the work a new meaning.

2. 4. "Banale dans" (Paul van Ostaijen) versus "Banale dans" (Lisette Ma Neza and Maja-Ajmia Yde Zellama)

The poem "Banale dans" ("Banal dance")[50] by Paul van Ostaijen shows a city which suffers terrible deterioration, but where there is dancing; a city which is in movement, and however banal it may appear, there is dancing for pleasure: "Leven giert / leven grijpt / en leven / valt / KnAK / dol draperen step / DANS van begeren".[51] However, dancing does not end up producing satisfaction; life has

48 deBuren: From *24u van Paul van Ostaijen*, 22.02.2021, 2h18m30s-2h28m32s YouTube, retrieved 17.01.2023, from https://www.youtube.com/watch?v=QKn-NyWq8BY&t=8330s.

49 "Darkness pushes".

50 The poem "Banale dans" by Paul van Ostaijen can be accessed on: Van Ostaijen 2021, n.p.; also on deBuren: *Banale dans* 2020 retrieved 17.01.2023, from https://deburen.eu/magazine/banale-dans; the critical study of the poem in De Ridder (2021, pp. 203–204). The English translation is of the original work by Paul van Ostaijen (Colmer 2016).

51 "Life screams / life seizes / and life / falls / CracK / crazed draping one-step / DANCE of desire".

fallen apart and the instruments and music, whether ancient or modern, end up being shattered, with a confirmation of death by cardiac event: "en leven / valt / altijd" […] "en DANS / valt / leven" […] "of violen of banjo's / VERTEERD WORDEN IN onBEKENDE GLOED / BANJ**O** BANJO BANJO zegt KNAK / en de / arts affection Cardiaque".[52]

Tom van Bauwel interprets and recreates the poem "Banale dans" by Paul Van Ostaijen on the stage of the *Elckerlijk* theatre in Antwerp.[53] At the same event the visual artists Lisete Ma Neza[54] and Maja-Ajmia Yde Zellama offer an artistic performance based on the same poem by Van Ostaijen[55] (Figure 3).

Fig. 3. Lisette Ma Neza and Maja-Ajmia Yde Zellama "Banale dans". In: De Ridder / Bongers-Dek (2021, pp. 144–146).

52 "and life / falls / al ways" […] "and DANCE / life / falls" […] "or violins or banjos / CONSUMED IN AN unKNOWN GLOW / "BANJ**O** /BANJO / BANJO / says CRACK / and the / doctor heart attACK".

53 deBuren: *Boem Paukeslag!,* 23.02.2021, 1h19m01s-01h20m51s, Youtube, retrieved 17.01.2023, from https://www.youtube.com/watch?v=KRY9bb5IKHs.

54 First woman writing in Dutch to win the Belgian *Poetry Slam* award.

55 deBuren: *Boem Paukeslag!,* 23.02.2021, 1h21m15s-1h29m30s Youtube, retrieved 17.01.2023, from https://www.youtube.com/watch?v=KRY9bb5IKHs; De Ridder / Bongers-Dek (2021, pp. 144–146).

A parallel is established between the world described in the poem by Van Ostaijen and the time in which the artists live. The creators admit that the inspiration for their own work mainly lies in the verses where the Flemish poet describes the dance of grey-haired people and young girls who know nothing of the reality of a collapsed city: "midden in dans vergrijzen haren / staan nog te midden jonge meiden / voortdansen over onze / VAL / Weten niets van werkelikheid / dromend door straten staan".[56] The young girls, say the artists, use the Internet during their lockdown and feel united, using *Tik Tok*, indicating that during the lockdown they did little more than eat, sleep and watch stories on *Instagram*. They share the sadness of losing their fathers, brothers or daughters: "jonge meisjes tiktokken / weten niets van werkelijkheid / verliezen hun vader" [...] "droom over de straten / vergeet dat er ooit toekomst was / eten slapen / eten slapen / eten slapen / *Instagram* / eten slapen" [...] "het verdriet van België zit in Brussel verstopt / 1234 / broeders die ons zijn ontnomen / 5678 / dochters om het leven gekomen / 5678".[57] The numbers in the poem establish a parallel between the thousands of deaths in Van Ostaijen's poem, the deaths of the pandemic and the deaths of the political violence in the United States, connecting it with the case of George Floyd.[58] The girls also share their joys, dreams, nightmares, dances, distancing and sisterhood. They know much more than we think about the reality that surrounds them and what is happening to their bodies, sharing many taboos: "klimmen op klimaatproblemen / zijn vrouwen nog voordat ze het weten / jonge meisjes hebben geen gender meer / weten alles over kleine dingen".[59] In the following verses, the girls dance a 'banal dance'. Why do they continue to dance? They dance even when they don't feel well, when they cry, when they are celebrating, when they are together online or offline, because they can't do anything else or know how to do anything else; because they are young

56 "hair turns grey mid-dance / still standing among young girls / dancing on over our / FALL / Knowing nothing of reality / dreaming through streets standing".

57 "young girls tiktok / know nothing of reality / lose their father" [...] "dream about the streets / forget there was ever a future / eat sleep / eat sleep / eat sleep / *Instagram* / eat sleep" [...] "Belgium's sorrow is hidden in Brussels / 1234 / brothers who have been taken from us / 5678 / daughters perished". The translation into English of the Dutch verses of "Banale dans" (De Ridder 2021, 144–146), is my translation. I would like to give my warmest thanks to Harry Rijnen for revising the translation.

58 deBuren: *Officiële opening Besmette Stad*, 04.02.2021, 4m14s-5m34s Youtube, retrieved 17.01.2023, from https://www.youtube.com/watch?v=2d6vUxs5I8Q&t=339s.

59 "climbing on climate problems / are women even before they know it / young girls no longer have gender / know everything about little things".

girls, girls who are afraid – because of this, they still dance: "redenen waarom we nog steeds dansen? / omdat we niet anders kunnen / omdat we niets weten / omdat we jonge meisjes zijn" [...] "omdat we niets anders kunnen / omdat we anders zijn / omdat ons angstig voelen / daarom dansen we / dansen we nog".[60]

The artistic proposal of Lisette Ma Neza and Maja-Ajmia Yde Zellama can be read on paper (De Ridder / Bongers-Dek 2021, pp. 144–146), but it has been created using the app *Tik Tok*.[61] According to Bongers-Dek, it went viral when it was published on the social media app.[62] Thus, they are inspired by what young people experience when they suffer a situation of pandemic and lockdown at a time when they are beginning to live and enjoy life. The poetic response to the coronavirus crisis is reflected by recycling this image expressed in the poem by Paul van Ostaijen, remediated and recreated in a postdigital era with its fears and hopes, a *Tik Tok* video-poem, where there is dancing and authentic images are used of the authors' friends and the poem also shows images that criticise political violence. Social media allow the work of Paul van Ostaijen to be transformed and recomposed, and in this way establish new connections and circulate again, spreading to infinity. They show an authentic and modern-day art, fundamentally of young people (although it may be extended to other generations) who depend on social media; or rather, have depended on it during the lockdown, using these media as a source of escape and a means to express their feelings. At any event, the artists admit that what they mainly wanted to reflect was what it means to be a young girl at this stage of the pandemic, how they see this world; and the means through which they express their experience, the social media platform *Tik Tok*, appeared to be the most obvious option for the artists to use.

3. Conclusions

With the premise of reusing the idea or vision of the city in *Bezette stad* by Paul van Ostaijen, those responsible for the macro-project "Besmette stad" gave complete freedom to the chosen artists to create their work, based on a

60 "reasons why we still dance? / because we can't do otherwise / because we know nothing / because we are young girls" [...] "because unable of anything else / because we are different / because feel anxious / that's why we dance / we still dance".

61 deBuren: *Besmette stad/ Banale dans* van Lisette Ma Neza en Maja Ajmia Yde Zellama', 05.06.2020, Youtube, retrieved 17.01.2023, from https://www.youtube.com/watch?v=1U4Cve6cPjE.

62 Statement communicated personally at a working meeting.

poem from the collection. However, there were some objectives which had to be furthered by each of them. The purpose of the new creation was, firstly, to provide an artistic response to the original poem; and, secondly, to respond to the crisis triggered by the COVID-19 pandemic in the spring of 2020. The aim of those managing the project was not for these new works to talk about the Flemish poet, but nevertheless, the title of van Ostaijen's collection features in the name of the project and subsequently in the works published on paper (De Ridder / Bongers-Dek 2021; De Ridder 2021; Eble et al. 2022). Many new works also use the titles of van Ostaijen's poems, adopt an approach similar to his, and moreover apply the concepts of a multimedia work and/or a collective work, with Flemish-Dutch artistic duos very often working together at the request of those responsible for the project. Van Ostaijen worked on his volume in Berlin, with the sculptor Oscar Jespers, who was in Antwerp. The latter was responsible for the reproductions of the woodcuts which appear in the collection and the typography and layout so characteristic of the poetical work.

The poetry of Paul van Ostaijen has been recycled in a variety of art forms, and through different media and social media, in which it is no longer possible to make a distinction between the analogue and the digital. Literature no longer has a single material location, as explained by Brillenburg Wurth (ed.) (2012, p. 1): "Literature no longer has a single material location, and one may wonder if it ever had one". The frontiers of events and meetings between artists, languages and spaces have also become blurred. The whole concept of this macro-project as it has grown has developed so many tentacles, as Matthijs de Ridder says in the preface to *De Aftocht* (Eble et al. 2022, p. 10), that all the creations become one, or form part of the whole. Moreover, the relations of materiality and virtuality have undergone considerable transformations in the last two decades (Brillenburg Wurth 2018, pp. 1–23), which has contributed to the fact that both complement each other, dilute each other and need each other.

In the creations of "Besmette stad", the characteristics of the postdigital are revealed, with a permanent connectivity, requiring interaction, dialogue and participation between artists and the general public. In the new artistic works, there is a multitude of postdigital features: emojis, neologisms inherent to the new technologies, apps, references to social media as agents of the pandemic: "Toen Facebook werd besmet en Twitter zich bemoeide met prognostiek" (Pfeijffer 2021, p. 16).[63] There are also apps to take you on a tour around the city of Antwerp,

63 "When Facebook got infected and Twitter meddled with forecasting" (De Ridder / Bongers-Dek 2021).

inspired by the stages of the life and work of Paul van Ostaijen and present in the collection *Bezette stad* exhibitions, concerts and meetings of creators and experts on the poet's life and work in Flanders, the Netherlands and recently in Germany.[64]

There are elements of postdigital recycling in the "Besmette stad" project which can be found in all the artistic works created in this collective work: elements such as collective reading and writing strategies. The result is the creative appropriation of a historical past, as well as a rewriting of both, the poems and the historical past, with the task of separating oneself from the context in which they are based to locate in a new context where a new project can begin. At the same time there is a recreation of the original work in the performance of the poems by the artist and composer Tom van Bauwel.

Often in "Besmette stad" the use of technology makes it possible for the work created to lend itself to repetition and interaction, and therefore to multiple interpretations and readings. Moreover, the use of social media to make artistic creations is very successful in this recycling framework, as it includes many characteristics that are intrinsic to the postdigital age, such as interaction, immediacy, reaching many people at the same time, the value of the authentic, remediation, reproduction, recontextualization and (re)circulation. In this way, the work becomes a dynamic phenomenon, traveling through new circuits of pooling and sharing.

That so many artists are simultaneously talking about something that is current and that can be conceived of holistically an artistic monument in itself, perhaps only possible in the postdigital age in which it is taking place. In general, these artists are in favour of a type of activist art and against artistic autonomy, which is considered exclusive and solipsistic (Ham / Vitse 2019b, p. 5). The desire for relationships and the sharing of artistic experiences through social media is thus a characteristic of making art which works within sociocultural contexts. Moreover, relations and identities are frequently relative and more than ever mediated. This responds to our condition of permanent digital connectivity (Op de Beek / Van Dijk 2019, p. 63).

In many artistic manifestations of the project "Besmette stad", there is a crossover between different arts and media, which is another characteristic of the postdigital age. This helps ensure that we are in contact with literature, which

64 The homage on 27 and 28 April 2022 to Paul Van Ostaijen in Berlin marks the start of a cultural and artistic tour across different cities of Germany, in *Neerlandistiek*, 24.04.2022, retrieved 17.01.2023, from https://neerlandistiek.nl/2022/04/27-28-april-2022-eine-hommage-an-den-flamischen-dichter-paul-van-ostaijen-in-berlin/.

against all predictions remains alive, entertains and provides enjoyment for us ('t Hooft (2016, pp. 14–18)).

It is no longer so important where this artistic creation is located: whether in a document, a poem, an exhibition or on the facade of a building. Nor is it crucial through which medium we find it. Kila van der Starre, who has for years collected poetry that is outside of books,[65] concludes that the results of her research tend to show (with minor exceptions) that most poetic manifestations are experienced, used and circulated outside of books. She adds that the dynamism of poetry is not linear but circular, so the recipients, readers or users of poetry adapt it and spread it in different situations and with the aid of different actors (Van der Starre 2021, 448).

The work *Bezette stad* by Paul van Ostaijen cannot be said to have fallen into oblivion in the last 100 years since its publication. Rather, for the average lover of Dutch-language literature, the work of the Flemish poet is linked to verses which have been repeated throughout the last century in different contexts and media and are found in the cultural imaginary of the people of the Netherlands and Flanders. The key phrase "Boem Paukeslag" has appeared on T-shirts, for example; woodcuts of the word "Zeppelin" in the form of a zeppelin, can also be seen on all types of mugs and other utensils. The implementation of the project has led to a rediscovery and recovery of the original work, with different strategies of recycling such as collaborative reading and transformation of the poems located on a map together with new creations, thus establishing a dialogue with the public visiting the website. Moreover, this material, which is accessible and digitally archived, implies that actions are being taken for the (re)circulation of the original text and its spread, and that ways of recovering the cultural memory are being promoted by means of postdigital participation.

This chapter itself also represents a form of (re)circulation of not only the work *Bezette stad*, but also of *Besmette stad*; because all the actors in society, whether artists, critics or receptors, contribute in one way or another, collaboratively, to keep alive, and give a new life to, the poetic art present in both anthologies.

---

65 Her website "Straatpoëzie", retrieved 17.01.2023, from https://straatpoezie.nl/ aims to create an inventory through *crowdsourcing* of 'poetry outside the book', poetry in the public spaces of the Netherlands and Flanders.

References

Andersen, Christian Ulrik / Cox, Geoff / Papadopoulos, Georgios (eds.): *A Peer Reviewed Journal About: POST-DIGITAL RESEARCH* vol. 3 (1) 2014, retrieved 17.01.2023, from https://aprja.net//issue/view/8400.

Brillenburg Wurth, Kiene / Driscoll, Kári / Pressman, Jessica (eds.): *Book Presence in a Digital Age*. Bloomsbury Academic: New York 2018.

Brillenburg Wurth, Kiene (ed.): *Between Page and Screen. Remaking Literature through cinema and Cyberspace*. Frodham University Press: New York 2012.

Bryant, Gabriele: "Peter Behrens y el problema del arte total en los albores del siglo XX". In: *Cuaderno de notas* (5) 1997, pp. 57–76, retrieved 17.01.2023, from http://polired.upm.es/index.php/cuadernodenotas/article/view/790/820.

Colmer, David [translator]: *Occupied City*. Smokestack Books 2016. Author: Paul Van Ostaijen: *Bezette stad*. Het Sinjaal: Antwerpen 1921.

Cramer, Florian: "What is 'Post-digital'?". *APRJA, A Peer-Reviewed Journal About:* POST-DIGITAL RESEARCH vol. 3 (1) 2014, pp. 10–24, retrieved 17.01.2023, from DOI https://doi.org/10.7146/aprja.v3i1.116068.

deBuren: *Besmette stad* (n.d.), retrieved 17.01.2023, from https://deburen.eu/besmette-stad.

De Ridder, Matthijs: *Boem. Paukeslag. Op strooptocht door Paul van Ostaijens* Bezette stad. Pelckmans: Kalmthout 2021.

De Ridder, Matthijs / Bongers-Dek, Willem (eds.): *Besmette stad. Vijfenzestig kunstenaars antwoorden op* Bezette stad *van Paul van Ostaijen*. Pelckmans: Kalmthout 2021.

Eble, Anna / Nagtegaal, Marleen / De Ridder, Matthijs / Bongers-Dek, Willem (eds.): *De Aftocht*. Pelckmans: Kalmthout 2022.

FARO. Vlaams steunpunt voor cultureel erfgoed vzw.: *Erfgoedapp* 2021 [Mobile app]. Google Play, retrieved 17.01.2023, from https://play.google.com/store/apps/details?id=be.faro.erfgoedapp; https://erfgoedapp.be/.

Forten.nl *FORTEN VERMAAK TIJDENS DE LOCKDOWN*, 19.12.2021, retrieved 17.01.2023, from https://forten.nl/forten-vermaak/.

Ham, Laurens / Vitse, Sven (eds.): *Het literair klimaat 2010–2019. Dietsche Warande en Belfort (DWB)* (3) 2019a.

Ham, Laurens / Vitse, Sven: "Het literair klimaat 2010–2019: een inleiding". In: Ham, Laurens / Vitse, Sven (eds.): *Dietsche Warande en Belfort (DWB)* (3) 2019b, pp. 5–10.

't Hooft, Niels: "Vloeibare literatuur in een digitaal tijdperk. Cross-overs tussen literatuur en games". In: Van Hamersveld, Ineke (ed.): *Boekman* 108 is in!,

Boekmanstichting: Amsterdam 2016, pp. 14–18, retrieved 17.01.2023, from https://www.boekman.nl/wp-content/uploads/2021/08/bm108_hooft-t-vloeibare_literatuur.pdf.

Llamas Ubieto, Miriam: 'Postdigital ahora'. (Serie: *Cuadernos del ahora* n. 1) 2020, pp. 1–13, retrieved 01.08.2023, from https://docta.ucm.es/entities/publication/cfb16b9c-fa20-4922-ab25-053e7d33d133.

Llamas Ubieto, Miriam / Goicoechea de Jorge, María (coords.): *Rec-Lit: Estrategias de reciclaje cultural y literario en la era postdigital.* Repositorio institucional, Universidad Complutense de Madrid: Madrid 2022, retrieved 06.07.2023, from http://repositorios.fdi.ucm.es/REC-LIT/view/paginas/view_paginas.php?id=1.

Op de Beek, Esther / Van Dijk, Yra: "Niña Weijers en Nina Polak: een nieuwe generatie auteurs maakt naam". *Dietsche Warande en Belfort (DWB): Het literair klimaat 2010–2019* (3) 2019, pp. 59–69.

Pakhuis de Zwijger: *LIVE / Amsterdam Vertelt #5: Besmette Stad on stage / Wat gebeurt er als makers van nu in dialoog gaan met Paul van Ostaijen? Tune in!* Facebook, 12.06.2020, retrieved 17.01.2023, from https://www.facebook.com/pakhuis.dezwijger/videos/277729296915276.

Pfeijffer, Ilja L.: "Bezette stad", In: De Ridder, Matthijs / Bongers-Dek, Willem (eds.): *Besmette stad. Vijfenzestig kunstenaars antwoorden op* Bezette stad *van Paul van Ostaijen*. Pelckmans 2021, pp. 15–19.

Souncloud: *Album Bezette stad*, 2021, retrieved 17.01.2023, from https://soundcloud.com/search?q=Bezette%20stad.

Soundcloud: "Banale dans", 2021, retrieved 17.01.2023, from https://soundcloud.com/deburen-eu/bezette-stad-16-banale-dans-door-tom-van-bauwel.

Soundcloud: "Bedreigde stad", 2021 retrieved 17.01.2023, from https://soundcloud.com/deburen-eu/bezette-stad-2-bedreigde-stad-door-tom-van-bauwel.

Soundcloud: "Rouwstad", 2021, retrieved 17.01.2023, from https://soundcloud.com/deburen-eu/bezette-stad-15-rouwstad-door-tom-van-bauwel.

Van der Starre, Kila: *Poëzie buiten het boek. De circulatie en het gebruik van poëzie,* Universiteit Utrecht 2021, retrieved 17.01.2023, from DOI: https://doi.org/10.33540/436.

Van der Starre, Kila: *Straatpoëzie,* 2007, retrieved 17.01.2023, from https://straatpoezie.nl/.

Van Ostaijen, Paul: *Bezette stad.* Boom Uitgevers: Amsterdam 2021.

Van Ostaijen, Paul: *Bezette stad.* Het Sienjaal: Antwerpen 1921.

Vlaanderen.be / Departement Cultuur, Jeugd & Media: "Manuscript 'Bezette Stad' aangekocht door Vlaamse Gemeenschap", 22.02.2021, retrieved 17.01.2023, from https://www.vlaanderen.be/cjm/nl/nieuws/manuscript-bezette-stad-aangekocht-door-vlaamse-gemeenschap.

Figures:

Figure 1. Van Ostaijen, Paul: "Bedreigde stad". In: Ostaijen, Paul van: *Bezette stad* [1921] 2021, n.p.; De Ridder 2021, p. 113.

Figure 2. Debroey, Shamisa: "Ragtime Nightmare". In: De Ridder, Matthijs / Bongers-Dek, Willem (eds.): *Besmette stad. Vijfenzestig kunstenaars antwoorden op* Bezette stad *van Paul van Ostaijen*. Pelckmans 2021, pp. 141–142; deBuren: 'Ragtime Nightmare', 03.06.2020, retrieved 17.01.2023, from https://deburen.eu/besmette-stad/33/shamisa-debroey.

Figure 3. Ma Neza, Lisette / Yde Zellama, Maja-Ajmia: "Banale dans". In: De Ridder, Matthijs / Bongers-Dek, Willem (eds.): *Besmette stad. Vijfenzestig kunstenaars antwoorden op* Bezette stad *van Paul van Ostaijen*. Pelckmans 2021, pp. 144–146.

Adrián Menéndez de la Cuesta González
Universidad Complutense de Madrid

From Memes to Literature and Vice-Versa: The Recycling Canon

Abstract: Nowadays, cultural recycling implies an increasing exchange between memetic and literary practices: social media memes remediate literary works and contemporary literature incorporates references to memes. This article considers a sample of both phenomena. Literary memes in social media are analysed within the corporative Twitter account of *@SparkNotes* (https://twitter.com/sparknotes), driven by community manager Courtney Gorter. The account has gained notoriety within the Twitter community and received widespread media coverage because of its success creating viral memes on classic literature. In parallel, the novels *Gideon the Ninth* and *Harrow the Ninth*, by Tamsyn Muir, have been chosen as an example of literature quoting memes. The abundance of such Internet jokes has been noted as one of the writer's main stylistic features by professional and lay reviewers, as well as by the author herself. The research questions guiding this article are: which canon of literary works is most likely to be recycled and how do literature and memes interact in this recycling loop?

Keywords: memes, canon, literary memes, cultural recycling in social media, *Gideon the Ninth*, *Harrow the Ninth*, Tamsyn Muir, memes and literature, postdigital.

1. Introduction

What is the relationship between literature and Internet memes? What does their intersection tell us about the current cultural ecosystem? What are the canons and dynamics that guide it? This article explores these questions. The results suggest a new paradigm in the way texts relate to other artifacts.

Firstly, the theoretical ground is structured around two apparently unconnected disciplines that come together in this phenomenon. In media studies, memetics are needed for a scientific understanding of what Internet memes are and how they work. In literary studies, canon studies provide background on previous and current dynamics shaping which authors and books are reworked, read and quoted the most. Two cases have been chosen for this article: a Twitter[1] account, *@SparkNotes,* posting literary memes and the novels *Gideon the Ninth* (2019) and *Harrow the Ninth* (2020) by Tamsyn Muir, which often include allusions to Internet memes.

---

1 Now X.

2. Theoretical framework

Even if far from discussing literary memes, Stephen Abblitt provides a sound framework for putting literature and memes in the same picture. When defining the "postdigital literary object", he draws attention to the context of current literary production and consumption: a print paradigm will no longer suffice to explain a cultural scene where traditional books coexist with digital culture. This setting invites the researcher to think of all forms of contemporary culture as belonging to the same network of contagions, influences and contacts shaped by "the advent of personal, mobile, ubiquitous computing" (Abblitt 2019, p. 101). This idea finds echoes in McDonald's suggestion that literature should not be isolated from other media synergies; they constitute external determinants that play a role in shaping the literary field (2016, pp. 41–42). As this article will prove, print novels and even classic literature take part in this synergetic, postdigital world.

2.1. Introduction to memetics

But what exactly is an Internet meme?[2] Limor Shifman defines it as "(a) a *group of digital items sharing common characteristics* of content, form and/or stance; (b) that were created *with awareness of each other*; and (c) were circulated, imitated, and/or transformed *via the Internet by many users*" (2014, pp. 7–8, her emphasis). Hence, mere textuality is not enough to explain the phenomenon: community and circulation are also key identifying features. Research has validated such a networked approach to memes (Segev et al. 2015). And it is this networked approach that allows the articulation of a research question like the one in this article: which is the canon – the most quoted or valued referents – in a given genre of memes? What can be understood by "canon" in such a context will be discussed in the next section.

Shifman distinguishes between founder-based memes – where a source can be identified as pre-existing to the several meme instances – and egalitarian memes – where meme instances repeat a shared formula in the absence of a single clear source (2014, pp. 58–59).

As an explanation of the recycling dynamics of Internet memes, Shifman coins the term "hypermemetic logic" (2014, p. 23). In postdigital culture, memes saturate both public and private spheres (2014, p. 30), as the individuals who are exposed to this meme-scape are well aware of (2014, p. 28). In this sense, they

2 For a wider discussion of the bibliography on the topic, see García Carcedo (2020).

are pervasive: they may arise from any event and be reproduced in all sorts of circumstances, even analogue (2014, p. 23). In other words, everything becomes a potential meme. However, how does literature interact or interfere with hypermemetic logic? Firstly, how do literary memes implement these dynamics? Secondly, what is the relationship between Internet memes and traditional literary recycling dynamics such as non-memetic quotations or allusions to other texts[3] when both strategies coexist within a book? This article attempts to answer these questions.

2.2. Canon and world literature

Asking, as this article does, what the most common references within literary memes are implies introducing the concept of the literary canon. From Auerbach to Bloom, much has been written on the topic. In more than one sense, there cannot be a single conception of the canon or even a single canon at all. In terms of its scope, it has been discussed in national (*The Cambridge History of American Literature*), European (Curtius [1948] 1990), Western (Auerbach [1953] 2003), or world (Damrosch 2003) frames of reference. Likewise, the nature and formation of the canon can be approached from an idealistic perspective, based purely on aesthetic criteria (Altieri 1983; Bloom 1994), or from a materialist perspective. In that case, the premise is that the perception of a literary phenomenon – in Damrosch's case, world literature – only exists inasmuch as there is an implicit list of "what is available to read, in classrooms and on bookstore shelves, on course syllabi and in anthologies for students and general readers" (2003, p. 111).

It is a materialist approach that guides this article. This understanding can be broken down even further according to the source of canon formation or reproduction. Some scholars' work has focused upon academic or pedagogical canons: reading lists "made up of the most frequently taught texts" across the "texts that are taught in college and university settings" (Gallagher 2001, p. 54). These canons can be distinguished from those deduced by the names and titles most referenced as canonical in surveys by media, publishers or booksellers, like the famous BBC Big Read Project (2003), or by literary prizes (Varela Zapata 2008). This article explores a recent source of canon reproduction: an account of

3 I am referring to the recycling dynamics analysed by literary studies under the label intertextuality, following Kristeva (1969, pp. 113, 145, 255), or transtextuality, following Genette (1982, p. 7). Any such allusion to a cultural product that does not fit into Shifman's definition is thus labelled as a non-memetic literary reference.

literary memes. Even if the choice will be discussed more in-depth in the next section, it should be anticipated that the canon that such a case study suggests – the most referenced literary works on a social media account – lies between these two sources. Its canonicity relies on both the para-academic authority of the account, belonging to a publisher of learning guides, and on the quantitative argument already present in Gallagher and Varela-Zapata. Given that, compared to the non-digital circulation of sources of canon reproduction, national or cultural frontiers are not as important in the online circulation of memes, the resulting canon may be a reflection of world literature – though the extent to which this is true will also be investigated in this article.

However, it has been argued that our age is postcanonical in a rather similar sense to how it is postdigital (Damrosch 2009, p. 510); not in the sense that it is defined by the abandonment of the canon, but that it is defined by the aftermath of its efforts to overcome it, rewrite it and, eventually, by the canon growing stronger in an evolved form. After the so-called "Canon Wars", the impact of postcolonial and feminist criticism informs our current understanding of the canon.

These efforts run parallel to the progressive opening of the Western canon – the object of study of Auerbach's generation – to include what would become known as world literature – the object of study of Damrosch's generation. Such evolution must be contextualised as the product of several proposals for restructuring Comparative Literature as a discipline, with the "Bernheimer Report" (1993) being probably the most influential and discussed (Bernheimer 1995). This trend in literary studies invited scholars to normalise the use of translations as the basis for the discipline (Bernheimer 1995, p. 44; Damrosch 2003, p. 111; 2009, p. 497) and to embrace multilingualism and diglossia (Pratt 1995, pp. 61–63). Taking it a step further, even monolingual studies were expected to embrace more diversity and explore the diversity within their fields. An antecedent for this would be Ashcroft, Griffith and Tiffin's focus on language diversity within British colonies, distinguishing between British English as it was inherited from the metropolis and "the english [sic] which the language has become in post-colonial countries" (1989, p. 8). In broader terms, Chow instated Comparative Literature to include a monolingual perspective, discussing internal borders such as those delineated by people of colour or gay and lesbian varieties (Chow 1995, p. 112).

What is the current state of the world literature canon as it is presented and recycled in literary memes? According to Damrosch, world literature stands in "four frames of reference: the global, the regional, the national and the individual" (2009, p. 496). From Goethe to our days, these frames of reference have come to interact ever faster and in more surprising ways. The most renowned anthologies show a growing interest in a global scale (2009, pp. 501–505). Other authors are more sceptical. Müller has pointed out that even if academic discussions and canons may be now increasingly global, influential Western media canons still consistently exclude the Global South (2019, p. 13). Research has confirmed this kind of distance between academic and non-academic canons, where the latter may be more inclined to cover middlebrow authors like J. R. R. Tolkien or Stephen King (Varela Zapata 2008, p. 110). In a similar tone, Herrero compares the multicultural optimism of the 1990s with the current state of literary and translation markets, where English retains its hegemony (2019, pp. 33–34). An example that confirms this dominance would be that, in 2019, English was 'translated from' 7.7 times more often than it was 'translated to' other languages, according to the *Index Translationum*. This inconsistency between the acclaimed advent of world literature and current research – suggesting otherwise or at least nuancing the claim – confirms that considering different sources for canon formation (anthologies, academic discussions, non-academic surveys, translation markets) profoundly shapes the conclusions of a study. Hence the importance of considering a new source for canon formation – literary memes – and the trends in the canon thus created.

In parallel, Damrosch also observed a rearrangement of canon systems. If the old canon for world literature was structured according to a two-tiered system (major authors versus minor authors), there are now three tiers: a hypercanon – a small subset of major authors who have become ubiquitous, – a countercanon – the result of critics reshaping and proposing alternative, more diverse canons –, and a shadow canon – composed of those authors who are still well known but now rarely discussed (2009, p. 512). This claim guides another secondary research question: how does this three-tiered canon system fit into literary memes? To be more specific, which tier is being reproduced? To what extent are feminist and postcolonial countercanons represented? These are the trends that are interrogated in the canon reproduced in literary memes.

3. Case studies

Recycling between memes and literature can happen in both directions and, consequently, this article requires two parallel case studies.

3.1. Memes recycling literature: @*SparkNotes*

The genre of memes that is analysed here is literary memes, i.e. Internet memes where the joke relies on a reference to literature. If memes are the epitome of current recycling practices and their production techniques are based on mimicry or remix (Shifman 2014, pp. 4, 19–21), then literary memes are those which work upon recycling literary heritage. Following Shifman's classification, all *@SparkNotes*' memes are thus necessarily founder-based, as they must point to a work of literature.

In representation of such literature-based memes, this research uses a randomised sample of 100 tweets from the Twitter account *@SparkNotes.*[4] The account, managed by Courtney Gorter, has already attracted attention because of its success at translating classic literature into Internet-digestible memes (Fitzgerald 2019; Quist 2020).

But in the case of this article, other reasons have been considered for choosing the account:

First, its specificity: it is one of the few accounts that is almost solely dedicated to publishing literary memes. Second, its scope: unlike other accounts posting this kind of content, it does not limit itself to a single author or book; instead, it tweets about a wide range of authors, genres, times and styles, covering what appears to be its own understanding of the literary canon. Third, its popularity: the high ratio of following/followers, as well as the high performance received by most of its tweets[5] indicates that the account is relevant and highly valued in the Twitter ecosystem. It may, therefore, be a good approximation to the preferences of a significant audience. Fourth, its relevance for canon formation; it is the corporate account of SparkNotes, a company engaged in publishing study guides on literature. It is more than likely that the books referenced by such an account are probably those deemed to be studied in schools and, thus, are recognised by the account as part of a tacit academic literary canon. However, the account is not affiliated with academic institutions or instructors, so it shares the more informal, mediatic aspect of non-academic canons.

By randomising the curation of the corpus,[6] the selection is kept as objective as possible, trying to avoid biases like temporal trends or the researcher's

4 The account can be found at the following link: https://twitter.com/sparknotes. For this article it was last consulted on 09.03.2022.

5 At the time this article is written, *@SparkNotes* follows 626 users and is followed by 376,741 users. Most of its recent tweets have thousands of likes and retweets.

6 The online tool *randomtweet* (https://randomtweet.com/) has been used to extract random tweets from the account analysed. Tweets thus obtained have been excluded from the corpus when the tweet is not memetic or when the meme lacks a literary source or refers to a generic literary source (e.g. a genre or a *topos*) instead of an identifiable work or author. When the tweet obtained is a reply, only the first tweet in the conversation is included in the corpus, and only if posted by *@SparkNotes*. No

subjectivity. For the sake of reproducibility, the full list of tweets included in the sample can be consulted in the appendix to this article.

For the sake of clarity, Figure 1 provides an example of the literary memes analysed here. The present tweet works as an example of the Internet meme "Guys Literally Only Want One Thing And It's Fucking Disgusting"[7] but relies on the allusion to the classic Gothic novel *Jane Eyre* (1847).

Fig. 1. Literary meme remixing Charlotte Brontë's *Jane Eyre* and an Internet meme (https://twitter.com/SparkNotes/status/1319658934228127744).

3.2. Literature recycling memes: *Gideon the Ninth* and *Harrow the Ninth*

To study how memes are incorporated into literary works, two novels have been chosen: *Gideon the Ninth* (2019) and *Harrow the Ninth* (2020), both by New Zealand author Tamsyn Muir.

Both novels have become well known for the abundance of Internet memes that appear in them, either founder-based or egalitarian. Professional reviewers (Grady 2020; Rowe 2019) and the author herself in interviews (Travis 2019) have mentioned their presence as one of the main stylistic features of the books.

Lay readers have also remarked on the importance of memes in Muir's writing. In reviews on the reading social media Goodreads the audience describes the book as "the sharpest, funniest, most shamelessly *meme-ridden prose* I've read in years"[8] (my emphasis) and its style as "extremely contemporary meme-speak[9]".

---

time filter has been used, so the tool has returned any tweet posted from the creation of the account in April 2008 to February 2022, when the corpus was selected.

7 Retrieved 9.3.2022, from https://knowyourmeme.com/memes/guys-literally-only-want-one-thing-and-its-fucking-disgusting.

8 Retrieved 9.3.2022, from https://www.goodreads.com/review/show/2695197956.

9 Retrieved 9.3.2022, from https://www.goodreads.com/review/show/2846162262.

Another user acknowledges that "there are more memes-per-capita in this book than any book I have read".[10]

These books constitute the first two volumes of the series "The Locked Tomb". In a combination of science fiction and fantasy, they narrate the adventures of several necromancers and cavaliers in an interplanetary feudalistic empire. This non-realistic setting holds little relation to the memes included within the narrative, as they are all metaleptic, i.e. they interrupt the diegesis and allude to the extradiegetic world shared by author and reader (Genette 1972, pp. 243–46).

For example, when the necromancer Harrow sardonically praises Gideon's swordsmanship saying "While we were developing common sense, she studied the blade" (2019, p. 53), Muir is alluding to the Internet meme "I Studied the Blade".[11] These memetic allusions coexist with non-memetic references: for example, the sentence "My whole House for a reliable food source" (2019, p. 368) mimics the famous Shakespearian line "My kingdom for a horse" in *Richard III.*

4. Methodology for analysis

First an analysis grid had to be developed to quantitatively study the *@SparkNotes* case. Its aim was to catalogue the literary sources of the memes. Several categories were devised based on the nature of the source referenced. This analysis assumes that at least one source can be identified for every reference, even for egalitarian memes – where the source would be a repeated formula instead of an original instance. Besides, it is important to note that memes usually have more than one source; they can reference several pre-existing objects or formulas. As the analysis will prove, this may result in several layers of references. According to this approach, the following features were identified for every reference in a meme: source, author, author's gender, source's genre, source's medium, source's national culture and source's time of publication.

However, the case study of novels recycling memes requires a qualitative methodology. Close reading is used to detect allusions, whether quotations, paraphrases, mentions or echoes of other cultural objects. The relationship between such references, their different levels and the impact of such recycling practices on the novels is then analysed.

The analysis of the novels covers all references, whether they be memetic – that is, to an object fitting into Shifman's definition – or non-memetic, to explore the relationship between them. An exhaustive list has been created, which has

10 Retrieved 9.3.2022, from https://www.goodreads.com/review/show/2749045909.

11 Retrieved 9.3.2022, from https://knowyourmeme.com/memes/i-studied-the-blade.

located 15 instances in *Gideon the Ninth* and 54 in *Harrow the Ninth*. Given that some of these are rather obscure, it is possible that a few may be missing. To minimise this risk, the insights of lay readers on the topic have been included. Therefore, this research owes a debt of gratitude to the disinterested work of the Reddit community[12] and the compiling blog post of Gin Jenny (2020). *KnowYourMeme*,[13] the online peer-to-peer encyclopaedia on Internet memes, has also constituted a valuable resource for identifying which references belonged to a confirmed meme family. Other researchers on the topic have also made use of its database for a similar purpose (Segev et al. 2015, p. 423; Shifman 2014, pp. 13, 89, 102; Katz / Shifman 2017, p. 829).

5. Memes recycling literature: *@SparkNotes*

5.1. Results

When analysing by author, the memes included in *@SparkNotes* give significantly more visibility to William Shakespeare than to any other writer – a third of the corpus references one of his works. Beside this author, there is a wide variety of writers, all of them far from the prominence of the English bard. Edgar Allan Poe is the second most-quoted author, followed by Jane Austen and Mary Shelley. Following them, there are another 18 writers, all mentioned between one and four times.

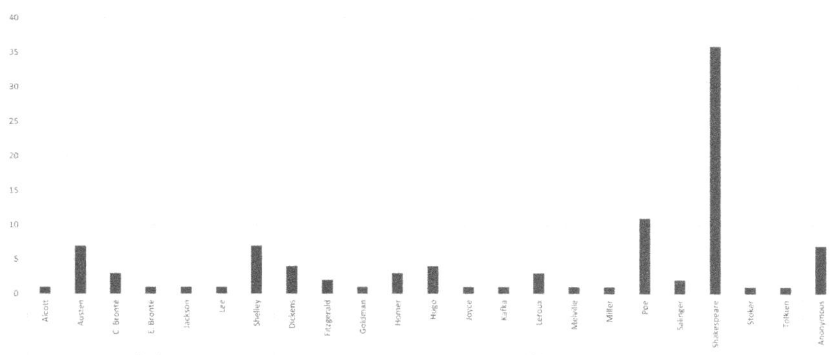

12 Reddit users share their comments, theories and fanart on Muir's books in the subreddit https://www.reddit.com/r/TheNinthHouse/.

13 The encyclopaedia can be consulted at the following link: https://knowyourmeme.com/. It was last consulted on 09.03.2022.

Most of those 18 names are to be expected, since they are clearly canonical and could be easily recognised by a wide audience: Charles Dickens, Charlotte and Emily Brontë, Francis Scott Fitzgerald, Victor Hugo, Homer, James Joyce and Franz Kafka. However, these authors coexist with a smaller subset of middlebrow authors who are still highly popular but less canonical: Louisa May Alcott, William Goldman, Gaston Leroux and J. R. R. Tolkien.

The corpus also displays an acute gender bias towards male authors, as they account for 72 % of the references versus 21 % for women and 7 % for anonymous texts. Nonetheless, even if women are less numerous, two of them (Shelley and Austen) are the third and fourth most quoted, as mentioned above.

An analysis by genre of the books referenced reveals an apparent co-prominence of theatre plays (37 %) and novels (39 %), which dominate almost the whole corpus. This data point may be misleading, as all but one play (Miller's *The Crucible* [1953]) are Shakespeare's, whose ubiquity skews this graph. Therefore, the novel is the genre that truly prevails in the corpus, in spite of the marginal appearances of more classic genres like the epic poem (Homer's *The Odyssey* [c. 8th C. BCE] and the *Epic of Gilgamesh* [c. 18th-17th C. BCE]) or poetry (monopolised by Poe's *The Raven* [1845]); short genres such as the short story and the *novella* (again led by Poe, but also including Shirley Jackson and Dickens), and even some premodern literature, such as romance (*Gawain and the Green Knight* [c. 14th C.]) and mythology (exclusively Greek). All the genres mentioned here are clearly literary, in contrast to the memetic object in which they are referenced.

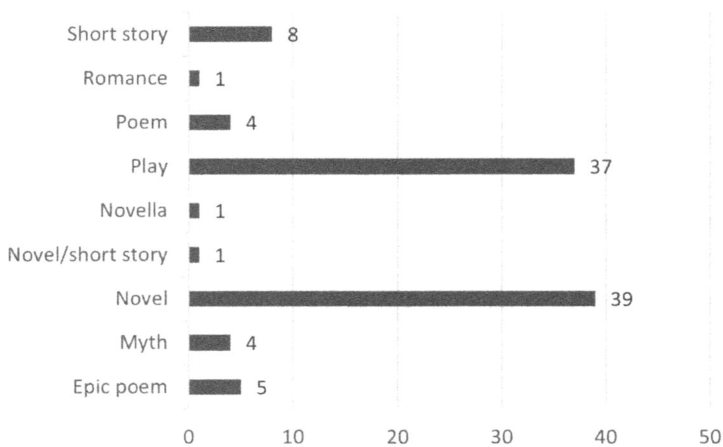

The data are also partial in terms of the national culture of the author quoted. The hypervisibility of the United Kingdom (62 %) and the United States (21 %) implies that Anglophone literature saturates 83 % of the corpus. Non-English literature is minimal: France is only represented by Hugo's *Les Misérables* (1862) and Leroux's *The Phantom of the Opera* (1910) (7 %); Greece is reduced to *The Odyssey* and anonymous mythology (7 %); Mesopotamia appears thanks to the *Epic of Gilgamesh* (2 %), and Kafka's *The Metamorphosis* (1912) stands not only for Czech, but also for all German and Central European literatures (1 %).

A timeline of the works mentioned by the corpus confirms a misrepresentation of literary history. Aside from Shakespeare, who constitutes the entirety of the 36 mentions to the 17th C., *@SparkNotes* focuses on 19th C. literature (43 %). Premodern literature is only present in the allusions to Antiquity already mentioned: *The Epic of Gilgamesh*, *The Odyssey*, and Greek mythology, with the anonymous romance *Gawain and the Green Knight* constituting the only Medieval referent. The 18th C. is significantly absent. The 20th C. accounts for 11 % of the allusions and becomes almost exclusively North American: apart from one mention of Kafka and UK writers like Joyce or Tolkien, this century is represented by classic US authors like Arthur Miller, J. D. Salinger, Francis Scott Fitzgerald and Harper Lee. Within the 20th C., mid-century authors are represented the most (6 mentions). The most recent text in the corpus is Goldman's *The Princess Bride* (1975).

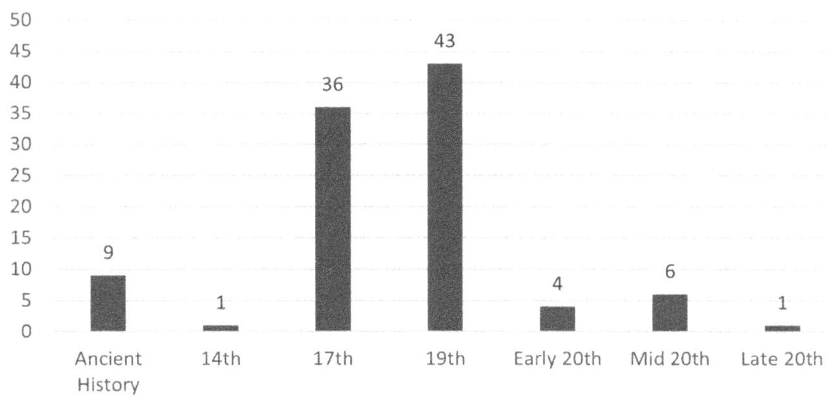

5.2. Interpretation

The selection of authors and texts quoted by the Twitter account analysed works as a "hypercanon", using Damrosch's aforementioned term. It reinforces the hypervisibility of an extremely reduced list of authors who are deemed easily recognisable and palatable to a mass audience, such as Shakespeare. This may explain the inclusion of middlebrow authors, such as Tolkien, Alcott, Goldman and Leroux. Furthermore, some works may have become popular not by themselves, but because of a mainstream, successful transmedia. This may be the case for Hugo's *Les Misérables* – first a Broadway musical (1985) and more recently a Hollywood movie (2012), Leroux's *The Phantom of the Opera* – famously adapted to the cinema on several occasions and also turned into a hit Broadway musical (1986), Goldman's *The Princess Bride* – turned into a Hollywood movie (1987), and possibly even Alcott's *Little Women* (1868–1869) –, which has seen several successful adaptations, with the most recent one (2019) gaining popularity among critics and public. If their popularity is indeed thanks to transmedia, it would confirm one of Damrosch's predictions: that the postcanonical era would be based on translations – not from one language to another as anticipated by Damrosch, but from one medium to another. McDonald's research also suggests the impact of film adaptations on the popularity of classic literature (2016, p. 41). Likewise, this update of the canon would explain the preference for novels – today's favourite genre – over other genres like poetry and tragedy that were traditionally more appreciated.

As is usual in traditional canons – Bloom's may be the clearest example (1994, pp. 2, 40, 62, 75, 521) – Shakespeare stands at the core as the indisputable star. This opens a line of continuity from previous canons. In *@SparkNotes*, the impact from the Canon Wars is barely visible. The canon is still indisputably biased towards English and none of the books mentioned are written by the colonial subalterns. And even within this Anglocentrism, the closest the account gets to adopting a postcolonial lens is the inclusion of Lee's *To Kill a Mockingbird* (1960), which only happens once in the corpus and feels insufficient in the absence of canonical and widely-read African-American authors like Toni Morrison and Alice Walker–the inclusion of Aschroft, Griffiths and Tiffin's "english" is thus minimal (1989).

There is a mild push by the feminist countercanon. As described above, even if the corpus overrepresents men, a few women writers (Shelley and Austen) are quoted more than the average. It is also remarkable that some female authors who traditionally were considered minor are reclaimed as part of the hypercanon, such as Alcott. This is all the more salient when realising that traditional major authors such as Percy Shelley and Lord Byron or novelists like William Thackeray, Daniel Defoe and Laurence Sterne are excluded. Curiously enough, Virginia Woolf, who was the only woman (or one of the few) included in many canons for some time (Auerbach [1953] 2003, pp. 463–88; Bloom 1994, pp. 433–46; Varela Zapata 2008, p. 110), is not included either, even if Joyce, her contemporary and an equally challenging author, is present.

Another feature of *@SparkNotes*' way of recycling literary heritage is its cautiousness towards its canonical sources. Temporally speaking, referenced works are located at a measured distance: they are old enough to be respectably canonical (mostly 19th C.), but not so old as to alienate readers (quotes to premodern texts are rare). Nonetheless, as can be appreciated from Figures 1 and 2, the memes belong to an unequivocally contemporary genre that remixes a canonical literary source with popular modern texts such as Internet jokes or blockbuster movies. The two elements of the remix are medially and temporally alien to each other. In this way, *@SparkNotes* establishes an unquestioned divide between a palatable, familiar literary heritage and the memetic, social media present.

This breach between literature and meme – content and form of the same object, but distinct and non-interchangeable – can be better understood considering that "simplicity" is a recurring feature of successful viral and memetic content (Shifman 2014, pp. 69, 81–82). The meme account is based on the translation of one extremely complex medium – literature – to another humorously simple medium – memes. Its success is due precisely to Gorter's genius in extracting easily digestible, recognisable messages out of complex object sources and inscribing them into simple memetic vehicles. This logic is clearly hypermemetic, as described by Shifman: pop culture cannibalises a foreign object and simplifies it to turn it into a meme.

Figure 2 exemplifies these dynamics. The meme factually paraphrases part of *Hamlet*'s act 4, scene 7. There are many markers that render this reference transparent even to those unfamiliar with the plot, the most obvious being the hero's name. In this way, *@SparkNotes* minimises the risk of its audience not recognising the meme's source. This is characteristic of hypercanon: not only does it refer to an extremely famous work, it does so in the most unequivocal way possible, alluding to its best-known details. With some exceptions, this is the rule throughout the corpus.

Fig. 2. Literary meme remixing *Hamlet and Star Wars: The Rise of Skywalker* (https://twitter.com/SparkNotes/status/1390759439087570944).

The clear distinction between the meme's literary source (*Hamlet* [1599–1601]) and its memetic format (a poorly edited screenshot of the movie *Star Wars: The Rise of Skywalker* [2019]) can also be appreciated in this tweet. There is a striking contrast between the two references: one of the most analysed texts in literary history and a blockbuster from a popular Hollywood franchise released only one and a half years before the tweet was posted. *@SparkNotes*' jokes rely on this anachronistic structure: remixing memes based on contemporary, popular culture that inscribe a comically-displaced reference to a literary classic.

6. Literature recycling memes: *Gideon the Ninth* and *Harrow the Ninth*

The references contained in Muir's two novels depict a rather distinct image, more ambivalent and multifaceted. Out of the references detected, around two thirds cannot be directly linked to a recognisable meme. However, many of those quotations do not refer to literary works but to the pop and Internet culture from which memes stem, thus blurring the line between the memetic and non-memetic.

The following excerpt illustrates Muir's recycling style. In this passage, the God-Emperor explains to the heroine Harrow that the survival of the solar system where the Nine Houses live – the whole population of the empire – depends on his survival. Therefore, he cannot face his enemies (the Resurrection Beasts and the Heralds) directly, as his death would be fatal to everyone. This *anagnorisis* is key to the novel's plot and relies deeply on science fiction and fantasy premises (e.g. necromancy and an interplanetary empire), which are objectively distant from the reader's world. Yet, the non-realistic setting of the scene is broken twice within the same page.

> "A myriad ago, I resurrected nine planets," he said. "And I reignited the central star, and I called it Dominicus. As a reminder. *Dominus illuminatio mea et salus mea, quem timebo*? God is my light. Harrowhark, if I went under – I'd enter that senseless state, and I am God. What if, forty billion light-years away, my people looked up to see Dominicus falter and go out? What if the very House beneath their feet died all over again, as I turned my back upon it?"
> […]
> "If I fought the Resurrection Beast I'd leave my Houses to die," he said. "If I fought the Heralds, I might well go mad, which would be the same thing. So I'm shut in here – walled in, really – to prevent the Nine Houses becoming none House, with left grief." (Muir 2020, p. 344).

Muir first quotes Psalm 26 from the Latin translation in the Vulgate Bible. The citation works as a metalepsis: it forces the reader out of the diegesis to an extradiegetic reality. Even if anachronistic – it cannot easily be assumed that in the world described by the novels Christianity or even Latin have ever existed – the quotation maintains a solemn tone that fits the scene. The metalepsis created by the second quote is even more abrupt: the expression "none House, with left grief" mimics the Internet meme "None Pizza with Left Beef" that crossed platforms like Reddit, Tumblr and Buzzfeed in about 2007.[14] This joke about a nonsensical custom pizza order resituates the reader even further from the diegesis – it alludes to a very specific contemporary piece of popular media and its irreverent tone differs widely from the tone of the diegesis. The proximity of these two quotations, both alien to the novel's plot, though in opposite ways, illustrates Muir's iconoclastic use of references.

---

14 Retrieved 9.3.2022, from https://knowyourmeme.com/memes/special-delivery-instructions.

The recycling style observed in the example is based on the incongruous juxtaposition of disparate sources – what could be labelled "anachronistic recycling", which may not be unprecedented but becomes highly characteristic of these contemporary practices. *@SparkNotes* remixed canonic literature with pop culture references in a memetic format (see Figure 2) and the novels display a similar eclecticism. Quotes by authors from classic literature – mainly Shakespeare, but also Andrew Marvell, Walt Whitman and Miguel de Cervantes, among others – share space with references to lowbrow and middlebrow cultural objects, e.g. Tina Fey's blockbuster *Mean Girls* (2004), Greg Daniels' TV show *The Office* (2005–2013), the Web series *Llamas with hats* (2009–2015) by Jason Steele, a tweet by the author Patricia Lockwood, or the musical *Firebringer* (2016) by Meredith Stepien and Mark Swiderski. References to Internet culture (e.g. 4Chan, Facebook, and Reddit) are also prominently displayed. Such heterogeneity can also be appreciated in the timeline of the references included in the novels: they span from Greek tragedy and medieval romance to classic and modern cinema and literature. Some of the referenced works are contemporary to the time of writing, while some Internet references from the early 2000s are still remembered and quoted. A wide range of classical pieces coexist with contemporary objects.

However, the most evident difference between the meme account and the novels is that, in Muir's work, the split between noble, canonical literature and fun, memetic format no longer exists. Literary and memetic sources are recycled at the same level. On the other hand, the *@SparkNotes*' memes on classic literature may be anachronistic, but they are respectful of the discontinuity between what is modern and what is classical. As seen in the example above, Muir's anachronisms are not: the novels juxtapose quotes from Shakespeare and from the latest Internet meme in the same extradiegetic humorous tone. Thus, Internet pop culture is elevated to the status of an intertextual-worthy source, while canonic authors are equalled to tongue-in-cheek jokes.

This equation of highbrow and lowbrow, classical and contemporary sources reveals a structure that is more complicated than that of *@SparkNotes*' memes. The novels are not plain objects simplifying complex ones, but rather elaborate objects of their own in dialogue with a heterogeneous set of sources. The author emphasises what is challenging about the memes quoted by referencing them at the same level of canonical texts. In this case, there is a conversation between the diegesis and the different sources, as well as between the different kinds of sources. This dialogue is based on anachronism at a much more radical level: the crude, incongruous juxtaposition of media, tones and registers.

Beyond this way of using memes, incongruity and displacement are central to the novels both stylistically and thematically, from the setting – mixing fantasy and science fiction – to the writing. The incipit of *Gideon the Ninth* exemplifies this point, as it sets archaisms, epic epithets and references to "dirty magazines" side by side:

> IN THE MYRIADIC YEAR OF OUR LORD – the ten thousandth year of the King Undying, the kindly Prince of Death! – Gideon Nav packed her sword, her shoes, and her dirty magazines, and she escaped from the House of the Ninth. (Muir 2019, p. 15).

A vaguely antique, sumptuous style, inherited from high fantasy literature, is often ruptured by allusions to pop culture, including pizza (2019, p. 57), comics (2019, pp. 67, 126; 2020, p. 464), romance novels (2019, p. 124; 2020, p. 310), and FAQs (2020, p. 490). Likewise, sunglasses (2019, pp. 68–69; 2020, pp. 433, 471, 488, 494) and guns (2019, pp. 204, 285; 2020, p. 396) are mentioned as anachronistic, displaced objects.

Which dynamics prevail in Muir's recycling and which of those refer to both the memetic and non-memetic content? This analysis detected more non-strictly memetic references (which could be called intertextual) than properly memetic ones. However, does this statement still stand qualitatively? I would argue it does not: the novels subordinate non-memetic, text-driven recycling to hypermemetic logic (Web-driven recycling). That is, the pervasiveness of the hypermemetic operates here to infect non-memetic content; once a memetic atmosphere is established with the first allusions to memes, any allusion to any object will be read as memetic.

There are several textual traces of hypermemetic recycling setting the tone for non-memetic references. For example, the aforementioned line "My whole House for a reliable food source" (2019, p. 368) recontextualises Shakespeare's *Richard III* with humour and language very similar to *@SparkNotes*' memes: it recovers and subverts an iconic, highly recognisable element. These memetic parodies often have several referential layers.

When one character complains of her situation saying, "I live in the *worst* of all possible worlds" (2020, p. 257), she is recycling Voltaire's parody of Leibniz's philosophy in *Candide* (1759). The non-sensical taste for discordant remixes is best appreciated when the full name of one of *Harrow the Ninth*'s villains is revealed: she is called "*Awake Remembrance of These Valiant Dead Kia Hua Ko Te Pai Snap Back to Reality Oops There Goes Gravity*" (2020, p. 465, her emphasis), later humorously shortened to "Commander Wake Me Up Inside" (2020, p. 468). This anthroponym juxtaposes Shakespeare's *Henry V* (c. 1599), the Māori version of the New-Zealand national anthem (1870), Eminem's *Lose Yourself* (2002), and

Evanescence's *Bring Me to Life* (2003). Even if parodies and pastiches are not new literary devices, the incongruity of those happening in Muir's novels resonate with memetic nonsense.

These references to memes speak of the *mise en abyme* of Muir's style. If memes can be understood as recycling devices, quoting memes implies another turn of the screw – the novels recycle such recycled objects. Writing is thus grounded in recycling practices taken from the Internet. Muir has been open about her past creating fanfiction, a transmedia practice in which (w)readers recycle a cultural object by writing stories that expand, shift or complement an existing fictional universe. Traces of this can be found in the novels: some chapters of *Harrow the Ninth* ironically adopt fanfic tropes such as Role Swap AU[15] – where necromancers become cavaliers and *vice-versa* (2020, pp. 367–371), Royal AU – where the setting suddenly becomes a period drama (2020, pp. 372–374), or Coffee shop AU – where the action takes place in a cafeteria and the characters become baristas (2020, pp. 375–378). Moreover, Muir recognises that writing fanfic and belonging to fan communities has shaped her style. She establishes a causal relationship between the influence of fanfiction and the mix of genres, references and tones that this article has described:

> We read everything, we wrote everything, genre had very little meaning. I feel this has had a huge impact on me and my writing now. Nobody gave a hot shit if you were writing a grimdark zombie apocalypse *Kingdom Hearts* story or a thing about Zidane doing a bakeoff. People only cared about *Ships*. [16]

These dynamics do not end with the author's writing: this loop of recycling dynamics, which follows a nested-doll principle, continues further at the hands of its readers. If the novels are driven by recycling artifacts such as Internet memes and fanfics, they also become the object of such recycling practices. There are now fanfics available based on Muir's fictional universe, as she is well aware,[17] and the author even encourages this by offering prompts.[18] Likewise, there is a fan community on Twitter and Reddit creating and sharing literary memes based

15 In fanfiction, an Alternative Universe (AU) is a narrative device in which the plot does not take place in the original setting, but in a different one chosen by the author of the derivative fanfiction.

16 Retrieved 14.3.2022, from https://www.reddit.com/r/Fantasy/comments/i45jq6/comment/g0gsaca/?utm_source=share&utm_medium=web2x&context=3.

17 Retrieved 14.3.2022, from https://www.reddit.com/r/Fantasy/comments/i45jq6/comment/g0gvouz/?utm_source=share&utm_medium=web2x&context=3

18 Retrieved 14.3.2022, from https://www.reddit.com/r/Fantasy/comments/i45jq6/comment/g0glnld/?utm_source=share&utm_medium=web2x&context=3

on *Gideon the Ninth* and *Harrow the Ninth*.[19] These fanfics and memes close the loop – postdigital novels recycling Internet objects are incorporated back into online recycling dynamics. Furthermore, they lead back to a complementary concept of "canon". In these fan communities, "canon" refers to the official, published source that is subject to transmedia recycling (Jenkins 2015, p. 371; Stanfill 2020, p. 131). In this context, Muir's novels become the canon on which such fanfics and memes are based.

7. Conclusion

This essay has explored two cases in which postdigital recycling connects Internet culture and literature. What do these analyses tell us about contemporary cultural recycling dynamics? Regarding what is being recycled, they suggest that the canon reproduced by literary memes is still, unsurprisingly, being negotiated and that feminist and postcolonial pushes have been modest in their impact. Likewise, the opening up to a world literature canon is still modest and Anglo-centric, though these conclusions should be verified with a more diverse corpus.

What may be more characteristic about our current relationship with this canon is that these retellings and quotations tend towards a deliberately anachronistic way of recycling. They revel in the abrupt, often ludic distance between these canonical sources, other contemporary referents and the diegesis. Research has found that memetic humour is often based on incongruity and decontextualisation (Shifman 2014, pp. 78–81, 90–92; Katz and Shifman 2017, pp. 834–35). This feature may go further than a particularly popular genre of jokes pointing to a sign of our postdigital times. Some thinkers have suggested terms like "hyperpresent" (Sierra-Paredes 2017, p. 33), "topological time" (Fernández Mallo 2018, pp. 171–172) and "archaeology of the present" (Carrión 2020, p. 131) to speak about the ways current recycling practices, especially those happening online, work aesthetically and conceptually by juxtaposing decontextualised fragments.

19 For example, https://www.reddit.com/r/TheNinthHouse/comments/szv4zc/made_this_for_my_best_friend_who_loves_this/?utm_source=share&utm_medium=web2x&context=3, https://www.reddit.com/r/TheNinthHouse/comments/sm1b41/ninth_house_doggo_meme/?utm_source=share&utm_medium=web2x&context=3, https://twitter.com/MaxxMorningstar/status/1500705862779822087?s=20&t=5PTLRrUz_TeWfFDqx6ElLA, or https://twitter.com/heliocharis/status/1232910125741957120, all retrieved 14.3.2022.

In this context, and as these cases suggest, it is productive to think about today's recycling dynamics in relation to hypermemetic logic. Even if not every form of cultural recycling needs to be shaped as a meme, it is theoretically and methodologically stimulating to rethink them in light of the way in which memes circulate and cannibalise other content and media. Such an analysis would regard any contemporary cultural object as (potential) part of the Web. It would offer an alternative to what has been called "the linguistic turn": the trend in the late 20th C. of describing and analysing all reality and social phenomena as text (Seigworth and Gregg 2010, pp. 7–8). Other classical theories about cultural recycling, such as Kristeva's intertextuality, rely on this linguistic bias: even if Kristeva is explicit about semiotics dealing beyond texts strictly speaking, it still looks at reality through a textual bias. For example, she takes text as its analytic unit (1969, p. 76), literature as its most illustrative case study (1969, p. 41) and linguistics as its methodological model (1969, pp. 62, 74–75). The goal of this study is not to problematise this approach, a task that has been undertaken much better by affect theory (Seigworth and Gregg 2010), but to stress the inappropriateness of using it to read a postdigital literary object. Muir's novels and *@SparkNotes*' literary memes belong to a current ecosystem that must be understood in relation to the Web: a multimedia, hypertextual and transmedia space shaped by social media like Twitter, Reddit, Facebook and 4Chan, which also incorporates text as one of its many components/layers.

References

Abblitt, Stephen: "A Postdigital Paradigm in Literary Studies". *Higher Education Research & Development* 38(1) 2019, pp. 97–109.

Altieri, Charles: "An Idea and Ideal of a Literary Canon". *Critical Inquiry* 10(1) 1983, pp. 37–60.

Ashcroft, Bill / Griffiths, Gareth / Tiffin, Helen: *The Empire Writes Back. Theory and Practice in Post-Colonial Literatures*. 2nd edition. Routledge: London and New York 1989.

Auerbach, Erich: *Mimesis. The Representation of Reality in Western Literature*. Translated by Willard R. Trask. Princeton University Press: Princeton and Oxford [1953] 2003.

Bernheimer, Charles: "The Bernheimer Report, 1993. Comparative Literature at the Turn of the Century". In: Bernheimer, Charles (ed.): *Comparative Literature in the Age of Multiculturalism*. (Parallax: Re-Visions of Culture & Society). Johns Hopkins University Press: Baltimore 1995, pp. 39–48.

Bloom, Harold: *The Western Canon. The Books and School of the Ages.* Harcourt Brace: New York 1994.

Carrión, Jorge: *Lo viral.* Galaxia Gutenberg: Barcelona 2020.

Chow, Rey: "In the Name of Comparative Literature". In: Bernheimer, Charles (ed.): *Comparative Literature in the Age of Multiculturalism.* (Parallax: Re-Visions of Culture & Society). Johns Hopkins University Press: Baltimore 1995, pp. 107–16.

Curtius, Ernst Robert: *European literature and the Latin Middle Ages.* [Translated by Willard R. Trask]. Princeton University Press: Princeton and Oxford [1948] 1990.

Damrosch, David: *What Is World Literature.* (Translation Transnation Series). Princeton University Press: Princeton and Oxford 2003.

Damrosch, David: "Frames for World Literature". In: Winko, Simone / Jannidis, Fotis / Lauer, Gerhard (eds.): *Grenzen der Literatur: Zu Begriff und Phänomen des Literarischen.* Walter de Gruyter: Berlin 2009, pp. 496–515.

Fernández Mallo, Agustín: *Teoría General de la Basura (Cultura, Apropiación, Complejidad).* Galaxia Gutenberg: Barcelona 2018.

Fitzgerald, Madeline: "Meet the 26-Year-Old Woman Behind SparkNotes' Genius Twitter Account". *Time* 30.7.2019, retrieved 1.3.2022, from https://time.com/5637311/sparknotes-twitter/.

Gallagher, Susan V.: "Contingencies and Intersections: The Formation of Pedagogical Canons". *Pedagogy* 1(1) 2001, pp. 53–67.

García Carcedo, Pilar: *Memes, reciclajes y escritura creativa digital.* Serie: "Cuadernos del ahora" n. 6, 2020, retrieved 1.8.2023, from https://hdl.handle.net/20.500.14352/11862.

Genette, Gérard: *Figures III.* (Poétique). Éditions du Seuil: Paris 1972.

Genette, Gérard: *Palimpsestes: la littérature au second degré.* (Poétique). Éditions du Seuil: Paris 1982.

Gin, Jenny: "Harrow the Ninth, Glossed". *Reading the End* (blog). 19.8.2020, retrieved 1.3.2022, from http://readingtheend.com/2020/08/19/harrow-the-ninth-glossed/.

Grady, Constance: "The Remixed Genre Tropes of Gideon the Ninth, Explained". *Vox*, 18.12.2020, retrieved 1.3.2022, from https://www.vox.com/22187746/gideon-the-ninth-tamsyn-muir-tropes-explained.

Herrero, Gustavo: "Literatura Mundial y Multilateralismo: Cambiando de Rumbo". In: Müller, Gesine / Siskind, Mariano (eds.): *World Literature, Cosmopolitanism, Globality: Beyond, Against, Post, Otherwise.* Walter de Gruyter: Berlin 2019, pp. 32–42.

Jenkins, Brett: "I Love You to Meaninglessness: From Mortal Characters to Immortal Character Types in P&P Fanfiction". *The Journal of Popular Culture* 48(2) 2015, pp. 371–384.

Katz, Yuval / Shifman, Limor: "Making Sense? The Structure and Meanings of Digital Memetic Nonsense". *Information, Communication & Society* 20(6) 2017, pp. 825–842.

Kristeva, Julia: *Semeiotiké: recherches pour une sémantique*. (Tel Quel). Éditions du Seuil: Paris 1969.

McDonald, Peter D.: "Instituting (World) Literature". In: Helgesson, Stefan / Vermeulen, Pieter (eds.): *Institutions of World Literature. Writing, Translation, Markets*. Routledge: New York 2016, pp. 39–52.

Muir, Tamsyn: *Gideon the Ninth*. Tor Dot Com: New York 2019.

Muir, Tamsyn: *Harrow the Ninth*. Tor Dot Com: New York 2020.

Müller, Gesine: "Debating World Literature without the World: Ideas for Materializing Literary Studies Based on Examples from Latin America and the Caribbean". In: Müller, Gesine / Siskind, Mariano (eds.): *World Literature, Cosmopolitanism, Globality: Beyond, Against, Post, Otherwise*. Walter de Gruyter: Berlin 2019, pp. 13–31.

Pratt, Marie-Louise: "Comparative Literature and Global Citizenship". In: Bernheimer, Charles (ed.): *Comparative Literature in the Age of Multiculturalism*. (Parallax: Re-Visions of Culture & Society). Johns Hopkins University Press: Baltimore 1995, pp. 39–48.

Quist, Rachel: "Twitter Reflection: Retweets, Memes, and a Return to SparkNotes". *Medium*, 8.3.2020, retrieved 1.3.2022, from https://medium.com/@RQ_spee26_dc/twitter-reflection-retweets-memes-and-a-return-to-sparknotes-19e04fe3e188.

Rowe, Adam: "Tamsyn Muir's Goony Fun 'Gideon The Ninth' Takes Sci-Fi Fantasy Prose into New Territory". *Forbes* 1.9.2019, retrieved 1.3.2022, from https://www.forbes.com/sites/adamrowe1/2019/09/10/tamsyn-muirs-goony-fun-gideon-the-ninth-takes-sci-fi-fantasy-prose-into-new-territory/.

Segev, Elad / Nissenbaum, Asaf / Stolero, Nathan / Shifman, Limor: "Families and Networks of Internet Memes: The Relationship Between Cohesiveness, Uniqueness, and Quiddity Concreteness". *Journal of Computer-Mediated Communication* 20(4) 2015, pp. 417–33.

Seigworth, Gregory J. / Gregg, Melissa: "An Inventory of Shimmers". In: Seigworth, Gregory J. / Gregg, Melissa (eds.): *The Affect Theory Reader*. Duke University Press: Durham 2010, pp. 1–25.

Shifman, Limor: *Memes in digital culture*. (MIT Press Essential Knowledge Series). The MIT Press: Cambridge 2014.

Sierra-Paredes, Germán: "Postdigital Synchronicity and Syntopy: The Manipulation of Universal Codes, and the Fully Automated Avantgarde". *Neohelicon: Acta Comparationis Litterarum Universarum* 44(1) 2017, pp. 27–39.

Stanfill, Mel: "Introduction: The Reactionary in the Fan and the Fan in the Reactionary". *Television & New Media* 21(2) 2020, pp. 123–134.

Travis: "An Interview with Tamsyn Muir". *The Fantasy Inn* 28.8.2019, retrieved 1.3.2022, from https://thefantasyinn.com/2019/08/28/an-interview-with-tamsyn-muir/.

Varela Zapata, Jesús: "The Canon Beyond Academia Alternative Sources of Canonicity in Twentieth Century Literature in English". In: Gabler, Hans Walter / Robinson, Peter / Subačius, Paulius V. (eds.): *Textual Scholarship and the Canon*. Brill: Leiden 2008, pp. 107–118.

9. Appendix: @*SparkNotes* corpus

The tweets from the account @*SparkNotes* included in the corpus are referenced by their 16-digit unique identifier.

1355192615692546051

1314642779990118401

1321500350994665472

1450850126105354246

1449020711004213293

1430543336792788997

1416135467846750210

1471526505222180865

1351621731841138690

1479484644043239428

1339656354194178054

1357767664337375238

1426208081160163331

1385335757959749632

1291467381198458880

1209562439647420419

1376913774960111620

1134516662785454080

1423730777846657034

1296121657984266241
1283102711882416128
1314593506267213826
1356633746854846465
1456647380837847041
1417855140036583432
1215354349259390978
1276225599045066753
1425532303489605635
1341496350085701633
1301229040246960128
1410983307546927112
1387056077490081793
1344738335961579520
1230884170752196608
1427664751329484803
1217847378792894464
1428364180390703116
1241088371059023878
1319658934228127744
1255148585017991171
1258783013275668484
1376596970656108544
1474043946594713601
1359949620584079366
1220765473907802112
1298710566010122240
1149686205249757184
1276570211332902914
1482371151066288128
1207702869937414144
1409910648797110283
1250475428915097600
1367906562090622976

1288525352780865538
1422213794244202497
1455550930825457670
1471925246462734338
1407376788528013317
1465725945759911937
1136642752400232448
1374766016434159616
1280567583675232257
1441412961646493707
1364678746976976898
1341775567469867008
1130906411100188673
1329831556538658818
1229492651419951105
1455955066045747202
1252313825132646400
1323660130861371393
1336755424897495041
1339255942966218755
1441060822202060802
1277619093454098433
1273676239895756810
1261360262096945152
1390759439087570944
1379553274718740484
1322266629179408384
1288857203185721344
984818317457313792
1133440202612121606
1131976624935768064
1365380710165438465
1367906562090622976
1244675520182267907

1091441768158167040
1354809580732047363
1435244966872289286
1315741113760780288
1173983480407048192
1263845659775512576
1260985532378734592
1252631255939723266
1286823023589425152
1468614753941696521
1222918115706703875
1274717321936986118
1461053745173827593

Antonio Domínguez Leiva
Université du Québec à Montréal

The Precession of Monoliths: Planetary Recycling of a Space Age Mythology[1]

Abstract: The strange planetary proliferation of monoliths since the first one was discovered in the Utah desert is an enigmatic homage to S. Kubrick and A. Clarke's classic *2001 A Space Odyssey* (1968), an extreme case of cultural recycling in a postdigital environment. We analyse this global performance / hoax through its relationship to the ambiguous meanings of the film's original artefact.

Keywords: monoliths, viral, *2001 A Space Odyssey*, postdigital, social media.

On 18 November 2020, biologists from the Utah Division of Wildlife Resources were flying by helicopter over the Southwest Mormon state to conduct a bighorn sheep survey, when they spotted a shiny, silvery metal structure standing tall among the hematite rocks in the middle of a canyon. The team's initial assumption was that it was the work of a "new wave artist or a big fan of *2001: A Space Odyssey*", a reference to the strange black monolith that dominates Stanley Kubrick's 1968 cult film, and which the metallic object appeared to mimic.

Two days later, the Utah Department of Public Safety (DPS) posted a photo of the enigmatic find on Instagram, followed on 23 November by videos and photos on its website. They did not reveal its exact location in order to deter pilgrimages of the curious to the Lockhart Basin, considered a dangerous area. The press release ("DPS Air Office encounters monolith in red rock country")[2] named the object as a "monolith" (although it was not a rock), allowing the connection to the cinematic reference.

Within hours, Reddit user Tim Slane geolocated the object on Google Earth, guided by the geological clues in the official videos (Robertson 2020). 48 hours

1 This article incorporates aspects of my research for my book *Monolithes. Retour viral d'une mythologie de l'Âge Spatial* (Paris: PUF 2022).

2 Department of Public Safety: *DPS Aero Bureau Encounters Monolith in Red Rock Country*. 23.11.2020. https://dpsnews.utah.gov/dps-aero-bureau-encounters-monolith-in-red-rock-country/.

later, several people had already arrived at the site and had started uploading photographs and videos of the monolith to social media, leading local residents to fear that the influx of visitors would not only damage the basin, but also the surrounding Native American sites and artefacts (including rock art protected by the Utah Department of Heritage and Arts). Then, on the night of 27 November, the strange structure disappeared. Four days later, a video ("We removed the Utah monolith") claimed the action in the name of the environmentalist ethic of "zero waste". The authors of the video immediately received death threats and hate messages on social media, forcing one of them, Andy Lewis, to show the intact monolith in his garden on Instagram as "proof of life" from its hijackers.

However, a day before this "rescue", another similar monolith appeared on the hill of Bâtca Doamnei in Romania, only to disappear again within 48 hours. On 2 December, a triangular column of reflective metal was erected on Pine Mountain in Atascadero (California). 48 hours later, three young men filmed themselves on DLive destroying it and replacing it with a large wooden cross, singing "Christ is King" to country music. "We don't want illegal aliens [whether from] Mexico or outer space," explained these supporters of the Groyper Army, named after a variant of the viral alt-right meme Pepe the Frog.[3] The next day, a group of four artists claimed authorship of the vandalised work and replaced it with a new one.

In the days that followed, dozens of monoliths began to proliferate first across the United States and after that in various other parts of the world. Since then, every continent (except, at the last count, Antarctica) has, to a greater or lesser extent, had its pillar (Wikipedia already counted a hundred of them a month and a half after the first discovery).[4] The Monolith Tracker[5] tracks new sightings on a daily basis, reporting over two hundred monoliths to date *urbi et orbi*.

The viral and global nature of the phenomenon immediately intrigued the traditional and social media, giving rise to a whole series of speculations. The fact that the first monolith (a kind of ironic "patient zero") was sighted a year after the outbreak of the global coronavirus pandemic in 2019 (COVID-19) – although Dutch journalist Nouska du Saar's research with Maxar satellite imagery showed

---

3 See Wakefield (2020), retrieved 03.04.2022, from https://uk.news.yahoo.com/trump-supporters-tear-down-mystery-163238074.html.

4 See Wikipedia's "List of works similar to the 2020 Utah monolith", retrieved 03.04.2022, from https://en.wikipedia.org/wiki/List_of_works_similar_to_the_2020_Utah_monolith.

5 https://monolithtracker.com.

that the monolith was erected between 7 July and 21 October 2016[6] – also contributed to its integration into the memetic mythology surrounding global zoonosis. From then on, the ostension of Kubrick's quotes became a kind of emblem, a commentary and a coronation of a year consecrated by the media as "the weirdest year" or "the year of the weird" (Rove 2020).

Identification with the enigmatic monolith that presides over the opening scene of *2001: A Space Odyssey* has endowed the strange artefact with an aura of hypermodern quotation, heir to the mythological status of its source. Unlike other recent global phenomena (such as the evil clown panic of 2016), which are framed in what anthropologists call "ostension" – a kind of acting out that aims to embody legendary fictions in real life[7] – the explicit film reference has conditioned the viralisation of the artefacts. Thus, the flying saucer community automatically distanced itself from the "trend", closing the way to an extra-terrestrial hypothesis (unlike, for example, the "crop circles", which continue to feed ufological interpretations), while the imitations were placed in a register ranging from "edutainment" to militancy, or even marketing and self-promotion.

However, if they failed to embody the aura of extra-terrestrial civilisations, the monoliths seem to illustrate the famous sentence with which Umberto Eco (one of the first theorists of semiotic "ostension") defined the postmodern condition:

> I think of the postmodern attitude as the attitude of someone who loves a very cultured woman and knows that he cannot say to her, "I love you desperately" because he knows that she knows (and she knows that he knows) that Barbara Cartland has already written those sentences. However, there is a solution. He can say, "As Barbara Cartland would say, I love you desperately". Then, having avoided false innocence, having made it clear that one cannot speak innocently, he will nevertheless have told this woman what he wanted to tell her: that he loves her and that he loves her in a time of lost innocence. (Eco 1985, pp. 74–75).

This is how the extra-terrestrial mythology surrounding Kubrick's monolith has been able to function beyond the scepticism of both those who despise any

---

6 See "Un 'mystérieux monolithe de métal' dans le désert de l'Utah: quand est-il apparu? Et qui a bien pu l'installer là?". *RTBF*. 25.11.2020, retrieved 03.04.2022, from https://www.rtbf.be/article/un-mysterieux-monolithe-de-metal-dans-le-desert-de-l-utah-quand-est-il-apparu-et-qui-a-bien-pu-l-installer-la-10639336?id=10639336.

7 The term was imported from semiotics by folklorists Linda Dégh and Andrew Vázsonyi in their 1983 article "Does the Word 'Dog' Bite? Ostensive Action as a Means of Legend-Telling" (1983, pp. 5–34) to refer to the ways in which real-life actions are guided by legends. On the panic of 2016 as spectacular (and spectacularised) ostension, let me refer to my book *Evil Clowns* (*Les clowns maléfiques*, Murmure: Dijon 2021).

mention to the "little green men" and of those who are rather wary of being compromised by a new media hoax. To understand the success of this bizarre cultural recycling operation, we must refer to the masterpiece of the brilliant British filmmaker.

Ironically, the monolith of *2001: A Space Odyssey* is itself a complex operation of cultural recycling. It first appeared in Arthur C. Clarke's short story "Sentinel of Eternity", published in the pulp magazine *10 Story Fantasy* (spring 1951). Following the usual practice of pulp literature, the paratext opens with an enigmatic illustration, centred here on the astronaut's anguished reaction to a mysterious radiation whose origin is not perceived. This is the recycling, in a science-fictional key, of the iconographic tradition of the encounter with the sacred, most particularly Moses's hierophany in front of the burning bush (Exodus 3:1–4). A small, equally enigmatic text accompanies this secularised hierophany, "Before there were men on Earth, that signal-sending pyramid had stood alone on a lifeless moon. What would happen now that its alarm was silenced?" (Clarke 1951, p. 41).

The narrator, a "selenologist", participates in an expedition to a *lunar terra incognita* "in the late summer of 1996", thus marking a double spatial and temporal "strangeness" in the tradition of interstellar transposition of tropes from the literature of colonial "discovery". He then encounters what will become one of science fiction's most iconic "novums": "a shiny, roughly pyramidal structure, twice the height of a man, which was embedded in the rock like a gigantic, multifaceted jewel" (Clarke 1951, p. 45). The choice of the pyramidal structure is anything but coincidental: the Egyptian pyramids had become, since James Bonwick's famous book (*Pyramid Facts and Fancies*, 1877), one of the sources of the most delirious speculations about the origins of 'civilisation'.[8]

The structure gives rise to a series of theories that recycle the fantasies of pyramidology in an extra-terrestrial context:

> Long ago, other races on the worlds of other suns must have scaled and passed the heights that we have reached. […] Everywhere there would be worlds, but they would be empty or peopled with crawling, mindless things. Such was our own Earth […] when

8 Thus, Ignatius Donnelly proposed as early as 1882 an Atlantean origin of these structures (of which he saw, pushing the diffusionist theories then in vogue to absurdity, equivalences in all cultures known and to be) in his classic *Atlantis, the Antediluvian World* (1882, p. 330). This theory was taken up by Grafton Elliot Smith in *The Ancient Egyptians and the Origin of Civilization* (1911) and then tirelessly repeated to this day by a large cohort of "pyramidologists" (or, to use Leonard Cottrell's more colourful term, "pyramidiots").

> that first ship of the peoples of the dawn came sliding in from the abyss beyond Pluto. […] So they left a sentinel, one of millions they have scattered throughout the universe, watching over all worlds with the promise of life. It was a beacon that down the ages has been patiently signalling the fact that no one had discovered it. Perhaps you understand now why that crystal pyramid was set upon the Moon instead of on the Earth. Its builders […] would be interested in our civilization only if we proved our fitness to survive – by crossing space and so escaping from the Earth, our cradle. (Clarke 1951, p. 47).

The enigmatic pyramid-shaped monolith thus becomes an interspatial telecommunication device, illustrating the new dominant paradigm of what McLuhan would call "the electronic age". Placed under the sign of the revolution introduced by radar in the Second World War, this "Sentinel of Eternity" is situated at the edge of the sacred and the machine. The end of the story is ambivalent, with no indication of the consequences of the discovery,

> Now its signals have ceased, and those whose duty it is will be turning their minds upon Earth. Perhaps they wish to help our infant civilization. But they must be very, very old, and the old are often insanely jealous of the young. […] We have broken the glass of the fire-alarm and have nothing to do but to wait. I do not think we will have to wait for long. (Clarke 1951, p. 47).

This open ending admirably sums up the ambivalence that presided over the figure of the extra-terrestrial at that time (and, in a way, up to the present day). On the one hand, the speculative tradition of cosmic palingenesis moved in the direction of universal brotherhood, with its ecumenical insistence on a kind of perpetual tutorship. But, on the other hand, Clarke also presents the other possible hypothesis, popularised by H. G. Wells' *War of the Worlds* (1898) and updated by the anxieties of the Cold War: that of an antagonism all the more ferocious because it would confront us with a pure otherness. This antagonism is symptomatically placed here under the Saturnian (and counter-oedipal) sign of the devouring of its offspring by the jealous Father. This seems to refer, implicitly, to another major paradigm, that of Lovecraftian cosmic horror (the adverb "insanely" being revealing in itself).

Kubrick contacted Arthur C. Clarke in 1964. He wanted to make, in the wake of his recent hit *Dr. Strangelove*, a science fiction film faithful to the ambitions of the genre as it had evolved in literature (and therefore at the antipodes of what it had become in the cinema, mostly geared towards the old formulas of "space opera" and "rampaging monsters"). Clarke suggested his short story "Sentinel" as a starting point for what was to become a real odyssey in more ways than one.

From the outset, the film was placed under the sign of the monolith, which in a way structures it or at least literally forms one of its pillars, at once a "cycle", rhyme and *leitmotif*, bridging its three main parts but also acting as an XYZ between the three great questions that the film seems to inherit from the famous painting by Gauguin (1898), "Where do we come from? What are we? Where are we going?". The strength of the monolith in the film comes above all, as has often been said, from its enigmaticity, as opposed to a regime of symbolic referentiality; hence the decision to move away from the pyramidal model of Clarke's short story, which is too heavily culturally connoted (Kubrick is rightly wary of the whole tradition of "pyramidologists", already mentioned). And what could be more enigmatic than the form finally adopted? In it are combined the powers of primordial lithophany and the most radical abstraction, the (literalised) "clean slate" and the Table of the Law (albeit without any written commandments), the Philosopher's Stone and the tombstone, avant-garde minimalism and primordial archaism. Above all, it remains a perfectly smooth surface onto which we can project all our desires and fears, but also all our interpretations (including the very common one of making it a cinema screen, when exactly the opposite is happening).

Its genesis shows a slow process of ascetic hollowing out: against the "shimmering" and "gemmy" aspect it had in the novella, and against the initial attempts to turn it into a slab of transparent Plexiglas, or even, precisely, a screen (in the guise of a "learning television machine", according to Kubrick's expression),[9] whereby the final choice took the form of the radical emptiness that has become such an obviousness for current spectators (Chion 2005, p. 254). Its austere elegance is, in itself, an image of this purification of which it is the result and, as such, brings it closer to that which governs the film as a whole (constituting, moreover, one of its recurring geometric motifs). This links it to the minimal art of its time ("a pretty fair example of minimal art", says Kubrick), as Jörg Heiser points out, noting its striking parallels with Anne Truitt's *Hardcastle* tomb sculpture of 1962 (once again the shadow of Thanatos looms) (Heiser 2002).

In the film, the monolith fulfils exactly the role of a 'McGuffin',

> It is the empty signifier that cannot be interpreted but which triggers the plot. At the same time, it is also – even if only in the cinematic space – oppressive, physically present as a fetish of power and technology. It is both the black box of progress and the uninscribed tombstone of history. (Heiser 2002).

Clarke and Kubrick had originally planned a kind of McLuhanian extrapolation of television, with images of monkeys materialising on the surface of the rectangle, to encourage their fellow monkeys to imitate them. But Kubrick wisely

9 Cited in "An Interview with Stanley Kubrick (1969)" (Gelmis 1970).

rejected such a didactic vision of "distance education" (ironically, the Open University was to be inaugurated in 1971 on BBC2). Furthermore, in the course of editing, he cut out the explanatory voice-over. Both of these decisions were precise applications of the lesson of minimal art.

The choice of black is emblematic in this respect, recycling, as Anne Truitt did, the radical abstraction embodied by Kazimir Malevich's famous *Black Square* (1915). Often considered the "zero point of painting", this monochrome canvas elided the thousand-year old figurative tradition of the West and paradoxically revived Jewish or Islamic religious aniconism, as the monolith seems to do as well (both have been compared with a tephilin). Malevich wrote, in a prose as enigmatic as his painting, "My new painting does not belong exclusively to the Earth. The Earth has been abandoned like a termite-infested house. And in fact, in man, in his consciousness, there is an impulse towards space. A desire to take off from the Earth."[10] This obsession, recurrent in the painter's work, could be read in the wake of the work of Konstantin Tsioklovsky and other "cosmists" who were to leave a lasting mark on the Russian (and then Soviet) fascination with outer space, culminating in the launch of the Sputnik, which triggered the Space Race, of which *2001* is in many ways an aesthetic extension.

The enigmatic nature of Kubrick's monolithic film provoked a reception that was paradoxical, to say the least, made up of both disorientation and hermeneutic infatuation. Two years after its release, Jerome Agel, the book designer of Marshall McLuhan's books *The Medium is the Message: An Inventory of Effects* (1967) and *War and Peace in the Global Village* (1968), published an unusual work under the somewhat misleading title of *The Making of Kubrick's 2001* (1970), which in its own way constituted a kind of critical monolith and was also a cultural milestone.

Following the model of the textual and visual collages that make up the previous McLuhanian works, Agel articulates a heterogeneous series of discourses generated by and around the film, discourses that have become, over time, a kind of portrait of its immediate cultural impact. Agel offers his own McLuhanesque collage of the terms used to refer to the monolith in a kind of "found poem", placed under the sign of *Citizen Kane*'s main symbol ("A rosebud by any other name!"), thus inheriting its fundamental ambiguity (McGuffin? Ultimate symbol? Freudian secret?):

> Here's what the artifact's been called: / Artifact / Metal prism / Pentalogue / Mies van der Rohe version of one-half / The Tablets of the Law / Black basalt column / Black steel

---

10 Cited in Douglas (1994, p. 26).

> door / Long cement board / Pillar / The block / Monololith / That damn two-by-four / Teaching machine / Candy bar / Calling card / Transistor radio / Handball court wall / Cracker Jacks box / Vibrating Metallic Bar / God. (Agel 1970, p. 289).

Following the phenomenal success of the film, monoliths began to proliferate, but discreetly, as esoteric signs of the pop semiosphere. Whether in the form of an action figure, the cover of the Who's *Next* album (1971), the mysterious members of SEELE in *Neon Genesis Evangelion* (1995–6) or in the design of the iPhone (2007). Between parody, quotation and reappropriation, various works have integrated them: for instance, the sketch comedy *The Groove Tube* (1974) transforms it into a simple television set, which is not without irony since we know that it was one of Clarke's ideas rejected by Kubrick. The primates, fascinated by their discovery, indulge in a kind of simian parody of Woodstock, playing rock music in front of a fire ("rock, not war"). The two antagonistic targets of the film (television and commodified counterculture) are thus merged in this scene.

Tim Burton, on the other hand, transforms the same scene into a *mise en abyme* squared in perfect accord with the metatextual nature of his film *Charlie and the Chocolate Factory* (2005). The monolith becomes a gigantic chocolate bar that Willy Wonka's scientific assistants shrink until it can be integrated into a kind of television where the scene from "The Dawn of Man" is played out (unless it literally happens there). The loss of the aura here also borders on the ridiculous, while Tim Burton himself seems to be playing the mad chocolatier. Is it that, behind the game of interlocking universes, classical cinema, reduced to living in the small screens of TV, has lost all its meaning, reduced to the reign of pure simulacra and pure merchandise? Is it Burton's work itself that laments it becoming an industrial sugar factory?

It is this iconic and semiotic proliferation that has been finally recycled in the monolith craze of 2020. Ironically, the mystery of the first monolith, attributed to a deceased minimalist artist – John McCracken – brings us back to the multiple connections between Kubrick's monolith, minimal art and Land Art, very specifically associated with the deserts of the Southwest.[11] It is significant that

11 As Gabriella Angeleti reminds us, "The wilderness of the southwestern United States has a rich and eventful history in Land Art, especially in works that retain their magic and mystery by being largely inaccessible or difficult to locate, from Robert Smithson's 1970 magnum opus *Spiral Jetty* in the Great Salt Lake to Michael Heizer's 1969 *Double Negative* near the Utah border in Nevada," both of which we've already mentioned in their connections to *2001* (Angeleti 2020).

the attribution of the monolith is shared between different possible artists, all working in the same area: names such as Petecia Le Fawnhawk or Derek DeSpain have been evoked but none has claimed authorship of the structure. McCracken's gallerist David Zwirner initially confirmed it was the former's work, but later retracted his statement, claiming it was a tribute by another artist. McCracken died in 2011 (shortly after finishing his monolith-like "Fair") and the earliest sighting of the structure in its present location dates from 2016. "Was this part of a well-orchestrated scheme to increase McCracken's market value or just a bit of art-world clout chasing?" asks Isabelle Hore-Thorburn (2020).

The question remains unanswered but, beyond these classical issues of authorship and attribution, it is the return to the foundational link between Kubrick's monolith and the artistic experiments of his time that appears to stand out most in this mysterious lithophany. With Kubrick's monolith, contemporary art thus rediscovers some of its origins, replaying in the same hypermodern quotation (quotation squared, or hyper-quotation) the evocation of the film and that of the works from which it was inspired or which it extended. Significantly, journalists intrigued by the global proliferation of monoliths have immediately focused on the "aesthetic" hypothesis rather than on the ufological "lunatic fringe" or simple pranksters. As Jonathan Jones wryly remarks, "It would be ironic if these structures were really the work of highly intelligent aliens trying to make first contact – but we're so jaded by artistic pranks and science fiction clichés that we take it for an elaborate stunt. 'Earthlings, we wanted to pass on the secret of the universe to you, but you're too cynical, they will lament as they annihilate us.' " (Jones 2020).

What's more, some of the monoliths are clearly advertisements (such as the one in Zenata, near Casablanca, placed by a logistics company to launch the campaign for their new robot, enclosed in the structure). "We've never had such a need for mystery", concludes Jones, "And for a while, for all their faults when examined as art, the sentinels were sublime. Please, whoever is responsible, stop now while there is still an ounce of wonder in this diversion from our banal apocalypse" (Jones 2020).

Now, in this plea, we can detect what may be at stake in this global "epidemic" of monoliths. Beyond the simple citation game, or even the will to materially embody this iconic fictional object (extending as it were the original cinematographic "trip"), something of the original monolith is still invoked. Is it the species' need to move, in a somewhat apocalyptic context, to another level of consciousness, as contemporary New Age movements continue to assert? Is it the renewed need to fantasise about the mysteries of outer space in the face of a daily life that has become absolutely claustrophobic?

In any case, it is clear that this is a curious case of postdigital recycling: it was the numerical proliferation of images that turned the Utah artefact into a planetary viral phenomenon, meta-recycling as it were the previous recycling of Kubrick's and Clarke's monolith that had been operating in the semiosphere since the release of the iconic 1968 film, whose shadow is still omnipresent in cyberspace.

References

Agel, Jerome: *The Making of Kubrick's 2001*. Signet: New York 1970.

Angeleti, Gabriella: "Alien visitors or avant-garde installation? Mysterious monolith discovered in the Utah desert". *The Art Newspaper*, November 24, 2020.

Chion, Michele: *Stanley Kubrick: L'Humain, Ni Plus Ni Moins*. Cahiers du Cinéma: Paris 2005.

Clarke, Arthur C.: "Sentinel of Eternity". *10 Story Fantasy*, spring 1951, pp. 41–47.

Dégh, Linda / Vázsonyi, Andrew: "Does the Word 'Dog' Bite? Ostensive Action as a Means of Legend-Telling". *Journal of Folklore Research* (20) 1983, pp. 5–34.

Department of Public Safety: *DPS Aero Bureau Encounters Monolith in Red Rock Country*. November 23, 2020, retrieved 3.4.2022, from https://dpsnews.utah.gov/dps-aero-bureau-encounters-monolith-in-red-rock-country/.

Domínguez Leiva, Antonio: *Les clowns maléfiques*. Le murmure: Dijon 2021.

Domínguez Leiva, Antonio: *Monolithes. Retour viral d'une mythologie de l'Âge Spatial*. PUF: Paris 2022.

Donnelly, Ignatius: *Atlantis: the antediluvian world*. Harper & Bros. Editorial: New York 1882.

Douglas, Charlotte: *Kazimir Malevich*. Abrams: H.N. New York 1994.

Eco, Umberto: *Apostille au Nom de la rose*. Grasset: Paris 1985.

Gelmis, Joseph: "An Interview with Stanley Kubrick (1969)". The Film Director as Superstar. Doubleday and Company: Garden City, New York 1970, retrieved 3.4.2022, from http://www.visual-memory.co.uk/amk/doc/0069.html.

Heiser, Jörg: "Dark side of the room. Plain surfaces". *Frieze* 65, March 4, 2002, retrieved 3.4.2022, from https://www.frieze.com/article/dark-side-room.

Hore-Thorburn, Isabelle: "Like Many Influencers, Utah's Vanishing Monolith Might Have Just Relocated to NYC". *Highsnobiety*, December 1, 2020, retrieved 3.4.2022, from https://www.highsnobiety.com/p/utah-monolith-john-mccracken-david-zwirner/.

Jones, Jonathan: “Mystery of the monoliths: if only it were aliens”, *The Guardian* 08.12.2020, retrieved 3.4.2022, from https://www.theguardian.com/artanddesign/2020/dec/08/monolith-makers-strange-objects-aliens-reflective-wildernesses.

Robertson, Adi: “Even Utah’s mysterious monolith may be no match for Google Earth”. *The Verge*, November 24, 2020, retrieved 3.4.2022, from https://www.theverge.com/2020/11/24/21656223/mysterious-utah-monolith-osint-google-earth-tracking.

Rove, Karl: “Election 2020: The Year of Weird Conventions are over, and voters may actually care about the vice president”. *The Wall Street Journal* 12.08.2020, retrieved 3.4.2022, from https://www.wsj.com/articles/election-2020-the-year-of-weird-11597269159.

RTBF (Radio-télévision belge de la Fédération Wallonie-Bruxelles): *Un “mystérieux monolithe de métal” dans le désert de l’Utah: quand est-il apparu? Et qui a bien pu l’installer là?* 25.11.2020, retrieved 3.4.2022, from https://www.rtbf.be/article/un-mysterieux-monolithe-de-metal-dans-le-desert-de-l-utah-quand-est-il-apparu-et-qui-a-bien-pu-l-installer-la-10639336?id=10639336.

Wakefield, Lily: “Trump supporters tear down mystery monolith because it’s ‘gay’ and they ‘hate illegal aliens from Mexico or outer space’”. *Pink News. Yahoo!news* 07.12.2020, retrieved 3.4.2022, from https://uk.news.yahoo.com/trump-supporters-tear-down-mystery-163238074.html.

Wikipedia. The Free Encyclopedia: *List of works similar to the 2020 Utah monolith*, retrieved 3.4.2022, from https://en.wikipedia.org/wiki/List_of_works_similar_to_the_2020_Utah_monolith.

Rafael Vidal Sanz
Universidad Complutense de Madrid

Recycling of Haunted House and Spiritualism Motifs in two Postdigital Narratives

Abstract: W.J.T. Mitchell, inspired by Marshall McLuhan, writes that "the content of a medium is another ancient medium". Throughout time, "the ghostly", the search for contact with a disappeared or invisible world, has nested in different media. At the end of the 19th Century, a new typology of photography emerged, "spiritual photography", which through overexposure sought to print spirits on the photosensitive plate. The technologies of the postdigital era, characterised by a dialectic between presence and absence, can serve as an emergency medium for the spectral phenomena. This article analyses the way in which films such as *Personal Shopper* (2016), by Olivier Assayas, or *Host* (2020), by Rob Savage, recycle elements such as spiritism and the haunted house from the gothic genre through the use of postdigital technologies.

Keywords: ghostly, spectral, spiritism, gothic, postdigital, *Personal Shopper*, Olivier Assayas, *Host*, Rob Savage.

1. Introduction

In the months following the lockdown decreed due to the COVID-19 pandemic, a meme went viral on social media in which four characters dressed in *fin-de-siècle* fashion sit around a turning table, above which is the following message: "Zoom meetings are just modern seances." There were times when telework was increasing and many meetings were held remotely through video conferencing apps such as Google Meet and Zoom itself. The meme is an ironic comment on the interruption during Zoom meetings, in the form of messages exchanged between those attending spiritualist seances, based on the phatic function of language defined by Jakobson ("Elizabeth, are you there?"). What is particularly interesting is how the recipient immediately understands the link between new communication technologies in the postdigital age and the formalities of spiritualism.

Fig. 1. Source: @artmemescentral on Instagram (Published on 31.01.2021).

Media of this type, particularly those linked to social media, which involve an immaterial link with beings who manifest a presence from their absence, may be positioned in the series of technical invention defined by Kafka and recognised by Deleuze and Guattari in their work *Kafka: pour une littérature mineure* [*Kafka: Towards a Minor Literature*], as "those that represent the vampirish revenge of the phantom where there is reintroduced 'the ghostly element between people' (the post, the telegraph, the telephone, wireless telegraphy)" ([1975] 1986, p. 30). There is a close link between the world of ghosts and technological evolution. As a medium in the film *Personal Shopper* by Olivier Assayas says, "spiritualism was always very close to the technological avantgarde" (Assayas 2016, 16:35). If we construct a brief genealogy in this respect, the telegraph developed in parallel with the spiritualist fashion of the 1840s in America and 1850s in Europe. The telegraph was reflected in the birth of spiritualist photography, which was first documented in 1861 by William H. Mumler (Chéroux 2004, p. 196). Thanks to the technique of overprinting on photosensitive plates, the technology of photography allowed this phenomenon of spectral hauntings, as if it revealed that the senses were more in focus under the lens. According to Jordy Ardanuy, "the arrival of modern spiritualism combined with photography made the new technology available to the belief in spirits, establishing an alliance between devices and apparitions, in an attempt to reconcile reason and belief" (Ardanuy / Csefkó 2018)[1]. Chéroux notes in this phenomenon the combination of an iconography of conviction and an iconography of recreation, as the belief in images of ghosts (many of them the result of technical ineptitude) was added to the idea of a trick or manipulation, as many photographers constructed them artificially as publicity (2004, p. 195). Other media such as painting were also explored in this respect, particularly by the painter Hilma af Klint, who used spiritualist sessions to try to contact an invisible or disappeared world which she wanted to portray in her canvasses (Sarriugarte Gómez 2005, p. 86).

The question is: what relationship can this link between technology and spiritualism have with the postdigital? An example can be found in the social media profiles of the dead, which continue open for a long time after death and through which posts are even uploaded, as if they were messages from a supernatural world. An example of this is the film critic Roger Ebert's account, which has been administered by his widow, Chaz, after his death. In his Facebook and Twitter profiles, new publications or retweets appear frequently.[2] This is a sign of the tense relationships of the process of grief and the technologies inherent to the postdigital era.

In *Understanding Media: The Extensions of Man* (1964), Marshal McLuhan describes the way in which the media serve as an extension of the subject: "The content of any medium is always another medium" ([1964] 2003, p. 19): This is the case of the spoken word, which is at the core of writing. This phenomenon is described by the concept of *nesting*, which was taken up by W.T.J. Mitchell in his study on the media and visual culture. *Nesting* refers to the case in which "one medium appears inside another as its content" (Mitchell 2005, p. 262), as in the case of TV conceived in terms of film. McLuhan's saying is slightly transformed in Mitchell by including an adjective: "The content of a medium is always an ancient medium" (2005, p. 262).[3] An emerging medium assumes content from other media by this nesting phenomenon, given that it does not have content

1 All translations from Rafael Vidal Sanz.

2 In his Twitter account, Roger Ebert retweeets all the publications with content related to the cinema by his wife, Chaz Ebert: https://twitter.com/ebertchicago.

3 Rather than a historical restriction of the idea, which could lead to a certain teleology in the evolution of the media, Mitchell proposes a possible anachronism in the configuration of the communication media: a subsequent and even speculative or imaginary medium may also be the content of a prior medium (2005, p. 262), in a kind of divining practice.

exclusive to it. It may be noted that ghosts are content which have nested in numerous earlier technological media, given the need for media support (Belting 2007, p. 3) for their appearance. The technologies of the postdigital age also take it up as a way of giving them a content that they previously lacked. This article explores the recycling of ghost narratives based on postdigital technologies such as Facebook or Zoom, given their adscription to communicative models with subjects immersed in a dialectic of presence/absence similar to what is produced in the attempt to contact spectral phenomena. It includes a brief summary of the notion of the "spectral turn" and an analysis of two recent films: *Personal Shopper* (2016), by Olivier Assayas, and *Host* (2020), by Rob Savage.

2. The spectral turn or the importance of the ghost

Ghosts are an elusive concept that refers to what is continually appearing and disappearing at the same time. For María Tausiet, "the ghost is an absence which, however, becomes present. Perhaps for this reason it is so ductile and suggestive when it comes to representing or evoking what is no longer there, but continues to be present, however much it is rejected: it is what refuses to disappear, precisely because it does not end up being known or understood properly" (Tausiet 2015). Based on the French philosopher Jacques Derrida's *Specters of Marx* ([1993] 2006), the so-called spectral turn has been developed in the academic world (Tausiet 2015; Hidalgo Urtiaga 2018, p. 33), in parallel with the increase and normalisation of digital technology. It is a change in the direction of the hermeneutic view which includes the category of ghost in the academic analyses of certain social, literary and historiographic phenomena. "This conceptual change turns the ghost into a meta-concept which serves as an instrument for interdisciplinary and intradisciplinary analysis" (Hidalgo Urtiaga 2018, p. 33). The interest of ghosts, whether in artistic or academic production, locates the concept in a privileged place for thought.

For Derrida, "the specter is always animated by a spirit" ([1993] 2006, p. 2), so we have to distinguish two ontological categories: the spirit, on the one hand, and its means of appearance in the world of the living, called the spectre or, more commonly, ghost, on the other hand. What makes the spirit different from the ghost for Derrida is "a supernatural and paradoxical phenomenality, the furtive and ungraspable visibility of the invisible, or an invisibility of a visible X" ([1993] 2006, p. 6). The ghost is the paradoxical operation by which the extremes of the binomial visibility/invisibility are interchanged: something visible is possessed by something invisible, or something invisible reappears among the visible. One of the fundamental procedures of the ghost, as described by Derrida, is haunting, similar to the return of what has been repressed. Ghosts will always return from their unsymbolised place to occupy our spaces and pass on their message. Although in their origin, ghosts were considered "the others" – the other side of enlightened rationality – with the birth of psychoanalysis, ghosts were interiorised and an attempt was made to explain them rationally by repressed drives or unresolved traumas which returned later in the life of patients. Hidalgo Urtiaga writes that "at the end of the 19th Century, the spectre was shifted to the disciplines of the mind, where it was emancipated as a metaphor of the psyche; in other words, a phantasmalisation of the mental" (2018, p. 23). Ghosts are expelled from representation and become mental images. In this respect, these ghosts which haunt us will serve as a projection of a series of fears that require a gothic or horror genre to transmit their repressed message. There are a number of aesthetic manifestations in which they do so through technologies of the postdigital age.

3. The medium as a medium: *Personal Shopper* by Olivier Assayas

Although at first it appears to be a film on spiritualism, this motif actually emerges as a result of unresolved mourning. Maureen (played by Kristen Stewart) works as a personal shopper. She is trying to find a means of communication with her twin brother, Lewis, who died recently as a result of a congenital malformation of the cardiovascular system, which she also has. Each operates as a mirror image of a single being in which one (the living body) embodies health and the other (the spectre) illness and the possibility of death. A subtle rift between the two emerges, which is produced between the medical image of the examination of the heart and the photograph taken with Maureen as a model. Maureen moves to the empty house where Lewis died to begin her supra-sensory contact with him. This space, filmed in contrasting shadows and light and avoiding subjective shots of Maureen, generating a feeling of surveillance over her, is the setting for a recycling of the motif of the haunted house so typical of the gothic genre. The house becomes a metonymic space for her psyche and maintains its own enunciation through the production of sounds which cannot be assigned to a human source, like a prosopopoeia. It is also the space of gothic writing that leaves messages from a supernatural world. Tausiet notes how gothic houses speak of "the lack of psychic independence often felt by their young occupants" (2015). In the case of Maureen, the house could symbolise a maternal meeting place with its disappeared twin given the impossibility of living one's own life.

In this negation phase of mourning, Maureen tries to exorcise the reality of absence by means of her conversion into a medium. For Freud, mourning arises from a retraction of the libido projected onto a loved object which no longer exists, either physically or as a tie, and whose absence we become aware of, which may sometimes lead to a hallucinatory psychosis:

> Reality-testing has shown that the loved object no longer exists, and it proceeds to demand that all libido shall be withdrawn from its attachments to the object [...]. This opposition can be so intense that a turning away from reality takes place and a clinging to the object through the medium of hallucinatory wishful psychosis. (Freud [1917] 1966, p. 244).

The process of this mourning is intimately linked to the figure of the ghost, an absence made present. Based on Freud, Tausiet refers to ghosts as "the dead who have not been forgotten" (2015). Derrida states that "[a]s in the work of mourning, after a trauma, the conjuration has to make sure that the dead will not come back" ([1993] 2006, p. 120), so if the process of mourning is a success, the ghost will no longer return. Maureen is immersed in a stage of negation of the death of her brother and her work as a medium will mean an attempt to bring closure to mourning by the assumption of the ghost as something which is part of her. In turn, she will operate as a spectre for her client Kyra, as she tries on the clothes she buys as if she were a ghost who found a medium as host in the changing rooms of her employee and masturbates with her in bed. The mirror condition of this narrative is heightened through intertextual references, such as the spiritualist history of Victor Hugo, who tried to find traces of his dead daughter in spiritualist sessions held between 1853 and 1855 during his exile from Paris. The characters become ghosts for others.

The contact with the absent figure of Lewis occurs through mysterious messages on a Facebook Messenger-like app on Maureen's smartphone.[4] The film sets up a shot/reverse montage between Maureen and the smartphone which supplants the inherently cinematographic form of the classical representation of conversation by a dialogue between a human being and the machine. The ghost becomes the reverse shot of the subject who is searching for it, by way of a detailed shot of the mobile's interface. The use of shot/reverse brings us to the concept of suture, a psychoanalytical notion developed by Jacques Allain-Miller (1969, p. 55) and adopted in film by Oudart ([1969] 1997, pp. 51–63). In

4 Paradoxically, Maureen contacts with the spectre through her mobile on the Eurotrain journey between Paris and London: within the framework of a means of locomotion typical of the industrial revolution, and analogous to the modern age of spiritualism.

Lacanian terms, a suture is a point which achieves closure of the symbolic plane with the imaginary plane; or, which is the same thing, the I of the statement with the I of what is stated.[5] Through the suture, the imaginary provides the symbolic chain with a unit in the discontinuity of its discourse. Translated into cinematographic terms, for Oudart the suture "represents the closure of the cinematic *énoncé* in line with its relationship which its subject [...] and then put in its place as the spectator" (1997 p. 51). This relationship consists of the projection by the spectator of a fantastic figure, called the Absent One, which combines filmic units – the shots – which the montage separates into discrete units (1997, p. 51). For Oudart, this continuity of the discrete is established in the dialectical relationship between the field and reverse field. The argument here is that the use of the shot/reverse shot in the relationship between Maureen and the mobile interface is Assays' way of producing a suture between presence and absence, and that the relationship that the spectator has with the Absent One in the film projection is analogous to that which is experienced through technologies of communication in the postdigital age, where a continuity is constructed in a discourse by means of the imaginary projection of a receptor who is absent. This is the reason for the appropriateness and effectiveness of the use of this form of film.

5 For Jacques-Alain Milller, there is a gap in which the continuity of the discourse is constructed, as "suture names the relation of the subject to the chain of its discourse; we shall see that it figures there as the element which is lacking, in the form of a stand-in. For, while there lacking, it is not purely and simply absent" (Miller 1969, p. 55).

Fig. 2 and 3. Shot and reverse-shot of the exchange of messages between Maureen and the ghost through an instant messaging app on the smartphone. Source: O. Assayas (2016). *Personal Shopper*. La Aventura Cine.

In a certain respect, these messages on the mobile's interface are like the e-image defined by Brea, whose basic feature is spectrality, as it is what comes to disappear immediately. It is everything which "is going" (2010, p. 67), only here the text would be what dissipates and what keeps vigil over the invoked image. We have to trace the link between the notion of medium and medium, which Belting relates through anthropology of the image based on necessity in ancient cultures, of having a medium for the cult of the dead and an image or an object with which the already absent body would be exchanged. Along the same lines, the medium existed in that "a relative latecomer to this tradition of death rituals was the modern medium of 19th-Century spiritualist seances. A living person offered his or her body to a dead person as a medium, who would transmit the voice of the departed." (Belting 2007, p. 38). In *Personal Shopper*, Maureen fails in her body-to-body contact with the ghost and requires a technological extension to serve as a host for the hauntings of the ghost of her twin brother. It is precisely the technologies of the postdigital age, like the smartphone and an instant messaging, which provide a communicative link with the lack of the power of a body. Hence the presence of these technologies could be considered a recycling of gothic and fantasy narratives, as they serve as a channel and mediation to the lost voice. In the train, Maureen asks him "Alive or dead?" (Assayas 2016, 41:28) by way of an invocation. This channel can only disappear by activating the Airplane mode.

This film was shot in 35 mm celluloid, so it generates a dialogue between two forms of being in images: digital and analogue. Assayas has a conservative view of cinema with respect to other arts. For him "cinema is not one of the multiple possible images; it is the only image which really has the capacity to see the Other, to face Otherness" (Faus 2017). That is why smartphone interfaces are normally presented within a larger image: the cinematographic narrative sutures the disparate images together based on an imaginary absence.

The film puts in play the relationship maintained by the subject with her loneliness through new communication technologies, in which social ties, including those of one's own images, are mediated by an interface. Maureen's isolation for the entire film is what triggers the desire for a re-encounter with a lost reality. Anaïs Guillet defines the film as a *thriller écranique* and notes that its discourse is closer to technological than spiritual: "l'enjeu communicationnel au cœur du film est moins spectral que technologique. Le tour de force d'Assayas est de filmer une Maureen le plus souvent seule et dont une grande partie des communications avec autrui sont interfacées (téléphone portable, ordinateur, mais aussi lettres manuscrites lues en voix off)"[6] (2018, p. 369). Here the spectral which haunts or nests through technology is a compensatory reflection of the virtual mediation of social ties. Paradoxically, through a fantasy excess the vicarious relationship maintained with others is remediated, as it functions as a form of self-knowledge. The film reverts to the *doppelgänger* motif, defined by Freud in his famous article on the uncanny or *unheimlich,* and which may be understood as the familiar "which has been repressed and then reappears" (Freud [1919] 2003, p. 152). The double twin who returns serves as a restoration of a lost reality and as a counterpoint to a precarious life founded on technological

6 "the communication issue at the heart of the film is less spectral than technological. Assayas' tour de force is to film a Maureen who is most often alone and whose communication with others is largely interfaced (mobile phone, computer, but also handwritten letters read in voice-over)".

mediatisation.[7] The only successful instant of communication with the spectral is produced in her trip to Oman, when the mourning is beginning to be overcome her and this phantasmagorical projection may be integrated in itself without technological mediation through a first close-up of her face which does not construct its reverse shot, because it is within herself. In her invocation to Lewis, Maureen uses a singular third-person pronoun to refer to herself: "Lewis, is it you? Or is it just me?" (Assayas 2016, 1:40:36). In a variation of Rimbaud's famous coinage, it could be said that this – the other, the thing, the spectre, the technology, what isn't me – is me.

4. Do you want to see a ghost? Lockdown and spiritualism in *Host* by Rob Savage

The popularity of the recent low-budget film *Host* (2020) is due to its ability to reflect, through the horror genre, the uncertainty provoked by the COVID-19 lockdown. The reasons lie in the analogy it creates between being locked in the home and the motif of a haunted house. The home itself, in the exceptional circumstance of a lack of communication with the outside world, becomes an organic being which obtains a spectral agency granted by the people who are locked in it. The haunted house motif of gothic literature and the horror genre serves as a narrative to reflect a state of reduced agency, offset by a spiritual broadening of the agency of the home. *Host* shows us that in an exceptional state, the intimacy which the home tends to metaphorise (Bachelard 2000, p. 27) may be inverted and converted into a disturbing event, like the Freudian *unheimlich*, as the home itself can be lived like a hostile entity. Furniture falling in the storage space of the house of Haley, the organiser, at the start of the film, functions as a portent of what is to come.

The plot is a simple and effective formula: a group of friends agree to a Zoom meeting with a medium for a session of spiritualism from home. The external impositions of the lockdown and its special features create the session and the

---

7 The film also includes a murder mystery plot which overlaps with the gothic and fantasy plot and functions also by way of a rational and reflective explanation of the story of ghosts. Kyra, the star dressed by Maureen, is murdered by her boyfriend, but they blame Maureen because of certain irrefutable evidence such as having slept in her boss's house and using her clothes without permission. The prosecution is based on the parasitic ghostly relationship between employee and employer. However, when they discover who committed the crime and reality discloses its sinister underbelly, Maureen can close the mourning process at last and contact Lewis.

film itself. The medium Seylan states that "there is no reason why spirits can't communicate with us over the Internet," (Savage 2020, 0:16:15) as they are made with the same virtual material as the medium through which they are invoked. While recycling of the Western idea of the haunted house, the film uses Eastern traditions in the materialisation of spectres. This is the case with the figure of the *tulpa*, which is Tibetan in origin, although it emerged as a hybrid between Buddhist tradition and Western theosophy. The *tulpa* "is a being that begins in the imagination but acquires a tangible reality and sentience. Tulpas are created either through a deliberate act of individual will or unintentionally from the thoughts of numerous people" (Mikes / Laycock 2019, p. 87). In *Host*, the tulpa is born from a trick: Jemma pretends to perceive the appearance of the ghost of Jack, a classmate who committed suicide at school, and the tulpa assumes the form of a fiction. That is why we can consider the Zoom meeting as a community of readers who try to escape the routine of confinement through the exercise of fiction. Thus, if we think of a spiritualist session as a community of readers[8] of a story, and the medium Seylan as an *informed reader* (Fish 2000, p. 21–67) who is competent in the language of the spiritualist tradition, the film may be interpreted as a symptom of the modification of social practice in the creation and reading of fiction through the technologies of the postdigital age, as a transformation is produced from the individual processes to experiences of a community nature, where the figure of expert (Seylan) even loses his symbolic capital, given the capacity for intervention of the subjects in the construction of the fictions.

Unlike *Personal Shopper*, where there is a relationship of an unequal nature between the interface of the postdigital device and the cinematographic image, *Host* aims to make the film narrative itself out of the poor image of the Zoom interface. In contrast with the conservative discourse of Assayas that creates a hierarchy of image types, *Host* manages to free itself from its prejudice of image quality and convert the events of the interface of the screen into the primordial source of the narrative. According to the film's producers, all filming was captured through a Zoom videocall, making it a product which recycles a cultural interface and makes it transparent by alluding to the material conditions produced by it. There is also a meta-cinematographic use of this interface, as the credits are shown through the list of participants in the Zoom meeting, including all the members of the filming team. In an ironic message, the duration of the

8 For more information on communities of readers in the postdigital age, see Menéndez de la Cuesta González (2020).

spiritualist session is limited to the time limit of a free videocall in the application, which is 40 minutes. It could be said that the limits of technology, at least in the non-premium version, are those of the film.

Host expands the dynamic screen that Manovich describes due to the split-screen phenomenon inherent to the computer interface. According to Manovich, "No single window completely dominates the viewer's attention" (2001, p. 97). This simultaneity of screens within one screen has already been explored extensively by both commercial cinema (particularly in the case of phone calls) and experimental films, in the search for a de-automation of the original conditions of film projection (such as in *We Can't Go Home Again*, by Nicholas Ray [1973]). In this case, the proposal is not to recycle the digital interface in the film image but quite the reverse: a recycling of film narratives through the cultural interfaces of the postdigital era. The aim is to normalise the everyday experience of the split screen and not subordinate it to the analogue experience of the cinema, normally based on a classic undivided screen. A film may also be a virtual interface,[9] but adapted to the codes of suspense associated with genres such as horror. As the title itself suggests, the image of the interface becomes the actual host of the ghost.

The editing is also guided by the sound source and not so much by the visual source. The application of Zoom itself produces the same process thanks to its detection of the sound of the user, so the close-up we see is always the person who is converted into a direct sound source, who produces an action.[10] The montage of the film is also like that of an analogue product translated into the codes of technology of the postdigital age: the split screen with all the participants of the spiritualist session may be interpreted as a distance shot and the isolated headshots would be the close-ups. This montage which interchanges the two types of shot by means of a sonic hierarchy is unified by the imaginary absence which sutures the film: the spectre, the belief which binds the whole community.

Film functions by a reflective projection, since when a film is viewed at home, the close-up observed of the characters would be the same as that obtained by the spectator observing the film. Horror functions by formally subsuming the

9 Along these lines, there is the recent film by Diego Kanblue, *Las continentes* (2020), a film produced exclusively based on the dynamic interactions with the interface of his Mac computer, representing a reflection about memory in the postdigital age through the notion of files and their processing.

10 In this respect, it would be interesting to compare how the Zoom recording device and that of any videocam integrated in the computer reproduce the notion of a close-up in film, making it an aesthetic recycling for a new functionality in the postdigital area.

identity of the recording and projection devices, as the computer generates both processes if we think of *Host* as a film designed specifically to be seen at home and not in the cinema.[11]

How is the spirit visualised as a ghost? While the sound is the first direct manifestation, it in turn requires technical mediation to make itself visible. *Host* uses technological innovations such as the designs of masks or virtual backgrounds in Zoom as a way of providing media support to the figure invoked.[12] In this way, the recycling of the motifs of spiritualism or the horror genre finds a source, not only in the technological mediation of Zoom, but as a reflection of the anxieties which the information society produces in those participating in it.

5. Conclusions

The postdigital age, characterised by a normalisation of the use of digital technologies, produces a recycling of classic stories adapted to the conditions of interconnectivity which characterise the information society. Through the analysis of two recent films, *Personal Shopper* and *Host*, we have tried to determine how elements of the gothic and horror genres, such as spiritualism and the haunted house, can find a place to nest in new technologies as a way of expressing contemporary social unease. We have chosen two films in which devices such as the smartphone, the computer, instant messaging apps like Facebook Messenger, and the videocall system Zoom – all of them everyday landscapes in social relations – serve as a channel and a compensation for the symbolisation of other mental worlds which have been lost in ours. They are extremely antagonistic proposals, given their authors' different personal histories. The career in film of Olivier Assayas spans almost four decades, starting from his initial years as a critic for *Cahiers du Cinema* in France and including his emotional education through the consumption and valuation of analogue cinema. His approach therefore comes from a predigital world which is renewed in *Personal Shopper* thanks to the introduction of technologies of the postdigital age as an everyday habit. By filming on 35 mm celluloid, a hierarchical relationship is glimpsed regarding the interface image of mobile devices which is not present in Rob Savage's *Host*, where the cinema is recycled from the devices of record and recording of the virtual applications. Savage was

---

11 Moreover, the sets in which the actresses live are real, as it was filmed in her home, which gives a greater reality to the filming.

12 There is also a retro moment when they try to capture the figure of the ghost through the use of an analogue Polaroid camera.

born in 1992 and belongs to the millennial generation. As a digital native, he knows how to construct a fully contemporary narrative thanks to the use of the cultural interface as a source of image and suspense.

Despite the differences between them, both films address repressed fears which return by means of ghosts nested in a technological channel. These fears may be loneliness in an age of digital mediation or the lockdown which uprooted the experience of bodily intimacy between people. In both cases, there is mourning for a person or a way of life that has been lost. The difficult process of mourning, which means dealing with an undesired absence, leads to a complex relationship with the technologies of the digital age, based on communicative links to an absent figure. That is why these cultural projects in which ghosts are invoked via the smartphone or Zoom are forms that compensate for a limitation on real life, as in the case of the death of Lewis in *Personal Shopper* or the lockdown in *Host*. By situating mourning within narratives of ghosts, haunted houses, spiritualism, motifs of gothic traditions and the horror genre, the films connect perfectly with the new conditions of communication inaugurated by modern technologies.[13] At the same time, they demonstrate the way in which a state of lost experience must be supplied with a vicarious mediation with the aim of reconstructing a reality that has disappeared.

References

Ardanuy, Jorge / Csefkó, Martí Flo: "Un tipo de documento visual descuidado en España: la fotografía espiritista". *Miscelánea* (17) 2018, pp. 481–508.

Bachelard, Gaston: *La poética del espacio*. Fondo de cultura económica: Buenos Aires [1957] 2000.

Belting, Hans: *Antropología de la imagen*. Katz Barpal Editores: Madrid 2007.

Brea, José Luis: *Las tres eras de la imagen*. Madrid, Akal 2010.

13 *Bleeding Edge* (2013), Thomas Pynchon's last novel, narrates a story of cyberterrorism which involves financial lobbies of the multinational neoliberal system with the 9/11 attacks. Through the gothic genre, as a recurrence of haunted houses or subterranean spaces, the economic subworld is used as a metaphor which governs the destination of individuals. Two brothers, Lucas and Justin, create DeepArcher, a Deep Web programme that serves as a refuge and sanctuary in which the ghosts of the victims of neoliberalism make themselves visible through an avatar, as is the case with Lester Traipse. Once more, the figure of the ghost serves as an analogy of the notion of mourning; and at the same time, the ghost is a stimulus for the politicisation of loss, as it is an absence motivated by economic speculation which is to be combatted.

Deleuze, Gilles / Guattari, Félix: *Kafka: Towards a Minor Literature.* [*Kafka: pour une littérature mineure.* Translated by Dana Polan]. University of Minnesota Press: Minneapolis, London [1975] 1986.

Derrida, Jacques: *Specters of Marx. The State of the Debt, the Work of Mourning and the New International.* [Translated by Peggy Kamuf]. Routledge: New York, London [1993] 2006.

Faus, Miguel: "Desnudando Personal Shopper con Olivier Assayas". *JotDown*, July 2017, retrieved 10.05.2022, from https://www.jotdown.es/2017/07/desnudando-personal-shopper-olivier-assayas/?fbclid=IwAR34uOPwMgLgealkhwX14MMjiQt_EjLIM-chSepoU1FtpWOOYKfXtMo8hkE.

Fish, Stanley Eugene: *Is there a text in this class? The authority of interpretive Communities.* Cambridge: Harvard University Press 2000.

Freud, Sigmund: "Mourning and Melancholia". In: *The standard edition of the complete psychological works of Sigmund Freud.* Vol. XIV. *A history of the psycho-analytic movement. Papers on metapsychology and other works.* The Hogarth Press and the Institute of Psycho-Analysis: London 1966, pp. 243–258. ["Trauer und Melancholia". *Int. Z. arztl. Psychoanal.* N. 6, 1917, pp. 288–301].

Freud, Sigmund: "The Uncanny". In: *The Uncanny* [Translated by David Mclintock]. Penguin Books: London 2003 [1919], pp. 123–162.

Guilet, Anaïs: "Les Spectres Interfacés: Des Corps et Des Écrans Dans Personal Shopper d'Olivier Assayas." In: Choinière, Isabelle *et al.* (eds.): *Par Le Prisme Des Sens: Médiation et Nouvelles Réalités Du Corps Dans Les Arts Performatifs: Technologies, Cognition et Méthodologies Émergentes de Recherche-Création.* Presses de l'Université du Québec: Montreal 2019, pp. 367–80. Retrieved 11.05.2022, from https://doi.org/10.2307/j.ctvq4bz0p.16.

Hidalgo Urtiaga, Ana: *La presencia espectral en la narrativa femenina transétnica desde 1975.* (Doctoral thesis) Universidad Complutense de Madrid: Madrid 2018, retrieved 01.08.2023, from https://docta.ucm.es/bitstreams/a5930df6-cffc-4d9c-b3d4-d48ca91171a1/download.

Manovich, Lev: *The Language of New Media.* MIT Press: Cambridge, Mass.; London 2001.

McLuhan, Marshall: *Understanding media. The extensions of man.* Ginko Press: Berkeley 2003.

Menéndez de la Cuesta González, Adrián: *Comunidades de lectores ahora.* [Serie: Cuadernos del ahora; No. 5] Docta-Complutense Universidad Complutense de Madrid: Madrid 2020, retrieved 01.08.2023, from https://docta.ucm.es/entities/publication/a3c50b37-e96f-4201-b7ba-6bfbe6627391.

Mikles, Natasha L. / Laycick, Joseph P.: "Tracking the Tulpa. Exploring the "Tibetan" origins of a Contemporary Paranormal Idea". *Nova Religio: The Journal of Alternative and Emergent Religions* 19(1) 2019, pp. 87–97.

Miller, Jacques-Alain: "La sutura. Elementos de la lógica del significante". *Significante y sutura en psicoanálisis*. Siglo XXI: Madrid 1973, pp. 52–69.

Mitchell, William John Thomas: "There are no visual media". *Journal of visual culture*. 4(2), 2005, pp. 257–266.

Oudart, Jean-Pierre: "La sutura". *Banda aparte* 6, [1969] 1997, pp. 51–63.

Sarriugarte-Gómez, Íñigo: "Mediumnismo y arte. El caso de Hilma af Klint: de la mano dirigida a la mano intuitiva". *La Colmena* (102) 2019, pp. 85–103.

Tausiet, María: "Mil y un fantasmas". *Revista de libros* 28.01.2015. Retrieved 15.05.2022, from https://www.revistadelibros.com/mil-y-un-fantasmas/.

Films

Assayas, Olivier (Director): *Personal Shopper*. [Film]. Arte France Cinéma, CG Cinéma, Vortex Sutra, Sirena Film, Detailfilm, ARTE, Arte France, Canal+, Ciné+, Westdeutscher Rundfunk (WDR), SCOPE Invest 2016.

Savage, Rob (Director): *Host* [Film]. Shadowhouse Films 2020.

Silviano Carrasco Yelmo
Universidad Complutense de Madrid

Incarnations of Little Red Riding Hood in Board and Video Games

Abstract: Since Charles Perrault put down his fairy tale version of *Little Red Riding Hood* in 1697, scholars have discovered that his was just one of many versions, and that the heroine has been constantly adapted into new media (for a brief overview of the process and strategies, see: Orenstein (2002, pp. 2–26) and Doughty (2006, pp. 36–51)). Susana Tosca has studied the phenomenon of adaptation when the fairy tale is translated into digital media (2013). The purpose of this chapter is to take into account the next step in the evolution of the tale: that is, LRRH in the postdigital period.

Keywords: Little Red Riding Hood, video games, board games, postdigital.

1. Little Red Riding Hood and board games

Although there is certainly a postdigital approach to *Little Red Riding Hood's*[1] themes and forms in contemporary films or songs, such as Lady Gaga's Monster (2009), the recent remake Illang (2018) or the anime adaptation Beastars (2019), the focus of this chapter will be on the current ludic field, and will thus consider LRRH as portrayed in board games and video games. I will try to unveil the underlying recycling strategies operating at each step to present LRRH to the players.

There are two main points I will try to convey through this section: firstly, the production market for board games has entered into a postdigital context, in which the lines between producer and consumer blur together. And secondly, more and more board games in the postdigital era tend to remediate video games. Such remediation is most noticeable in their aesthetics, but also in the implementation of certain non-traditional board gaming elements, such as apps, which provide narration; audio-visual clues; hidden information or an AI that acts as the opponent of the players. I will discuss some examples of both cases.

1 LRRH hereinafter.

1.2. Little Red Riding Hood meets crowdfunding

Crowdfunding (sometimes also referred to as *kickstarting*) is a practice in which creators ask for funding from individual backers interested in the project, who often contribute to the project with their vision, thus creating a semi-collaborative piece of work. The two most relevant platforms for crowdfunding board games are *Kickstarter*[2] and *GameFound*.[3]

The most successful campaigns aimed at producing board games via crowdfunding now collect millions of dollars from enthusiastic backers.[4] Reaching these impressive figures requires a deep knowledge of the crowdfunding system and platforms: these are spaces of interaction between creators and their public that are constantly open to suggestions. This effectively blurs the lines between authors/producers and clients/consumers, leading unequivocally to the age of the *prosumer* and *prosumption* (mixing production and consumption). This is a phenomenon that, although as old as humanity, has become heavily accentuated in the postdigital entourage, which excels in and promotes this kind of relationship. See, for instance, the claims made by the creators in the game Legend Academy (2022) (a game about LRRH that I will examine later) in GameFound:

> We want to work together as a community to make this game as great as possible! If you want to play the game now or become part of the playtesting community, watch the Playtester video below. […] *We will also be naming all playtesters (that give feedback) in the rulebook because you helped improve the game!* [italics in the original].[5]

The above paragraph means that the creators are directly inviting their backers into the playtesting phase of production, which is a key part of the development of the game and requires expertise, feedback and creative thinking on the backers' part. A nominal reward is offered in exchange for their effort (crediting their names in the rulebook), but above all, this means producers will be tailoring the product to the immediate needs of the consumers, who are the ones creating the

---

2 https://www.kickstarter.com.

3 https://gamefound.com.

4 See for instance, campaigns up to 12 million dollars here: *Most funded gaming projects*, retrieved 15.06.2022, from https://www.statista.com/statistics/283843/crowdfunding-most-funded-gaming-projects/#:~:text=Frosthaven%20was%20the%20highest%20funded,upgrades%20to%20improve%20their%20performance.

5 Retrieved 15.05.2022, from https://gamefound.com/projects/el-dorado-games/legend-academy?previewPhase=CrowdfundingEnded.

final rules with their comments on playtesting. The same trend can be appreciated in the Kickstarter project *Paradise Lost*[6] (2022), another game featuring LRRH:

> What other stories would you like to see? Give us a shout and let us know.
> To hear more about history embedded in board game design, join us later today for an interview with Gabe Barrett on his show, Board Game Design Lab: http://www.boardgamedesignlab.com/
> Let's keep it going!
> Tom & Team Green Feet Games [...]
> Thanks for all your continued inputs and support. We are good listeners :)[7]

Trying to lure the backer into different channels besides the simple webpage in Kickstarter or GameFound, and offering videos or pics in YouTube or Instagram, chats in Discord, etc., is common practice in the postdigital era, where the user is assumed to navigate across different platforms and share the experience, thus contributing to the process of going viral, another characteristic feature of the postdigital recycling strategy.

Although the difference between production and consumption has always been an artificial, purely conceptual one, as Marx (1981 [1884]) or Baudrillard ([1970] 1998) remarked, the fusion between the two reaches its climax with the digital and postdigital paradigm. Ritzer and Jurgenson put the emphasis on the "absolutely crucial technological change that needs to be highlighted separately", which is "the increasing importance of the computer and the Internet for the process of prosumption" (2010, p. 13). In an article from 2012, Ritzer also remarks:

> Prosumption on the Internet has increasingly occurred through user-generated content on what has become known as Web 2.0 (in Web 1.0, such as AOL or Yahoo, content is generated by the producer, leaving little room for prosumption). Web 2.0 includes the social web with sites such as Facebook and Twitter, the blogosphere, Wikipedia, content-sharing sites such as Flickr and You Tube, and much else where users not only consume but also produce content. It is in the immaterial worlds of Web 2.0 that it is hardest to distinguish between producers and consumers, where the hegemony of prosumers is clearest. (Ritzer et al. 2012, p. 385).

It should be quite obvious now that prosumption, or offering the consumer the chance to take part in designing and producing the board game, is used in the

---

6 See https://www.kickstarter.com/projects/piraterepublic1/paradise-lost-0, retrieved 15.05.2022.

7 Retrieved 15.05.2022, from https://www.kickstarter.com/projects/piraterepublic1/paradise-lost-0/posts/2476026.

postdigital era as a marketing strategy. Making the public feel like they belong in the same team as the creators of the board game instills pride, confidence and happiness in the backer, who will gladly fund the project and/to? see their names credited in the box or manual.

I will purposely omit from my study some older incarnations of LRRH in board games, such as *Little Red Riding Hood* (2003); *Wherewolf* [sic.]: *Red Riding Hood* (2012); *Fairy Tale Assassin League: Red Riding Hood Rampage* (2013); *Dark Tales: Little Red Riding Hood* (2015); *Tales & Games: Little Red Riding Hood* (2015) or *Little Red Riding Hood: Full Moon Rising* (2019), either because they present recycling strategies that may be found in a non-postdigital context or because they are too simple to be of any interest to us. I will now examine some recent board games about LRRH and their strategies to recycle the fairy tale (or at least the characters from it).

2.2. *Twisted Fables* (2021)

One of the more extremes incarnations of LRRH in board games can be found in the kickstarted game *Twisted Fables*[8] (2021). The game describes itself this way:

> Welcome to a universe where fairy tale heroines exist. These aren't the helpless damsels waiting for their prince, though: these are dangerous, relentless warriors, and they will not be denied. Coming not from high towers or grandmothers' cottages, these champions emerge instead from cyberpunk dystopias, interstellar war zones, and strange steampunk cities. The old stories have been shattered. In their place have arisen Twisted Fables.[9]

The description tries to be empowering, but fails to acknowledge that the tradition it is supposedly contesting is nothing but another version (and a relatively modern one) of an earlier version, i.e., Disney's version of the tales, which itself ignores a far more vast oral tradition in which these heroines are indeed empowered: see, for instance, The Grandmother's Tale (Orenstein, 2002, pp. 63–84). Nevertheless, the visual presentation of LRRH in *Twisted Fables* draws our attention immediately (and the creators know it, since she is featured as the prominent image for the project in the webpage): in a very similar pose as the figurine from the board game *Unmatched*,[10] LRRH displays a cybernetic

8 See https://www.kickstarter.com/projects/diemensiongames/twisted-fables, retrieved 15.05.2022.

9 See https://www.kickstarter.com/projects/diemensiongames/twisted-fables/description, retrieved 15.05.2022.

10 See https://restorationgames.com/shop/little-red-beowulf-unmatched, retrieved 15.05.2022.

arm and is holding a sub-machine gun. The Riding Hood is now also a red hood covering her face, that plays with the similarity of another anti-hero from DC comics: The Hood (thus appealing once again to the crossover and intertextual logic). Next to the description of the game, LRRH's character is detailed as:

> RED RIDING HOOD
> The Cybernetic Assassin
> Her body was ripped apart then reassembled with cybernetic components; her life returned to her but not to her family. Red Ridin Hood had so many questions and no answers. Why her? What made her special? Then the wolf's voice spoke from inside her. It taught her how to survive, how to thrive, and how to get her revenge.[11]

Notice that, as in *Paradise Lost,* she's "little" no more. The producers have replaced her body with a cyborg one, and the description hints at the mental process of the victim of a rape (by needing a rational explanation under the question "why her" and in the need for further answers as to why this happened): it is not quite clear who the criminal was, but she empowers herself by shifting her perspective from that of victim to executioner, and the wolf's voice now is her inner self craving for revenge (the reader will want to revisit again the Unmatched figurine and appreciate the detail of the wolf's ears above the riding hood). The underlying logic of this is the heroine's empowerment through violence and the ability to kill as the mark of her superiority and victory over the offender. This is a common strategy in American revenge films and series such as Hard Candy (2005), which is another notably contemporary incarnation of LRRH's trope;[12] *The Brave One* (2007), a *Law Abiding Citizen* (2009), *The Foreigner* (2017), *Peppermint* (2018), or the famous *The Punisher* (2004, 2008, series 2017–2019). This focus on violence can also be linked to Duclos' famous essay *The Werewolf Complex: America's Fascination with Violence* (1998), in which he argues that every American is obsessed with and afraid of their inner beast, a potential serial killer hidden under a thin mask of civilization.

Finally, LRRH's mini is displayed as wielding a huge Gatling gun. Her cyborg limbs can be clearly appreciated. As with many pop revisions, the message pretends to be feminist via empowerment, but sadly the poses of the heroines are utterly sexualised for the male gaze.[13] The recycling strategies, mixing the theoretical revision of the postfeminist ideology with prosumption via

---

11 See https://www.kickstarter.com/projects/diemensiongames/twisted-fables, retrieved 15.05.2022.

12 For a detailed analysis see: Delvaux (2009, pp. 27–31) and Hayton (2011).

13 As described in Mulvey (1975, pp. 6–18).

Kickstarter (as detailed above) may be a commercial success (the game funded at a respectable 162.330$) but fails from a hermeneutic perspective, as it doesn't dig properly into the deeper meanings of the fairy tale, nor does it offer a novel revision of the tale.

2.3. *Legend Academy* (2022)

The publicity of the GameFound campaign for this board game went straight to the point with a brief and hilarious presentation: "Attend a prestigious institution where characters train to become tomorrow's legends. A competitive, deckbuilding, card crafting, worker placement, adventure game".[14]

The main page notably features two heroes with their action figures: Robin Hood is leaping and drawing his bow in the background, while the foreground is consecrated to LRRH. She is wearing her hood and cape, and stares fiercely at us, but the most shocking part is that she is actually riding the wolf, which is about twice as big as her and seems to howl while looking at us, too. The same previous strategies about empowering the heroine through physical domination are obviously at play here, but there are more details about the characters:

> You are a folklore character before their story was told. Legends can be trained completely differently every game depending on which classes you take, how well you do during training sessions, and what kind of attributes you improve.[15]

There are indeed four main characters in the game: Paul Bunyan, Little Red Riding Hood, Alice (from Wonderland) and Robin Hood. Thanks to the prosumption approach, encouraging participation in the comments section, the creators were able to detect that some backers (i.e. Europeans) didn't know anything about one of the playable characters, Paul Bunyan: "This morning, you unlocked ***The Tales of Paul Bunyan Mini-Expansion***! A few people from Europe mentioned that they didn't know who Paul Bunyan was."[16] An update was then provided in order to explore the lore around this American-centered folklore character, so the prosumption approach served its purpose, allowing the creators to reach an audience not fully familiarised with the character. The recycling strategy concerning LRRH is a mix of the crossover episode and the original

---

14 Retrieved 15.05.2022 from https://gamefound.com/projects/el-dorado-games/legend-academy.

15 See https://gamefound.com/projects/el-dorado-games/legend-academy, retrieved 15.05.2022.

16 See: https://gamefound.com/projects/el-dorado-games/legend-academy/updates/3, retrieved 15.05.2022.

story, a strategy which is prolific nowadays in the superhero movies and series. More information about LRRH's playstyle is provided and the player will find that there is a fixation with the content of her basket as a defining trait for the character, since the heroine is presented as "Specialized in movement. She can lay traps and lure enemies to them using her basket."[17] Her looks are those of an adult, and she seems to have teamed up with her nemesis, so this incarnation is a mix between the little girl presented in Paradise Lost and Unmatched, and the cunning cyborg in Twisted Fables. The success of Gamefound's recycling strategy is supported by the amazing number of backers and dollars (212.310$) on their campaign.

Every new incarnation of LRRH so far focuses on the heroine's empowerment through feminism, so ideology is the strategy the creators (or rather prosumers) seem always to have in mind when redesigning the character, be it in a crossover, origin story or dystopian future. Appealing to cross-platforms (Discord, Instagram, Facebook, other websites like BGG) in order to know about, comment, and share the information about the product, and inviting the consumer to participate in the creation process through beta-testing or giving instant feedback throughout the crowdfunding campaign are recurrent strategies in the recycling process.

2.4. *One Night Ultimate Werewolf* (2014)

The most interesting iteration of LRRH in board games for the purpose of this chapter will now be examined. The chosen example shows perfectly the trend of fusing classical board games with digital technologies, incorporating video game aesthetics or AI features for the gameplay. In *One Night Ultimate Werewolf*, the game tries to convey the horror experience of a hidden traitor game (such as in *The Werewolves of Miller's Hollow* (2014)). Little Red Riding Hood is arguably represented in *The Werewolves of Miller's Hollow* by the character of "the Little Girl" in the village. She possesses the special ability to open her eyes during the night to spy on the werewolves' characters, thus reinforcing the theme of daring transgression and finding pleasure along with fear in her breaking of the rules. This is reinterpreted in *One Night Ultimate Werewolf* as the little girl holding a teddy bear, who receives the name of "Insomniac". However, the most interesting element in the game is not in the werewolves or little red riding hood character, but in the fact that, unlike its predecessor *The Werewolves of Miller's Hollow*,

17 See https://gamefound.com/projects/el-dorado-games/legend-academy?previewPhase=CrowdfundingEnded#/section/whats-in-the-box-2960, retrieved 15.05.2022.

One Night Ultimate Werewolf can be played without resorting to one person being the narrator of the story, thanks to the incorporation of an app which does the reading and revealing parts of the game for the players. The creator knows this is a strong selling point, and the game is announced accordingly: "No moderator, no elimination, ten-minute games". The app is remediating the role of the physical narrator, but this is surprisingly an element that is not always well received in the board gaming community. A thread in the most famous board gaming webpage in the world (*Board Game Geek*, aka *BGG*) illustrates the general distrust.[18] The users debate whether the app is optional or mandatory in order to enjoy the full experience of the game, and the consensus is that, of the two, being optional is the more desirable. This is not an isolated case, and almost identical opinions may be found in every entry for games that require apps (such as *Descent: Journeys in the* Dark (2021), *Lord of the Rings: Journeys in the Middle Earth* (2019), *XCOM: the board game* (2016) or current projects being crowdfunded like The Dark Quarter (2023)). The board gaming public constantly perceives that the remediation from the app puts in danger the longevity of the game, as it depends on the software being compatible with future devices and being updated. Another common complaint is that they play board games in order to take a break from the computer (usually pervasive at their jobs), so digital remediation is generally not well received. This is paradoxical, since board games seem to be living a revival as the go-to product when it comes to enjoying leisure because of their social aspect, in contrast to the loneliness of the computer or game console player. In other words, postdigital remediation in an older medium such as the board game is not always well received, and seen more as a danger for enjoying the medium than as the logical next step, namely, a postdigital development. Paradoxically, video games in the postdigital era tend to remediate, in retro style, the mechanics, dynamics and aesthetics of board games.

3. Little Red Riding Hood and video games

Video games are obviously by their nature digital. Surprisingly, in the postdigital environment, they are (d)evolving into predigital forms, combining their aesthetics, dynamics and mechanics[19] with traditional board games or the most primitive forms of video games in the 80's and 90's, craving for nostalgia and

18 See https://boardgamegeek.com/thread/2847571/requires-app, retrieved 15.05.2022.
19 For the MDA approach to game design see: Hunicke / Leblanc / Zubek (2004).

hence resorting to a retro-remediation recycling strategy. Another postdigital aspect of the video games under consideration is the market into which they are being sold: I will take into account mostly video games available on *Steam*, an online platform dedicated to selling games in their exclusively digital form. Their physical version no longer exists in this market (if it ever existed there in the first place), thus negating the opposition between physical and virtual content when it comes to this medium.

The storytelling aspect of these postdigital products will be examined next, but firstly some precision about recycling folklore tales is needed. Folklorist Amie A. Doughty establishes the distinction between *retellings* (which include minor differences, due for instance to nuances in translations or even the iteration of the oral retelling itself which would vary some details) and *revisions*. According to this difference, "[r]evisions of folktales, however, are versions of folktales, usually written, that take traditional tales, often well-known ones, and alter them in a much more elaborate manner than retellings." (Doughty 2006, p. 14).

This distinction is useful when it comes to examining why LRRH video games often result in utterly failed adaptations, as the gameplay lacks depth (most of them are platform games that can be played with just a D-pad and a couple of buttons, or even more simply, they display static shots and, being puzzles, require only a mousepad). The games also lack innovative storytelling and any meaningful recycling strategy, being merely retells as opposed to far more elaborated revisions. It seems as if the creators fail to find meaningful plots for LRRH (admittedly the fairy tale consists of a too-short plot to make it into something unusual/surprising without altering too much), and when they choose to deviate from the simple formula, they cannot come up with anything remarkable. Alas, the prehistory of video games about LRRH is nothing to write home about: in 1989, for instance, Nintendo produced a video game for the NES system under the name of Little Hood. Red The title has not become famous, and this is for a reason: LRRH has to navigate maps while collecting fruits and avoiding enemies: no wolf is present in the story at all (goblins, however, are present); combat is pointless most of the time; and exploration is almost impossible due to the difficulty of the stages, with no clues to guide gamers. Last but not least, the game is riddled with glitches.[20]

Decades have passed and graphics and sound may have improved, but not necessarily the inventiveness required to recycle the fairy tale: the best Nintendo

20 See the full mocking of the game at: https://crappygames.miraheze.org/wiki/Little_Red_Hood, retrieved 15.05.2022.

could come up with in 2007 for their Nintendo DS was an action rail shooter game named Little Riding Hood's Zombie BBQ. Red The game opens with the proverbial introductory narration:

> Once upon a time… After saving her grandmother from the clutches of the wolf and its army of evil, everything seemed to have returned to normal… [heavy metal music plays now in the background] but nothing could be further from the truth. The woodcutter has tragically died in battle and now just recently the dead has risen and a zombie invasion once again puts peace on Earth in danger. But Red " Ready to Rock" Riding Hood knows how to deal with zombies. And she's even got Momo "Kamikaze" Taro with her to fire up the grill.[21]

LRRH plus traditional Japanese folklore character Momotaro, plus zombies, machine guns and the end of the world: if the reader is intrigued about how the story unfolds in stage two, the player is confronted with a boss battle in which LRRH will have to kill her own zombified granny, who is tied to the bed and vomiting zombie dogs (instead of the proverbial wolf). Stage three takes you to the town of Hansel and Gretel, and so on. LRRH is the hero chosen to end the plague because "her legend precedes her". A ridiculous translation into English makes the game even more bizarre, and the player cannot play this game without a mix of chuckles and compassion for the poor quality that often chracterises B-series. On top of the nonsensical plot, a gross Little Red Riding Hood, overtly sexualized for the male gaze and designed in manga style, puts this adaptation on a very inferior level to the board games we have previously examined. The main recycling strategy is a collage mixing video game genres (third person shooter, adventure) with a crossover of folklore characters from diverse cultures (both western and eastern). The game may be of interest because it exploits the characteristics of the Nintendo DSi XL console: a double screen allowing for different shots simultaneously, and the use of the stylus (a responsive digital pencil which allows the player to aim by touching the screen with the instrument).

More considerations about narration, themes and adaptation of LRRH in video games will be examined later on, but before that it is important to study a case of relevance in the video game medium when it comes to recycling the moral of a tale. Only when the user understands the ludic nature of the medium can video games be appreciated by their specific features and not by their storytelling abilities or lack thereof. This is particularly important regarding the next LRRH video game example: The Path (2009). The game can be ascribed to the psychological horror genre: it is clear from the art box that the player is

21 Quoted from the introduction screen of the game.

confronted by this genre. A dark forest in the background serves as the frame for little girl in black and red with a sinister look, breaking the fourth wall as she stares at the spectator. The title is written in black, with a gothic looking font that twists and intertwines with the red color, as if it were bleeding. Without any narrative introduction whatsoever, the game presents the player with a choice among six characters (all of which are girls ranging from 9 to 19 years old): Ginger, Rose, Scarlet, Ruby, Robin, Carmen (the wordplay with Little Red Riding Hood is obvious). Once the player selects their character, they will be assigned the task (under the form of the title over the screen): "Go to Grandmother's house and stay on the path". The real talent of the designers lies in the fact that the player is tacitly invited to disobey the instruction deliberately so as to generate meaning while playing. Indeed, if the player follows the instruction and walks directly to the Grandmother's house without deviating from the path, they will enter the house (the camera will then shift to a first person perspective), visit some rooms in which nothing particularly interesting happens and will finish the game receiving a D rank. They will then realise that they did not collect any special items, did not unlock any special rooms and did not encounter the wolf. A big "FAILURE!" will sanction the playthrough and the player at that point would understand that being obedient to the rules did not provide any significant payoff. The model player is assumed to subvert the given rules. This logic is linked to the psychology of the explorer's profile among video game players, as famously classified by Bartle in 1996. The second point subverting expectations in the video game is also related to the gameplay, and more specifically to the concept of "player agency". The concept may be defined as follows:

> Player agency is about giving players the interactivity to affect and change the game world. Through agency, players have power to influence and change what is happening in the game. It provides them control (or at least of sense of it) of what will happen next.[22]

Player agency is assumed to be actively pursued through action (although Sarah Stang challenged this notion, as well as the relevance of real control over the game, hence "at least the sense of it" in the previous definition; see Stang (2019)). The Path illustrates perfectly this misalignment when the player is told that, in order to interact with the objects of people they will find in the forest, once they leave the path they have, surprisingly, to let go. Only when the player gives up control will they create meaning through interaction with the relevant game objects. In this way the game conveys the hidden, deep moral of the tale (curiosity pays off, disobeying orders is what makes possible the adventure,

22 See Eng (2020).

letting go of the rational side and giving up to idleness means embracing the true nature of the adventure and achieving a successful ending) through gameplay actions (and, paradoxically, lack of them) and not through narration. The model player will understand when he has to cooperate with the game and how, and when he has to disobey, but any non-gamer member of the public would be at a loss and would have to undergo a process of what could be defined as postdigital literacy, since, from 2009, video games no longer assumed that the player needed specific instructions. A contemporary gamer should not expect great improvements over their previous experiences of Nintendo in 1987 and 2007. The current adaptations are either aimed at children and have the worst possible adaptation of the fairy tale structure, since they are all cheap productions which would have looked look poor even in the 90s, as very simple *hack and slash* productions (as in RED, 2016). Others are simple conversational adventures with static backgrounds which simply re-enact the elemental plot – maybe with minor, more or less meaningless twists – or create another generic adventure which uses the traditional characters as placeholders for "action heroine" and "villain", such as in BRG's Riding Hood Red (2019); 1/2 Riding Hood Red (2021); Return of Riding Hood Red (2018); Dark Parables: The Riding Hood Sisters Red (2016); The Hood Red (2022). – The list could go on without a single remarkable title, or even worse yet, the theme can be just an excuse to justify pasted-on game mechanics which bear no relationship whatsoever with LRRH, such as in: Fairytale Solitaire: Riding Hood Red (2019), a digitised version of the traditional solitaire card games; *Picross Fairytale – nonogram:* Red *Riding Hood secret* (2018), which consists of jigsaw puzzle games with fairy tale themes; and *Night of Full Moon – Little* Red *Ridding* [sic.] *Hood's Diary* (2019), a card game about fighting enemies, a la Pokemon.

Both lists could go on and on, but the reader will notice the lack of any critically acclaimed or famous title in the repertoire, which leads us to another recurrent question: why do video games seem always to adapt narratives so poorly? Maybe the answer is that this is the wrong question. Maybe the answer lies in the obsession of philologists to turn to the medium in search of narrative content, when in fact video games are not essentially a representational medium: they were never intended to convey stories in the first place, but to develop gameplay. Ludologists have traditionally denounced this colonisation (or at least what they perceived as such) of the now consolidated game studies by the seekers after narratives, films, ideology, etc.[23]

23 For an exposition of the problematic, see: Juul (2001); Eskelinen (2001) or Frasca (2003).

When the video game dares to stride away from the path, it is not the content of the basket (as it was in the board games we have examined), but rather the question of the parenthood of LRRH that is often a focal point for the beginning of the story being told: "My name is Red Riding Hood: I have no father, no mother, no fear", LRRH states in a defiant voice in Woolfe: Diaries the Hood Red (2015), which is a hack and slash adventure in which LRRH is on a mission to avenge her dead parents armed with an axe. The video game is upfront about its content:

> Woolfe – The Red Hood Diaries is a cinematic fable featuring a vengeful Red Riding Hood. All grown up, cried out and armed with an axe, our noble heroine embarks on an odyssey to avenge the death of her parents. Buckle up for a surprising take on the traditional Red Riding Hood tale, mixed with some good old-fashioned action platforming, fun combo-based hack 'n slash combat and rewarding environment puzzles that explore the attractive fantasy universe.[24]

In the same vein, the page on Steam announces, stressing the pun: "THIS IS NOT A FAIRYTALE, THERE'S NOTHING FAIR ABOUT IT".[25] The same violent twist has been applied previously in critically acclaimed games like *Alice: Madness Returns* (2011), but besides that, there is no inherent quality of originality, particularly in applying the display of violence as the main selling point in order to bring a folklore character into a digital medium.

In RED (2016) the mother of the protagonist (named "Green") falls in love with the wolf (a likeable, humanised character in manga style) and she gives birth to a daughter whose psyche is divided into three different personalities (one of them being a feral werewolf, of course). These revisions do not stand any deeper scrutiny from a symbolic perspective and again miss their opportunity to try something different or interesting with the source material, so the only strategy to be found here will be a marketing one: the need to resort to something familiar to the user to sell the product.

4. Conclusion

In conclusion, the corpus examined in which the figure of LRRH is being recycled confirms the initial hypothesis: board games funded via crowdfunding platforms always resort to prosumption, which leads to consumers modifying

24 See the presentation of the game in Steam: https://store.steampowered.com/app/281940/Woolfe__The_Red_Hood_Diaries/, retrieved 15.05.2022.

25 See second trailer on the website https://store.steampowered.com/app/281940/Woolfe__The_Red_Hood_Diaries/, retrieved 15.05.2022.

substantial parts of the board game, such as the rules. Multi-platforms are also regularly used as a marketing strategy to hook the consumer and help the game go viral. Neither of these strategies could be possible in the so-called Internet 1.0, so they may be labelled as postdigital. The same digital approach that worked in the promotion and production steps, however, does not work when touching the structure of the board game itself: users state again and again that they feel the presence of apps or hybrid board games to be invasive in board gaming. Some may welcome electronic components, while others are happy with them as long as they are always optional. Obsolescence is one of the main concerns, and that implies that the board game is falsely perceived as eternal or impervious to aging, while any technology brings the danger of outdating itself. Concerning video games properly speaking, no video game about LRRH has been a great hit in the market, and this reveals a lack of successful recycling strategies (at least in economic terms): the crossover logic (mixing LRRH with other characters), the origin story (digging into LRRH's parenthood), the post feminism approach (empowering LRRH via deadly weaponry or cyborg bodies) and copy pasting puzzle mechanics onto LRRH's theme have been employed many times. The process by which video games (especially modest ones) try to remediate older card or puzzle games is easily recognizable, but none of these low-budget indie video games seems to capture the essence of the folktale. The Path is an exception because the game incorporates the meaning into the ludic nature of the video game (that is, its dynamics and mechanics). It is nevertheless a relatively unknown video game, so the potential recycling of LRHH in this postdigital medium is yet to be exploited.

References

Bartle, Richard: "Hearts, Clubs, Diamonds, Spades: Players Who Suit MUDs". 1996. Retrieved 15.06.2022, from https://mud.co.uk/richard/hcds.htm.

Baudrillard, Jean: *The Consumer Society*. Sage: London [1970] 1998.

Delvaux, Martine: "Peur et tremblements: autour de Hard Candy et The Brave One". *Frontières* 21(2) 2009, pp. 27–31.

Doughty, Amie A.: *Folktales retold: A Critical Overview of Stories Updated for Children*. McFarland & Company: Jefferson, NC 2006.

Duclos, Denis: *The Werewolf Complex: America's Fascination with Violence*. Oxford International Publishers: New York 1998.

Eng, Dave: "What is Player Agency?", University XP, Games-Based Learning, August 2020. Retrieved 15.06.2022, from http://www.universityxp.com/blog/2020/8/20/what-is-player-agency.

Eskelinen, Markku: "The Gaming Situation". *Game Studies. The International Journal of Computer Game Research* 1(1) July 2001. Retrieved 15.06.2022, from http://www.gamestudies.org/0101/eskelinen/.

Frasca, Gonzalo: "Ludologists Love Stories Too: Notes from a Debate that Never Took Place". *Level Up – Digital Games Research Conference*, November 2003 [conference]. Retrieved 15.06.2022, from http://www.digra.org/wp-content/uploads/digital-library/05163.01125.pdf.

Hayton, Natalie: "Unconscious Adaptation: *Hard Candy as Little Red Riding Hood*". *Adaptation*, 4 (1), March 2011, pp. 38–54. https://doi.org/10.1093/adaptation/apr001.

Hunicke, Robin / Leblanc, Marc / Zubek, Robert: "MDA: A Formal Approach to Game Design and Game Research". *AAAI Workshop – Technical Report* (1) 2004. Retrieved 3.3.2022, from https://users.cs.northwestern.edu/~hunicke/MDA.pdf.

Juul, Jesper: "Games Telling stories? A brief note on games and narratives". *Game Studies. The International Journal of Computer Game Research* 1(1) 2001. Retrieved 16.06.2022, from http://www.gamestudies.org/0101/juul-gts/.

Marx, Karl: *Capital: Volume Two*. Vintage Books: New York [1884] 1981.

Most funded gaming projects. Retrieved 15.06.2022, from https://www.statista.com/statistics/283843/crowdfunding-most-funded-gaming-projects/#:~:text=Frosthaven%20was%20the%20highest%20funded,upgrades%20to%20improve%20their%20performance.

Mulvey, Laura: "Visual pleasure and narrative cinema", *Screen*, [Oxford Journals], vol. 16, n. 3, autumn, 1975, pp. 6–18.

Orenstein, Catherine: *Little Red Riding Hood Uncloaked*. A Member of the Perseus Book Group: New York 2002.

Ritzer, George *et al.*: "The Coming of Age of the Prosumer". *American Behavioral Scientist*, vol. 56, no. 4, Apr. 2012, pp. 379–398.

Ritzer, George / Jurgenson, Nathan: "Production, Consumption, Prosumption: The Nature of Capitalism in the Age of the Digital 'Prosumer' ". *Journal of Consumer Culture*, vol. 10, no. 1, Mar. 2010, pp. 13–36.

Stang, Sarah: "'This Action Will Have Consequences': Interactivity and Player Agency". *Game Studies. The International Journal of Computer Game Research*, volume 19, issue 1 May, 2019, retrieved 15.06.2022, from http://gamestudies.org/1901/articles/stang.

Tosca, Susana: "Fairy tale trans-migrations: the case of Little Red Riding Hood". *Intersemiose, Revista digital*, Año II, n. 4 (II), 2013. Retrieved 15.06.2022, from https://www.neliufpe.com.br/wp-content/uploads/2014/02/11.pdf.

Films and series

Bright, Matthew: *Freeway*. The Kushner-Locke Company, distributed by Republic Pictures 1996.

Ji-woon, Kim: *Illang: The Wolf Brigade*. Lewis Pictures, distributed by Warner Bros, Korea 2018.

Jordan, Neil: *The company of wolves*. Palace Pictures, distributed by ITC Entertainment 1984.

Matsumi, Shinichi: *Beastars*. Studio Orange, licensed by Netflix 2019.

Slade, David: *Hard Candy*. Vulcan Productions, distributed by Lionsgate 2005.

Songs

Lady Gaga: "Monster". In: *The Fame Monster*. Darkchild Studio 2009.

Board games

Alspach, Ted / Okui, Akihisa: *One Night Ultimate Werewolf*. Bézier Games 2014.

Aronson, David: *Legend Academy*. El Dorado Games 2022 (in production).

Butler, Tom: *Paradise Lost*. Green Feet Games 2020.

Centell-Dunk, Kara / Hajek, Nathan I. / Michlitsch, Todd: *Descent: Journeys in the Dark*. Fantasy Flight Games 2021.

Cohen, Noah / Daviau, Rob / Jacobson, Justin D. / Neff, Brian: *Unmatched: Little Red Riding Hood vs. Beowulf*. Mondo Games 2020.

Evan, Derrick: *The Dark Quarter*. Lucky Duck Games 2023 (in production).

Hajek, Nathan I. / Holdinghaus, Grace: *Lord of the Rings: Journeys in the Middle Earth*. Fantasy Flight Games 2019.

Lang, Eric M.: *XCOM: the board game*. Fantasy Flight Games 2016.

Wang, Gang / Gao, Xiang: *Twisted Fables*. Diemension Games 2021.

Video games

1/2 Red Riding Hood. Succubella Games, PC, 2021.

BRG's Red Riding Hood. Brave Rock Games, PC, 2019.

Dark Parables: The Red Riding Hood Sisters. Blue Tea Games, PC, 2016.

Fairytale Solitaire: Red Riding Hood. Somer Games, PC, 2019.

Van, Joy: *Little Red Hood*. Sachen, NES, 1989.

Jose M. Iñiguez: *Little Red Riding Hood's Zombie BBQ*. Ikari Studio, Nintendo DS,2007.

Night of Full Moon – Little Red Ridding Hood's Diary. Giant Games,PC, 2019.
Picross Fairytale – nonogram: Red Riding Hood secret. Somer Games, PC, 2018.
RED, STILILA, PC, 2016.
The Path. Tale of Tales, PC, 2009.
The Red Hood. Egutidze, PC, 2022.
Return of Red Riding Hood. NLB Project, PC, 2018.
Woolfe: The Red Hood Diaries. GriN Gamestudio, PC, 2015.

Teresa Cañadas García
Universidad Complutense de Madrid

Literary Recycling of Traditional Tales. The Path towards the Postdigital Traditional Tale

Abstract: This contribution seeks to analyse, from a theoretical standpoint, the ways traditional tales are recycled as an important part of children's and young adult's literature. This article is based on the idea that traditional tales have their origins in such defining features as orality, universality and cohesive capacity, features that enhance their propensity for re-elaboration, re-appropriation and re-use processes. Furthermore, intertextuality and recycling will be considered as narrative strategies that belong to children's literature in the way conceived by Gianni Rodari in his *Grammatica della fantasia* ([1973] 2018) [*The Grammar of Fantasy*], ideological and politically correct strategies like those of James Finn Garner (1994) and acculturation strategies such as the ones that have become highly recurrent in recent years and that adapt traditional tales to today's technological and postdigital world, as in the novels starring princesses by Nina MacKay (2016).

Keywords: traditional tale, literary recycling, (post)digital literature, tales and ideology, literature and folklore.

1. Traditional tales: origin and characteristics

Traditional tales, also known as folk tales, are fictional narrative stories associated with the oral traditions of different peoples, and are thus anonymous; they are characterised by their brevity, fast-moving action and simple language. The fact that folk tales originating from distant geographic points or from distant times reflect the same plots is striking and points to a potential shared past.

Historicist trends justify these similarities as a result of the migration of peoples, while anthropological trends explain the analogies through universality and the unity of human thought beyond culture, geographical points or the century they hail from, since tales narrate and play host, above all, to fantastic events that contain vital experiences.

From these (vital) experiences, whether the characters in the tales are human beings, fantasy or imaginary beings or animals – stem such characteristics as timelessness and perpetuation, universality, cohesive capacity, the heterogeneity of their listeners or readers and emotional capacity (Cañadas García 2020, pp. 19–22).

Timelessness and perpetuation manifest themselves in the fact that, although oral tradition complicates the identification of a particular origin of the tale – society, culture, the time they appear – their key elements are perpetuated throughout time and reflect past uses and customs.

Universality, along with perpetuation, shows that although the content of the tales is not fully identical to the habits of today's world, they are home to feelings that are shared by all human beings – fear, hope, humour, hatred, dislike, ambition, jealousy – and common pursuits, such as the desire for power, all-conquering love and intergenerational or fraternal conflicts, which surpass any historical context. Cohesive capacity manifests itself in the fact that the tales form part of a tradition that introduces us to the human community and to a common cultural heritage that is perpetuated whenever a tale is or has been repeated, whether listened to, read or told. The heterogeneity of listeners or readers indicates that the original public of the tales were both adults and children, although in their modern conception they are primarily aimed at the latter. Lastly, the emotional capacity of the tales is noteworthy, since they create a bond between the story-teller and the listener; the former understands in depth what they are telling and what may be awakened in the listener, and the latter perceives the repetitive structure shared with other tales – simple and recognisable – that creates a sense of security when listening to it. The reader of the tale, in turn, establishes parallels between their own experiences and the fictitious story and gets emotionally involved in the array of universal values shared by many civilisations at different stages of human life.

The conscious and voluntary incorporation of folk tales in literature – literalisation – is performed by the Brothers Grimm in *Children's and Household Tales* (Vega, 2009), with the knowledge of having discovered treasures in the tales told by different peoples.

Writing these tales, which traditionally were passed down orally, down, was a means to prevent them from being lost to time, and a way to avoid them no longer being told once their "tellers" would die, in cases where they weren't passed down from generation to generation.

Intergenerational transmission implies not only tales potentially being forgotten but also their modification and adaptation due to changes in customs and social uses, and due to additions that the story-teller may make.

This move from the oral to the written tale, from folklore to literature, known as culture, meant the loss of spontaneity in the tale and helped establish more stable versions, always taking into account the person who wrote them down.

In this regard, we talk about the "X" tale by Perrault, Andersen or Grimm, etc., although their true author may be unknown and the tale is backed only by the people and tradition that conserved it.

The contact between traditional tales and media and modern technology has also created new channels to tell tales. The traditional channel was the family or local meeting, but tales have evolved and have been told in books (texts on paper), radio, television, cinema, and now even on digital screens of all forms (videogames, computers, tablets) and even in a virtual reality format. In short, the move by tales from oral to paper has meant that folk tales have changed to become literary or cultural tales.

2. Folklore, literature and recycling

To talk about recycling, a profound reflection is required of the origin of tales and their relationship with folklore and written literature. As mentioned before, tales were originally handed down orally. In the case of children's and young adult's literature, children too began their literalisation through oral tales (songs, rhymes, cartoons, tales and *aleluyas*) coming from the mouths of their families and friends, along with their teachers and carers. Children themselves also integrate these stories, rhymes and songs into their own games with other children. However, their spoken nature can make tales or the transfer to hearing or learning something fleeting, since it is all too easy to introduce variations and add or remove elements, which leads to new variants of the same tale.

When folklore is written down, it becomes literature or "written folklore" (Ewers 2012, p. 73) and is then characterised by its compilatory and unifying nature, bringing together variations on a text based around a theme or applied to a concrete situation (church songs, lullabies, bedtime stories), which are all versions of a series of a similar nature.

When writing is not folkloric, it stamps a permanence onto a text and also delimits it with(in) its own other characteristics: text as a literary work, fixed, established and limited by the written word, individualisations through an author (not a group), the exemplary nature of the text as unique, a reference and original. The maximum exponent of the literalisation process is known as copyright, which is even backed by the universal declaration of human rights.

As Ewers points out, (2012, pp. 80–83) the process can go in both directions: the literalisation of folklore and the folklorisation of literature. The first case is represented in such works as *Hausmärchen* by the Brothers Grimm and the folk tales of Perrault, who captured popular tradition into writing to the point that tales or certain versions are now attributed to them ("Perrault's Little Red Riding Hood" or "the Brothers Grimm's Little Red Riding Hood"). The second case is represented by works that become so well-known that they turn into a popular ensemble and again become an oral tale to the point that the origin and author are long forgotten. Examples of this would be sayings and cartoon characters from literary works that are so well-known that their origin becomes blurred and is ignored by the public, or as sometimes happens, for example, with Pinocchio or Peter Pan, the characters of which have become very popular without many people knowing they originated from tales or stories by named authors.

At any event, it seems that children's and young adult's literature accepts these processes of folklorisation and literalisation including its changes, modifications and versions much more than adult literature. In some cases, such as folk tales, one could even talk about a consecutive process of literalisation and folklorisation where, as in the case of the folk tales of the Brothers Grimm, they linked their name to the oral and popular traditions by writing them down and in doing so created classical versions, which in turn are now popularised and diversified again as folklore.

Literary work	**Popular work**
One author, one origin	Several authors – collective work
The text is unique and fixed	The text starts from a series with its variants
Cannot be reproduced without referring to the author	Reproducible

Although traditional tales originally had a host of listeners, such as the *Hausmärchen* of the Brothers Grimm, geared towards children, adults and the elderly, i.e. for all those who inhabited the house (*Haus*), (Ewers 2012, p. 61), with the passage of time children and young people have appropriated these tales, with versions adapted and popularised specifically for them. In the literature we are talking about here, adults are not considered as its readers but as mediators, transmitters and filters. (Ewers 2012, p. 57) However, the difficulty in defining the public that the tales are designed for lies in the fact that, originally, these were not tales geared at children and young people but rather, above all, at adults. Getting together around a warm fireplace was one of the highlights of their rural lives, and included both adults and children – the whole family.

3. Literary recycling and the recycling of folk tales

The paradox of traditional tales is that on the one hand, as already explained, they are timeless and perpetual while on the other hand, they are prone to modifications and adaptations stemming from their oral nature and caused by their neglect, the passing of time, socio-cultural changes and the taste of the story-teller. Knowing this, oral narrators from the Ashanti people added the following proviso to their tales, "This is the story I have told, whether it is pleasant or not; take part of it elsewhere and leave the other part to return to me."[1] (Mandela 2007, pp. 11–12).

This highlights, together with orality and their neglect, one more reason for the change and transformation of folk tales, which is the taste of the reader or listener, who may reproduce the tale they have heard or read, adapting or modifying whatever they did not like, "both whether it is pleasant or not".

The decisive factor for the establishment of traditional tales has been writing them down. Perfecting textual reproduction methods has overcome what Don Juan Manuel feared in *El Conde Lucanor* (*The Count Lucanor*):

> Observing that there are many copying errors in books, as the letters are very similar to each other and the copyists, by confusing them, change the meaning of many passages, and then readers blame the author of the work, Don Juan asks for those who read any copy of one of his books, if they find a word misused, not to blame him until such time as they consult the original written by his hand which will have been corrected, on many occasions, in his own handwriting.[2] (Don Juan Manuel [1331–1335] 2004, p. 28).

It is easy to imagine that if in the past a text would undergo modifications when copied, it would undergo even more changes when passed on orally from person to person. In the case of folk tales, as the author is unknown and its origin is attributed to the cultural imagination of people of the past, there are no grounds to make any claims about the author as happens with Don Juan Manuel.

Even when a traditional tale is modified, its essence still remains in the new version, as Valentina Pisanty warns in the words of Gadamer, "in the intended mutation of all things, much more of the past is conserved than anyone could

---

1 "Ésta es la historia que he relatado, tanto si es agradable como si no lo es; llevaos una parte a otro lugar y dejad que otra parte vuelva a mí" (Mandela 2007, pp. 11–12).

2 "Como don Juan ha visto y comprobado que en los libros hay muchos errores de copia, pues las letras son muy parecidas entre sí y los copistas, al confundirlas, cambian el sentido de muchos pasajes, por lo que luego los lectores le echan la culpa al autor de la obra, pide don Juan a quienes leyeren cualquier copia de un libro suyo que, si encuentran alguna palabra mal empleada, no le culpen a él, hasta que consulten el original que salió de sus manos y que estará corregido, en muchas ocasiones, de su puño y letra". (Don Juan Manuel [1331–1335] 2004, p. 28).

imagine, which is then united with the new, taking on a renewed validity."[3] (Pisanty 1995, p. 16).

However, the author points to the feelings of alienation and distancing readers experience when they read versions that go against the grain of those accepted by their cultural, historical or social environment, even when pleasurable to the reader. "The pleasure gained from the story stems from the combined action of 'constriction and liberty'; in other words, from the demand for security on the one hand (the security of what is familiar) and from being pushed towards the unknown, on the other hand."[4] (Pisanty 1995, p. 31).

However, the distancing when receiving a tale may be so strong that on many occasions it has led to multiple retellings that seek to adapt it to a more current environment, presenting other models of behaviour, rejecting attitudes reflected in some tales by considering them to be inadequate and teaching new lessons and values, in this case created by a specific author.

These intentional modifications are examples of recycling which, as pointed out by Miriam Llamas Ubieto in a lecture on recycling in the postdigital era (2020), can be defined as a practice that seeks to reintroduce previously used resources into a new life cycle, which thus implies the reinsertion of something into a new useful circle of life. They would thus become creations based on something that previously existed by reusing one or more elements, with the subsequent product containing parts that are reiteration and repetition and other parts that are variation and innovation.

The concept of recycling is associated with other terms like intertextuality, appropriation, re-elaboration, re-writing, adaptation and re-contextualisation. Intertextuality not only refers to the linguistic quality granted by textuality to the written discourse, but also implies the relationship established, as pointed out by poststructuralism, between the texts.

In the words of Umberto Eco, this intertextual dialogue is "the phenomenon by which a given text echoes previous texts" (Eco 2005, p. 197), such that "we have a work that speaks of itself: not a work that speaks of the genre to which it belongs, but a work that speaks of its own structure, and of the way in which it was made." (Eco 2005, p. 199).

3 "En la pretendida mutación de todas las cosas se conserva del pasado mucho más de lo que cualquiera pueda imaginar, y se une a lo nuevo adquiriendo una renovada validez" (Pisanty 1995, p. 16).

4 "El placer del cuento deriva de la acción combinada de 'constricción y libertad', o sea, de la exigencia de seguridad por un lado (la seguridad de lo ya conocido) y del impulso hacia lo desconocido por el otro" (Pisanty 1995, p. 31).

Literary works, by possessing a marked intertextual nature, clearly show their process of (re)-elaboration and their process of recycling, making use of content and forms from other original works and adopting new characteristics, and point to the express desire of the author to modify, and even correct, something which is already known but has become obsolete, is judged as improvable or opens up new aesthetic-narrative possibilities.

In this way, the new author appropriates something pre-existing and adapts it to their own needs or to those of their readers and that way re-contextualises it. Previous elements are combined with new elements, thus giving rise to a new work.

The recycling process happens even more frequently when the work it echoes belongs to classical literature or is based on folk traditions of peoples; in the modern world, where copyright is defended and preserved, recycling may be considered to be plagiarism, and thus the thin line between what is legal and illegal becomes blurred, as Linda Hutcheon indicates in her article "Literary Borrowing … and Stealing: Plagiarism, Sources, Influences and Intertexts", adding that when speaking about literary loans or textual allegiance, not only are the texts important but also the author, their intention and the reader's interpretation (1986, p. 231).

In this regard, intertextuality is the result of the re-elaboration or recycling process carried out by the author, albeit not always recognised by the reader. In folk traditions, with unknown or anonymous authors, all kinds of adaptations, re-elaborations and recycling may take place without resulting in accusations of plagiarism, which exclusively occurs with traditional tales.

Some studies relating to the recycling of traditional tales take stock of this phenomenon, for example, *Recycling Red Riding Hood* (Becket 2002), *Little Red Riding Hood Uncloacked* (Orenstein 2002) or *Die Geschichte vom Rotkäppchen. Ursprünge, Analyse, Parodien eines Märchens* (*The story of Little Red Riding Hood, Origins, Analyses, Parodies of a Fairy Tale*) (Ritz 1981), and this is without mentioning the large number of films that have adapted traditional tales or developed their plot for their main story.

In this regard, cinema has enhanced the creation of multiple versions and re-elaborations, and is seen as one of the main agents of literary recycling; films also involve the phenomenon of remediation, where the main elements of the traditional tale are not only re-elaborated but recycled (story, plot and characters), but it also made accessible through another format – film-making.

In this work, we will stick to a few examples of the recycling of traditional tales on paper and we will (fundamentally) consider three movements or types of recycling: ideological recycling, aesthetic-literary recycling and technologically updated recycling.

4. Types of recycling

Ideological recycling seeks to denounce values established in traditional tales by replacing them with those that are more in line with modern and contemporary movements that promote and advocate more modern values such as feminism, political and economic power, values of solidarity, the condemnation of violence, the promotion of environmental awareness, etc.

This movement was made popular and given visibility through James Finn Garner's work, *Politically Correct Bedtime Stories. Modern Tales for Our Life and Times* (1994). The title points to a *correction*, which implies the existence of a previous item that is classified as erroneous and requires improving.

This is not just any type of correction but a matter of respect for what is politically correct; in other words, a diplomatic use that is respectful of everyone and does not harm sensitivities or cause offence, and may even seem to contradict its previous iteration, to adhere more closely to what is popularly known as progressive thought.

This respect refers to what is modern and current, thus justifying the need to correct these tales and stories to adapt them to modern-day sensibilities. The author indicates in the introduction that the tales originally sought, successfully, to serve certain purposes: "to entrench the patriarchy, to estrange people from their own natural impulses, to demonize 'evil' and to 'reward' an 'objective' 'Good'". (Garner 1994, p. 3) Despite being a work replete with humour, irony and sarcasm, the author points out that "today, we have the opportunity – and the obligation – to rethink these classic stories so they reflect more enlightened times." (Garner 1994, p. 3).

Garner's statements indicate why classic ideas are circumvented and, to some extent, rejected. Aware of social sensitivities, which is what promotes and paves the way for this type of recycling, Garner appeals to the reader and apologises in advance in the following manner:

> If, through omission or commission, I have inadvertently displayed any sexist, racist, culturalist, nationalist, regionalist, ageist, lookist, ableist, sizeist, speciesist, intellectualist, socioeconomics, ethnocentrist, phallocentrist, heteropatriarchalist, or type of bias as yet unnamed, I apologize and encourage your suggestions for rectification. In the quest to develop meaningful literature that is totally free from bias and purged from the influences of its flawed cultural past, I doubtless have made some mistakes. (Garner 1994, p. 4).

And again, the author sarcastically proposes a complete list of "biases" he may have fallen into and which could generate offence or harm sensitivities. This irony questions all modern ideological versions as it shows the ease with which a tale may lead to discord and misinterpretation to the point where we may ask whether there even truly exists a tale everyone likes.

Not always using sarcasm, many works still have followed this ideological recycling movement, as in the Spanish example of *Érase dos veces* (*Twice upon a time*) by the publisher Cuatro Tuercas, the *Cuentos clásicos para niñas y niños de hoy* (Gaudes / Macías 2014) (*Contemporary classic tales for boys and girls*) adapted by Manuel Calvente and Kike de los Reyes by the publisher Ocala or *Cuentos clásicos feministas* (2018) (*Classic feminist tales*) by Ángela Vallvey, in German *Moderne Märchen für Kinder* (2011) (*Modern tales for children*), by Hans-Peter Bischof, or in English *Power to the Princess. 15 Favorite Fairytales Retold with Girl Power* (2018), by Vita Murrow.

Aesthetic-literary recycling is very common in children's literature, whereby the funny, playful or humorous elements of the tale take on a dominant role. To achieve their playful end, authors who make use of aesthetic-literary recycling need to ensure that readers are familiar with the original stories and can appreciate the differences and changes produced in the new version. If the reader does not recognise the underlying work, even though they are reading an independent and complete tale that may be read separately from the original, the playful and humorous effect will not be fully achieved. This effect is illustrated by Gianni Rodari in the following way:

- Once upon a time there was a girl called Little Yellow Riding Hood.
- No, red!
- Ah yes, red. Her father calls her and …
- No, it wasn't her father but her mother.
- That's true. She calls her and says, go to Aunt Rosita's house and take her…
- Go to her grandmother's house, she said, not her aunt's house

Etc.[5] (Rodari 2018, p. 77).

These works follow the line of those presented by Gianni Rodari in his *Gramática de la fantasía* ([1973] 2018) (*The Grammar of Fantasy* and *Cuentos por teléfono*) ([1962]

---

5 - Había una vez una niña que se llamaba Caperucita Amarilla.
- ¡No, roja!
- Ah, sí, roja. Pues, su papá la llama y …
- Que no, que no era su papá, era su mamá.
- Es verdad. La llama y le dice: ve a casa de la tía Rosita a llevarle…
- ¡Ve a casa de la abuelita; le dijo, no a la de la tía!
Etcétera (Rodari 2018, p. 77).

2012) (*Tales on the phone*) where he implements techniques such as "transforming stories", "stories the other way round", "what happens next", "imitating tales" and "concoction of stories" (Rodari 2018, pp. 77–100).

This phenomenon is explained by Little Red Riding Hood to the wolf in *Little Red Reading Hood*:

> You don't like an ending? Red Reading Hood said.
> "Then change it, arrange it again in your head.
> Just switch it and stitch it up some other way." (Lowland / Mantle 2018).

These aesthetic-literary recycling versions may maintain the structure or plot of the traditional tale, but may sometimes go so far as removing the main character, placing them in a completely different environment. In the first case, versions that maintain the structure or plot of the traditional tale would include *Revolting Rhymes* (1982) by Roald Dahl or the collection *Des-cuentos* by Enric Lluch (2014) (*Un-tales/Talebacks*) in which the titles themselves point to the change to the original tale: *Caperucita y el Lobo Bobo* (2014a) (*Little Red Riding Hood and the silly wolf*), *La trompeta de* Cenicienta (2014b) (*Cinderella's trumpet*), *El saxofonista de Hamelín* (2014c) (*The saxophonist of Hamelin*), *Los músicos que braman* (2014d) (*The blaring musicians*), *Tres cerditos duros de roer* (2014e) (*Three little pigs hard to break down*), *Los dos genios de* Aladino (2014 f) (*Aladdin's two genies*), *Las increíbles botas del gato* (2014g) (*Puss's incredible boots*), etc. They all maintain the structure of the tale, which they re-elaborate, while often also playing with characteristics of the main characters, symbolic objects of the tale, and the tale's language.

Another example would be *¿Qué me cuentas, Caperucita?* (2019) (*What's up, Little Red Riding Hood?*) by José Carlos Andrés, in which the main character, fed up with having to always do everything, decides to put on a cape of different colours and cycle to the forest, or *Cappuccetto Rosso Verde Giallo Blu e Bianco* (1981), by Bruno Munari and Enrica Agostinelli, where the main character appears in different scenes (forest, city, sea, snow) taking on the wolf in each of them.

The second case, with versions starring the central character of the traditional tale against a backdrop with a completely different storyline, would include modern tales that use characters from traditional tales[6], like *Iu, el Lobo, y Berta, la Caperucita verde* (2017) (*Iu, the Wolf and Berta, Little Green Riding Hood*), by Paula Ramos Rey, in which a tale of friendship between the two main

6 Film versions would also fall into this category. This type of recycling is seen most frequently in children's and adult's literature: harnessing characters already created in traditional tales inserted into a new fictitious world.

characters is told in a version with a vegan Little Red Riding Hood, who speaks five languages as well as being able to read sign language, who is a defender of animals, an aid worker, committed to the environment and who protects the wolf from hunters, or *Rotkäppchen hat keine Lust* (2016) (*Little Red Riding Hood doesn't feel like it*), by Sebastian Meschenmoser, where Little Red Riding Hood, in a bad mood, carries bricks, socks and chewing gum in her bag and hates going to see her grandmother, finally going to live in the wolf's cave and becoming a thief. In *Cinderella and the Hot Air Balloon* (1992), by Ann Jungman, Cinderella does not go to the ball in the palace, but arranges her own party at home so that all the servants can have a good time. She dresses up in her house clothes, does not like elegant dresses and prefers to run around and climb trees. At the end of the tale, she bumps into another rebellious prince and they 'run' away together in a hot-air balloon.

Lastly, we will look at technologically updated recycling, in which not only values, ideas and customs are updated, as in ideological recycling, but where there is also a technological and digital component in line with the postdigital era, offering new aesthetic and narrative possibilities.

As pointed out by Seth Lerer in his book *Children's Literature: A Reader's History, from Aesop to Harry Potter* (2008), we find ourselves in an "ironic age" (Lerer 2008, p. 305) in which "no canons can be taken at face value" (Lerer 2008, p. 306) and he describes the backdrop of

> the late twentieth-century child in books. No longer are we traveling the seas, exploring continents, or staking out our homesteads on the prairie. Much recent children's literature locates its boys and girls on city streets, in high apartments, in schoolyards that abut boulevards and highways. (Lerer 2008, p. 306).

Through the term "irony", Seth Lerer characterises the state in which the child finds itself represented in current literature: "this mix of urban disaffection, snarky wisdom, and 'been there, done that' distance that the modern child affects" (Lerer 2008, p. 307), which converts the young reader, in turn, into an "ironic" observer. This brings to mind the words of Jedediah Purdy when he says, "Everything we encounter is a remark, a rerelease, a ripoff, or a rerun" (Lerer 2008, p. 307). These terms clearly allude to concepts close to the recycling we have been discussing.

It is perhaps at this point that we should look more in depth at the nature of the young (and young adult) reader of the 21st Century, the so-called Generation Z, or the centennials, those born in the 1990s, or even the next generation – Generation Alpha – born after 2010. Anna Dolot (2018, p. 45) mentions a quote by Singh Dangmei where he states that the members of Generation Z grew up "during the most profound changes in the century, who exist in a world with Internet, smart phones, laptops, freely available networks and digital media" (Dolot 2018, p. 45), and are as used to living in the real world as in the virtual world of a fully digitalised society, and hence, a postdigital society. Generation Z

> uses different mobile devices, they comment on reality, the environment, and the surroundings they live in, they manifest their opinions and attitudes using Twitter, blogs, and internet forums, and they share photos (Instagram, Pinterest, Snapchat) and films (YouTube, Instagram, Snapchat). Facebook can be used for all of abovementioned activities. (Dolot 2018, p. 45).

Unlike Generation Z, Generation Alpha, who were born later, are entirely digitally native, as they were born with the Internet, social media and screens already completely developed and implemented; technology forms part of these people's life from their first breath, when they were probably photographed with a smartphone. They take digital technology for granted, and it is fully integrated in their daily lives, just as it has been for Generation Z from a certain age onwards.

Given the clear socio-cultural changes that have arrived with globalisation, multiculturalism and technological progress, which have created new expectations and needs for readers, Elena Consejo Pano asks, "Is it thus fair then to continue to offer them the same literary discourse as a few decades ago?"[7] (2011, p. 111).

Technologically-updated recycling encounters the changes alluded to by Lerer and the question asked by Consejo Pano. By this, I am not referring to the formal changes that readers may have experienced, through tablets, computers, mobile phones and even video-consoles, but rather – as has been seen in other types of recycling mentioned earlier – to the appreciable changes in content, above all in the features of the main characters, in the world in which they interact, in the language they use and in the type of plot which, by employing technology, modifies the potential events and outcomes. Applied to the traditional tale, in its original version, Little Red Riding Hood didn't have the option of calling the police when the wolf attacked her because mobile phones did not exist and Snow White's stepmother could not trace her footsteps with a GPS tracker. However, this is possible through the recycling of updated technology in traditional tales. In *Lobo solo buscaba wifi* (*The wolf was just looked for Wi-Fi*), by Pilar Serrano and Mar Azabal (2017), the much-feared wolf leaves the forest because he didn't have any reception there and, when bumping in to other characters from

7 "¿Es justo, entonces, seguir ofreciéndole el mismo discurso literario ahora que hace unas décadas?" (consejo Pano 2011, p. 111).

other tales that he has treated badly, defends himself by stating that "He was just searching for Wi-Fi!" The wolf's interest in other tales in waylaying other animals and characters has been replaced by his need to connect to the Internet; his character has changed.

In the anthology of tales for adults, *Grimms Märchen Update 1.2* (2012), the different authors "have addressed what Grimm's tales would be like if they had been written today"[8] (Erpenbeck 2012, p. 5). The term that appears in the title – update – which belongs to the world of IT, alludes to the technological and digital presence that will be part of the recycled tales in this anthology.

For its part, in the novel by Nina McKay *Rotkäppchen und der Hipster-Wolf* (2016) (*Little Red Riding Hood and the hipster wolf*), which begins a tetralogy always starring a princess (Little Red Riding Hood, Cinderella, Rapunzel, Sleeping Beauty), the princesses carry smartphones with them, together with a selfie stick, wherever they go; the magic of the mirror consists of having a GPS system incorporated and they can hack other devices, the witches have their own social media to stay in touch, etc. This in turn leads to a change in the language which – just as in daily life – translates into literature. The technicisms and neologisms abound when something is "mainstream" (MacKay 2016, p. 6), the characters "tweet" ["twittern"] (2016, p. 15), "give likes" ["like"] (2016, p. 29), "scroll" ["scrollen"] (2016, p. 29) and "blog" ["bloggen"] (2016, p. 30) or "post" ["posten"] (2016, p. 37).

5. Conclusion

Technologically-updated recycling is fully incorporated in children's and young adult's literature nowadays, with readers that belong to Generation Z or Alpha immersed in a postdigital world from an early age. Although this type of recycling is the most current, the three types of recycling considered here may take place at the same time and are not mutually exclusive. The renewal of classic folk tales has been a part of their very nature since their origin, and at the end of the first quarter of the 21st Century, this is no different. Tales are dressed up in modern apparel, whether through play, ideology or technology.

8 "[…] sind der Frage nachgegangen, wie Grimms Märchen wohl aussehen würden, hätte man sie heute geschrieben" (Erpenbeck 2012, p. 5).

References

Afanásiev, A. N.: *El pájaro de fuego y otros cuentos populares rusos*. Ed. Vega, Carlos. Alianza: Madrid 2009.

Andrés, José Carlos: *¿Qué me cuentas, Caperucita?* Algar: Alzira 2019.

Beckett, Sandra: *Recycling Red Riding Hood*. Psychology Press: New York 2002.

Bischof, Hans-Peter *et. al.*: *Moderne Märchen für Kinder: Anthologie*. Net-Verlag: Chemnitz 2011.

Calvente, Manuel / de los Reyes, Kike: *Cuentos Clásicos para niñas y niños de hoy*. Ocala: Madrid 2017.

Cañadas García, Teresa: "El cuento tradicional y su percepción actual". *Educación y Futuro* (42) 2020, pp. 15–36.

Consejo Pano, Elena: "Peritextos del siglo XXI. Las guardas en el discurso literario infantil". *Ocnos* (7) 2011, pp. 111–122, retrieved 2.2.2022, from DOI https://doi.org/10.18239/ocnos_2011.07.09.

Dahl, Roald: *Revolting Rhymes*. Jonathan Cape: London 1982.

Dolot, Anna: "The characteristic of Generation Z". *e-mentor* 2018, pp. 44–50, retrieved 2.2.2022, from DOI http://dx.doi.org/10.15219/em74.1351.

Don Juan Manuel: *El Conde Lucanor*. Vicedo, Juan (Ed.). Biblioteca Virtual Miguel de Cervantes: Alicante [1331–1335] 2004, retrieved 2.2.2022, from http://www.cervantesvirtual.com/obra-visor/el-conde-lucanor--0/html/00052e2a-82b2-11df-acc7-002185ce6064_1.html.

Eco, Umberto: "Innovation & Repetition: Between Modern & Postmodern Aesthetics". *Daedalus* 134(4) 2005, pp. 191–207.

Erpenbeck, Charlotte: *Grimms Märchen Update 1.2*. Machandel: Haselünne 2012.

Ewers, Hans-Heino: *Literatur für Kinder und Jugendliche. Eine Einführung*. Wilhelm Fink: Paderborn 2012.

Garner, James Finn: *Politically Correct Bedtime Stories: Modern Tales for Our Life and Times*. John Wiley & Sons Inc.: New Jersey 1994.

Gaudes, Belén / Macías, Pablo: *Cuentos clásicos para niños y niñas de hoy*. Cuatro Tuercas: Madrid 2014.

Hutcheon, Linda: "Literary Borrowing … and Stealing: Plagiarism, Sources, Influences, and Intertexts". *English Studies in Canada* 12(2) 1986, pp. 229–239, doi:10.1353/esc.1986.0020.

Jungman, Ann: *Cinderella and the Hot Air Balloon*. F. Lincoln: London 1992.

Lerer, Seth: *Children's Literature: A Reader's History, from Aesop to Harry Potter*. University of Chicago Press: Chicago 2008.

Llamas Ubieto, Miriam: "El concepto de reciclaje en la era postdigital". Jornadas *Reciclaje, postdigital, postglobal: definiciones para el ahora*. Universidad Complutense de Madrid: 29.01.2020.

Lluch, Enric: *Des-cuentos. Caperucita y el Lobo Bobo*. Algar: Alzira 2014a.

Lluch, Enric: *Des-cuentos. La trompeta de Cenicienta*. Algar: Alzira 2014b.

Lluch, Enric: *Des-cuentos. El saxofonista de Hamelín*. Algar: Alzira 2014c.

Lluch, Enric: *Des-cuentos. Los músicos que braman*. Algar: Alzira 2014d.

Lluch, Enric: *Des-cuentos. Tres cerditos duros de roer*. Algar: Alzira 2014e.

Lluch, Enric: *Des-cuentos. Los dos genios de Aladino*. Algar: Alzira 2014f.

Lluch, Enric: *Des-cuentos. Las increíbles botas del gato*. Algrar: Alzira 2014g.

Lowland, Lucy / Mantle, Ben: *Little Red Reading Hood*. MacMillan: London 2018.

MacKay, Nina: *Rotkäppchen und der Hipster-Wolf*. Drachenmond: Leverkusen 2016.

Mandela, Nelson: *Mis cuentos africanos*. Siruela: Madrid 2007.

Meschenmoser, Sebastian: *Rotkäppchen hat keine Lust*. Thienemann: Stuttgart 2016.

Munari, Bruno / Agostinelli, Enrica: *Cappuccetto Rosso Verde Giallo Blu e Bianco*. Einaudi: Turín 1981.

Murrow, Vita: *Power to the Princess: 15 Favorite Fairytales Retold with Girl Power*. Frances Lincoln: London 2018.

Orenstein, Catherine: *Little Red Riding Hood Uncloacked*. Basic Books: New York 2002.

Pisanty, Valentina: *Cómo se lee un cuento popular*. Paidós: Barcelona 1995.

Ramos Rey, Paula: *Iu, el Lobo y Berta, la Caperucita verde*. Dekimba: Madrid 2017.

Ritz, Hans: *Die Geschichte vom Rotkäppchen. Ursprünge, Analyse, Parodien eines Märchens*. Muriverlag: Kassel 1981.

Rodari, Gianni: *Cuentos por teléfono* [*Favole al telefono*]. Juventud: Barcelona [1962] 2012.

Rodari, Gianni: *Gramática de la fantasía* [*Grammatica della fantasía*]. Planeta: Barcelona [1973] 2018.

Serrano, Pilar / Azabal, Mar: *Lobo solo buscaba wifi*. Amigos de Papel: Madrid 2017.

Vallvey, Ángela: *Cuentos clásicos feministas*. Arzalia: Madrid 2018.

Vega, Carlos: *Aleksander Afanásiev. El pájaro de fuego y otros cuentos populares rusos*. Alianza: Madrid 2009.

Pilar García Carcedo
Universidad Complutense de Madrid

The Creation of Memes Based on Traditional Folk Tales in a Teacher-training Degree Classroom

Abstract: Traditional folk tales constitute a special case for literary re-writings, as they have been the object of a wide variety of versions and transformations through the ages, as has already been studied by specialists in the field, such as Zipes or Rodríguez Almodóvar. The only part that does not vary in traditional oral stories is their skeleton, structure and archetypes; the garb that overlays it adopts different forms in each location and culture, whether through versions or recycling. But the structural elements and more symbolic details of the tales are universal, and therefore known by the wider public: Cinderella's slipper, the kiss that wakes up Sleeping Beauty, etc. It is precisely this extensive propagation among recipients that makes the stories perfect material for modern digital recycling. Our research has focused on the analysis of the memes created by students of the Faculty of Education at Complutense University, based on various versions of some or the best-known folk tales in the world (*Cinderella*, *Little Red Riding Hood* and *Sleeping Beauty*), as well as on a lesser known tale in the Hispanic tradition, (*Blancaflor*). This study will also look at the memes from a gender perspective.

Keywords: recycling, Comparative Literature, traditional folk tales, Gender studies, critical thought.

1. Introduction

This chapter presents the results of research focused on humorous digital recycling by students of the Faculty of Education at Complutense University, based on the traditional versions of some of the most well-known folk tales. We will see that, despite the comic aspect of these brief creations, there is still no lack of a spirit of protest. In any case, these memes are new forms of writing, as the digital technologies of the 21st Century have led to an expansion of (other) visual texts, and to the combining of words with a variety of different codes. The students' creations are a form of digital rewriting, making use of a whole range of multimedia possibilities through merging words and image.

These new creations give the tales a new perspective, thus bringing them closer to current students, increasing their motivation to engage with these traditional texts.

The specialist Sánchez-Aparicio (2016) uses the term "escrituras del software" ("software writings") for this, which he defines as "disruptive poetics"[1]. Alex Saum-Pascual has coined the term "escritura #postweb" ("post-web writing") to refer to a literature that "has been generated by and for the digital media. It has fully assumed the web as something that is no longer a novelty or the future, and has become the present" (Saum-Pascual 2018, p. 10). Digital writing certainly helps preserve "the possibility that what emerged once leaping out of our perception does so again from the page" or the screen (Rivera Garza 2010, p. 16). At any event, it is a cultural recycling activity for everyone. As Carroll (1998) says, technical reproduction and accessibility are both sufficient and necessary conditions to define *mass art*.[2] This article deals with the possibility available to all students to recycle literary texts, in this case traditional folk tales, giving the texts a new digital life through *memes*.

The term 'meme'[3] was included in the *Diccionario de la Real Academia Española* (*Dictionary of the Spanish Royal Academy*) in 2018, with two main definitions, of which the second is currently best known on social media: the meme as "an image, video or text, in general distorted for the purpose of caricature, which is mainly disseminated through the Internet". The first definition takes us to the historical origin of the term, as coined by Dawkins in 1976, "A feature of a culture or conduct that is transmitted by imitation from one person to another, or from generation to generation" (DRAE).[4] Thus, following Dawkins, a meme would be, in its origin, a term that serves as the cultural counterpart of biological

---

1 All Spanish sources are translated by the author.

2 To reflect on the dichotomy between what specialists call mass art and elevated art, you need only look at the studies by Carroll on *mass art*, defined as follows, "x is a mass artwork if and only if 1. x is a multiple instance or type artwork, 2. produced and distributed by a mass technology, 3. which artwork is intentionally designed to gravitate in its structural choices (for example, its narrative forms, symbolism, intended affect, and even its content) toward those choices that promise accessibility with minimum effort, virtually on first contact, for the largest number of untutored (or relatively untutored) audiences." (Carroll 1998, p. 196).

3 For more details on the concept of memes, see Zipes (2012), Ruiz Martínez (2018) and García Carcedo (2020a, 2020b), as well as the chapter of this work entitled "From Memes to Literature and Vice-Versa: the Recycling Canon" by Adrián Menéndez de la Cuesta.

4 So, from an historical perspective, 'meme' is a term coined by Richard Dawkins in his work *The Selfish Gene* [1976]. Dawkins' thesis is based on an analogy to Darwinian

genes; and just as in the Darwinian theory of evolution, the mutated genes and the memes that are the most advantageous (we will talk more about this below) are those that are successful.

In the 21st Century, digital technologies and social media have contributed to the exponential multiplication of memes across almost the entire world, as viral digital content. What the modern public understands as a 'meme' is any event in the news that has been distorted through an immediate proliferation of images accompanied by humorous texts; artistic objects geared to amusement that arouse emotions by formulaic serial repetition (Ruiz-Moscardó 2018, p. 38). Shifman calls this modern impulse to convert all events into memes "*hypermemetic* logic, in which almost every major public event sprouts a stream of memes" (2014, p. 128). Understood in this way, memes are similar to cartoons, but nearly always imply transcendent protest and much more complex semiotics than is immediately apparent. Moreover, memes do not function independently. To understand them, we have to be aware of a whole series of prior or simultaneous references, in what Rowan has called "constellations" (Rowan 2015, p. 797). What is more, memes contribute to structuring the current public discourse, and even create states of opinion (Shifman 2014, p. 123)[5].

2. The corpus of memes created by students

The overwhelming presence of memes in social media means that they are a tool for recycling that is particularly well known by students, and thus very motivational.

The memes were part of a more extensive creative writing project consisting of a number of phases, which had as its initial objective to bring students closer to the model of traditional folk tales through a motivational approach.

For more than three years, students of the "Literature and Education", "Reading and Creative Writing", "Stories and Poetry" and "Children's Literature" modules at the Faculty of Education at the Complutense University (which are all part of the courses of the Master's Degree in Children's Education and Master's Degree

evolution according to which cultural features or memes are replicated in a similar way to genes (Dawkins [1976] 2016).

5 Jorge Bustos wrote that Spain is "a democracy dedicated to memes" (Bustos 2016). The tremendous current importance of memes in social media is what makes them a tool that is familiar and accessible to students. See "Esto no es serio" ("This isn't serious"). *El Mundo*, 22.01.2016, https://www.elmundo.es/opinion/2016/01/22/56a129a1268e3ed2018b4575.html.

in Primary Education) have been given exercises where they digitally rewriting folk tales, and the resulting memes they created were collected at the end. This has left us with an extensive corpus of more than three hundred memes. We have made a selection out of the hundred we felt are most representative, and we will analyse them in the following pages.

The tales chosen by the students as referents for their memes were, in order of preference, *Cinderella*, *Sleeping Beauty* and *Snow White*. Most of the images selected by the students belong to the Disney films which adapted the stories; although among those who have chosen a gender perspective, the images of *Feminista ilustrada* were very popular.

Fig. 1. Meme created by *Feminista ilustrada*, chosen by the student Noelia Alcalde. (Text in English: "I woke up and he was kissing me. What was he thinking? Me too! How did he know whether I wanted to?").

The Complutense University students were given complete freedom to choose whatever app they wanted to use to create the memes. Some used *Meme creator,*

Memasik or *Meme Generator*, but, in fact, the most common move was to create them directly within the actual social media they are familiar with, above all Instagram. Before starting our analysis in the following section, we would like to point out that meme typology has been analysed in several studies, including by Elad Segev et al. (2015), in which Shifman also participated (2015, p. 423). This study reaches the conclusion that what confers unity to memes are two main forces: firstly, the essential qualities of each family of memes, and, secondly, the special nature of the individual form and content.

Thus, at least three different aspects must be taken into account when analysing Internet memes: first, their content and references; second, their form and the decontextualisation between the graphic and textual aspects; and finally, the attitude the receivers and spreaders have towards this meme, which will have a direct impact on the success of the meme.

3. Traditional tales, recycling and memes

> *"If there is any single genre that has captured the imagination of people in all walks of life throughout the world, it is the fairy tale" (Zipes 2012, p. 9).*

Traditional folk tales can be defined as brief fictional stories that have been passed down orally, with numerous different versions, and which are part of our common heritage (like myths, epics and legends). The mystery of their origins, their influences and their fertile spread closely resemble the viral effect of the Internet recycling we are dealing with here, and numerous specialists have analysed the specific ways traditional tales have expanded orally in different parts of the world: Opie / Opie (1974), Rodríguez Almodóvar (2004), Hernández and Llamas (2014) and García Carcedo (2018, 2020a).

We would like to highlight the research by the scholar Zipes (2012) in his work *The Irresistible Fairy Tale: The Cultural and Social History of a Genre* which, based on Dawkins' notion of a meme, focuses on traditional tales and their oral transmission. Zipes reflects on the popular tales that compete across the generations of cultural evolution until only the most resilient have survived. In fact, he states that the tales of oral tradition are memes in and of themselves: "'Cinderella,' 'Snow White,' 'Bluebeard,' 'Little Red Riding Hood,' […] are so well known and have spread so widely in the world in all kinds of mediated forms that they appear to be universal memes" (Zipes 2012, p. 29). He concludes that what allows a tale to be spread and persist is its power to "determine and influence social practices". For this reason, from a gender perspective, one of the questions in this research could be based on discovering whether there were brave and active women in traditional tales, or, as some sectors now criticise, the leading female characters were always passive.

The memes created during the students' exercises, which, as we will also see, tend to be based on a gender approach, can be classified as a subtype of digital recycling, which is mainly based on *approximation, remediation and recirculation* of existing images depicting traditional folk tales, through their decontextualisation by the use of new and surprising texts. To examine these concepts in more detail with respect to recycling, we refer to the research space and database of "Cultural and literary recycling strategies in the post-digital era", which explores and classifies recycling strategies, as well as to examples of popular, artistic and literary recycling[6]. This study, carried out within the framework of the REC-LIT project on recycling typology and strategy, forms the basis for our analysis of the memes created in the teaching degree classroom.

The types of recycling proposed in REC-LIT include, but are not limited to, the following: appropriation, rewriting, remediation, circulation and recirculation, recovery, recreation and reproduction (Llamas Ubieto / Goicoechea de Jorge 2022). Among these, as has been mentioned, appropriation and recirculation are key when it comes to memes. In the case of our memes, the most important possible strategies used for recycling, as proposed on the LEETHI website, are based on the *decontextualisation* and *recontextualisation* of the images used as a reference to traditional folk tales. For each meme we have to explain whether it is a *composition* or juxtaposition of existing images with new texts, or whether there has been a *transformation* of the images to adapt them to the aims of the meme. In the following section, these typologies and strategies will be applied to understand the operation of a selection of the memes from the corpus that has been analysed. We do in fact consider that because of their universality, traditional tales constitute particularly appropriate material for *memetic recycling*. We will now analyse some of the examples created.

4. Analysis of the memes created in the project

Creating digital memes based on traditional folk tales in the teaching degree classroom has been a highly motivating form of developing creativity. The memes are a next step in the writing workshops that have been expanding in line with the suggestions of such teachers as Gianni Rodari (2010). There are two keys to the complex aspect of the reception and success of a meme: whether

6 Created within the framework of the REC-LIT project, which can be consulted on this link: http://repositorios.fdi.ucm.es/REC-LIT/view/ls_ov_clasificacion.php.

the recipient understands the implicit references in the meme, and whether they identify with it: a meme will achieve its goal and be spread if it manages to meet both requirements. Memes are strongly intertextual discourses, because some are developed in relation to earlier ones, and the references must still be current if they are to be successful with the intended recipients. In this sense, traditional folk tales are ideal as a basis for these memes because everyone is familiar with the references.

For the internal description of memes, scholars suggest three basic properties: longevity, fecundity (capacity to be reproduced) and fidelity to the original (Shifman 2014, p. 240). Thus, the success of a meme depends on it being communicable and malleable at the same time (Davidson 2012, pp. 124–126); in any case, what is important is that memes should continue to be recognised despite the variants. Memes based on traditional and well-known folk tales will always be recognised, especially if they use images that are well known, such as those of Disney films. For a statistical analysis of the memes created in the faculty, we will focus on showing the results from a thematic point of view. Surprisingly, most of the memes only focused on two themes: feminism (62 % of the memes) and aspects related to the lockdown due to the current pandemic (33 % of the memes); while only 5 % of students created memes on other subjects, as can be seen in the chart:

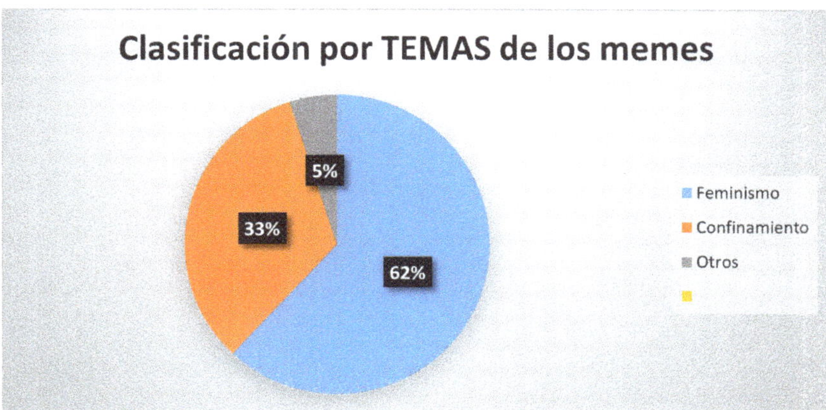

Classification of memes by THEMES: Feminism / Confinement / Other

With respect to the form, memes in general and those in this sample in particular are based on fixed patterns which, moreover, appear in the applications used to create memes, or they make use of familiar images that have been recovered by the creators, such as stills from Disney films. For example, we frequently see two or three images in the graphic part; and the textual part is also divided, with a textual setting in the upper part of the image and a newly-created conclusion or paradox below, which decontextualises the illustration. The meme is therefore based on a graphic element which is recognisable at first sight, but introduces a textual incongruency that produces humour (by some other type of surprising recontextualisation or by the obvious clash between image and text). It is a type of juxtaposition that aims to destroy traditional expectations and create new meanings, often satirical in nature, thus creating a certain similarity to the way rhetorical figures or tropes function.

The characteristics of the memes that we are going to comment on are therefore based on the detextualisation of well-known images, which are then recontextualised to trigger surprise or humour through new texts that modify the referent of the image. At this point, to continue to analyse the memes from a comprehensive perspective, we consider it necessary to include some complete visual examples. Below, we have included a very small sample of memes created by the students, which represent the two basic issues of feminism and lockdown. The first two examples are in the form of feminist protest, although they also include other social themes, such as the problem of youth unemployment in the case of the first meme, which, despite the seriousness of the issue, produces humour by the inversion of the expectations of *Cinderella:*

Fig. 2. Meme created by the student Cristina Palomino, from the folk tale *Cinderella.* (Text in English: "Forget the prince, I want a job"*).*[7]

7 Figures 2, 3, 4, 5, 6 and 7. Memes created as part of the REC-LIT research project, with Professor García Carcedo at the Complutense University.

The social media success of this first meme seems guaranteed, because the referent is based on a fragment of the folk tale *Cinderella,* which everyone knows: it is the moment when Disney's fairy godmother gives the protagonist a dress to go to the ball. It is an image that has not been transformed: the strategy of recycling has consisted of the simple juxtaposition of the Disney image with a text by a student who recontextualises it. Moreover, the new theme introduced by the text also guarantees success on social media, as it calls for female independence, an issue dear to almost all female social media users. Cinderella does not want a prince; she hopes to achieve things for herself through a decent job. In this case, the purpose of the meme is not so much humour but social protest from a gender perspective.

The second meme selected also has a feminist viewpoint, but this time the focus lies on humour. It is based on a visual template of three images in the form of a comic strip, two of which introduce a new text. The first text reflects, without any novelty, what is expected from the tale *The Frog Prince* – that the animal will become a prince when kissed; it is in the third drawing where expectations are broken, when the girl is clear about not wanting a prince – she prefers to keep an entertaining talking frog:

Fig. 3. Meme by student Tiffany Hurtado Gutiérrez, based on *The Frog Prince.* (Text: "If you kiss me, I'll turn into a handsome prince… I prefer to have a talking frog").

It is precisely this tale – *The Frog Prince* – which was chosen by the scholar Jack Zipes to reflect on the meme theory in his article "What Makes a Repulsive Frog So Appealing? Memetics and Folk tales". Zipes insists, like Dawkins, that "any cultural artifact can become a meme [...] [but] a meme is not eternal and it cannot endure outside systems of cultural evolution" (2008, p. 112). And, as we have seen in the new text of the meme, for today's recycling the repulsive but comic talking frog is more appealing than the traditional Prince Charming. Another element that recontextualises the image of the meme is the title "A Real Tale", which clearly contrasts with the leading character's princess dress.

Next, we present a selection of memes from the students' second most popular thematic group: the consequences of lockdown during the pandemic. We have chosen two very different examples referring to the two most popular sub-topics. The first meme deals with concerns about limitations on night-life, which have, of course, particularly affected the young:

Fig. 4. Meme created by Noelia Alcalde Castro, based on the folk tale *Cinderella*. (Text "23.45h Madrid...Returning home before curfew").

The midnight curfew imposed in the city of Madrid during lockdown is related comically in this meme to Cinderella's forced departure at midnight, which was in fact a curfew imposed explicitly on her by the fairy godmother. In this case, the original image is used without any transformation, showing a princess who was already subject to a curfew in the traditional folk tale. It has become one of the most popular memes among the students from the point of view of humour; the kind humour more in line with what is commonly seen in memes on social media.

The second meme relating to the effects of the pandemic focuses on another issue that has seriously affected the students: online lessons rather than classroom/in-person teaching.

Fig. 5. Meme created by Ainhoa Urbaneja, based on the folk tale *Sleeping Beauty.* (Text "Me going to sleep at 3am/My 9am online class").

A number of recent studies have demonstrated the devastating effects of the lack of classroom teaching and students' clear preference for a return to classroom-based normality[8]. This meme demonstrates the lack of interest in attending an online class first thing in the morning, and is related to the referent of the folk tale *Sleeping Beauty*. From the point of view of recycling strategies, there has been a transformation of Disney's image, because in the film the prince obviously does not appear pulling on the princess's leg. In fact, it also has an implicit gender perspective, as the prince is the metaphor of this online class which does not interest the female character in the slightest.

Finally, we include two examples of other memes that are not based on very universal folk tales, but rather on a tale that is far less well known. It is the tale *Blancaflor, la hija del diablo* (*Blancaflor, the Daughter of the Devil*), which acquired significant status due to its extensive dissemination in the Spanish oral tradition. However, it is rather autochthonous or exclusive, in the sense that it does not appear as such in other European countries. We consider it a representative folk tale that should be rescued from oblivion. One of the reasons being its defence of gender equality within the oral tradition itself, since the leading female character is the real heroine of the tale and it is she who successfully completes the three impossible tests which the Devil gives to the male character, who cannot manage anything on his own. We wanted to end with these memes in order to reflect again on the causes of the online success and fecundity of these examples of digital recycling. The memes based on this tale, which is almost unknown today need a *#hashtag* for the folk tale to be recognised. There is no Disney film that has made it universally recognisable, or stereotyped images to identify the referent. The next meme once again returns to the subject of confinement/lockdown, this time based on the *Blancaflor* tale. But this time, the recycling strategy could be considered a failure, and it does not generate humour or public understanding. It is not at all a misjudgement on the part of the creator, but rather a daring proposal by the professor. However, it might be a failure of communicability, caused by the use of a folk tale that is not well known. Moreover, the text created by the student includes a highbrow reference to the contemporary collector of Spanish folk tales – Rodríguez Almodóvar – specifically his marvellous work *Cuentos al amor de la lumbre* I y II (1983).

---

8 For example, the *Informe Volvemos a clase* (*Back to School Report*, issued by the IDEA Institute, which is part of the SM Foundation), based on a sample taken from a thousand schools, shows that 75 % of students prefer classroom/in-person teaching.

Fig. 6. Meme created by the student Justo Sotelo. (Text in English: "Here I am, waiting for them to lift the local lockdown so that I can go out and buy the tales of Almodóvar" #RECLIT).

Having concluded that this last meme would not be as successful or fertile at the level of general online dissemination, we would like to open up the possibility of its success in a specific educational environment. In other words, although the referent is not as well-known at a general level, it may be used appropriately within a certain group that does share its background.

We refer to the fact that *Blancaflor* has been a frequent subject in many of the modules of the teaching degree in which this recycling project has been taught, so the memes based on this folk tale are successful in the closed circuit of the 400-plus students who take these modules, and the creators have shared them both on social media (Twitter and Instagram) and in the wikis of the Complutense University virtual campus. This extends the educational possibilities of circulating digital recycling based on more complex texts, or ones that are less well known by the general public, such as the marvellous heroine of the tale *Blancaflor, la hija del diablo*; who in this last ironic meme shows herself sceptical because she is the one who solves everything, rather than the self-proclaimed hero.

Fig. 7. Meme created by the students Alba, Roberto and Lidia, based on the folk tale *Blancaflor*. (Text: "Out of the way Blancaflor! I'm going to confront the devil. / Of course, sweetie (emoticon)").

5. Conclusions

We can say that in the 21st Century, most people will recognise the well-known referents of the stories of *Cinderella* and *Sleeping Beauty* (albeit in their simplified film versions). This is the reason that traditional folk tales constitute excellent material for *mimetic recycling*. The classroom project for a teaching degree at Complutense University complied with its initial objective, that of being a creative and motivating approach to connecting with the different versions of traditional folk tales. The experience consisted of a number of different phases, which can be summed up as follows: based on a reading of multiple different versions of the tales, students undertook writing exercises (traditional creative writing and collaborative and digital writing); and finally, the memes resulting of the final phase (of the module) were published on social media like Twitter and Instagram, platforms that cater to a younger audience (especially Instagram).

With respect to the memes, it could be questioned to what extent the literary aspect can be recycled in depth this way, and it could be argued that the exercise never went beyond the superficial level.

That is why in the preliminary phases, the focus was much more on extensive re-writing of the aforementioned versions of the traditional tales.

We also consider that the motivation generated by using a format such as memes, which younger people are fluent in, justifies their didactic use.

The analysis of the ways the students have constructed their memes allowed us to understand their use a little better; the *appropriation*, and even the *transformation*, of Disney's images for their own ends through their *recontextualization* with new texts. In any event, the results of the workshops have demonstrated the enormous interest of students in this type of digital recycling; Additionally, all students participated enthusiastically, whether male or female.

This type of creative recycling in the classroom demonstrates that the humour of these brief, apparently superficial memes, does not prevent them from carrying a strong element of protest.

From a thematic point of view, it is particularly noteworthy that most of the memes created based on traditional folk tales have only focused on two themes: first, support for female equality against the stereotypes of the patriarchy; and second, a variety of aspects related to lockdowns due to the current pandemic. In 60 % of memes with a feminist focus, the students tried to provide the princess with modern empowerment, demonstrating that she is not interested in being dependent on a prince or on continuing to sleep, waiting for the kiss of a man. With respect to the gender perspective of the memes, we should add that, despite the current criticism from certain sectors of feminism, the more traditional versions of the folk tales also present us with brave and decisive female characters, like in *Blancaflor, la hija del diablo*.

This autochthonous Spanish tale provides a way to dismantle the simplified belief that folk tales have always been sexist and filled with passive female characters like in many of the Disney films. This is why we wanted to include this lesser-known folk tale in the models for the recycling project, even though the fact that it was unknown to some of the recipients could lead to the resulting memes being less successful (outside the scope of the class in which the folk tale had already been studied). What we would like is for these other traditional and enriching versions of folk tales to be disseminated far and wide and gain more popular renown, because in them the female characters are saved by themselves and help other people, "saving" the world as real heroines. And one of the best ways of making more people aware of these heroines, in the classroom and outside of it, is through creative recycling.

References

Carroll, Nöel: *A Philosophy of Mass Art*. Clarendon Press: New York 1998.

Davidson, Patrick: "The Language of Internet Memes". In: Mandiberg, Michael (ed.): *The Social Media Reader*. New York University Press: New York 2012, pp. 120–134.

Dawkins, Richard: *The extended selfish gene*. Oxford University Press: Oxford 2016 [*The extended selfish gene* 1976].

García Carcedo, Pilar: "Escritura creativa e igualdad: versiones de los cuentos tradicionales", en *Didáctica. Lengua y Literatura* (30) 2018, pp. 87–103. Retrieved 01.08.2023, from https://doi.org/10.5209/DIDA.61956; https://revistas.ucm.es/index.php/DIDA/article/view/61956.

García Carcedo, Pilar: *Entre brujas y dragones. Travesía comparativa por los cuentos del mundo*. Verbum: Madrid 2020a.

García Carcedo, Pilar: *Memes ahora*. (Serie: Cuadernos del ahora n. 6). Docta-Complutense, Universidad Complutense de Madrid: Madrid 2020b. Retrieved 01.08.2023, from https://docta.ucm.es/entities/publication/e8b51a8f-4af1-4f16-8e3c-fd01af3cc4c9; https://docta.ucm.es/rest/api/core/bitstreams/9c18f36f-6ee4-4a2c-b74b-9e70446a52ec/content.

Hernández González, Isabel / Llamas Ubieto, Miriam (eds.): *Los hermanos Grimm en contexto: reescritura e interpretación de un legado universal*. Síntesis: Madrid 2014.

Llamas Ubieto, Miriam / Goicoechea de Jorge, María (coords.): *Rec-Lit: Estrategias de reciclaje cultural y literario en la era postdigital*. Repositorio institucional, Universidad Complutense de Madrid: Madrid 2022, retrieved 06.07.2023, from http://repositorios.fdi.ucm.es/REC-LIT/view/paginas/view_paginas.php?id=1.

Opie, Iona / Opie, Peter: *The Classic Fairy Tales*. Oxford University Press: New York, London 1974.

Rivera Garza, Cristina: "La página cruda". In: Estrada, Oswaldo (ed.): *Cristina Rivera Garza. Ningún crítico cuenta* esto. Ediciones Eón: México 2010, pp. 15–17.

Rodari, Gianni: *Gramática de la fantasía* [*Grammatica della fantasía*]. Planeta: Barcelona [1973] 2010.

Rodríguez Almodóvar, Antonio: *Cuentos al amor de la lumbre* I y II. Anaya: Madrid 1983.

Rodríguez Almodóvar, Antonio: *El texto infinito. Recopilación actualizada de ensayos sobre el cuento popular*. Madrid: Fundación Germán Sánchez Ruipérez 2004.

Rowan, Jaron: *Memes. Inteligencia idiota, política rara y folclore digital*. Capitán Swing: Madrid 2015.

Ruiz Martínez, José Manuel: "Una aproximación retórica a los memes de Internet". *Revista Signa* (27) 2018, pp. 995–1021. https://doi.org/10.5944/signa.vol27.2018.21856.

Ruiz-Moscardó, Javier: "The greatest understanding for the greatest number: Noël Carroll's approach to 'mass art'". *Revista Guillermo de Ockham* 16(1) 2018, pp. 37–44.

Sánchez-Aparicio, Vega: "Software Allegorical Writings: Aesthetic Breakdown, Ethic Rearticulation, from Mexican Sphere". *Caracteres: estudios culturales y críticos de la esfera digital* 2(5) 2016, pp. 80–113.

Saum-Pascual, Alex: *#Postweb! Crear con la máquina y en la red*. Iberoamericana/ Vervuert: Madrid, Frankfurt 2018.

Segev, Elad *et al.*: "Families and Networks of Internet Memes". *Journal of Computer-Mediated Communication* (20) 2015, 417–433.

Shifman, Limor: *Memes in Digital Culture*. MIT University Press Cambridge: Massachusetts 2014.

Zipes, Jack: "What Makes a Repulsive Frog So Appealing: Memetics and Folk tales". *Journal of Folklore Research* 45 (2) 2008, pp. 109–143.

Zipes, Jack: *The Irresistible Fairy Tale: The Cultural and Social History of a Genre*. Princeton University Press: Princeton 2012.

Begoña Regueiro Salgado
Universidad Complutense de Madrid

Cervantes and Bécquer in the 21st Century: Literary Recycling of Texts as Educational Tools

Abstract: According to the concept of literary education, one of the main aims of literature classes in secondary education is to ensure that an encounter takes place between readers and texts. To achieve that, different resources have been employed, including adaptations. However, not all reviewers agree on the suitability of using those, given that at no time the desired relationship with the original text is established. Based on this idea of needing to achieve a meaningful contact between readers and text, in this chapter we propose literary recycling as an educational tool. This allows contact with the text as it was originally conceived by the author and, through an active methodology related to reading and creative writing, students themselves can create an adaptation in which the text approaches the moment it was produced to facilitate them taking on board the main message, which is the true hallmark/test of literary proficiency.

Keywords: literary education, literary proficiency, the teaching of literature, literary recycling.

1. Literary education

What does studying literature consist of? Why (even) study literature? What is literature and what can it give us? Many of us have spent years studying literature, yet on probably only very few occasions have secondary-level or non-specialised students stopped to wonder why they are doing all this. As C.S. Lewis said, literature is art and, as art, produces pleasure.

> Our experience of the work as Poiema is unquestionably a keen pleasure. Those who have had it want to have it again. And they seek out new experiences of the same sort although they are not obliged to do so by their conscience, nor compelled by their necessities, nor allured by their interests[1] (2000, p. 133).

1 All Spanish sources my translation.

However, it seems that we have forgotten this and, to some degree, we betray literary authors when we convert the study of their works into what they should never have been. "The study of literature is not the learning of a succession of movements, dates, authors and works, not a simple list of influences and 'style traits'", indicates Mendoza Fillola (2006, p. 5), adding,

> The content appears to students as unclear and barely attainable abstractions, because they perceive it as content of little importance to them and hard to understand when listed in a manual [...]. This surrogate [...] prepared from historical, biographical remnants and characterisations from schools, eras and genres, garnished with critical opinions, [...] is perceived by them as alien to their capabilities and interests (Mendoza Fillola 2006, p. 5).

Literature can produce intense pleasure and it is through this pleasure that literature stimulates thought and provides knowledge which, as indicated by Guadalupe Jover (2007), gives rise to a new type of citizenship and, as Ribeiro (2021) claims, contributes to educating a fairer and more supportive society; it is also through (the reader's) recognition of and identification with the literary text that literature can help personal reconstruction following adversity, as Petit (2009) indicates, and possibly even help with the creation of personal image and personality. It is thus through pleasure that a true encounter with the text can be found.[2]

Beyond our desire for literature classes at all educational levels to foster this kind of experience for our students, this is what is our duty as teachers. Under Spanish legislation, which may serve as a good example, we see that Royal Decree 1105/2014[3]and Decree 48/2015[4] speak, first of all, about:

1. The free reading of works of Spanish and universal literature and young adult literature as a source of pleasure, of personal enrichment and of worldly knowledge to develop their own literary tastes and interests and reading autonomy.

---

2 It is true that not all literature shares ideological assumptions that foster the values we mentioned. However, in these cases, the encounter with the text and what López Valero *et al.* (2021) call educational reading would contribute to the formation of critical minds. Furthermore, in the case of reading for younger people, the figure of the mediator would take on greater importance, since they would be in charge of selecting works according to certain ideological assumptions, and of raising pertinent questions to foster the critical judgement mentioned.

3 Retrieved 12.05.2022, from https://www.boe.es/buscar/act.php?id=BOE-A-2015-37.

4 Retrieved 12.05.2022, from https://www.bocm.es/boletin/CM_Orden_BOCM/2015/05/20/BOCM-20150520-1.PDF.

2. Develop reading autonomy and an appreciation for literature as a source of pleasure and knowledge of other worlds, times and cultures.

Only in third place mention is made of an "approximation to literary genres through reading and the explanation of meaningful fragments and complete texts", and in fourth and fifth places the decrees talk about the "critical analysis and interpretation of fragments and complete meaningful works". In other words, as Bertochi (1995) indicates, the ultimate aim is to provide students with a positive attitude towards literature and a personal enjoyment of reading.

Thus our primary mission must be to develop reading autonomy and the formation of competent readers, in line with what the concept of literary education calls for, in the understanding that a competent reader is one that is able to contextualise the work, recognise the codes of each genre, develop a system of expectations, assimilate the literary playbook, comprehend cultural reminiscence and recognise specific intertextuality to better appreciate texts by recognising their relationship with other preceding works.

2. The classics and introducing readers to the classics: difficulties and problems

With the decrees in mind, the next question would be: how can this be reconciled with reading the classics? What do we do with them? It is obvious that the mention of meaningful works refers to the canonical and classical works, and the need to read them is hard to deny, both from a legal framework and from the wish to comprehensively educate students The law requires that in the first cycle of compulsory secondary education (ESO) (at 12, 13 and 14 years of age), students are introduced to the works most representative of Spanish literature from the Middle Ages to the Spanish Golden Age, and an introduction to Spanish literature from the 18th Century to present-day is indicated for the fourth year of ESO.

Both of these eras are revisited in advanced secondary education (Bachillerato) to be studied more in depth, with the reading and explanation of meaningful fragments as the methodology to achieve this, along with complete texts, as and when appropriate.

Furthermore, from a less legalistic and more humanistic approach, we can raise of the question whether studying the classics provides anything to 21st Century students, to which the answer appears to be positive as well.

We do not need to look at all 14 reasons argued by Italo Calvino (2012) to justify reading the classics, just the second reason will do, which talks about the wealth offered to those who have read them, and the third reason, which recalls the influence they exercise "when imposed, as they are unforgettable or when hidden in the corners of the memory, blending with the collective or individual sub-conscious" (Calvino 2012).

It is enough to recall that the classics – the works that have endured centuries or even millenniums to reach us – remain in our lives and in our culture because they speak about universal issues like love, death and liberty… that remain valid and speak to the 21st Century reader in the same way as they spoke to the reader or spectator in the 17th Century or in the 1st or 2nd Century B.C.

However, we would be kidding ourselves if we claimed that the classics can be read by a 12 year old and, without the need for mediation, reach the reader with their full force, plenitude and meaning.

It is obvious that the language is a major obstacle, as indicated by Blanca Hernández Quintana (2016) in relation to Cervantes, and more general, in the case of Spanish literature, understanding the very early Spanish of *El cantar de Mio Cid*, or 15th Century Spanish, still in formation, is extremely difficult for teenagers that are still developing their linguistic skills.

Additionally, as indicated by Caro and González, another reason for a lack of interest may be "that the classics are read by imposition, in a distant fashion – conceptual and historicist – and are rarely employed in editions and versions that offer truly motivating bonds for learners" (2013 pp. 100–101).

3. Adaptations – a subject of debate

The acceptance of these two considerations – the need to introduce the classics to students, on the one hand, and the difficulty in doing this, on the other – has led specialists to propose different solutions. The first of these, and probably the most widespread, is the use of adaptations of works in the classroom.

Adaptations facilitate access to more complex reading; however, the suitability of their use has been and is a subject of much debate. Detractors argue that the title and the signature are might deceive readers into thinking they have read the real thing, that the work does not countenance the breakdown into or removal of parts, that the reader cannot enjoy the language of the time or another language (Witdouck 2014, p. 12) and that the new texts are impoverished, are of poorer quality than the original and detract from their message (Fernández Andino 2014, p. 8). In contrast, the proponents of adaptations argue in their favour that the new versions contribute to stimulate enthusiasm, help literacy (Soriano 1995, pp. 38–40) and offer "literary texts that are closer to the interests and comprehensive abilities of students" (Colomer 1991, p. 23).

From a less radical standpoint, Marc Soriano (1995) recognises that "the adaptation of a book for children that wasn't written for them means subjecting it to a host of modifications, in general through cuts and removals [...] which makes it more approachable to this new public" (Soriano 1995, p. 198), but this adaptation which "undoubtedly makes the effort easier for young readers, [...] can make them more passive. In the future, would the reader still make the effort of reading the full version if they (erroneously) thought they already knew it?" (Soriano 1995, p. 198). Taking it a step further, and taking into account that the specificity of literature also consists of its language, to what extent can an adaptation replace the reading of the original work? It is true that different types of adaptation exist, whereby some are closer to the original, or a more summarised and commercial interpretation is sought,[5] and it is also true that, at lower educational levels, the adaptation may serve to bring us closer to the universe of a literary work and thus ensure that students incorporate in their imagination and cultural baggage works that are true references and, as Calvino indicated, form part of the collective or individual imagination. But, should we look for the same XYZ in compulsory and advanced secondary education? Or should we also look to bring students closer to the literary phenomenon and to cultural manifestations of other times? The works closest to the interests and comprehensive ability of students (in the words of Colomer, 1991) would probably be better selected from among the works of current young adults' literature and these would be the works that students could read freely or "on impulse", in the terminology of Lluch (2010). However, the classics also contribute to learning about other historical periods, other languages and, if you like, another function of language and another register, at least in your own mother tongue. Wouldn't it be possible to bring us closer to these texts in a more meaningful fashion?

4. Recycling as a teaching methodology

At this point literary recycling comes into play. This concept, currently still in its settlement phase, is starting to be used as a new paradigm that could define the 21st Century's approach to the literary traditions.

If, in the *Ancien Régime*, imitation pointed to the origin and, in Romanticism, the search for originality translated into the presence of influences that authors, in some way, rebelled against; if structuralism spoke about intertextuality,

5 Witdouck talks about three strategies in adaptations: faithfully respecting the original, the elaboration of an innovative and creative version, and the summarised and commercial interpretation" (2014, p. 63).

establishing a relationship between the past and the future; then, in the 21st Century, the studies by Miriam Llamas Ubieto (2020), through the LEETHI Group, point to recycling as a new paradigm in which the relationship with previous works is established through focussing on the present.

Along this line, Llamas Ubieto, accepting the most technical meaning of the term, defined literary recycling as "reiteration, renewal, the processing of the pre-existing, a mixing with other materials", with the aim of "inserting something again into a useful life cycle or circle" (2020, n.p.). In other words, recycling takes the past again and transports it to the present, from a modern perspective that indicates and incorporates the present and which, through contemporary culture that judges what it sees, is legitimised to select what it feels can be rescued from the past and modifies what it considers opportune based on its perception of reality.

So there is one more step to rewriting, given that updating and a rapprochement with the subject of enunciation have become essential again, whereby literary recycling[6] seeks to create a text that feels distant and alien and make it admissible, comprehensible and enjoyable; recycling would thus be a form of translation in which linguistic and cultural variants are not taken into account for diatopical reasons, but rather, the linguistic and cultural variants, due to the passing of time, are precisely what make understanding the classics difficult for our students.

Conceived in this way, recycling is not just a new paradigm of textual analysis that detects the elements that the 21st Century has decided to rescue from the past in a conscious and active manner; rather, from this perspective, it can also become a teaching methodology which, in this case, is related to reading and creative writing, adding a series of nuances to the new written version.

Along this line, we understand creative writing as something undertaken with the intention of re-writing the text, of seeking those cracks that separate us from it and modifying them. From the theoretical point of view, Charles (1995) speaks about the emergence of "possibilities",

> and not just the possibilities of writing but also, and above all, the possibilities of reading [...]. The real text will be considered as effective both for what it does not use and abandon, and for what it actually introduces; the real text will be considered as surrounded by virtual texts and penetrated by them [...]. On the one hand, this thus does away with the principle of the authority of the text [...]. On the other hand, a dimension is introduced into the commentary that *a priori* seemed inadmissible: creativity, what

6 According to the studies being carried out in the ELLI and LEETHI groups at Complutense University of Madrid, different types of recycling exist whereby not all of them reproduce the complete work, and nor is the original work always clear.

> will be addressed is no more and no less than the production of other texts (virtual, but describable) based on the text examined (Charles 1995, pp. 107–108).

From a teaching standpoint, this type of reading is highly recommendable since, as can be seen in the quotation from Charles, when speaking about the "text examined", this is a question of analysing the text, reading it in close detail, but not with a submissive attitude that means you cannot have any criticism and that the only thing asked for is an analysis of the resources of this discourse; through creative writing, we achieve the dialogue with the classics that we should seek to develop for literary proficiency; if the proficient reader is capable of detecting the relationship between literature and his own life, then we must let young readers forge a dialogue with the text, understand what it says and assimilate what seems opportune to them, but also disagree with or deny what is distant from their experiences. As Alonso indicates,

> Abstracts, guided commentaries, files, tables, opinions by specialists can all help the study, but without comprehensive reading that produces real communication between the reader and the text, the effect will end up being the opposite because it avoids or replaces the act of reading itself (Alonso 2001, p. 57).

We want this personal reading to take place, which can be achieved by what Citton (2007) calls "actualising reading", the aim of which is not so much to extract what the author wishes to say from the text but rather to extract what is insightful in the analysis done in the present, a reading, so to spaek, that is "applied" to the present situation of the interpreter who, far from condemning the anachronism, exploits it as a creative element.

This is beneficial for the reader, since it helps him better understand the time he lives in, but also for literature, since it justifies its current validity – "a text remains literarily alive to the extent that an interpreter updates it" (Citton 2007, p. 394). The next step, as is only right, would be actualising the re-writing; in other words, what we have called "recycling", by means of which students create their own adaptation, an adaptation that feels closer to their own interests and comprehensive ability, but which still required direct contact with the text to also perceive the characteristics of the era it was set in. Recycling may employ analogue or mixed textual codes but we should take into account that, in a postdigital society in which everything is digital to the point that it is normal to use these formats, recycling may also opt to reuse digital codes and resources, with remediation in addition to re-writing leading students to, from a teaching perspective, develop not only linguistic and literary proficiency, but also digital proficiency.

5. Some examples of literary recycling

Everything said so far falls within the realm of speculation; however, its efficacy needs to be proven in the classroom. Accordingly, following a research-action methodology, in the academic years 2020–2021 and 2021–2022 several groups of students were asked to recycle some works. As regards the different years of compulsory and advanced secondary education, 76 students from the Didactics of Literature subject, part of the Master's Degree in Teaching Training at Complutense University of Madrid, were asked, in groups of between three and five people (17 groups in total), to recycle a classical work that they could freely choose from among those studied during this course,[7] with the aim of bringing these works closer to pupils in the intended age group. In other words, they were asked to rewrite the text, in an analogue or digital format, updating their values and drawing them closer to the 21st Century, in such a way that they would become more accessible to a teenage public. Furthermore, after recycling the text, they were asked for a metacognitive reflection on what they had learned during the recycling process, and for an assessment of the experience.

From the works recycled, two were selected for this article, based on the quality of the recycling and the importance of the author or the work chosen. These will be presented in this work and will form part of the TROPOS repository of Digital Creative Writing for teaching Literature.[8]

5.1. Recycling of "El celoso extremeño" ["The Jealous Extremaduran"]

One of the authors most frequently chosen by students for recycling of his works is Miguel de Cervantes. This is not a surprising choice for two reasons: the first is the importance of this author and the concerns that exists regarding finding ways to bring him closer to compulsory and advanced secondary education classrooms; the second reason is related to the modernity of his message. Despite the fact, as pointed out by the critique of Hernández Quintana (2016), that the language of 17th Century Cervantes may be an obstacle to make his work more readable, it is clear that his messages remain fully valid.

7 As seen previously, the curriculum for this education cycle includes representative works from the Middle Ages to the 20th Century, as established in Royal Decree 1105/2014 and Decree 48/2015.

8 Retrieved 12.05.2022, from http://repositorios.fdi.ucm.es/Tropos.

This is the case of the *novela ejemplar* (12 short stories known as the exemplary novels) "El celoso extremeño" ("The Jealous Extremaduran"), in which the extreme jealousy of Filipo de Carrizales is criticised. He is married to a woman 35 years younger than him whom he decides to lock away to isolate her from the world and mould her to his whims. This subject of male jealousy, which would seem to have been overcome in the 21st Century, ties in, however, with contemporary male violence and new control mechanisms.

When recycling this work, the students, who maintained the structure and the main subject, eliminating just a few details, opted for the digital format of WhatsApp. Accordingly, the story was conveyed based on WhatsApp conversations held between the different characters. This update through the postdigital element is fundamental, as it not only implies that the medium in which the new text is presented is digital, but also that the digital format modifies the standpoint offered to us and introduces the perspectivism and voice of different characters, which ties into postmodern narrative techniques as well. This also represents the hyper-updating implied by recycling, as it places a new form of communication at the heart of the work, a communication that includes text messages, but also photographs, emoticons, memes and gifs (which themselves constitute another type of related recycling, in this case with intertextual references).

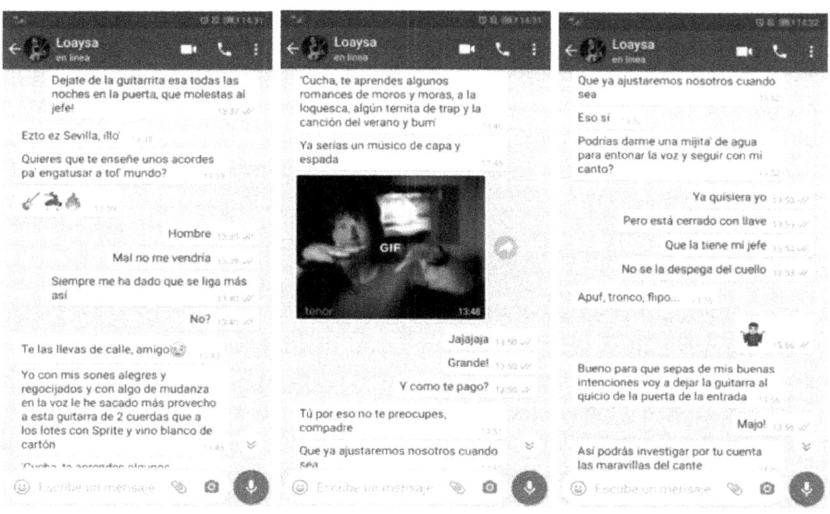

Fig. 1.

An update also takes place in the field of translation, known as "cultural markers" (Marcelo Wimitzer 2007) or "cultural references" (Mayoral 1994); in other words, cultural references that may make comprehension harder for the reader in the era the work is received in, both due to unfamiliarity with the references and unfamiliarity with the implications or connotations that a reference may contain. In this case, the recycling was carried out along two lines. Firstly, the ways in which men control women is updated, no longer talking about a man who locks up his wife under the custody of a guard, but referenced to the type of control exercised in the 21st Century, such as the supervision of the clothes worn by the woman, the time she can connect to social media, her online profile, the endless missed calls when she does not answer the telephone or the insistent messages when she is not there. It is also interesting to add that, although this is not an update, there is another element that changes as a result of the recycling and that may foster better identification by a teenage reader – if, in the work, the age gap is significant, in the recycling this is not mentioned. This, which may be perceived as a mistake, given that it is an important feature in the original work, encourages teenage readers to see the way in which these forms of control can take place in their own relationships, even though they are the same age; in other words, this helps establish a connection between literature and life when we are seeking to develop literary proficiency.

Another one of the cultural references or markers updated is music. Music is important in the work because it is one of the tools that Loaysa employs to access the house; in this case, music maintains its leading role, which plays the same function as in the reference work, but it becomes popular music and the reference to Moorish romance is maintained by adding allusions to 'trap' or summer songs, in other words, current popular music.

Lastly, something crucial in the update: the language is modernised and 21st Century slang is used.

5.2. Recycling of "El rayo de Luna"

Another author that forms part of the compulsory and advanced secondary education curriculum, and who is important to study due to the relevance of his work in the history of Spanish literature is Gustavo Adolfo Bécquer, thus the second example we have selected is related to his work. In this case, students doing a Master's Degree in Teacher Training chose to work with one of his legends which, interestingly, are rarely studied in the classroom.

The way in which this recycling was carried out is also important. On this occasion, the medium was not a digital application or platform, but a Power

Point presentation comparing images related to the text in terms of the context of the work and the time in which it is set (16th Century and the Middle Ages, respectively) to images of the 21st Century that would visually "translate" the references. For example, the format of a party or the model of the lone hero, so common in Romanticism, are iconographically rendered as imagined by 21st Century students, along with what these new readers consider the concept's current equivalent.

Fig. 2.

Furthermore, the obsession of Bécquer's Manrique in his search for a shadow in the night becomes a state of melancholy that is conveyed here by means of reference to cultural products, related to both poetry and music. To comprehend this change, which is fundamental for the update, it is important to also take into account the space in which the story unfolds, which provides the framework for (and contextualises) the whole update: what in the original legend was a reflection in the middle of the night has become someone anonymous who gets in touch via social media; in other words, the postdigital world once again infiltrates to portray the Internet as a dark forest where it is impossible to find the person you are looking for, and converts the glimpse of the supposed mysterious woman into a digital message of an unknow person.

Returning to updating cultural references, the desperation of Manrique can be seen on this occasion through the music he listens to, in Spotify playlists, which include such songs as "*Triste*" by Kase O, "*Todo está bien*" by Carlos Sadness and Manuel Medrano, "*En el muelle de San Blas*" by Maná, etc. (see figure 3) and in the memes of poetic phrases that are read as another form of recycling:[9]

Fig. 3.

The translation of the references is completed when the supposedly mysterious lady who, obviously in the Internet universe could not be a ray of moon-light, is presented as an Internet bot (that is, an account with no-one behind it).

The translation of the legend into the postdigital world of the 21st Century is performed completely and coherently, clearly portraying the current validity of the subject matter addressed by Gustavo Adolfo Bécquer, while including one of the elements considered as a mark of the postdigital world: the criticism of the dangers posed by this digital world (Regueiro 2020).

On this occasion, it was not the imagination or the desire of the main character that led them to betrayal. Hence, the main issue is not the romantic disillusion as linked to Neoplatonism, which creates these romanticist dreams of ideals that do not exist in reality; on this occasion, the disillusion is caused by external factors. As in the case of Don Quixote, we have gone from a character

9 Pilar García Carcedo has studied memes as evidence of cultural recycling. For more information, read García Carcedo (2020).

that changes reality to a reality that is already changed so that the character lives through the deception until the truth is revealed.

These paradigm shifts are also reflected in two other details which, at first sight, do not seem very important. Firstly, it is the Internet bot that addresses the character, it is "she" who takes the initiative, as is fitting of a 21st Century woman. Secondly, the main character socialises and shares what has happened to him, telling his friends on social media. When there is overexposure to intimacy through social media, it is important that even the lone hero we see in the initial slides shares his story via WhatsApp.

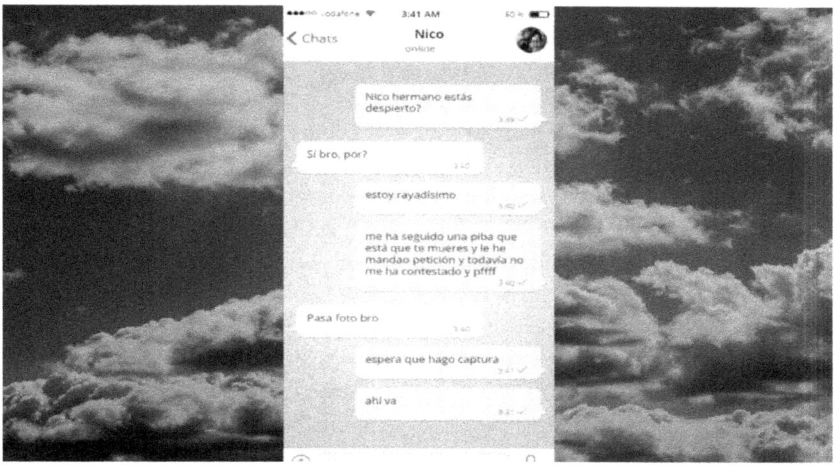

Fig. 4.

The added fact that the friend with whom the story is shared is a well-known media personality is no more than a touch of humour by the students, but it, in turn, contributes to the hyper-updating of the legend; in other words, the extreme update that includes details from the time the recycling is performed.

Accordingly, the recycling of this legend constitutes, in our opinion, a clear example of what Citton calls "actualising reading", the aim of which is not so much to extract what the author wants to say from the text but rather what is edifying in the modern-day analysis, what could be called an "applied" reading to the present situation of the interpreter. So, in this case, the legend has been updated by applying its message to the 21st Century, in which the deceit does not take place (at least in most cases) because we construct a reality out of nothing, but rather the postdigital world fosters the creation of non-existent ideas by establishing relationships with people, or bots in this case, about whom we know nothing, but on whom it is easy to project all our expectations.

If the first work we analysed, resulting from the recycling of "El celoso extremeño" was interesting when it comes to working with teenagers due to the updating of the model of the toxic relationship, this work is more anchored in the postdigital context, given that it warns of the dangers one can encounter on social media.

6. Conclusions

In light of these examples, we can affirm that, as we indicated at the start, literary recycling, in which the updating of the original text is a key element, can work as a wonderful teaching tool.

Firstly, faced with the problem of the lack of contact with the text as an artistic and cultural product, which is often blamed on the use of adaptations in the classroom, recycling would actually make this contact necessary. Students would have to work on the language of the time of the text in question, along with the cultural references, which would open a window to other eras, and then, as Citton (2007) indicates, would have to use these elements as a source of creativity and a blank page to fill with their own references.

Secondly, updating would imply, also in line with what Citton states, a better understanding of the time in which we live. This can be seen in the examples proposed, as the recycling of these two canonical works of Spanish literature from the 17th and 19th Centuries, respectively, has led the students to reflect on two problems from their own time: toxic relations and the dangers of the digital environment. We would thus be covering everything needed to develop the literary proficiency of the students: they would be verifying the validity of the messages from the literary works of the past and relate them to their own lives and circumstances; and they would be working on the unhurried and analytical reading of "previous models, the recognition of intertextual relations and the internalisation of literary codes by handling, exploring and applying them", as García Carcedo (2011) indicates in relation to creative writing. Lastly, the students' feedback reflects that, with the freedom offered by active reading and the handling of the texts, they have enjoyed reading more. A good example is the feedback of Mario Gutiérrez – one of the students who recycled *El rayo de luna*, who, in his reflection, explained what happened in the following terms:

> We moved from a palatial environment in Soria to a wealthy neighbourhood of Madrid. From a lone, taciturn nobleman to a sad young man who is a fan of tearful songs. In this

> regard, we should mention how much fun it was to draw up a Spotify playlist adapted to the personality of the main character through songs such as *En el muelle de San Blas*, by Maná; *Tú me dejaste de querer*, by C. Tangana, and *Rosas*, by La Oreja de Van Gogh. Details like this contribute an intermedial and fun side to recycling that could be more enjoyable for students.
>
> As well as the creation and narrative instrumentalisation of the aforementioned Instagram account – @rayodeluna567 – the incorporation of new technologies was based on strategies such as the recreation of a WhatsApp conversation between Manrique and a friend of his […]; this is a very valuable resource in terms of incorporating it into the classroom. It allows you to incorporate others languages and semiotic codes, like emojis, Gifs and stickers. Additionally, it gives free rein to the creativity of students through a platform they know better than anyone. Together with this familiarity with the medium, the shortness of each message makes writing easier and simplifies a quite complex process: understanding relationships between the characters, acquiring their vocabulary and idiolect and re-writing and adapting their dialogues.

Accordingly, literary recycling presents itself as one of the best tools for teaching literature. By means of literary recycling through an active methodology which provides a leading role to the students, we foster the creation of new readers who enjoy literature in a conscious and critical fashion.

References

Alonso Blázquez, Francisco: "Didáctica de la escritura creativa". *Tarbiya: Revista de investigación e innovación educativa* 2001, pp. 51–64.

Bertochi, Daniela: "La aproximación al texto literario en la enseñanza obligatoria", *Textos de didáctica de la lengua y la literatura* (4) 1995, pp. 23–38.

Calvino, Italo: *Por qué leer a los clásicos*. Vol. 19. Siruela: Madrid 2012.

Charles, Michael: *Introduction à l'étude des textes*. Seuil: Paris 1995.

Citton, Yves: *Lire, interpréter, actualiser. Pourquoi les études littéraires?* Amsterdam Editions: Paris 2007.

Colomer, Teresa: "De la enseñanza de la literatura a la educación literaria". *Comunicación, lenguaje y educación* (3.9) 1991, pp. 21–31, retrieved 12.05.2022, from https://www.researchgate.net/publication/28269247_De_la_ensenanza_de_la_Literatura_a_la_educacion_literaria.

Fernández Andino, Débora: *Adaptaciones literarias dirigidas al público infanto-juvenil. El caso del Lazarillo de Tormes*. [TFG Escuela Universitaria de Bilbao]. Bilbao 2014.

García Carcedo, Pilar: *Educación literaria y escritura creativa*. Geu Ediciones: Granada 2011.

García Carcedo, Pilar: *Memes ahora*. (Serie: Cuadernos del ahora n. 6). Docta-Complutense, Universidad Complutense de Madrid: Madrid 2020, retrieved 01.08.2023, from https://docta.ucm.es/entities/publication/e8b51a8f-4af1-4f16-8e3c-fd01af3cc4c9; https://docta.ucm.es/rest/api/core/bitstreams/9c18f36f-6ee4-4a2c-b74b-9e70446a52ec/content.

González Caro, María Teresa / González García, María: "De la mano de Cervantes: la lectura moderna de los clásicos". *Ocnos* (9) 2013, pp. 89–106, retrieved 12.05.2022, from https://www.redalyc.org/pdf/2591/259126460005.pdf.

Hernández Quintana, Blanca: "Don Quijote en las aulas del siglo XXI". *El Guiniguada* (25) 2016, pp. 17–21.

Jover, Guadalupe: *Un mundo por leer*. Octaedro: Barcelona 2007.

Lewis, C.S: *La experiencia de leer*. Alba editorial: Barcelona 2000.

López Valero, Amando / Encabo Fernández, Eduardo / Jerez Martínez, Isabel / Hernández Delgado, Lourdes: *Literatura infantil y lectura dialógica. La formación de educadores desde la investigación*. Octaedro: Barcelona 2021.

Llamas Ubieto, Miriam: "Estado de la cuestión sobre reciclaje". In: Llamas Ubieto, Miriam (coord.): *Jornadas: Reciclaje, postdigital, postglobal: definiciones para el ahora*. Facultad de Filología de la Universidad Complutense de Madrid 29.01.2020.

Lluch, Gemma: "Las nuevas lecturas deslocalizadas de la escuela". In: Lluch, Gemma (ed.): *Las lecturas de los jóvenes. Un nuevo lector para un nuevo siglo*. Anthropos: Barcelona 2010, pp. 105–128.

Marcelo Wirnitzer, Gisela: *Traducción de las referencias culturales en la literatura infantil y juvenil*. Peter Lang: Frankfurt 2007.

Martín Rogero, Nieves: "El uso del Quijote en el aula. Revisión histórica de ediciones escolares y paratextos didácticos". *OCNOS. Revista de estudios sobre lectura* (3) 2007, p. 77–90.

Mayoral, Roberto: "La explicitación de información en la traducción intercultural". In: Hurtado Albir, Amparo (ed.): *Estudis sobre la traducció*. Universitat Jaume I: Castelló 1994, pp. 73–96.

Mendoza Fillola, Antonio: *La educación literaria. Bases para la formación de la competencia lecto-literaria*. In: *Biblioteca Virtual Universal* 2006, retrieved 12.05.2022, from https://www.cervantesvirtual.com/obra-visor/la-educacin-literaria---bases-para-la-formacin-de-la-competencia-lectoliteraria-0/html/.

Petit, Michèle: *A arte de ler – ou como resistir à adversidade*. Editora 34: São Paulo 2009.

Regueiro Salgado, Begoña: "El reciclaje de los cuentos tradicionales y populares en los *Cuentos clásicos feministas*, de Ángela Vallvey. Una mirada postfeminista y postdigital a la tradición". In: Saneleuterio, Elia (ed.): *La agencia femenina en la literatura ibérica y latinoamericana*. Iberoamericana / Vervuet: Madrid 2020, pp. 339–358.

Ribeiro Otani, Bruna: "Educação literária no ensino de línguas". *Porto Das Letras* 7.1.2021, pp. 323–341.

Soriano, Marc: *La literatura para niños y jóvenes. Guía de exploración de sus grandes temas*. Ediciones Colihue SRL: Buenos Aires 1995.

Sotomayor, María Victoria: "Literatura, sociedad, educación: las adaptaciones literarias". *Revista de Educación*, N. Extra 1, 2005, pp. 217–238.

Witdouck, Sally: *Las adaptaciones infantiles de Lazarillo de Tormes*. [Masterproef voorgelegd de Faculteit Letteren en Wijsbegeerte voor het behalen van de graad van Master in de Taal – en Letterkunde Frans – Spaans] 2014.

www.ingramcontent.com/pod-product-compliance
Ingram Content Group UK Ltd.
Pitfield, Milton Keynes, MK11 3LW, UK
UKHW021921120926
8556IPUK00042BA/1093

9 783034 345477